Reading Assessment

Principles and Practices for Elementary Teachers

A Collection of Articles From *The Reading Teacher*

Shelby J. Barrentine

E d i t o r
University of North Dakota
Grand Forks, North Dakota, USA

International Reading Association
800 Barksdale Road, PO Box 8139
Newark, Delaware 19714-8139, USA
www.reading.org

The International Reading Association attempts, through its publications, to provide a forum for a wide spectrum of opinions on reading. This policy permits divergent viewpoints without implying the endorsement of the Association.

Director of Publications Joan M. Irwin
Assistant Director of Publications Jeanette K. Moss
Senior Editor Matthew W. Baker
Assistant Editor Janet S. Parrack
Assistant Editor Tori Mello
Publications Coordinator Beth Doughty
Association Editor David K. Roberts
Production Department Manager Iona Sauscermen
Art Director Boni Nash
Electronic Publishing Supervisor Wendy A. Mazur
Electronic Publishing Specialist Anette Schütz-Ruff
Electronic Publishing Specialist Cheryl J. Strum
Electronic Publishing Assistant Peggy Mason

Project Editor Tori Mello

Library of Congress Cataloging in Publication Data
  Reading assessment: Principles and practices for elementary teachers / Shelby J. Barrentine, editor.
    p.   cm.
  Includes bibliographical references and index.
  1. Reading (Elementary)   2. Reading—Ability testing.   I. Barrentine, Shelby J.   II. International Reading Association.   III. Reading teacher.
LB1573.R2793   1999   99-21205
372.4—dc21
ISBN 0-87207-250-9
Fourth Printing, June 2003

Contents

Section One

Principles and Possibilities for Assessment

Section Two

Integrating Assessment and Instruction

Section Three

Performance and Portfolio Assessment

Section Four

Miscue Analysis

*Section
Five*

Formal Assessment Instruments

Acknowledgments

I am grateful to the authors of the articles included in this compilation for their compelling and scholarly work on reading assessment. Two colleagues who have directly influenced my holistic view of assessing readers are Dr. Deanna Strackbein and Dr. Elizabeth Franklin. It is a pleasure to have taught and thought alongside each of them, and I thank them for their influences.

For her considerate and expeditious assistance, I thank Tori Mello, Assistant Editor of Books at the International Reading Association. I appreciate her suggestions, frequent correspondence, and ability to keep the work rolling forward.

Finally, I credit Lucretius with offering encouragement throughout the project.

Introduction

Shelby J. Barrentine

I t is not an easy task to know and understand the readers in our classrooms. Rather, it is challenging to observe the consistency with which a reader monitors comprehension, to see patterns in the ways a reader is constructing or disrupting meaning, and to identify the effectiveness of a reader's predictions. It requires specialized knowledge to profile which individuals need more instruction on making effective use of semantic, syntactic, and graphophonic cues. We need to know what to listen for to ascertain the effectiveness of a reader's ability to retell text. Practical protocols are needed to determine attitude factors that enhance or deter reading growth, to understand how our students view themselves as readers, to know how aware they are of their own reading strategies, and to help them set literacy learning goals. It is challenging to inquire, amass, organize, interpret, and use assessment information to enlighten our instructional decisions. The task is ambitious, but knowing the readers in our classrooms is essential if we are to foster the development of people who can and do read, and who turn to books for information, ideas, escape, and pleasure (Cambourne,1988).

A Look at the Challenge

We know what it is we want our readers to be able to do: We want them to be able to read for meaning. But, like most simple statements, the underlying concepts are not simple. To ascertain whether or not our students are learning to read for meaning requires that we possess a rich body of professional knowledge about reading and about reading assessment. Merely possessing the requisite knowledge, however, does not make the path of assessment barrier free. Difficulties can be alleviated by teachers' willingness to try alternative assessments, to implement compatible instruction and assessment methods, and to view assessment as a long-term process that reveals patterns in a reader's development.

Incompatible assessment and instructional methods, rigid and short-term performance standards, and inflated views of the importance of phonics-oriented decoding can all become barriers to implementing assessment that supports full knowledge of our readers. Currently, one large obstacle that encompasses the difficulties mentioned earlier relates to the pressures of standardized testing. In the sections that follow in this Introduction, aspects of the professional reading knowledge we use when assessing our students and the influence of standardized testing on assessment are explored in more depth. Then, the role of this collection of articles, in a push for meaningful assessment, is addressed.

Professional Knowledge About Reading

To establish a shared view of what and how we are assessing, it is useful to briefly survey the most essential of the professional knowledge that facilitates knowing our readers. Uncovering what a reader can do—the central task of reading assessment—is facilitated by using our professional knowledge about the reading process, behaviors of effective and ineffective readers, and literacy development. Knowledge of the tools that help us uncover what a reader can do also will help establish shared understandings about meaningful assessment.

The Reading Process

The shift from viewing reading as a word recognition task to conceptualizing reading as a meaning-making process resulted from Ken Goodman's 1964 report on miscue analysis, which he presented at a meeting of the American Educational Research Association (Bloome & Dail, 1997; Goodman, 1996). This meaning-making process, now commonly called "the reading process," is generally viewed by reading educators as essential knowledge for successfully teaching and assessing reading. The reading process provides an explanation of "how reading happens" (Cambourne, 1988). To construct meaning, readers draw on, or sample, the language information available to them (see Figure 1).

The available language information consists of sounds and symbols (graphophonic cues), language structure or grammar (syntactic cues), and knowledge—that which is presented in the text and that which is a part of the reader's background (semantic cues). As readers interact with print, they access and process these language cues through actively making and confirming predictions. They check their predictions for sense as they blend or integrate them into a meaningful interpretation of the text. We know that effective readers use these language cues interdependently, or in ways that mutually support comprehension (Cambourne, 1988; Goodman, 1996; Rhodes & Dudley-Marling, 1996). For example, effective, proficient readers unconsciously use semantic, syntactic, and graphophonic cues to check that a word has meaning, makes grammatical sense, looks right, and contains the right sounds.

When assessing readers, teachers use this knowledge about "how reading happens" to make observations about how well readers are controlling the active strategies (such as sampling, predicting, confirming, and integrating) and the knowledge associated with the language cueing systems. The more control readers have over the reading process, the more readers control their own meaning construction (Cambourne, 1988). Because meaning is valued over word calling, teachers are particularly observant about readers' abilities to use semantic language cues. At times, it is difficult to focus on the value of semantic cues because they are abstract compared to graphophonic cues. Nevertheless, it is well documented that effective readers rely on meaning cues to propel them successfully through text (Cambourne, 1988; Goodman, 1996; Martens, 1997; Rhodes & Dudley-Marling, 1996). To illustrate this idea, consider the following reading example. Imagine this sentence appears in a story:

My eyes were fixed, staring at the lake.

Imagine further that a reader miscues (deviates from the text) and substitutes the word *starting* for the word *staring* as she reads the sentence. A teacher who is assessing the reader and over-values phonics would tend to focus on the reader's inaccurate processing of sounds and symbols. This teacher would ask the reader to re-examine the word for the accurate sound-symbol match. A meaning-oriented teacher, however, would urge this reader to repair meaning. This teacher would ask the reader to think what the sentence is about, look for picture cues, and supply a word that makes sense with the story and also looks and sounds right. Thus, the meaning-oriented teacher will use knowledge

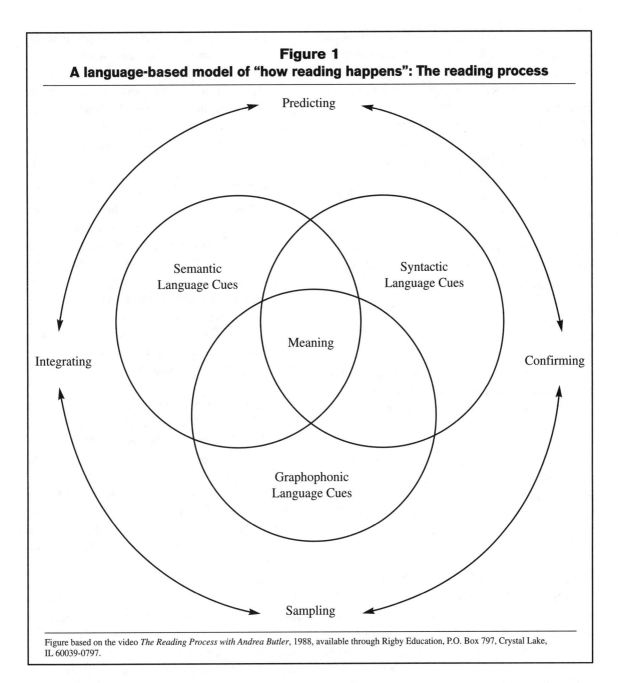

Figure 1
A language-based model of "how reading happens": The reading process

Predicting

Integrating

Semantic
Language Cues

Syntactic
Language Cues

Meaning

Confirming

Graphophonic
Language Cues

Sampling

Figure based on the video *The Reading Process with Andrea Butler*, 1988, available through Rigby Education, P.O. Box 797, Crystal Lake, IL 60039-0797.

about the reading process to document readers' control over comprehending text.

Ineffective and Effective Readers

As teachers, we want to assess whether or not our students are developing the attributes of ef-

fective readers. Observations on how well readers control the reading process reveal that ineffective readers do not or cannot process printed language as well as effective readers (Cambourne, 1988; Martens, Goodman, & Flurkey, 1995; Rhodes & Dudley-Marling, 1996). In an attempt to construct meaning, ineffective readers draw on fewer or less useful cues from the language information available to them. In addition, the information ineffective readers do sample is not processed as well as it is by effective readers. In the example presented earlier, a reader substituted *starting* for *staring*. Although the reader used graphophonic information, she overlooked the sound and symbol cues in the middle of the word and did not monitor the meaning for sensibility within the context of the story. An effective reader would not let that miscue go because it disrupts meaning. The word prediction cannot be confirmed and thus, the effective reader goes back to the language systems for more information (cues).

In addition to how well they control the process of reading, effective and ineffective readers possess other differences that we want to assess (Cambourne, 1998). We assess readers for attributes such as confidence, risk-taking, sustained engagement with text, connecting personally with text, retelling, application of strategies to derive and repair meaning, ability to choose books, and even ability to use text to make a difference in their lives. As we assess the effectiveness of our readers, we gather evidence that reveals the presence or absence of these attributes.

Knowledge About Development

What developmental milestones are evident in a reader's growth? Because of individual differences, it is always risky to associate specific developmental expectations with specific ages or grade levels. Nevertheless, development is not chaotic. There are patterns of growth in literacy development that can be described (Hill & Ruptic, 1994). For example, in their continuum of reading development, Hill and Ruptic note that readers progress toward greater competence as they read and retell highly predictable stories, as they read silently and retell less predictable

text, and as they independently apply reading strategies to construct meaning with complex text that is laden with unfamiliar content. At times it is useful for teachers to determine if reading development is rapid, steady, or delayed. Such observations help us make decisions about how to proceed with instruction.

Assessment Practices

We know what to assess when we observe readers because of our professional knowledge about how reading happens, attributes of effective readers, and development of reading abilities. It is especially challenging that most of what we want to know about readers is invisible. How they process print, what meaning-making strategies they use, their personal connections, or their confidence is not readily obvious. Thus, it is up to the assessment tools to make the invisible visible.

What are some of the assessment practices that make tangible that which is by nature intangible? Most commonly, they are the artifacts of daily reading experiences. For example, learning logs and response products such as story reflections, illustrations, character maps, and Venn diagrams (Yopp & Yopp, 1996) yield useful assessment information. They help teachers appraise and reflect on what students have learned and are ready to learn.

Other more specialized practices, however, are necessary to help teachers observe readers more thoroughly. Practices such as anecdotal record keeping, holding conferences, interviewing, surveying, miscue analysis, and retelling are needed to trace a reader's developing ability to comprehend and discuss text confidently. These practices also help determine what is difficult for the reader, how he or she processes print, or what reading strategies are employed.

Contrary to the arguments of those who promote standardized reading tests, alternative assessments do not yield subjective, imprecise bits of information (Calkins, Montgomery, & Santman, 1998; see also Appendix). These assessment practices are carefully selected and implemented to identify and analyze a reader's processes and products for the purpose of informing instruction (Rhodes, 1993). By nature, the assessments allow for inquiry into the reader's literacy knowledge and provide ongoing information about a reader's growth over time (Crafton, 1994; Yoshioka, 1997). Organized into personalized portfolios for analysis and reflection by teachers, students, and caregivers, these multidimensional assessments yield high-quality information and aim to improve teaching and learning by meeting the needs of diverse learners, respecting the complex nature of literacy learning, and drawing from the voices of students, parents, and teachers (IRA & NCTE, 1994).

An Obstacle to Meaningful Assessment

More and more often teachers do not receive support for developing the professional knowledge or for implementing assessments that help us understand the readers in our classrooms. Currently, teachers endure pressures from centralized powers who promote the practice of preparing children for high-stakes standardized testing. The development of national, state, and local performance standards in almost all academic fields, combined with the on-going school reform movement that began in earnest in the 1980s, has ushered in the expansion of high-stakes testing, especially in the area of literacy (see Appendix). We are receiving reports about large-scale standards-driven assessment programs that are now operational and have involved classroom teachers (Falk & Ort, 1998). Through active involvement with the standards and reform movements, however, policy makers have discovered that, in particular, standardized testing is a mechanism they can use to control

how reading is taught. Calkins, Montgomery, and Santman (1998) illustrate this control by reporting stories about teachers who are abandoning child-centered ways of teaching and are instead "begin[ning their] day by writing sentences filled with errors on the board and then asking the children to correct these sentences, just as if they were working on a standardized reading test" and "fall[ing] into line, opening their school days with a drill on contractions and apostrophes" (p. 4). The authors argue that the "national fixation on test scores" (p. 6) has taken curriculum and pedagogy out of the hands of teachers and placed it in the hands of those removed from daily work with children—district office administrators, textbook publishers, and other outside policy makers.

Teachers are "falling into line" and "teaching to the test" not because they agree with instruction that is driven by standardized testing, but because the consequences of low test scores are so great. Generally viewed by the public as rigorous, objective, scientific, and informative because of their statistical properties, standardized tests are granted the power to set numerous consequences in motion. Severe penalties associated with low test scores can include a school's loss of accreditation, a district's loss of control to the state government, a teacher's low evaluation, and a student's retention from the next grade level (see Appendix).

The ongoing dilemma is that "teachers find the results from standardized tests minimally useful to them in instructional decision making" (see Appendix, p. 249). So, even when a school district is involved in high-stakes testing, teachers are still compelled to know the readers in their classrooms. Because standardized tests provide limited information about what a reader can do, teachers are still turning to alternative, more authentic forms of assessment, such as daily work, interviews, conferences, anecdotal record keeping, miscue analysis, and development of student portfolios.

The Articles in This Collection

Building our knowledge when confronted with challenges is often our best recourse for protecting children's interests and moving forward with confidence. The articles in this collection aim to refresh and support teachers' efforts to understand the readers in their classrooms. At the center of this collection is my belief that teachers, aiming to "live thoughtfully in the presence of tests" (Calkins et al., 1998), desire practical, child-centered resources to help them know their students in order to make informed decisions about instruction.

The articles are organized into five sections, each centered around an assessment-related theme. The articles are drawn from the last 10 years of *The Reading Teacher*, resulting in a comprehensive survey of topics on assessment for the elementary classroom teacher. To enrich the collection I have provided a list of relevant additional readings after a brief introduction at the beginning of each section.

The primary criterion applied to choosing each article for inclusion in the collection was whether or not it had the potential to help teachers know and understand the readers in their classrooms. Several articles were included to supply thoughtful ideas and lead the way as teachers form and articulate their beliefs about assessment. Most of the articles were included for their practical nature: They contain descriptions of assessment practices that can be adapted for use by individual teachers, or they are assessment protocols that when implemented reveal specific literacy information about individual learners. Further, the articles in this collection were chosen for their compatibility with the thinking laid out in *Standards for the Assessment of Reading and Writing* (IRA & NCTE, 1994), because these standards foster decision making about assessment that foremost serves the interests of children.

Specifically, to be included in this collection, the ideas in the articles were required to serve the interests of diverse populations of learners. It is important to note that while the assessment tools in this collection are potentially useful with all children, readers who struggle greatly or whose reading development journey is very tangled deserve specialized diagnosis and assistance. Completely meeting the needs of these most troubled readers is not within the scope of the information provided in this collection. It was also a goal to avoid unnecessary overlap of information, and hopefully, the unique niche that each article fills within the collection will provide a new context for any repetitious information.

In this climate of accountability, with reading perpetually used as the barometer for measuring school success, teachers need to credibly explain their practices and articulate the difference those practices make in the reading lives of children. This book's overall aim is to supply elementary classroom teachers with practical articles that also provide an adequate foundation of information on which to build solid explanations about why particular and alternative assessment practices make a difference in teaching children. It is also my intent to renew, inspire, and support teachers as they continue their efforts to use assessment that supports literacy learning, that empowers readers, and that equips them with the tools necessary to meet the challenge of implementing assessment that leads to lifelong literacy development.

References

Bloome, D., & Dail, A.R. (1997). Toward (re)defining miscue analysis: Reading as a social and cultural process. *Language Arts, 74*(8), 610–617.

Calkins, L., Montgomery, K., & Santman, D. (1998). *A teacher's guide to standardized reading tests: Knowledge is power.* Portsmouth, NH: Heinemann.

Cambourne, B. (1988). *The whole story: Natural learning and the acquisition of literacy in the classroom.* Auckland, New Zealand: Ashton Scholastic.

Crafton, L.K. (1994). (Ed.). Inquiry-based evaluation. *Primary Voices K–6, 2*(2).

Falk, B., & Ort, S. (1998). Sitting down to score: Teacher learning through assessment. *Phi Delta Kappan, 80*(1), 59–64.

Goodman, K. (1996). *On reading: A common-sense look at the nature of language and the science of reading.* Portsmouth, NH: Heinemann.

Hill, B.C., & Ruptic, C. (1994). *Practical aspects of authentic assessment: Putting the pieces together.* Norwood, MA: Christopher-Gordon.

International Reading Association & National Council of Teachers of English (1994). *Standards for the assessment of reading and writing.* Newark, DE: International Reading Association; Urbana, IL: National Council of Teachers of English.

Martens, P. (1997). What miscue analysis reveals about word recognition and repeated reading: A view through the "miscue window." *Language Arts, 74*(8), p. 600–609.

Martens, P., Goodman, Y., & Flurkey, A.D. (Eds.). (1995). Miscue analysis for classroom teachers. *Primary Voices K–6, 3*(4).

Rhodes, L.K. (1993). *Literacy assessment: A handbook of instruments.* Portsmouth, NH: Heinemann.

Rhodes, L.K., & Dudley-Marling, C. (1996). *Readers with a difference: A holistic approach to teaching struggling readers and writers.* Portsmouth, NH: Heinemann.

Yopp, H.K., & Yopp, R.H. (1996). *Literature-based reading activities* (2nd ed.). Needham Heights, MA: Allyn & Bacon.

Yoshioka, E. (Ed.). (1997). Assessment as inquiry. *Primary Voices K–6, 5*(1).

Section One

Principles and Possibilities for Assessment

The articles in this section lay the foundation for developing assessment plans that are compatible with child-centered, developmentally appropriate, language-based literacy programs for a pluralistic society. Through the views of several educators, readers gain varied but harmonious information about what to consider when developing an assessment plan, as well as thoughts on the value of shifting from external, one-dimensional, standardized assessments to classroom-based, multidimensional, and child-centered assessments. The articles will help readers to consider the critical pieces in the assessment puzzle and to explore ways of cooperating in order to honor varied interests. They also shed light on what assessment information is useful to various constituents, how to use the information to inform instruction, and methods to communicate assessment information in meaningful ways to parents, students, and other stakeholders.

Additional Readings

- Calkins, L., Montgomery, K., & Santman, D. (1998). *A teacher's guide to standardized reading tests: Knowledge is power.* Portsmouth, NH: Heinemann.
- Gersten, R., Vaughn, S., & Brengelman, S.U. (1996). Grading and academic feedback for special education students and students with learning disabilities. In T.R. Guskey (Ed.), *Communicating student learning* (pp. 47–57). Alexandria, VA: Association for Supervision and Curriculum Development.
- International Reading Association & National Council of Teachers of English. (1994). *Standards for the assessment of reading and writing.* Newark, DE: International Reading Association; Urbana, IL: National Council of Teachers of English.
- International Reading Association & National Council of Teachers of English. (1996). *Standards for the English Language Arts.* Newark, DE: International Reading Association; Urbana, IL: National Council of Teachers of English.
- Learning First Alliance. (1998). *Every child reading: An action plan.* Washington DC: Author.
- Moore, A. (1996). Assessing young readers: Questions of culture and ability. *Language Arts,* 73(5), 306–316.
- Peckron, K.B. (1996). Beyond the A: Communicating the learning progress of gifted students. In T.R. Guskey (Ed.), *Communicating student learning* (pp. 58–64). Alexandria, VA: Association for Supervision and Curriculum Development.
- Routman, R. (1996). *Literacy at the crossroads: Crucial talk about reading, writing, and other teaching dilemmas.* Portsmouth, NH: Heinemann.

Literacy Assessment Reform: Shifting Beliefs, Principled Possibilities, and Emerging Practices

Robert J. Tierney

February 1998

Developing better assessment practices requires more than simply choosing a new test or adopting a packaged informal assessment procedure. Indeed, it is difficult to imagine "plastic wrapped" versions of what these new assessment systems intend. Unfortunately, some assessment practices may be repackaged versions of old tests rather than new ways of doing assessment. And some assessment practices, regardless of the label (authentic assessment, alternative assessment, student-centered assessment, responsive evaluation, classroom-based assessment, or constructive assessment), may be compromised as they are made to fit tenets or principles out of character or inconsistent with the aspirations of these possibilities. Contributing to the confusion may be reverence for certain technical attributes espoused by some pyschometricians and a predilection or political climate that tends to perpetuate top-down assessment and curriculum reform. Not surprising, professionals may differ in whether or not new forms of assessment live up to their promise.

In hopes of helping to sort out some of these dilemmas—the oxymorons, compromises or, at the very least, different views of assessment, learners, and learning—I have tried to make the ramifications of my definition of assessment more explicit with the articulation of a number of principles, which I describe in this article.

These principles for assessment emanate from personal ideals and practice as much as theory and research—a mix of child-centered views of teaching, pluralistic and developmental views of children, constructivist views of knowing, and critical theoretical views of empowerment. The view that I espouse strives to be in harmony with Bruner's (1990) notion that a democratic society "demands that we be conscious of how we come to our knowledge and be as conscious as we can be about the values that lead us to our perspectives. It asks us to be accountable for how and what we know" (p. 31). Likewise, my goal is aligned with constructivists' ways of knowing and the notion of responsive evaluation that Guba and Lincoln

10

(1989) as well as others (e.g., Lather, 1986; Stake, 1983) have espoused:

> Responsive evaluation is not only responsive for the reason that it seeks out different stakeholder views but also since it responds to those items in the subsequent collection of information. It is quite likely that different stakeholders will hold very different constructions with respect to any particular claim, concern, or issue. As we shall see, one of the major tasks of the evaluator is to conduct the evaluation in such a way that each group must confront and deal with the constructions of all the others, a process we shall refer to as a hermeneutic dialectic. (Guba & Lincoln, 1989, p. 41)

I also find my views aligning with critical theorists (e.g., Baker & Luke, 1991; Freire & Macedo, 1987; Gee, 1990; hooks, 1989, 1994) who suggest that the point of literacy is to reflect upon, and be empowered by, text rather than to be subjugated by it—that literacy contributes to social transformation as we connect with what we read and write, not in acquiescence, but in reaction, reflection, and response.

In accordance with these notions, I contend that to be both accountable and empowered, readers and writers need to be both reflective and pragmatic. To do so, readers and writers need to be inquirers—researching their own selves, considering the consequences of their efforts, and evaluating the implications, worth, and ongoing usefulness of what they are doing or have done. Teachers can facilitate such reflection by encouraging students to keep traces of what they do, by suggesting they pursue ways to depict their journey (e.g., webs, a narrative, or listing of steps) and by setting aside time to contemplate their progress and efforts. These reflections can serve as conversation starters—conversations about what they are doing and planning to do and what they did and have learned. I suggest moving toward conversations and notes rather than checklists, rubrics, and more formal evaluations, which seem to distance the student from what he or she is doing, has done, or might do.

These principles stem from a concern that new assessment efforts need to be principled and thoughtful rather than faddish. They reflect a need for a major paradigm shift as regards how we assess, why we assess, and the ways these assessments manifest in the classroom. Some ramifications include a new type of professionalism on the part of teachers, a shift in the relationship between testing and teaching, and between teacher, students, and parents. In general, these principles call for a willingness to recognize complexity and diversity and an approach to assessment that begins from inside rather than outside the classroom. Are we succeeding in terms of shifting such values? Currently, there are several efforts occurring that are simultaneously studying and supporting such shifts (see, for instance, Tierney, Clark, Fenner, Wiser, Herter, & Simpson, in press). I am optimistic enough to think we have the makings of a movement that is beginning to establish its own identity—one that is aligned with contemporary views of learning, and more consistent with pluralistic and constructivist ethics (see especially Moss, 1996).

The Principles

Principle 1: Assessments Should Emerge From the Classroom Rather Than be Imposed Upon it

Classrooms are places where wonderful ideas are encountered every day; where children engage with one another in a myriad of social interactions; where learning can occur as the culmination of a unit of work, in conjunction with an experiment, or as students work with others or watch others work. Learnings may be fleeting, emerging, reinforced, and challenged. Oftentimes teachers expect certain learnings; at other times, teachers are surprised at what is learned.

The learnings that occur in classrooms are difficult to predict. Children are different not only in their interests and backgrounds, but also in terms of their literacies. While most teachers may begin the year with a sense of what they want to cover, generally they do not consider their plans to be cast in stone. Indeed, they are quick to adjust to their assessment of their students' needs and even to discard and begin afresh. They are more apt to begin with a menu of possibilities and an open-ended agenda, which allows for learning that is opportunistic and individualized.

With the movement to more child-centered approaches, teaching and learning have become less prescriptive and predetermined and have given way to notions of emergent literacy and negotiated curriculums. Most teachers espouse following the lead of the child. Unfortunately, testing practices tend to abide by a different orientation. Many forms of traditional tests do not measure what is valued and what is occurring in classrooms. Changes in testing have not kept pace with shifts in our understanding of learning and literacy development. Moreover, they often perpetuate an approach to assessment that is from the outside in rather than from the inside out. Indeed, I often argue that one of the reasons for emergent assessment is to ensure that assessment practices keep up with teaching and learning rather than stagnate them by perpetuating the status quo or outdated views of literacy learning.

Compare, if you will, these two scenarios:

Students in one classroom are engaged in a wide array of reading and writing experiences, projects, book talks, conferences, and workshops. In conjunction with these activities the students keep journals in which they discuss their reflections, including their goals and self-assessment of their achievements. In addition, each student maintains a log of his or her reading and writing activities, as well as a folder that contains almost everything. Portfolios, in turn, are used to keep track of the key aspects of their work over time. During teacher conferences with the students, the teacher encourages the students to note what they have achieved and want to pursue further. The teacher keeps his or her own informal notes on what is occurring, focusing on a menu of different aspects drawn from a menu of possibilities that the teacher and some colleagues developed. The menu supports but does not constrain the notes that the teacher keeps on the students. As part of the process, these notes are shared with the students, who are encouraged to add their own comments to them. At parent-teacher conferences and student-led parent conferences both the teacher and the student refer to these notes, portfolios, etc. to remind themselves of and share what has occurred.

The students in another classroom are engaged in a wide array of activities but are not encouraged to monitor themselves. Periodically the teacher distributes a checklist to each student with a preset listing of skills that the child has to check. Likewise the teacher may interrupt the flow of activities and check the students in terms of these preset listing of skills. The skills on the list bear some relationship to some things that are done, but there are a host of things that are not included and some other things that are included that do not seem to apply. The listing of skills was not developed by the teacher nor is it open ended. Instead, the list was developed by a curriculum committee for the district. In some ways the list reflects a philosophy and approach that do not match the current situation. Nonetheless, the teacher is expected to keep the checklist and file it. After the checklist is completed and filed it is not reexamined or revised.

The first example is representative of an inside-out approach; that is, what is assessed and the manner in which the assessment of various learnings is carried out and originates from within the classroom. An inside-out approach does not involve overly rigid a priori determinations of what should be looked for nor does it restrict the types of learning to be examined. In addition, assessment is negotiated among the parties that are involved.

Our second example may give the illusion of being inside out, but it actually perpetuates the outside-in approach. In this classroom the teacher uses informal assessment procedures, but they do not fit with or emerge from the classroom, and there is no negotiation between teacher and student. While the second type of classroom may represent an improvement over classrooms that depend upon standardized assessments and periodic checks, it has some major shortcomings in terms of what is being done and how these things are negotiated. Such a classroom does not invest in or trust the professionalism and problem-solving abilities of teachers, as well as the need for student involvement.

Principle 2: Effective Testing Requires Teacher Professionalism With Teachers as Learners

Many of the assessment practices in schools (especially standardized tests) have a dysfunctional relationship with teachers and learners. Whereas in most relationships you expect a give and take, actual testing practices in schools seem more estranged than reciprocal, more detached than intimate. This should come as no surprise, for oftentimes testing personnel have separated themselves and their instruments from teachers and students. Testing divisions in school districts generally have detached themselves from teachers and students or have forced teachers and students to work on their terms. In some districts, the testing division may use tenets tied to notions of objectivity and reliability to leverage control of what is tested as well as how, when, and why testing occurs.

If teachers become involved in making assessment decisions, the complexity of dealing with individual differences and differences across classes and schools is apt to surface. It may become problematic to assume that differ-ent students can be assessed with the same test, that comparisons across students are straightforward, or that students' performance and progress can be adequately represented with scores derived by periodical administrations of tests.

Quite often teachers will make reference to the tests that they are required to use, principals will allude to the district and state policy, and the district and state lay the responsibility on the public. Some systems seem to be either resistant to change or entrenched in their commitments.

But, teachers relinquishing control of assessment leads to a loss of self-determinacy and professionalism, which is problematic for a number of reasons. It seems to accept and reinforce the view that teachers cannot be trusted. It removes responsibility for instructional decisions from the hands of those who need to be making them. As a result, it decreases the likelihood that assessment will be aligned with teaching and learning and increases the separation between how learning is occurring in classrooms and how it is tested and reported. It depersonalizes the experience and serves as an excuse for relinquishing responsibility. Essentially, the external control of testing and standardization of testing procedures tend to perpetuate teacher and student disenfranchisement.

Teachers are in a better position to know and learn about an individual's development than outsiders. They are with the student over time across a variety of learning situations. As a result they become aware of the subtle changes and nuances of learning within and across individuals. They are sensitive to student engagement, student interests, student personalities, and the idiosyncrasies of students across learning activities. They are less likely to overstate or ascribe too much significance to results on a single test that may have an alienating impact upon a student. They are in a better position to track and assess learning in the context of teaching and child watching, and therefore to help students assess themselves. Effective teachers are effective learners themselves; they are members of a community of learners in a classroom.

So how might assessment be changed? Teachers, in partnership with their students, need to devise their own classroom assessment systems. These systems should have goals for assessment tied to teaching and learning. These goals should be tied to the types of learning and experiences deemed desirable and, therefore, should be established by those most directly invested in the student's education—the teachers and the students themselves. These standards/ features should be open ended and flexible enough to adjust to the nuances of classroom life. Tied to these goals might be an array of assessment activities from formalized procedures to very informal, from student self-assessment activities to teacher observations to periodical assessments via portfolios or other ways of checking progress.

Teachers and students need to be willing to change and recognize that there exists no quick fix or prepackaged way to do assessment. Indeed, prepackaged assessments are apt to be the antithesis of what should be developed. Unfortunately, teachers, students, and caregivers may have been enculturated to view assessment as predetermined rather than emergent and as having a look and feel quite different from more direct and classroom-derived assessments.

More direct forms of assessment might involve ongoing monitoring of students by sampling reading and writing behaviors, maintaining portfolios and journals, holding periodic conferences, and keeping anecdotal records. Several teachers and state efforts suggest that the community will support, if not embrace, such changes. We have numerous affidavits from teachers to that effect, which are corroborated by published reports of others such as Shepard and Bliem (1995), who found community support for performance assessments or more direct methods of assessment over traditional assessments was forthcoming and con-

siderable when caregivers were presented with examples of the options.

Principle 3: Assessment Practices Should be Client-Centered and Reciprocal

The notion that assessment should empower students and caregivers suggests an approach consistent with a more client-centered approach to learning. A client-centered approach to assessment is not novel. In areas such as psychotherapy and medicine, client-centered orientations are more the rule than the exception. In a court of law the judicial process hinges upon the notion of advocacy for a client. In attempts at being client-centered, teachers are apt to consider what students take away from tests or teacher-student conferences. A shift to client-centered approaches addresses how assessment practices are helping students assess themselves—i.e., the extent to which students might know how they can check their own progress. Indeed, the development of assessment practices with such provisions may have far-reaching consequences. It suggests that we should shift the whole orientation of assessment from developing better methods of assessing students toward better methods of helping students assess themselves.

So how might client-centered assessment look? It would look like child-centered learning. Teachers would strive to help students assess themselves. Their orientation would shift from subjecting students to assessment practices to respecting students for their self-assessment initiatives. This entails a shift from something you do *to* students to something you do *with* them or help them do for themselves, a form of leading from behind.

A number of classrooms have in place the beginnings of student self-assessment vehicles via the use of journals, logs, and portfolios. But this is just a beginning; self-assessment should extend to every aspect of the classroom, from helping students formulate their own learning goals, to helping students make decisions on what they can handle and need, to having them collaborate in the development of report cards and parent-teacher conferences. Also, the involvement of students in their own assessment helps with the management of such activities. This might entail having students set their own goals at the beginning of a unit (not unlike what is proposed with K-W-L); hold conferences with teachers, parents, or peers as they progress or wrestle with issues; look at their efforts and study their progress; and set future goals at the end of a unit in conjunction with parent conferences, or as alternatives to report cards.

There are numerous ways to start these conversations. I ground my conversations about assessment for and with students in the actual portfolio without the intrusion of a grade or score. Scores and grades only give the illusion of accuracy and authority; conversations connected to portfolios or other forms of more direct assessment unmask the bases for decision making and spur the conversation toward a consideration of the evidence, an appreciation of assumptions and the negotiations of goals. "Let's look," "I can show you," "It's like this," "I see what you mean," and "Do you think" displace more general and removed conversations, which tend to be categorical rather than contributory.

Various forms of self-analysis can complement portfolios and be wonderful springboards for such conversations. For example, sometimes I will have students represent their progress and goals with bar graphs or other visual representations (e.g., Venn diagrams, landscapes) in a fashion akin to "then," "now," and "future" and use these graphs as conversation starters. In turn, the visuals serve as the basis for having students delve into their portfolios and examine evidence about what they have achieved and what they might focus upon or set their sights on.

Principle 4: Assessment Should be Done Judiciously, With Teachers as Advocates for Students and Ensuring Their Due Process

A useful metaphor, if not rule, for rethinking assessment can be derived from aligning assessment with judicial processes. In a court of law, an individual on trial is given an advocate who presents evidence, including testimony, to present a case on behalf of the client. The client and the lawyer work in tandem. The trial is judged upon whether or not the client was given a just hearing and whether or not his or her representation was adequate. The client has the right to see the evidence presented for and against him or her, the right to reports developed, the right to present his or her own evidence and arguments, and the right to appeal. Also, in the event the client is not satisfied with his or her representation, the client has the right to request someone else to support his or her making a case or, if concerned about procedure, to request a retrial.

Now consider how students are put on trial in our school systems. They may or may not have an advocate, they may or may not be given adequate representation, and the evidence that is presented may or may not best represent their cases. They may not see the reports that are developed. Indirect indicators such as standardized tests, of questionable (if not circumstantial) quality, serve as the basis for decisions that restrict opportunities. In a host of ways assessment activities appear less judicious than they should be. Indeed, students are rarely given the right to appeal or to provide their own evidence. It is as if the students' right to due process is violated.

An examination of the law governing public schools raises some interesting concerns regarding schooling. Over the last 30 years, some key U.S. Supreme Court decisions have been offered that should direct our thinking. In *Tinker v. Des Moines Independent School District*, 393 U.S. 503 (1969), a case involving freedom of speech, the Court established some key principles undergirding students' rights. The Court wrote, "In our system, state operated schools may not be enclaves for totalitarianism.... Students in schools, as well as out of school are possessed of fundamental rights which the State must respect." This position was reaffirmed in the case of *Goss v. Lopez*, 419 U.S. 565 (1975). As Justice White stated, "young people do not 'shed their constitutional rights' at the schoolhouse door"; the right to due process is of particular importance when the impact of an event "may interfere with later opportunities."

I would hope that legislators pursue practices that place students' rights at a premium rather than displace such a goal with practices that serve first to protect themselves against legal challenges. At a minimum, I would hope that any assessments afford students better due process, including the right of disclosure and presentation of evidence on behalf of the student, as well as the right to appeal the use of indirect or circumstantial evidence. Moreover, I would hope my appeal for judicious assessment shifts the pursuit of such to being both a goal and a right.

Unfortunately, some U.S. state legislators may be more intent on protecting themselves against possible litigation than ensuring that students' rights have been fully supported. For example, they might consider that the spirit of due process has been satisfied when students have been given advance notice of tests and what these tests will entail; that is, in lieu of opportunities to appeal or students providing their own "alternative" evidence of progress or proficiencies. Also, an insipid development occurs when teaching to the test is used to maximize the legal defensibility of tests. In particular, states will often try to finesse the possibility of legal challenges of test bias by ensuring that students have had the opportunity to learn the content covered on tests. To avoid litigation and appear to address local needs, they will establish programs to prepare students for the tests and therefore "make" their tests unbiased by definition. The attitude of most institutions and states is to emphasize legal defensibility ahead of protection for and advocacy on behalf of students.

Principle 5: Assessment Extends Beyond Improving Our Tests to the Purposes of Assessment and How Results From Assessment Are Used, Reported, Contextualized, and Perceived

Any consideration of assessment needs to be broadly defined to encompass an exploration of the relationship between assessment and teaching, as well as facets such as report cards, parent-teacher-student conferences, and the student's ongoing record. These facets should not be viewed as exempt from scrutiny in terms of the principles described herein. They should be subjected to the same guidelines.

Just as the goals for developing better classroom-based assessment procedures are tied to the principles discussed herein, so report cards, records, and other elements must be examined in terms of whether they adequately serve the ends for which they are intended. Take, if you will, report cards. Do report cards serve the needs of the student, teacher, and parent? Do they represent a vehicle for ongoing communication and goal setting? Are they done judiciously? If not, how might the method of reporting be changed to afford such possibilities? Or, take, if you will, the student's records. For what purposes are the records used? Are the records adequate for these purposes?

Changes in assessment should be viewed systemically. When teachers contemplate a shift in classroom assessment, it is rarely a matter of simply making selected adjustments or additions. What a teacher does with one facet should and will affect another. For example, a teacher who incorporates a portfolio approach is likely to become dissatisfied with traditional forms of reporting progress. The solution is not to shy away from such changes, but to realize that they will need to occur and, if they do not, to realize that the failure to make such changes may undermine the changes already made. Teachers start to feel as if their new assessment initiatives are being compromised. Students may begin to sense mixed messages if teachers advocate student decision making and then reassert their singular authority via the determination of a grade without any student input or negotiation. That is, teachers move in and out of assessment practices tied to very different underlying principles. I feel as if the worth of assessment efforts such as portfolios may be diminished if the portfolios are graded or graded inappropriately, either without any student input or without consideration for diversity and richness, especially what the portfolio might mean to the student. We need to keep an eye on achieving students' engagement in their own learning as we negotiate future goals and possibilities against the type of judgments that are made and reported.

We should not underestimate the importance of parent or caregiver involvement in such efforts. Rather than keep the parent or caregiver at arm's length in the negotiations over reform, we need to embrace the concerns that parents have and the contributions that they can make. In those situations where teachers pursue alternatives to report cards, parent contributions may be crucial. Parents need to be informed of the goals and engaged in contributing to the efforts. Because not all parents might see the advantages, they may need choices. And, there are ways to avoid holding all parents hostage to what one parent or a small number express as concerns. For example, in pursuit of student-led conferences as an alternative to report cards, Steve Bober (1995) presented parents in Massachusetts with a description of two alternatives and offered them a choice—student-led conferences or more traditional report cards. Parents choosing student-led conferences were also expected to write letters to their children after each conference. Apart from the distinctiveness of the practice, what is notable is how Bober engaged parents as informed partners in the practice.

Principle 6: Diversity Should Be Embraced, Not Slighted

Oftentimes those assessing students want to remove any cultural biases rather than recognize diversity and support individual empowerment. They often pursue culture-free items and analysis procedures as a way of neatening and comparing. In pursuit of straightforward comparisons they assume that to be fair more items are needed, and therefore, the use of authentic assessment procedures will create problems, especially since the "time-consuming nature of the problems limits the number" (Linn, Baker, & Dunbar, 1991, p. 18). In addition, they seem to support as a given the use of the same analysis systems for the responses of all students. They expect a respondent to interpret a task in a certain way and respond in a set manner and may not tolerate variation in response, even if such variation might be justified. Whereas they might allude to the context-specific nature of any assessment, they tend to retreat from considering individuals on their own merits or in their own ways.

The term culture-free tests seems an oxymoron. I suspect that it is well nigh impossible, and certainly questionable, to extract cultural influences from any test or measure of someone's literacy. Literacy, your own and my own, is inextricably connected to cultural background and life experiences. Culture-free assessments afford, at best, a partial and perhaps distorted understanding of the student. In other words, assessments that do not build upon the nature and nuances of each individual's experiences should be viewed as limited and perhaps flawed. Just as teachers attempt to engage students by building from their background of experiences, so assessment should pursue a goal of culture sensitivity. Classroom teaching does not occur by ignoring or removing diversities. Nor should such a view of assessment be dismissed because of its ideological or sociopolitical considerations: Recognition or validation of one's own experience would seem a basic human right.

We need to aspire to culturally based assessment practices. In some ways I see this pursuit consistent with John Ogbu's (1988, 1991) notions about beginning to meet the needs of African American students, namely an approach to educational reform that has a cultural ecological orientation. I envision cultural ecological assessments that build upon, recognize, and value rather than displace what students have experienced in their worlds.

For a number of years literacy educators have been willing to sidestep complex issues of culturally sensitive assessments by appealing to the need to make straightforward comparisons. For years standardized test developers and the National Assessment of Educational Progress have retreated from dealing with issues of nonuniformity and diversity as they have pursued the development of scales for straightforward comparisons across individuals. In conjunction with doing this, they have often revised their assessment instruments to ensure that results fit their models or views of literacy. For example, they are apt to exclude items on topics tied to specific cultural interests and to remove items that show an advantage for one group over another. Even recent attempts espousing guidelines for new approaches to performance assessment (e.g., Linn et al., 1991) or exploring bias in testing minorities (Haney, 1993) may have fallen prey to the same view of the world.

Principle 7: Assessment Procedures May Need to Be Nonstandardized to Be Fair to the Individual

As teachers try to avail students of every opportunity within their control, they are constantly making adjustments as they "read" the students—their dispositions, verbal abilities, familiarities, needs, and so on. We look for ways to maximize the learning for different students, and we know that different students may need different amounts of encouragement and very different kinds of support. If we standardized our teaching, we know what would apt to be the end result: Some students with wonderful potential would reveal only certain sides of themselves and might not achieve their potential or even reveal who they are and what they might contribute and learn.

Allowing for individual or even group differences creates havoc with the desire to standardize assessment. Standardization approaches each individual and group in the same way; that is, students perform the same tasks at the same time, and then their responses are assessed using the same criteria. But if different students' learning repertoires are different and different students enlist different strategies and have different values, etc., and different approaches to testing, then what may be standard for one student may be unique for another.

Studies across cultures, across classrooms, and within classrooms suggest that different students respond in different ways to different forms of assessment depending upon their cultural, classroom, or personal histories. As my previous principle suggested, how students respond should be looked at as different across situations and against a "comparative canvas, one that takes into account the nature of the community that students inhabit, both the community of the classroom and the community of society with all of its past and present conditions and hopes for the future" (Purves, 1982, p. 345). Green and Dixon (1994) have emphasized that students construct "situated repertoires associated with particular models for being a student...not generic ones" (p. 237). We have ample demonstrations as to how the responsiveness of various groups and individuals in testing situations depends on their view of the social dynamics of the situation (Basso, 1970; Crumpler, 1996; Ogbu, 1988; Philips, 1983).

Indeed, there is always a tension between a need for uniformity across individuals and groups and the use of procedures that are sensitive to the different literacy developments of students, as well as the students' own predispositions to respond differently to different people in different ways at different times. On numerous occasions my assessment of some students has been revised as a result of pursuing more than one mode of response, as well as establishing different kinds of partnerships with them or watching them interact over time in different situations with different individuals or groups. In turn, what may serve as a vehicle for uncovering the literacies of one student may not be a satisfactory method for uncovering those of another student or those of the same student at another time. Teachers need to be willing to use different means with different students whether they are assessing or teaching.

The decision-making process may also be complicated by certain of our own predilections. In conjunction with my work on portfolios, I am always surprised at the analyses that learners have done of their progress and the types of goals that they choose to pursue. They ascribe significance to elements in their portfolios that I may have overlooked or not have been able to see. And their decisions to proceed are often at variance with what I would have suggested.

Principle 8: Simple-Minded Summaries, Scores, and Comparisons Should Be Displaced With Approaches That Acknowledge the Complex and Idiosyncratic Nature of Literacy Development

Straightforward comparisons across individuals are usually arbitrary, biased, and narrow. Assuming an approach to assessment with a new openness to complexity, respect for diversity, and interest in acquiring a rich picture of each student, then how might decisions be made about students? Those decisions that require reflection upon the individual's progress and prospects will likely be bountiful. Teachers who pursue an open-ended and diverse view of students will find little difficulty negotiating new areas of pursuit with and for individual students. Decisions that demand comparisons from one individual to the next will be problematic, but these difficulties are not insurmountable. They require a willingness to deal with uncertainties, to entertain possibilities, and to negotiate decisions, including the possibility that there will be lack of agreement. The problems with comparisons are confounded when people assume that straightforward continuums or single scores can adequately describe students.

Comparisons based upon scores are so problematic for a host of reasons: (a) Each student's development is unique; (b) the literacies of one student will be different from another, and even the same literacies will involve differing arrays of facets; and (c) some of these facets will be unique to a certain situation. Literacy development is sufficiently different from one student to the next that the types of comparisons that might be made are quite complex and multifaceted. The term literacy *abilities* rather than literacy ability seems in order. If you were trying to portray the character of these developments, you might find yourself gravitating to describing individuals on their own terms. Unfortunately, the terms of comparison in place with standardized tests and NAEP assessments and implicit in many of the attempts to score portfolios and other classroom-based data are often insensitive to such complexity. Looking at different individuals in terms of a single score masks variability and individuality. Again, test makers err on the side of a level of simplification not unlike a massive "conspiracy of convenience" (Spiro,

Vispoel, Schmitz, Samarapungavan, & Boerger, 1987, p. 180).

The drive for uniformity is quite pervasive. Our assessment and instructional programs oftentimes include long lists of skills as outcomes to be assessed, taught, and mastered. It is assumed that skills are neatly packaged and discrete and that each makes a uniform contribution to literacy development. It is assumed that students acquire these skills to mastery and that their ability to use them is uniform across literacy situations. In authentic reading and writing situations within which genuine purposes are being pursued, this is unlikely. Across literacy situations certain attributes may be more likely to be enlisted than others, and they are apt to be enlisted as clusters rather than one by one or discretely.

Too often literacy educators have ignored the complexities of the issues and have fallen back on convenience rather than exploring possibilities. Take, if you will, the attempts to wed some of the data emerging from performance assessment (e.g., portfolios) with rubrics. The data generated from portfolios might involve a rich array of samples or observations of students' work across situations and time. These samples are apt to represent the students' pursuit of different goals, utilizing different resources, including content, under varying conditions. In some ways student classroom samples may vary as much as the works of art from an artist's portfolio. Each sample may represent very different achievements and processes. When you hold them, examine them, and discuss their significance you are in touch with the actual artifact and not some distant derivative.

It is at this point, some would argue, that we can use a rubric to affix a score or scores or a sum total score to the student's work. But we need to examine a question that is the reverse of what is often asked. Instead of asking how we rate the portfolio, we should be asking whether the rubric measures up to the portfolio or to the assessment of complex performance. Moreover, in classrooms do we need a measure that is a distant derivative when we have the primary sources—the actual samples—to examine and reexamine using an array of lenses or perspectives? Whereas I argue for the context-specific nature of any assessment, advocates of rubrics seem to want to dismiss idiosyncrasies and variation; they would retreat from being willing to consider individuals on their own merits or in their own ways. Unless rubrics are used to prompt a consideration of possible ways to analyze work or as conversation starters in conjunction with revisiting the students' work samples, I see few advantages to their use in classrooms.

Sometimes assessment of reading and writing becomes more far-fetched by adding together a set of subscores. A key assumption often undergirding the use of such scores—especially the suggestion that they can be added and used as the basis of comparative decision making—is that the full and detailed portrait of an individual's literacies has been afforded. Unfortunately, these dimensions are not exhaustive, these determinations of degree are not accurate, and they should not be added. To be able to do so, we would have to do the following:

1. include all of the attributes or be assured that the partial listing that was developed is representative;

2. determine how these attributes are configured across situations;

3. assume that ample evidence will be provided for assessing these attributes;

4. develop scales for assessing attributes; and

5. generate an algorithm that works across individuals by which we might combine the elements and their dimensions.

I would posit that we do not have such samples, sampling procedures, ways of procuring evidence, adequate scales, or algorithm. And it is problematic to assume that an algorithm that simply represents sums would ever be adequate. The complexity of literacy is such that we cannot assume a basis for generating or combining scores.

Literacy assessments cannot and should not be so rigid. Perhaps there are some benchmarks that are appropriate across all students. Perhaps there are benchmarks appropriate to some readers and not others. But such benchmarks are likely to represent a partial view of any student's literacies. The use of scores and continua as ways of affording simplification and comparability has a tendency to camouflage the subjectivity of assessment and give test developers the allusion of objectivity. The use of scores and continua is not more objective; it is arbitrary. Guba and Lincoln (1989) have suggested the shift toward accepting the inevitability of relativism and the complexities across different settings may require the ongoing, ecumenical, and recursive pursuit of shared possibilities rather than a single set of absolute truths.

Principle 9: Some Things That Can Be Assessed Reliably Across Raters Are Not Worth Assessing; Some Things That Are Worth Assessing May Be Difficult to Assess Reliably Except by the Same Rater

Oftentimes, test makers and researchers will perseverate on whether or not they can consistently measure certain abilities. They tout reliability as the major criteria for whether or not a test is valid. The end result is that some things that are worth measuring are discarded and some things that are not worth measuring or valuing achieve an elevated level of importance. Typically, complex and individualistic learning tends to be shortchanged whereas the currency of learnings that are easier to define may be inflated. For example, in writing assessment, constructs such as style or voice may be short-

changed, while spelling and punctuation may be inflated. In reading, constructs such as self-questioning, engagement, and interpretation may be shortchanged, while speed, factual recall, and vocabulary may be elevated.

Unfortunately, reliability is translated to mean that two different scorers or raters will be able to assess the same thing in the same way. Unless a high degree of agreement across raters is achieved, test makers will deem a measure unreliable and therefore question its worth. In so doing, they may be making the mistake of assuming that reliability equates to agreement when verifiability may be a better approach.

We should be willing to accept differences of opinion in terms of how certain abilities are rated or discerned. Some abilities and strategies are difficult to pin down in terms of clear operational definitions. Different raters or even the same raters at different times are apt to develop different constructions of the same phenomena. Sometimes these shifts arise as a result of the different predispositions of the raters. Sometimes they arise as different facets of the phenomena are taken into account either by different raters or the same rater. Sometimes they arise as a result of differences in how students enlisted certain abilities. Such differences should not be viewed as surprising, for they coincide with two key tenets of most current views of learning: the notion of an ongoing constructive nature of knowing; and the situation-specific nature of learning. Differences are apt to exist across and within an individual's literacies (e.g., reading a newspaper for purposes of locating an advertisement versus reading a romance novel for pleasure) and from one individual to the next. In other words, some features may or may not apply to some students' literacy, and some facets may apply uniquely to individuals.

One should not be seduced into thinking that variables that are easy to define should be looked at to the exclusion of those that are difficult to assess. It may be foolish to exclude some facets because they are difficult to assess or because they look different either across students or situations or by the raters. Likewise, one should not be seduced into thinking that every reading and writing act is the same and involves the same variables. If the only literacy facets scored are those common across students and those that can be scored with high reliability across different students' responses, then certain facets will be given more weight than they deserve, and some important facets may be excluded.

Principle 10: Assessment Should Be More Developmental and Sustained Than Piecemeal and Shortsighted

To assess how well a student is doing, our vision or vistas need to change. If assessment goals are tied to development, then we need to look at patterns and long-term goals. What we see or look for in a single selection or case may not be helpful in looking for patterns across cases, selections, or circumstances. For example, as a reader or writer reads and writes a single selection, we might look for engagement and active involvement. Across situations we might want to consider the extent to which the interest and engagement are maintained across a range of material for different purposes. We also might be interested in the extent to which the student has developed a value for reading and writing that is reflected in how he or she uses reading and writing inside and outside the class. This may be apparent in his or her self-selection of books or self-initiated writing to serve different purposes.

Within areas such as the students' abilities to read with understanding, our goal for a single selection might be the extent to which a reader understands the main idea or theme or can draw conclusions using selected details. Across selections or in the long term, we might be interested in how the students use different books to contribute overall understandings tied to units or

projects or their own developing understandings of the world. Or, we might be interested in self-assessment. With a single selection we could focus on the reader's or writer's ability to monitor reading and writing, to set goals for a specific selection, and to problem-solve and wrestle with meaning making. Across selections we might be interested in the reader's or writer's ability to set goals and assess progress across several selections. In looking across selections, you should not expect that students will always appear to reveal the same level of sophistication with skills and strategies or necessarily use the same skills and strategies. See the Table for other short-term and long-term contrasts.

A shift toward assessment that examines students over time aligns assessment with classroom practices that pursue sustained engagement and aim to help students derive an understanding of patterns. It shifts our teaching and learning to long-term possibilities rather than the specific and short-term objectives of a lesson.

Principle 11: Most Interpretations of Results Are Not Straightforward

Assessment should be viewed as ongoing and suggestive, rather than fixed or definitive. In many ways teaching involves constant redevelopment or continuous experimentation and adjustments to plans, directions, and future goals. To appreciate the complexities and sophistication of teaching, consider the image one conjures up for a sportsperson. In certain sports involving eye-hand coordination with racquets or bats, players will begin their swing and constantly be making subtle adjustments as balls with different velocities, rotations, and angles are thrown at them. But sporting events pale in comparison with the dynamics of teacher-student interactions—the adjustments, just-in-time decision making, and ebb and flow of activities that occur. Teachers deal with students whom they may be trying to respond to, moti-

Table
Short- and long-term contrasts in assessment

Short-term/single instance	Long-term/multiple situations
Affect	
Engaged	Value
Active	Self-seeking ongoing
Thoughtful	Habit
Strategies	
Planning	Flexible, reflective, coordinated, selective,
Fixing up and troubleshooting	customized
Making connections	
Looking back, forward, and beyond	
Collaborating	Community building
Outcomes	
Main idea	Overall understandings, intertextual connections
Details	Projects
Conclusions	Applications
Implications	Range of problems and activities
	Overall understandings and themes
Self-assessment	
Self-monitoring	Self-scrutiny, goal setting, self-determinations
Online problem solving	Overall goals, progress, patterns

vate, mobilize, develop, and coach while understanding their needs, beliefs, strategies, and possible ways of responding as they are interacting with one another and dealing with the rest of their lives. Not surprising, teachers have to be a mix of ecologist, developer, advocate, coach, player, actor-director, stage manager, mayor, and sometimes counselor. Teachers are always planning and recognizing the need to make constant adjustments to what they are doing and what they might do next.

For these purposes, the typical assessment data (e.g., scouting reports of students provided by school records, premeasures of abilities, standardized or even informal assessments) may provide limited guidance to teachers in terms of the moment-by-moment decision making and even planning for the next day or week or even month. Too often typical student records seem as limited as a mug shot taken of the learner; you may be able to identify the learner (depending upon your ability to see likenesses) but may not. Certainly, the mug shot will not afford you an appreciation of the character of the student, nor will it help you understand the range of things that the student can do, nor will it support your ability to negotiate either long-term or short-term learning goals.

Most classroom-based assessments offer more promise but are still limited. Classroom-based assessment procedures may give teachers a better sense of how students will proceed in like circumstances and may also afford a fuller picture of the student across time. Portfolios, for example, are equivalent to scrapbooks involving multiple snapshots of the learner in a variety of contexts. Such assessments might afford a fuller and richer depiction of the learner and his or her pattern of development, but judgments—especially prescriptions—are never as straightforward as they might appear. The possibility of obtaining a complete vision of a learner is complicated by our inability to constantly monitor a learner, delve into and interpret his or her innermost thoughts, and achieve more than one perspective on the learner. It is also tied to the ever-changing nature of learning. Apart from the fact that our snapshots of classroom learning tend to be still shots of the learner, these images are tied to a place and time that has become more historical than current. Such limitations might be viewed as a problem if we were to perseverate on wanting to pin down what to do next with a student and be sure to stick to a set course. Instead, they should be anticipated and viewed as tentative bases for where and when one might begin. While we can develop short- and long-term goals and plans, we should not approach our teaching as if our prescriptions should not be altered, assessment fixed, nor directions more than suggestive.

Likewise, we should not approach assessment as if our results need be final or base our subsequent actions as if we have derived a decision that is any better than a hunch. We should avoid assuming that our assessments do anything more than afford us information that we might consider. No assessment should be used as restrictively or rigidly as decisions made in courts of law, yet I fear that many are. Instead we should reinforce what needs to occur in classrooms—constant adjustments, shifts, and ongoing decision making by teachers who are constantly watching, learning, coaching, and responding to students, peers, and others.

Principle 12: Learning Possibilities Should Be Negotiated With the Students and Stakeholders Rather Than Imposed via Standards and Assessments That Are Preset, Prescribed, or Mandated

The state within which I reside (along with many other states) has been seduced into thinking that standard setting may be the answer to improving education by ensuring that teachers teach and students learn certain basic skills. I find myself quite discouraged that our professional associations have aligned with similar efforts. Historically, standard setting (and the proficiency testing that it spurs) has tended to restrict access and experimentation at the same time as it has tended to support agendas tied to gatekeeping and exclusion.

The standard-setting enterprise and the proficiency-testing industry have the potential to perpetuate the view that we can set targets that we can easily reach. Unfortunately, it is problematic to assume that development is simply setting a course for the student from A to B-, especially when A is not taken into account and B is tied to views of outcomes looking for expertise rather than individual assessment of development. Without ample consideration being given for where students are and how and why they develop and their aspirations, we are apt to have our targets misplaced and our learning routes poorly aligned. I was in attendance at one of the many sessions on standards sponsored by the International Reading Association and the National Council for Teachers of English, when a speaker talked about standards using the analogy of a basketball player of the caliber of Michael Jordan as the "standard." As the speaker discussed the worth of setting standards based upon what we view as aspirations, I mulled over my height and my skill and what I might do to improve. Then I reminded myself of my reasons for playing basketball and where I am insofar as my background in basketball. I play basketball for fun, to be with my sons, and for exercise. We need to realize that we should be asking "Who is deciding? Whose standards are being represented?" In some ways the quest for educational improvement via standards and in turn proficiency testing places a premium on uniformity rather than diversity and favors prepackaged learning over emerging possibilities.

In a similar vein, advocates of standards emphasize the importance of the role of making judgments by comparisons to Olympic skating and other activities where success is measured by the trophies one achieves or the graded measures that are applied. I think we need to challenge this metaphor and question the emphasis on judgment rather than support. I prefer to think of a teacher as a coach rather than a judge—a supporter and counselor versus an enforcer and award- or grade-giver. I would like to see teachers view their role as providing guidance, handholding, and comments rather than As, Bs, and Cs or some score. In my view of a more ideal world, I see teachers, students, and caregivers operating in a kind of public sphere where they are part of the team negotiating for a better self. In this regard, I find myself fascinated with several classroom projects: with the kind of self-reflection and analysis occurring amidst the community-based preschool efforts of Reggio Emilia (Forman, 1993, 1994) where teachers, students, and community work together developing and implementing curriculum plans, ponder the right questions to ask to spur students' reflections, develop insights, and learn; with the work of Short, Harste, and Burke (1996) on developing inquiry in Indianapolis schools (as they engage students and teachers in considering the anomalies, patterns, and ways of looking at themselves); with the work of the Santa Barbara Classroom Discourse Group (1992a, 1992b), a community of teachers, researchers, and students interested in understanding how life in classrooms is constructed and

how expectations and practices influence opportunities to access, accomplish, and learn in school; and with the work of Fenner (1995) who uses a general form of Toulmin's (1958) analysis of argumentation to examine classroom conversations and student self-assessments with portfolios and looks for ways to help students look at themselves in terms of evidence, assumptions, claims, and goals. Fenner's approach to self-assessment moves us away from the typical checklist that asks students to detail in rather vague and unsubstantiated fashion their strengths and goals in a kind of "hit and miss" fashion.

Unfortunately, rather than language that suggests a view of classrooms as developmental and nurturing, oftentimes the metaphors adopted by those involved in the testing, proficiency, and standards enterprises seem more appropriate to developing consumer products connected to prescribed guidelines and uniform inspection procedures. That is, they seem to fit with our views of industry rather than nurturing human potential (Wile & Tierney, 1996). With this in mind, I would suggest that we should assess assessment based on whether it is parsimonious with a society's bill of rights and our views of individual rights, opportunities, and freedoms.

I fear that standards will perpetuate the effects uncovered when Ellwein, Glass, and Smith (1988) surveyed the history of the effects of various statewide proficiency testing—gatekeeping and the removal rather than enhancement of opportunities. Indeed, in Ohio and I would suspect other states, Ellwein et al.'s (1988) findings are being replicated. With the introduction of proficiency testing more students are dropping out. Ironically, the tests were intended to improve instruction, but fewer students are taking them, which in turn suggests that more students are passing them. So by keeping these dropouts invisible, advocates of proficiency testing and legislators claim the reform is having positive effects; that is, as more students leave or drop out, abhorring or deterred by the situation, legislators and advocates (including the media) erroneously suggest or advertise falsely that more students are passing.

Closing Remarks

My principles for assessment emanate from a mix of child-centered views of teaching, developmental views of children, constructivist views of knowing, critical theoretical views of empowerment, and pluralistic views of society. I view them as suggesting directions and guidelines for thinking about the why, how, where and when, who, and what of assessment.

Why?

To develop culturally sensitive versus culturally free assessments

To connect assessment to teaching and learning

To connect assessment to students' ongoing goal setting, decision making, and development

To become better informed and make better decisions

To develop assessment that keeps up with teaching and learning

How?

Collaborative, participatory, client centered

Coach-like, supportive and ongoing rather than judgmental, hard-nosed, and final

Supplemental and complementary versus grade-like and summative

Individually, diversely, not prepackaged

Judiciously

Developmentally

Reasoned

Where and when?

Amidst students' lives

Across everyday events and programs

In and out of school

Opportunistically, periodically, continuously

Who?

Students, teachers, and stakeholders

What?

Ongoing learning: development, resources, and needs

Complexities

Individuals and groups

Evidence of progress and decision making

Programs, groups, individuals

In describing the essence of my proposition, I would like to return to where I began. I believe an overriding principle, which is perhaps my 13th or more of a penumbra, is assessment should be assessed in terms of its relationship with teaching and learning, including the opportunities learners are offered and the rights and respect they are accorded.

Shifts in my own thinking about assessment began occurring when I asked myself this question: If I were to assess assessment, what criteria might I use? My answer to this question was that assessment practices should empower teachers, students, and their caregivers. In other words, assessment practices should enrich teaching and learning. As I explored how tests might be used as tools of empowerment for teachers and learners, I became interested in whether this type of assessment actually helped teachers and students (as well as the student's caregiver, resource teachers, principal, and others) achieve a more expanded view of the student's learning. I also wanted to know whether testing contributed to developing goals and formulating plans of action, which would suggest that assessment practices were empowering. My view of empowerment includes:

• Teachers having a fuller sense (expanded, refined, different) of the students' abilities, needs, and instructional possibilities;

• Students having a fuller sense of their own abilities, needs, and instructional possibilities;

• Teachers integrating assessment with teaching and learning (this would entail the dynamic/ongoing use of assessment practices, as well as assessment tailored to classroom life);

• Accommodating, adapting, adjusting, customizing-shifting assessment practices to fit with students and their learning and adjusting teaching in accordance with feedback from assessments;

• Students engaging in their own self-assessments as they set, pursue, and monitor their own goals for learning in collaboration with others, including peers, teachers, and caregivers; and

• Communities of teachers, students, and parents forming and supporting one another around this assessment process.

The use of standardized tests, tests accompanying the published reading programs, and even teacher-made tests do not expand teachers' views of their students' learning over time, nor suggest ways the teacher might help them. Nor are such tests integrated into classroom life. They tend to displace teaching and learning activities rather than enhance them.

Likewise, students rarely seem to be engaged in learning how to assess themselves. When my colleagues and I interviewed teachers with whom we began working in assessment 10 years ago, most teachers did not conceptualize the goal of testing to be helping students reflect or obtain feedback on their progress, nor did they envision tests as helping students establish, refine, or achieve learning goals. When we interviewed students, we found that students in these classes tended to have a limited and rather negative view of themselves, and they had set few learning goals. Attempts to examine the impact of more learner-based assessments yielded quite contrasting results. In classrooms in which portfolios were becoming an integral part of classroom life, teachers and students had developed a fuller sense of their own abilities (Carter,

1992; Carter & Tierney, 1988; Fenner, 1995; Stowell & Tierney, 1995; Tierney, Carter, & Desai, 1991).

A study by Shavelson, Baxter, and Pine (1992) provides other confirmation of the worth of aligning assessment to the teaching and learning in classrooms. In their attempts to examine variations in instructional programs, they concluded that direct observations and more emergent procedures captured the shifts in learning while traditional methods (multiple choice, short answer) did not. Such findings should come as no surprise to those of us who have been involved in research on the effects of teaching upon learning; that is, very few literacy researchers would rely upon a standardized test to measure the effectiveness of particular teaching strategies with different students. Instead, we are apt to pursue a range of measures, and some of us would not develop our measures a priori. In fact, several efforts have demonstrated the power of new assessment approaches to evaluate and guide program development and teacher change effectively (see Tierney et al., 1993).

Designing these new assessment approaches has to do with a way of teaching, testing, and knowing that is aligned with a set of values different than what has been and still is espoused by most educational reformers. Unfortunately, the power of some of the psychometricians and their entrenched values related to testing make the emergence of alternative assessment procedures difficult. Indeed, I see the shift as involving a cultural transformation, a shift away from what I view as a somewhat totalitarian practice tied to "old science" and metaphors that equate student learning to quality control.

Mike Rose (1995) suggests in *Possible Lives* that classrooms are created spaces, and the successful ones create spaces where students feel safe and secure; they are the classrooms in which students are willing to stretch, take risks, and pursue their interpretive authority for themselves and with others. In a similar vein, Kris

Gutierrez and her colleagues (Gutierrez, Rymes, & Larson, 1995), in discussing teacher-student discourse, assert the need for spaces where students and teachers can connect or transact with each other, rather than pass by one another. The key is finding ways to effect involvement and transaction rather than detachment and monolithic responses.

Assessment must address making futures possible and pursuable rather than impossible or improbable. We must create spaces where students, teachers, and others can achieve futures and spaces wherein the dynamics and practices are such that they challenge but do not undermine the ecology of who students are and might become.

References

Baker, A., & Luke, A. (1991). *Toward a critical sociology of reading pedagogy*. Philadelphia: John Benjamin's.

Basso, K. (1970). "To give up on words": Silence in Western Apache culture. *Southwest Journal of Anthropology, 26*, 213–230.

Bober, S. (1995, July). *Portfolio conferences*. Presentation at Lesley College Literacy Institute, Cambridge, MA.

Bruner, J. (1990). *Acts of meaning*. Cambridge, MA: Harvard University Press.

Carter, M. (1992). *Self-assessment using writing portfolios*. Unpublished doctoral dissertation, The Ohio State University, Columbus.

Carter, M., & Tierney, R.J. (1988, December). *Writing growth: Using portfolios in assessment*. Paper presented at the National Reading Conference, Tucson, AZ.

Ellwein, M.C., Glass, G.V., & Smith, M.L. (1988). Standards of competence: Propositions on the nature of testing reforms. *Educational Researcher, 17*(8), 4–9.

Fenner, L. (1995). *Student portfolios: A view from inside the classroom*. Unpublished doctoral dissertation, The Ohio State University, Columbus.

Forman, G. (1993). Multiple symbolizations in the long jump project. In C. Edward, L. Gandini, & G. Forman (Eds.), *The hundred languages of children* (pp. 171–188). Norwood, NJ: Ablex.

Forman, G. (1994). Different media, different languages. In L. Katz & B. Cesarone (Eds.), *Reflections on the Reggio Emilia approach* (pp. 41–54). Urbana, IL: ERIC/EECE.

Freire, P., & Macedo, D. (1987). *Literacy: Reading the word and the world*. South Hadley, MA: Bergin & Garvey.

Gee, J. (1990). *Social linguistics and literacies: Ideologies in discourse*. New York: Falmer Press.

Green, J., & Dixon, C. (1994). Talking knowledge into being: Discursive and social practices in classrooms. *Linguistics and Education, 5*, 231–239.

Guba, E.G., & Lincoln, Y.S. (1989). *Fourth generation evaluation*. Newbury Park, CA: Sage.

Gutierrez, K., Rymes, B., & Larson, J. (1995). Script, counterscript, and underlife in the classroom: James Brown versus Brown v. Board of Education. *Harvard Educational Review, 65*, 445–471.

Haney, W. (1993). Testing and minorities. In L. Weis & M. Fine (Eds.), *Beyond silenced voices* (pp. 45–74). Albany, NY: State University of New York Press.

hooks, b. (1989). *Talking back*. Boston: South End Press.

hooks, b. (1994). *Teaching to transgress: Education as the practice of freedom*. New York: Routledge.

Lather, P. (1986). Research as praxis. *Harvard Educational Review, 56*, 257–277.

Linn, R.L., Baker, E.L., & Dunbar, S.B. (1991). Complex performance assessment: Expectations and validation criteria. *Educational Researcher, 20*(8), 15–21.

Moss, P. (1996). Enlarging the dialogue in educational measurement: Voices from interpretive research traditions. *Educational Researcher, 25*(1), 20–28.

Ogbu, J. (1988). Literacy and schooling in subordinate cultures: The case of Black Americans. In E. Kintgen, B. Kroll, & M. Rose (Eds.), *Perspectives on literacy* (pp. 227–242). Carbondale, IL: Southern Illinois University Press.

Ogbu, J. (1991). Cultural perspective and school experience. In C. Walsh (Ed.), *Literacy as praxis: Culture, language and pedagogy* (pp. 25–50). Norwood, NJ: Ablex.

Phillips, S. (1983). *The invisible culture: Communication and community on the Warm Springs Indian reservation*. New York: Longman.

Purves, A. (1982). Conclusion to an international perspective to the evaluation of written composition. In B.H. Choppin & T.N. Postlethwaite (Eds.), *Evaluation in education: An international review series* (Vol. 5, pp. 343–345.). Oxford, England: Pergamon Press.

Rose, M. (1995). *Possible lives*. Boston: Houghton Mifflin.

Santa Barbara Classroom Discourse Group. (1992a). Constructing literacy in classrooms; literate action as social accomplishment. In H. Marshall (Ed.), *Redefining student learning: Roots of educational change* (pp. 119–150). Norwood, NJ: Ablex.

Santa Barbara Classroom Discourse Group. (1992b). The referential and intertextual nature of classroom life. *Journal of Classroom Interaction*, *27*(2), 29–36.

Shavelson, R., Baxter, G.P., & Pine, J. (1992). Performance assessment: Political rhetoric and measurement reality. *Educational Researcher*, *21*(4), 22–27.

Short, K.G., Harste, J.C., & Burke, C. (1996). *Creating classrooms for authors and inquirers*. Portsmouth, NH: Heinemann.

Spiro, R.J., Vispoel, W.L., Schmitz, J., Samarapungavan, A., & Boerger, A. (1987). Knowledge acquisition for application: Cognitive flexibility and transfer in complex content domains. In B.C. Britton & S. Glynn (Eds.), *Executive control processes* (pp. 177–200). Hillsdale, NJ: Erlbaum.

Stake, R. (1983). The case study method in social inquiry. In G. Madaus, M. Scriven, & D. Stufflebeam (Eds.), *Evaluation models* (pp. 279–286). Boston: Kluwer-Nijhoff.

Tierney, R.J., Carter, M., & Desai, L. (1991). *Portfolio assessment in the reading-writing classroom*. Norwood, MA: Christopher-Gordon.

Tierney, R.J., Clark, C., Fenner, L., Wiser, B., Herter, R.J., & Simpson, C. (in press). A portfolio discussion: Assumptions, tensions and possibilities. *Reading Research Quarterly*.

Tierney, R.J., Wile, J., Moss, A.G., Reed, E.W., Ribar, J.P., & Zilversmit, A. (1993). *Portfolio evaluation as history: Evaluation of the history academy for Ohio teachers* (occasional paper). National Council of History Education.

Toulmin, S. (1958). *The uses of argument*. Cambridge, England: Cambridge University Press.

Wile, J., & Tierney, R.J. (1996). Tensions in assessment: The battle over portfolios, curriculum and control. In R. Calfee & P. Perfumo (Eds.), *Writing portfolios in the classrooms: Policy and practice, process and peril* (pp. 203–218). Hillsdale, NJ: Erlbaum.

A Framework for Authentic Literacy Assessment

Scott G. Paris, Robert C. Calfee, Nikola Filby, Elfrieda H. Hiebert, P. David Pearson, Sheila W. Valencia, and Kenneth P. Wolf

October 1992

Assessment is fundamental to the improvement of education; it provides measures of success for students' learning, for educators' leadership, and for continuous evaluations of instructional programs. Many researchers and educators have argued that traditional psychoeducational tests are no longer adequate for these diverse assessment purposes (e.g., Resnick & Resnick, 1990; Valencia & Pearson, 1987). The proposals offered to improve literacy assessment include a wide variety of suggestions from new national tests based on performance measures to classroom assessments of individuals based on portfolios of work samples. It is unlikely that a single test or alternative assessment will meet the needs of all stakeholders, but it seems clear to us that the efforts are stimulating many new and useful approaches to assessment.

The purpose of this article is to describe a framework for literacy assessment that can be adapted to suit the assessment needs of particular schools and districts. The framework involves five phases of decision making that policy makers should consider as they revise assessment practices. Because the decisions about what outcomes are valued, how to assess literacy achievements, and how to use the data directly affect teachers, parents, and students, we believe that the decision making should be shared among the various stakeholders. In this manner, all the participants are informed about the goals and criteria of assessment, and they are motivated to participate fully in assessment. Although this article describes a process of decision making about authentic literacy assessments that was created by the authors for an external program evaluation, we encourage educators to emulate this process in schools and districts because it can establish an informed consensus among local stakeholders about the literacy outcomes and processes that will be assessed and valued in each community.

Our team was assembled as a group of consultants to the Far West Laboratory for Educational Research and Development charged with designing a framework for the evaluation of literacy achievement in the Kamehameha Elementary Education Program (KEEP). The overall evaluation, conducted by the Southwest

Regional Educational Laboratory, is part of a U.S. federally funded project designed to assess the effectiveness of the K–3 KEEP literacy curriculum and to compare the achievement of KEEP students at the end of third grade to similar students in other classrooms in Hawaii. What began as a program evaluation of a "whole literacy" curriculum grew into the creation of alternative literacy assessments because of the limitations of standardized tests to capture critical aspects of the curriculum objectives of both KEEP and the Hawaii Department of Education (DOE) curricula (Giuli, 1991). The situation provided a unique opportunity for our team to work together on a specific practical problem. We believe that both the process and the outcome can serve as models for others to design authentic literacy assessments.

The Hawaiian Context of KEEP

KEEP began in 1972 as an experimental project at the Kamehameha School to foster literacy among native Hawaiian students (Tharp & Gallimore, 1988). It is now disseminated in eight schools throughout the islands of Hawaii and serves annually approximately 3,000 students in K–3 classes. The curriculum has recently been extended to some Grade 4, 5, and 6 classrooms also. The KEEP curriculum has been revised several times and may be described most appropriately as a dynamic rather than static set of guidelines for curriculum, instruction, and assessment. For example, the KEEP *Literacy Curriculum Guide* (Au, Blake, Herman, Oshiro, & Scheu, 1990) describes instruction that includes language experience and whole literacy activities relevant for native Hawaiian children.

The *Guide* also describes a portfolio assessment system of observations and checklists that teachers can use to assess students' progress against developmental benchmarks. The checklists summarize children's literacy in four broad areas: ownership and voluntary reading, reading comprehension, writing processes, and emergent literacy (Au, Scheu, Kawakami, & Herman, 1990). Although the *Guide* provided us with valuable information about the goals of the KEEP curriculum and assessment, our suggestions for authentic assessments were not constrained by extant practices. The portfolio system described by Au et al. is used primarily by paraprofessional aides for diagnostic purposes, although teachers are gradually learning about the system so that they can record similar observations. In contrast, the assessment system that we were charged to create will be used by external evaluators to make quantitative comparisons between the achievements of KEEP and non-KEEP students.

The *Language Arts Program Guide* (Hawaii Department of Education, 1988) describes an integrated language arts curriculum that is similar to the KEEP framework but less oriented to whole language instruction and the sociocultural backgrounds of native Hawaiian children. Learner outcomes for each grade level and domain of language arts are specified in more detail than the KEEP benchmarks, but the objectives of both curricula are generally congruent. It is important to note that we used the curricular goals and activities of both KEEP and the DOE to determine which aspects of literacy are emphasized in daily instruction and which outcomes are valued.

The assessment problems in Hawaii are similar to those faced by most school districts—that is, how to create assessments that (a) measure critical features of the curriculum, (b) are consistent with instructional practices, (c) motivate students, and (d) provide measures of accountability (Winograd, Paris, & Bridge, 1991). The traditional practice in Hawaii has been to test all students above second grade every spring with the Stanford Achievement Test, which does not measure many of the goals in the KEEP and

Hawaii DOE curricula. Many teachers spend months preparing their students for the Stanford with materials and activities that are inconsistent with their regular curriculum. Likewise, many students regard the Stanford as the goal of literacy learning and the pinnacle of the academic year. Administrators report a "canyon effect" of low motivation for the last month of school following the Stanford. The Stanford results have been used historically to evaluate the KEEP program without regard for the variable time that teachers and students have participated in actual KEEP classrooms or for the misalignment between the Stanford and the curricula.

Given these problems, it is not surprising that evaluations of KEEP using scores from the Stanford and the Metropolitan Achievement Test (Yap, Estes, & Nickel, 1988) revealed poor performance of KEEP students and frustrated KEEP staff. There was a clear and compelling need to design alternative assessments to measure literacy development in KEEP classrooms. The assessments needed to measure reading and writing proficiency as well as students' literacy ownership, habits, attitudes, and strategies in a manner that reflected the interactive, collaborative, and constructive nature of learning in Hawaiian classrooms. This is the problem we tackled.

Negotiating a Framework for Alternative Assessment

We began meeting in January 1991 as a group, met periodically during the year, collected pilot data, and corresponded regularly about the framework. As with many new projects, we realized the shape of the task and the solutions only after being immersed in them for many months. In the end, we can identify five discrete phases to our decision making that may be heuristic for others.

Phase 1: Identifying Dimensions of Literacy

Our discussions about alternative assessments always hinged on issues of curriculum and instruction because we all agreed that "authentic assessment" must reflect daily classroom practices and goals. Thus, the initial task was to decide which aspects of students' literacy development are important to measure in Hawaiian schools and, correspondingly, which aspects are not assessed by current procedures. We began by considering various taxonomies that included elements such as knowledge, skills, and attitudes of reading, writing, listening, and speaking. None of these were satisfactory because they failed to capture the interconnectedness and the psychological characteristics of motivated literacy that were central to the curricula. From discussions with educators from KEEP and the DOE, as well as our observations and knowledge of KEEP, we gleaned a list of 5–10 dimensions that were the basis for continuing discussions. We subsequently identified seven critical dimensions of literacy, described in Table 1, that we considered to be at the core of both curricula. These dimensions embody a view of literacy that is interactive, social, constructive, metacognitive, motivated, and integrated with functional language uses. The assessment of these dimensions transcend the Stanford scores and traditional emphases on basic reading skills.

The results of this phase of decision making included both a product and a process. The process of examining the curricula, observing classroom instruction, and operationalizing the objectives of "whole literacy" took several months and involved brainstorming, clarifying values, and building consensus among our team. We also discussed our assessment proposals with Kathy Au and Chuck Giuli at KEEP and with Betsy Brandt at the DOE. It was remarkably illuminating to negotiate the alignment of

Table 1
Critical dimensions and attributes of literacy

1. Engagement with text through reading

A critical aspect of literacy is the extent to which readers and writers interact with the ideas conveyed in text. They need to relate their background knowledge and experiences to new textual information and integrate the ideas. Thoughtful engagement with text implies that readers construct meaning sensibly, that they employ strategies as they read, and that they reflect on the meaning and style of the text. Comprehension is a key element of engagement, but the dimension also includes the demonstration of thinking strategies and personal responses to text that extend the basic interpretation of text.

2. Engagement with text through writing

Writing is a constructive expression of ideas that are communicated coherently and accurately. Students' involvement with writing and reading should provide mutual support for effective literacy strategies, habits, and motivation. Writing should be embedded in everyday activities and based on genuine communicative purposes. It should allow students to compose their ideas on a variety of topics with different genres and styles. Students' writing should include their personal opinions, reflections, and elaborations to texts they have read. The message and voice should be clear. The technical aspects of writing such as spelling, word choice, punctuation, grammar, and organization should be appropriate for the students' grade level.

3. Knowledge about literacy

Students should understand that language can be expressed through reading and writing according to literacy conventions and that adherence to these conventions helps people to understand each other through written communication. For example, effective readers and writers understand the different purposes and structures of various literary genres and know how strategies can be used while reading and writing. Their knowledge about literacy also includes their metalinguistic understanding of the nuances of language, such as ambiguity and figurative language, as well as their understanding about the connections among reading, writing, listening, and speaking.

4. Orientation to literacy

Reading and writing require more than engagement with text and the construction of meaning. They also require motivation so that children can read, write, and learn independently. Learners must set appropriate goals for literacy and persevere in the face of difficulty. Motivated readers seek challenges in what they read just as motivated writers extend themselves to compose more text, to write in various genres, or to write creatively. A positive orientation to literacy also includes feelings of confidence, optimism, enjoyment, and control so that children regard their achievements with pride and satisfaction.

5. Ownership of literacy

Good readers develop independent reading habits, identify their favorite topics and books, and monitor their own progress and achievements. In this sense, they develop "ownership" of their reading that reflects pride in their accomplishments and their enjoyment in recreational reading. Likewise, good writers engage in writing independently, read their own compositions, and develop preferences for writing about some topics or writing with particular genres. This sense of ownership fosters lifelong literacy habits and is evident in children's preferences for reading and writing, their independence, and their initiative for literacy.

(continued)

6. Collaboration

Reading and writing are not always private activities; they often involve discussion and cooperation so that meaning can be negotiated among individuals. The social construction of meaning is especially important in school where instructional activities may involve shared reading and writing, cooperative learning, and peer tutoring arrangements. Effective readers and writers can work with others in "communities of learners" to create meaning, revise compositions, present and share their ideas, and solve problems while they read and write. Frequent participation with other students in school is one mark of collaboration; social respect for others and mutual benefits for learning are also desirable consequences of collaboration.

7. Connectedness of the curriculum

Reading and writing are pervasive activities in school and are fundamental for learning across the entire school curriculum. It is important, therefore, that children read and write in order to learn in subjects such as social studies, science, and mathematics and that the skills, motivation, and collaboration evident in literacy instruction are reinforced in content areas. It is also important for children to understand the connections among reading, writing, listening, and speaking so that they regard language arts as integrated, purposeful, and pragmatic. Literacy also needs to be connected between school and home so that families can support school-based literacy skills and habits and so that teachers can be sensitive to the unique backgrounds and talents of each child.

---

curriculum and assessment, and we were all struck by the value this process can have for teachers and administrators. Indeed, students who understand the connections between daily activities for learning and assessment might also become more informed about the purposes of assessment and the criteria for success. Knowing what counts in literacy performance in the classroom can help create a shared vision for teaching and learning.

Phase 2: Identifying Attributes of Literacy Dimensions

As we identified potential dimensions we also discussed the kinds of literate performance that distinguish skilled from less skilled students on each dimension. These attributes could be described at general or specific levels. For example, in the dimension of Engagement With Text Through Reading, we discussed how good readers are constructive, strategic, reflective, and evaluative. For each of these general attributes, we generated three specific literacy indicators that could be verified empirically from students' performance, such as using appropriate strategies for monitoring comprehension or making inferences. Each of these indicators is described in Table 2 and provides a tangible referent point for evaluating students' literacy. These indicators lie on continua, but anchored descriptions are provided only for the high and low ends. More detailed standards and scoring rubrics can be generated for each indicator.

One virtue of this activity for educators in general is that the participants share their theories of literacy with each other so that ideas about literacy development are reconsidered within this collaborative context. We believe that this exercise is extremely valuable for

Table 2
Performance indicators for each attribute and dimension of literacy

ENGAGEMENT WITH TEXT THROUGH READING

Low engagement	High engagement
Reading is constructive	
a. Fails to build on prior knowledge	a. Integrates new ideas with previous knowledge and experiences
b. Few inferences or elaborations; literal retelling of text	b. Exhibits within text and beyond text inferences
c. Focus is on isolated facts; does not connect text elements	c. Identifies and elaborates plots, themes, or concepts
Reading is evaluative	
a. Fails to use personal knowledge and experience as a framework for interpreting text	a. Uses prior knowledge and experience to construct meaning
b. Is sensitive to the author's style, assumptions, perspective, and claims	b. Is sensitive to, and may even question, the author's style, assumptions, perspective, and claims
c. Fails to examine or go beyond a literal account of the ideas in the text	c. Expresses opinions, judgments, or insights about the content of the text

ENGAGEMENT WITH TEXT THROUGH WRITING

Low engagement	High engagement
Writing is constructive	
a. Writes disconnected words or phrases with few identifiable features of any genre	a. Writes well-constructed, thematic, cohesive text that is appropriate to the genre
b. Fails to use personal knowledge as a base for composing text	b. Draws on personal knowledge and experiences in composing text
c. Little evidence of voice, personal style, or originality	c. Creative writing reveals a strong sense of voice, personal style, and originality
Writing is technically appropriate	
a. Writing includes numerous violations of the conventions of spelling, punctuation, and usage	a. Displays developmentally appropriate use of the conventions of spelling, punctuation, and usage
b. Inappropriate or inflexible use of grammatical structures	b. Writing exhibits grammatical structures appropriate to the purpose and genre
c. Limited and contextually inappropriate vocabulary	c. Rich, varied, and appropriate vocabulary

(continued)

Table 2
Performance indicators for each attribute and dimension of literacy (continued)

KNOWLEDGE ABOUT LITERACY

Low knowledge	High knowledge

Knowledge about literacy conventions and structures

a. Unaware of the functions of print conventions and punctuation in written communication	a. Understands the functions that print conventions and punctuation play in written communication
b. Unaware of text structures and genres	b. Can identify and use several specific text structures and genres
c. Unaware of the subtleties of language use; does not understand or use connotative meaning, ambiguity, or figurative language	c. Understands that words have multiple meanings; can use and understand ambiguity and figurative language

Knowledge about strategies

a. Unaware of the strategies that can be applied while reading and writing	a. Knows strategies that can be applied before, during, and after reading and writing
b. Limited understanding of how strategies can be applied while reading or writing	c. Can explain how strategies are applied or might be used
c. Naive about the value of strategies; does not use strategies selectively	c. Understands how and when strategies can be used and why they are helpful

ORIENTATION TO LITERACY

Low orientation	High orientation

Motivation for reading and writing

a. Goals for literacy are task completion and extrinsic rewards	a. Goals are intrinsic and mastery oriented
b. Gives up easily in the face of difficulty	b. Persists when confronted with obstacles or difficulties
c. Chooses tasks where success or failure are certain	c. Chooses challenging tasks on the edge of current abilities

Attitudes about reading and writing

a. Negative attitudes about reading and writing	a. Exhibits enthusiasm for reading and writing
b. Exhibits embarrassment, passivity, and insecurity about self as a reader or writer	b. Exhibits pride and confidence about self as a reader or writer
c. Views literacy events as under the control of others	c. Views self as in charge of own literacy and feels that others respect contributions

(continued)

Table 2
Performance indicators for each attribute and dimension of literacy (continued)

OWNERSHIP OF LITERACY

Low ownership	High ownership
Interests and habits	
a. Expresses little or no preference for different topics, genres, and authors	a. Exhibits clear preferences for topics, genres, and authors
b. Avoids reading and writing as free choice activities	b. Voluntarily selects reading and writing as free choice activities
c. Does not choose texts to read or topics to write about appropriately	c. Chooses appropriate texts to read and topics for writing
Self-assessment of reading and writing	
a. Rarely evaluates own work, learning, or progress	a. Frequently assesses own work, learning, and progress
b. Shows little initiative in evaluating own work	b. Takes initiative to review and monitor own performance
c. Uses single, vague, or unclear criteria in assessing own work	c. Employs appropriate criteria to evaluate what has been read or written

COLLABORATION

Low collaboration	High collaboration
Cooperation among peers	
a. Little participation with others; engages in isolated activities	a. Frequently engages in collaborative literacy activities
b. Unwilling to engage in the collaborative construction of meaning	b. Initiates discussion, dialogue, or debate about text meaning
c. Reluctant to give or seek help; does not encourage the literacy development of peers	c. Provides positive support, affect, and instructional scaffolding for peers
Community of learners	
a. Does not share goals, values, and practices with others	a. Shares goals, values, and practices with others
b. Does not participate, or plays only a limited array of roles, in the learning community	b. Plays a variety of roles (performer, audience member, leader, supporter) with the learning community
c. Is unaware of the contribution others can make to one's own literacy development	c. Values the contributions of others; respects others' opinions and help

(continued)

Table 2
Performance indicators for each attribute and dimension of literacy (continued)

CONNECTEDNESS OF THE CURRICULUM

Low connectedness	High connectedness
Within school	
a. Views reading and writing as decontextualized activities	a. Understands that reading and writing are tools for learning and personal insight
b. Views reading, writing, speaking, and listening as independent of each other	b. Views reading, writing, speaking, and listening as mutually supportive activities
c. Sees little relation between reading and writing and other content areas	c. Understands that what one learns in reading and writing is useful in other content areas
Beyond school	
a. Rarely engages in reading and writing outside of school	a. Reading and writing are part of daily routine activities
b. Views the school literacy curriculum as unrelated to one's own life	b. Connects school literacy activities with reading and writing in daily life
c. Feels discouraged and unsupported for reading and writing outside of school	c. Feels encouraged and supported to read and write outside of school

groups of teachers, administrators, and parents who design assessment. A second virtue of identifying specific attributes of literacy is that it forces us to consider jointly the questions "What is important?" and "How can we measure it?" Although the ease and economy of measurement are important, we need to ensure that new forms of assessment are aimed at critical aspects of students' learning and development and not just those skills that are readily tested. Of course, the dimensions, attributes, and indicators are interrelated, so they all must be negotiated together. We often expanded and reduced the lists we produced because there appeared to be an imbalance in the level of detail or emphasis. We cannot emphasize too strongly the importance of the *process* of negotiating what is important to assess because it allows local stakeholders to create a shared set of values and concepts about literacy development.

Evaluating Literacy Performance

The next three phases in the design of alternative assessments translate the values and specific attributes identified in phases 1 and 2 into assessment procedures. There are several options available to decision makers at this point for gathering evidence about students' learning, including conventional tests, checklists, structured lessons, observations, etc. We chose to analyze students' ordinary literacy artifacts and activities rather than their responses to specific instruction or uniform content for three reasons. First, we wanted the literacy assessment to reflect authentic activities in classrooms, including the variety and quality of students' literacy experiences. Second, we wanted to design a prototypical assessment model based on students' work samples that could be used flexibly and adapted by other educators. Third, the overall

KEEP evaluation plan includes several other assessments of children's literacy development that are not based on students' daily performance.

Phase 3: Methods for Collecting Evidence About Literacy Proficiency

Work that students produce in class every day reveals their usual learning and motivation. Such work samples are authentic performance measures that reflect instructional opportunities afforded in classrooms as well as achievements of students. Ordinary work samples, therefore, are not pure ability measures, but they can provide illuminating evidence about students' typical and best work in class. Conversely, a paucity of outstanding work samples may indicate a lack of opportunities in the classroom, an "instructional deficit," rather than some kind of deficit in the student. Additional information about students' achievements, including their perceptions, understanding, and self-assessment, can be gained when students are given opportunities to reflect on their strengths, weaknesses, and progress. The method of reflective interviews about work samples is consistent with portfolio approaches, but it is an equally fair assessment in classrooms where portfolio systems are not used.

The method we devised was to collect all literacy work samples produced in one week by children who represented a range of achievement levels in each classroom. The artifacts included reading logs, journal entries, letters, essays, spelling lists, worksheets, and book reports. In the pilot project, teachers collected work samples from four students in each class who were then interviewed about their work as well as their literacy habits and attitudes. In our pilot project with four teachers and 16 third graders, there was an abundance of diverse materials that reflected the curricular units and literate activities occurring in each classroom.

At the end of the week, an interviewer discussed the materials with students individually for 20–30 minutes. Approximately 20 questions were assembled in a structured yet conversational interview, described fully in Wolf et al. (1991), that was designed to yield information about the attributes and indicators of each dimension so that a score could be assigned. For example, students were asked questions such as:

• Here is a sample of your writing that you did this week. Are you finished with it? What do you like about this piece? What would you change to make it better? Did other students in the class help you to write or revise it?

• What book have you read this week? Tell me about it. How did it make you feel? Was there anything surprising in the book?

• Do you think you are a good reader and writer? What makes someone a really good reader? When you think of yourself as a reader, what would you like to do differently or better?

The interview was tape recorded and transcribed later so that we could discuss the students' answers as we created the scoring system. In the future, we anticipate that trained interviewers can score the students' reflections and work samples during the interview so that the process is speedy and efficient.

Phase 4: Scoring Students' Work Samples

The next phase in our project was to score the pilot data from 16 students to determine if the system could yield reliable and informative measures of differences among students. We gathered the data in May and discussed whether the data should be scored at the level of indicators (the 42 "a, b, c" items in Table 2) or at the level of attributes (the 14 subcategories in Table 2, e.g., "Reading is constructive") or at the general level of dimensions (the 7 major entries in Table 2, e.g., "Engagement With Text Through Reading"). We settled on an intermediate level of attributes as most appropriate for the holistic, quantitative judgments that we wanted to make. However, teachers who use a similar system may elect a more holistic evaluation or choose to record narrative comments rather than quantitative scores.

The scoring procedure involved reading the transcript of the student's interview, examining the work samples, and assigning a score of 1–4 for each attribute. The four-point scale was anchored at both ends with descriptions of the attributes (e.g., "Integrates new ideas with previous knowledge and experiences"; see Table 2) which aided the judgments considerably because they were tangible examples of students' knowledge, attitudes, or behavior for each attribute. The scores can be aggregated across the two attributes per dimension (values range from 2–8) and across the seven dimensions (values range from 14–56) to give summary scores about the literacy performance of individual students. As we evaluated different students' work samples, we achieved greater consensus in scoring. Although the evaluations were conducted by our team, we are optimistic that trained and knowledgeable teachers can use this holistic scoring procedure to obtain trustworthy assessments of students' literacy development.

An example might help to illustrate the scoring procedures. Alice's collection of work included nearly 20 pages of her own writing, including poems, a response journal, and a long story entitled "Ghost Dad." During her interview, Alice told how she liked to choose her own journal topics and how she chose her best poems to include in a portfolio. She also identified her favorite books and described how she enjoyed reading frequently. These remarks, coupled with the tangible evidence, earned her a score of three out of four points for the attribute of "Interests and Habits" within the dimension of "Ownership" (see Table 2). The other attribute in that dimension, "Self-Assessment," only received two points because Alice said that

her writing goal was to write faster, a negative piece of evidence that was offset modestly by her discussion of choosing her best poem. In a similar fashion, Alice's comments and reflections, coupled with a review of her work samples, were used to determine scores for each of the 14 attributes.

Because this was a pilot project and the scoring system was generated and refined as we examined students' work, we do not have numerical indices of the validity and reliability of the performance assessments. However, we believe that this model yields data that are authentic and trustworthy because the work samples are derived from daily curricular activities and interpreted by students (cf. Valencia, 1990). Traditional notions of reliability, based on the similarity of scores from tests to retest, may no longer apply to performance assessments that provide opportunities for reflection and learning. Indeed, low test-retest reliability may be desirable if students benefit from the process of assessing their own literacy.

Assessments grounded in performance may provide dynamic descriptions of students' rates of learning and degrees of change. Furthermore, Linn, Baker, and Dunbar (1991) have suggested that performance-based assessments be judged by expanded notions of validity that include concepts such as the consequences of assessment, the fairness of tasks and scoring, the generalizability of results, and the quality and complexity of the content of the assessments. We think that evaluations of students' work samples like we have done will encourage teachers and students to produce complex, high quality, diverse, and fair collections of literacy artifacts. The consequences of such assessment will stimulate motivated learning by students as well as effective instruction by teachers that is aligned with curricular objectives.

These brief comments about reliability and validity illustrate the need to expand traditional psychometric definitions. We believe that various assessment models, such as the one we designed for KEEP, should be examined against standards of validity and reliability, but we also recognize that those psychometric constructs are being redefined as new kinds of assessment are created. Revisions of assessment and criteria for evaluating assessment are intertwined, so we encourage researchers to substantiate the usefulness of new assessment procedures against a wide variety of criteria.

Phase 5: Interpreting and Using the Data

We have not yet had an opportunity to implement the system and use the data derived from the interviews and work samples. However, the framework we created was guided by certain intended uses of the data, and we strongly believe that stakeholders must consider the uses and consequences of assessment *before* creating alternative measures. The data derived from the interviews and artifacts can be reported in several ways. One option is to report the scores for each attribute or dimension. These can be compared directly across students, classrooms, or programs. Another option is to report the percentage of students meeting some criterion (e.g., a "High orientation," see Table 2), on each dimension. A third option is to aggregate the data across dimensions and report single scores for each student, although this mixes evaluations from quite different dimensions of literacy. A fourth option is to record students' achievements with narrative comments rather than numerical scores, noting areas of particular talent or weakness.

Regardless of the format of the data, the results of authentic assessments can serve a variety of purposes, all of which can improve opportunities for students to learn. First, alternative assessments can provide richer diagnostic information about students' development because the assessments are tied directly to the curriculum objectives and to instructional procedures and goals in the classroom (Calfee & Hiebert, 1990). In this model, assessment and instruction become overlapping and symbiotic activities. A second use of the data is to inform parents about their children's progress as well as the curriculum objectives and instructional practices. We believe that parents can become more involved in their children's literacy when they understand how they can support and extend instructional efforts at school. Third, authentic assessments help students to engage in monitoring and evaluating their own work, to reflect on their efforts and accomplishments, and to gain insights into the processes of learning that will help them in future tasks (Tierney, Carter, & Desai, 1991). Fourth, we think that authentic assessments can yield summative data for administrators who must provide quantitative indicators of accountability. These multiple functions can be served by authentic assessments when they are designed with these purposes in mind.

Modifying and Applying the Framework

The strength of the five-phase framework is that it can serve as a dynamic, flexible system for any district or state revising or creating alternative assessments of educational progress. Our project illustrates the feasibility of the framework for large-scale literacy assessments. We see the coherence, flexibility, and local control as strengths of the process. For example, a district might identify different dimensions of literacy than we did, but the process of identifying what is valued in a curriculum and building consensus among stakeholders clarifies what needs to be assessed.

The specification of characteristics and attributes of literacy can also be negotiated to reflect the level of specificity desired for different purposes. Teachers who want fine-grained assessments to use diagnostically may use the evidence in a different manner than administrators who may need only general descriptions; however, the same kinds of dimensions and evidence undergird both assessments. For example, a teacher who reviews a student's work in an interview may notice that the student is unaware of text structures, genre, and specific comprehension strategies suitable for expository text. The teacher might design specific projects involving documents and library research skills to improve the student's knowledge about literacy. An administrator who notices low scores on this dimension across many students may look for concomitant low reading scores in social studies and science and may suggest instructional strategies for content area reading.

There is also flexibility in the ways that evidence is collected and scored. We believe that a broad array of evidence is needed to augment traditional test scores, evidence that should include students' daily work samples collected periodically throughout the year. The collection of evidence need not be disruptive nor undermine the curriculum if assessment, instruction, and curricula are mutually supportive. Local decision makers can choose to score students' work quantitatively or qualitatively. In our project there was a need for quantitative data to make yearly comparisons among programs so the data could serve summative evaluation purposes. If the data are used primarily for formative purposes, then qualitative descriptions might suffice.

We consider the local control and implementation of assessment reform to be essential, but at the same time, we see a need for districts to generate coherent frameworks to guide their decision making. As districts move away from using "off-the-shelf, one-size-fits-all" commercial tests of literacy, they need to clarify what they value, what they measure, what standards will be used for evaluation, how they will collect the evidence, and how the data will be used. Our framework for creating alternative literacy assessments provides a starting point that can be expanded and revised to fit the needs of any district. We are enthusiastic about the opportunities that exist today for designing new kinds of educational assessment, not just new tests, but whole new systems of assessing teaching and learning in schools. Creative solutions to long-standing problems of assessment hold great promise for enhancing students' learning, motivation, and achievement.

Authors' Note

This report is based on research supported by the United States Department of Education (USDOE) pursuant to Public Law 100-297, through federal funds granted to the Kamehameha Schools/Bishop Estate (KS/BE) by Grant Number S208A90001. The views expressed are the authors' and not necessarily shared by the USDOE or KS/BE. We appreciate the intellectual stimulation and opportunities for dialogue provided by our colleagues at KS/BE and thank especially Chuck Giuli and Kathy Au.

References

Au, K., Blake, K., Herman, P., Oshiro, M., & Scheu, J. (1990). *Literacy curriculum guide*. Honolulu, HI: Center for the Development of Early Education, Kamehameha Schools.

Au, K.H., Scheu, J.A., Kawakami, A.J., & Herman, P.A. (1990). Assessment and accountability in a whole language curriculum. *The Reading Teacher, 43*, 674–578.

Calfee, R., & Hiebert, E. (1990). Classroom assessment of reading. In R. Barr, M. Kamil, P. Mosenthal, & P.D. Pearson (Eds.), *Handbook of reading research* (2nd ed., pp. 281–309). White Plains, NY: Longman.

Giuli, C. (1991). Developing a summative measure of whole language instruction: A sonata in risk-taking. *The Kamehameha Journal of Education, 2*, 67–65.

Hawaii Department of Education. (1988). *Language arts program guide*. Honolulu, HI: Office of Instructional Services.

Linn, R.L., Baker, E.L., & Dunbar, S.B. (1991). Complex, performance-based assessment: Expectations and validation criteria. *Educational Researcher, 20,* 15–21.

Resnick, L., & Resnick, D. (1990). Tests as standards of achievement in school. *The uses of standardized tests in American education* (pp. 83–80). Princeton, NJ: Educational Testing Service.

Tharp, R.G., & Gallimore, R. (1988). *Rousing minds to life: Teaching, learning, and schooling in social context.* New York: Cambridge University Press.

Tierney, R.J., Carter, M.A., & Desai, L.E. (1991). *Portfolio assessment in the reading-writing classroom.* Norwood, MA: Christopher-Gordon.

Valencia, S.W. (1990). Alternative assessment: Separating the wheat from the chaff. *The Reading Teacher, 44,* 60–61.

Valencia, S., & Pearson, P.D. (1987). Reading assessment: A time for change. *The Reading Teacher, 40,* 726–733.

Winograd, P., Paris, S., & Bridge, C. (1991). Improving the assessment of reading. *The Reading Teacher, 45,* 108–116.

Wolf, K., Filby, N., Paris, S., Valencia, S., Pearson, D., Hiebert, E., & Calfee, R. (1991). *KEEP literacy assessment system.* Final report from the Far West Laboratory for Educational Research and Development.

Yap, K.O., Estes, G.D., & Nickel, P.R. (1988, September). *A summative evaluation of the Kamehameha elementary education program as disseminated in Hawaii public schools.* Northwest Regional Educational Laboratory, Evaluation and Assessment Program.

Putting It All Together: Solving the Reading Assessment Puzzle

Roger Farr

September 1992

Reading assessment has become a genuine puzzle. Confusion and debate continue about what the goals of school assessment of reading should be and about what types of tests and other assessments are needed to achieve those goals. That debate should focus on the purposes for assessment and whether current tests achieve those purposes. Too often, however, the focus of the debate is on the latest testing panacea. In this article, I first examine the complex components of the assessment puzzle. Next I propose a solution to the puzzle that involves linkages among various assessment audiences and approaches. I conclude with a few remarks about how school districts in the United States might pull together all the pieces and solve the assessment puzzle for themselves.

Examining the Pieces of the Assessment Puzzle

The pieces of the puzzle represent many types of assessments, critical attitudes about them, and attempts to challenge or improve them. One of the truly puzzling aspects of reading assessment to many educators is that the amount of testing appears to increase at the same time that criticism of it intensifies (Farr & Carey, 1986; McClellan, 1988; Salganik, 1985; Valencia & Pearson, 1987).

Criticism of Schools Has Led to More Assessment

Public disappointment with student achievement has led to extensive criticism of U.S. schools. This disapproval intensified in the 1950s with a focus on reading. Reading assessment conducted to prove or disprove the criticism has received a great deal of attention ever since. Could Johnny read or not, and how well or how poorly? By the 1960s, and beyond, score declines on tests used to predict how well high schoolers would do in college compounded public concern and criticism (The National Commission on Excellence in Education, 1983).

The conviction that many students were receiving high school diplomas and yet were almost totally illiterate became firmly established in the public's mind (Purves & Niles, 1984). The Peter Doe case in California exemplified that concern (Saretsky, 1973). The case concerned a high school student who sued the school district for graduating him without teaching him to read. As a result of this kind of dissatisfaction with educational outcomes, the use of standardized, norm-referenced assessment intensified, and state minimum competency testing programs proliferated (Madaus, 1985; Salmon-Cox, 1981).

The data to determine whether scores on reading tests were deteriorating over time are sketchy at best and tend not to substantiate dramatic declines in the reading performance of U.S. students over the years (Farr & Fay, 1982; Farr, Fay, Myers, & Ginsberg, 1987; Stedman & Kaestle, 1987). Nonetheless, the public has remained convinced that performance has dropped rather dramatically. Further, the prevalence of minimum competency programs has not significantly altered the conviction of the public and press that student achievement, particularly in reading, continues to deteriorate.

This unabated critical concern was at least partly responsible for the establishment of the National Assessment of Educational Progress (NAEP), an ongoing federally mandated study that now provides some reading performance data over time. Any declines it has depicted are small compared to the public's determined assumptions (Mullis, Owen, & Phillips, 1990). And although careful analyses of the ACT and SAT score declines has cited several reasonable causes other than poor schools, that phenomenon did much to sustain and cement public conviction and the demand for accountability testing (Popham, 1987; Resnick, 1982).

The continuing debate about the quality of U.S. schools has now given rise to a new focus on standards and assessment. At the same time that they reaffirm their conviction that children are not learning in school, critics like Chester Finn (1992) echo the call from the White House "for new American achievement tests" that compare student performance to "world class standards" that would be set as criterion references. President Bush (1991) has called for "voluntary national tests for 4th, 8th, and 12th graders in the five core subjects" to "tell parents and educators, politicians and employers, just how well our schools are doing."

The Search for Alternative Assessments Has Also Led to More Assessment

In addition to dissatisfaction with the schools, there has been a quest for assessments that are closely aligned with more holistic views of language development. Some curriculum theorists concerned with the mismatch between curriculum and assessment have determined that if curriculum is to change, the reading tests must change. This has brought about a proliferation of new assessments—both formal and informal (Brown, 1986; Burstall, 1986; Priestley, 1982; Stiggins, Conklin, & Bridgeford, 1986).

Included in this mix have been modifications of conventional tests with new item formats and the addition of the assessment of behaviors not often included on traditional tests, such as background knowledge, student interests and attitudes, and metacognition. Other assessments in reading have taken an entirely different approach to assessment, relying entirely on student work samples collected in portfolios (Jongsma, 1989; Valencia, 1990; Wolf, 1989). Portfolios have themselves taken many different forms from *show portfolios*, which include only a few carefully selected samples, to *working portfolios*, which include a broad sample of work and which are used to guide and organize daily instruction. In addition, numerous professional publications have published articles calling for the use of a broader range of teacher observations and informal assessment techniques (Cambourne & Turbill, 1990; Goodman, 1991).

Different Audiences Need Different Information

Thus, it seems that the increased amount of testing has resulted from greater accountability demands as well as from attempts to find alternatives to traditional assessments. In order to bring some sense to this proliferation of assessment, we need to understand that tests have only one general purpose: Tests should be considered as nothing more than attempts to systematically gather information. The information is used to help children learn about their own literacy development and to give teachers and others concerned with students' literacy the information they need for curriculum planning. *The bottom line in selecting and using any assessment should be whether it helps students.*

A book that I first authored more than 20 years ago regarding the assessment of reading was entitled *Reading: What Can Be Measured?* (Farr, 1970; Farr & Carey, 1986). I have always felt that the title gave the wrong focus to the review of assessment issues. That book should have been entitled *Reading: Why Should It Be Measured?* We need to consider who needs information about reading, what kind of information is needed, and when it is needed. Only then can we begin to plan for more sensible assessment.

In order to think more clearly about overall assessment plans, we need to know why we want to test. There are, of course, different groups that need information. Without considering these groups and their information needs, the assessment program in any school system will remain as a set of jumbled puzzle pieces. The general distinctions between audiences are covered in Figure 1.

The public. Members of the general public, who make decisions through their elected officials, including school boards, have a vested interest in the future of children and in their effective and cost efficient instruction. It is recognized as vital to Americans' and their nation's future that schools produce educated students. Indeed, the most recent federally supported efforts to improve education have been on establishing standards that presumably will result in the development of assessments related to those standards. At the present time, those involved with establishing the standards are moving in the direction of holistic kinds of performance assessment.

Administrators. Ideally school administrators would rely most heavily on performance assessments that are criterion referenced. These performance measures should compare student performance against a clearly defined curriculum. Since we live in a complex world where mobility and diversity are the reality, administrators also need norm-referenced comparisons of their students' performance.

Parents. While parents share the public's interests, they have a vested interest in their own individual children. In order to monitor their children's progress and to be active in their education, parents want criterion-referenced reports; additionally parents are also typically interested in how their children perform on normed tests in comparison to children from across the United States.

Teachers. A teacher's primary concern is helping students learn. While teachers are necessarily aware of normed assessment's comparative reports as a kind of bottom-line accountability, they are primarily interested in the kind of information that will support the daily instructional decisions they need to make. This kind of information has been generated by criterion-referenced tests and by other types of assessment that can be utilized more effectively in the classroom as a part of instruction.

Students. Students need to become good self-assessors if they are to improve their literacy skills. They need to select, review, and think about the reading and writing they are doing. They need to be able to revise their own writing and to revise their comprehension as they read.

Figure 1
Assessment audiences

Audiences	The information is needed to:	The information is related to:	Type of information	When information is needed:
General public (and the press)	Judge if schools are accountable and effective	Groups of students	Related to broad goals; norm- and criterion-referenced	Annually
School administrators/staff	Judge effectiveness of curriculum, materials, teachers	Groups of students and individuals	Related to broad goals; criterion- and norm-referenced	Annually or by term/semester
Parents	Monitor progress of child, effectiveness of school	Individual student	Usually related to broader goals; both criterion- and norm-referenced	Periodically; five or six times a year
Teachers	Plan instruction, strategies, activities	Individual student; small groups	Related to specific goals: primarily criterion-referenced	Daily, or as often as possible
Students	Identify strengths, areas to emphasize	Individual (self)	Related to specific goals; criterion-referenced	Daily, or as often as possible

If students understand their own needs, they will improve. Students should, in fact, be the primary assessors of their own literacy development.

The Wall Between Understanding

It is important for each of these audiences to recognize, understand, and respect the needs of the others if we are to pull the assessment puzzle together. Audience needs cluster around those of teachers and students on the one hand and those of other decision makers on the other.

The assessment needs of these two general groups tend to be dramatically different and even contradictory, and if the users of assessment do not recognize one another's needs, it is because these distinctions create a kind of wall depicted in Figure 2. It is essential that we breach that wall if we are to get our assessment act together!

Some Tests Attempt to Do It All

No single assessment can serve all the audiences in need of educational performance information. Yet developments in standardized tests have attempted to do so. The tests have added criterion-referenced interpretations, special interpretations for teachers, special reports for parents, individual score reports, and instructional support materials of various kinds. These developments have made the tests longer, more expensive, more time-consuming, and more confusing. Consequently, teachers are expected to justify these investments by making more instructional use of the test results.

At the same time, the increased investment in assessment time and money has tended to give these tests even more importance in determining school accountability and in making high-stakes educational decisions. Specifically, four potential problems have arisen.

Teaching to the test. As accountability became more and more of a concern, teachers have felt pressured to place emphasis on what the standardized tests covered, regardless of what the school curriculum called for. Over time, reading curricula have begun to reflect the skill breakdown of many tests, and reading textbooks have tended to emphasize the skills tests cover as well.

Contaminating the evidence. Standardized reading tests used to mean something. They were genuine indications that a student who performed adequately on them could read. This was so because they *sampled* reading behavior. But now that indication is contaminated. If teachers are deliberately stressing the sub-behaviors that they know are on the tests, the assessments are no longer sampling reading behavior—they are,

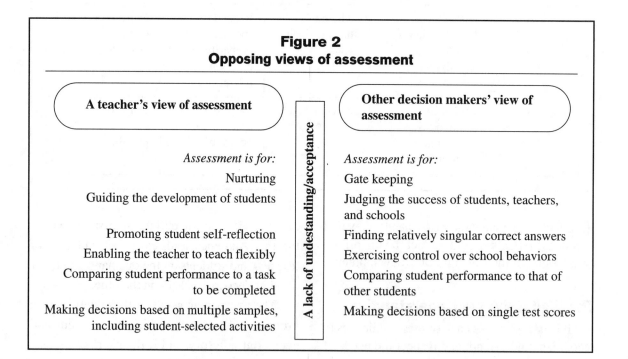

Figure 2
Opposing views of assessment

A teacher's view of assessment	A lack of undestanding/acceptance	Other decision makers' view of assessment
Assessment is for:		*Assessment is for:*
Nurturing		Gate keeping
Guiding the development of students		Judging the success of students, teachers, and schools
Promoting student self-reflection		Finding relatively singular correct answers
Enabling the teacher to teach flexibly		Exercising control over school behaviors
Comparing student performance to a task to be completed		Comparing student performance to that of other students
Making decisions based on multiple samples, including student-selected activities		Making decisions based on single test scores

in effect, covering a very limited definition of it. A good score on a standardized reading test no longer indicates that the student can read in general. It means only that the student can do those limited things the test covers.

Crunching objectives. Attempts to make reading assessment tests more encompassing have tended to make them much longer. Even so, tests are forced to cover the numerous subskills they contain with only a few items each. "What does it mean," a teacher may legitimately ask, "if a student misses one of three items that report on comprehending cause-and-effect?"

The potential for a mismatch. Teachers have long noted that nationally normed tests do not reflect particular emphases in their classrooms. How can a standardized reading test, they have correctly argued, tell them much about a particular curriculum they are following? What can it tell the public about how well the teacher has done using the curriculum?

The more a teacher adheres to instruction related directly to the needs, interests, and backgrounds of his or her particular students, the less assured is the match of that instruction to standardized test content—and the less likely the test's scores will serve that instruction.

Good Reading Theory Recommends Authentic Performance Assessment

Most published tests have not adequately responded to emerging reading theory, which explains reading comprehension as a meaning-constructing process. Any subskills factored out of the process are not discrete; if they actually exist as behaviors, they appear to operate in such an intricate fashion that it is difficult if not impossible to isolate them.

Authentic assessment. Relatively wide acceptance of a constructivist, context-specific definition of reading has promoted a careful analysis of current reading and language arts test content and format to see how authentic the test-

ing experience is. This analysis has led to the conclusion that the reading required on most tests is not much like the reading behavior that our new understanding describes. How valid is the content of a reading test in terms of reader purpose, interests, and background, which we now believe are primary influences on reading behavior?

Performance assessment. Attention to authenticity has accompanied and helped generate the development and use of performance assessment. A student's language behaviors need to be assessed, it is contended, as they are used in real-life situations. Students do not comprehend something read, for example, as a multiple-choice response, and marking those answers has nothing to do with the way reading is actually used, except in taking tests. Reading performance assessment must look at the reading act in process or judge comprehension of a text as it is applied in some realistic way.

Observation. Observation is one way to do this and can lead teachers to meaningful insights about the progress and needs of individual students. Yet teachers need to be trained in regard to what they can look for and what those signs suggest. They need to develop useful ways to make discrete notes about observations and to synthesize what they find. Observation generates many details in relatively random order, and they seldom become clearly useful until they are gathered into patterns that can direct instruction.

Portfolios. Another highly valuable form of performance assessment is the portfolio. For these collections, students and teachers select numerous samples from drafts and final versions of various kinds of a student's writing. The idea is to demonstrate the student's progress and development in the combined process of reading, thinking, and writing. Thus many of the samples in the portfolio are responses to reading. The portfolio is reviewed and discussed regularly by the teacher and student, who may arrange it for others to examine.

Integrated assessment. Assessments in which thinking, reading, and writing are integrated have been developed in recent years. Such assessments have been developed by classroom teachers, school districts, and publishers in an attempt to integrate reading and writing and to assess reading and writing with more realistic activities. These vary widely, but for most of them the student is given a writing task related to a text that is supplied. The task has been deemed to be authentic because it is typical of something the student might do in real life, including the kinds of activities often used for learning in the classroom. It is designed to emphasize the use of information in the reading selection in a realistic and interesting writing task.

For example, one such test asks students to read a nonfiction article that categorically discusses and describes how insect-eating plants lure, capture, and digest their victims. The task is to write a fictional piece telling what a mother bug might say to her children in cautioning them about these plants. Teachers use what the students write to assess students' understanding of the text. They rate other integrated behaviors as well, such as the students' organization and application of the text's content to the task and factors related to writing.

Such reading/writing assessments encourage students to develop a variety of responses based on their interpretation of the reading selection, their background knowledge, and the direction they choose to take in constructing a realistic response. These kinds of performance assessments provide teachers with valuable insights regarding a student's ability to read, write, and construct a meaningful response to an interesting task. Prewriting notes, first drafts, and teacher observation notes all make the assessment a valuable source of information.

In addition, the final drafts can be scored to serve as information that can help determine accountability. The responses can be scored following a "rubric," a list of criteria that describes several levels of performance in each of the categories to be analyzed. Samples of actual student papers ("anchors") that represent each score level described by the rubrics can also be used in scoring. Thus these tests are criterion-referenced. Yet the guides to scoring are somewhat equivalent to normed scores in the sense that the anchor papers were taken from many gathered in field testing and were judged to be typical of the range of responses described in the rubric.

A Combined Solution to the Assessment Puzzle

None of the preceding types of assessment should be argued to be the single solution to the testing puzzle. Figure 3 depicts how performance assessments can provide direct linkage among the main users of assessment and how the three major types of assessment are linked. The chart is a plan for pulling the pieces of the assessment puzzle together into a solution that can inform all the decision makers involved in a student's development into an effective reader and language user.

Solving the Puzzle Will Require Cooperation

Pulling the assessment puzzle together will require tolerance and compromise on the part of many critics of particular types of assessment. The process would be facilitated if:

• Critics of the schools would become aware that assessment must serve more than school accountability. Ideally, critics will inform their concerns with a better understanding of what schools are trying to accomplish.

• Decision makers would understand that assessment is more than numbers on a test paper. They would begin to understand and use the kinds of assessments that are based on real classroom activities and that represent the types

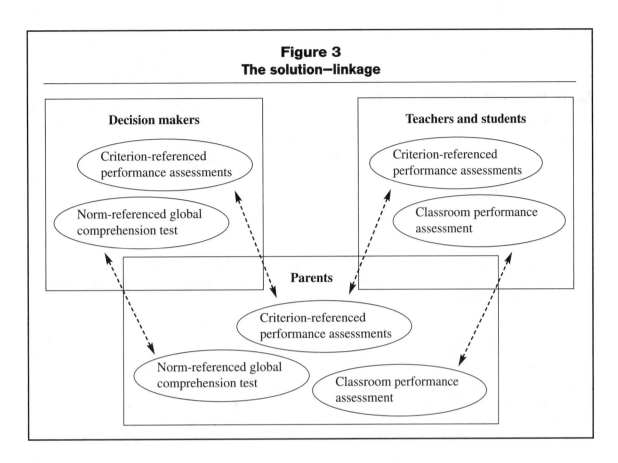

Figure 3
The solution—linkage

Decision makers

Criterion-referenced performance assessments

Norm-referenced global comprehension test

Teachers and students

Criterion-referenced performance assessments

Classroom performance assessment

Parents

Criterion-referenced performance assessments

Norm-referenced global comprehension test

Classroom performance assessment

of activities in which students who are effective readers and writers should become proficient.

• The most idealistic of the critics of assessment would become more realistic and flexible, tempering their insistence on authentic performance assessment. It seems fruitless, in particular, for some critics to insist that all assessment revolve around observation of activities that are apt not to involve all children and that reveal language use in highly varying degrees.

• Producers of assessments would acknowledge that no one assessment is going to suffice as a school's examination of reading. This would mean that they would no longer promote any of their products as such a test. It would also mean that future revisions of standardized reading tests would undo much of the complexity they now contain.

None of this is to suggest that critical analysis of reading assessment should stop, nor should attempts to improve tests in response to criticism cease. Efforts to develop and institute the new accountability assessments in Illinois (Pearson & Valencia, 1987), where the assessment allows for multiple correct responses within each multiple-choice item, and in Michigan (Michigan State Board of Education, 1987), where the assessment relies on longer passages followed by more numerous items, have been interesting, if not conclusive, efforts to contribute to a solution to the assessment puzzle. So have attempts to construct items that will reveal students' awareness of how they are processing texts. Although longer reading test passages, different question formats, etc. will not solve the assessment puzzle, they can certainly shape the parts we pull together for a better fit.

Norm-Referenced Tests Need to Change

To solve the assessment puzzle, it will be necessary for teachers and other educators to admit that norm-referenced test results can be of some value to the public and other decision makers, including parents. But these standardized tests should not be of the form that has evolved in response to criticism.

Test authors and publishers should begin to plan assessment *programs* that address multiple audiences. Teachers and schools will need assistance in developing portfolios, planning performance assessments, and integrating assessment information. What are not needed are large single test batteries that promise to meet all of a school's assessment needs from classroom diagnosis to accountability. That attempt, especially linking accountability assessment and instructional assessment, has led to a narrowing of the curriculum.

For the large-scale assessments, this suggests the elimination of the designation of items by subskills and reporting on those sub-behaviors as if they truly are separable and distinct. More publisher efforts should go into the development of a variety of creative and useful curriculum assessments in which students have to actually perform the behaviors the school is attempting to teach.

What large-scale assessment can and should do is to report a global comprehension score, with no special subtests on traditional focuses like word recognition and vocabulary. Without the time-consuming battery of accompanying tests, reading tests can be shorter while using longer passages of a variety of types. These passages must evoke different purposes for reading that reflect the real reasons students read in and out of school. Thus, the reading test will be more authentic.

Without the burden of reporting on a host of specific reading and thinking subskills, test makers can write items that truly reflect the balance of a passage, the students' probable purpose for reading such a text, and the aspects of the writing that make the text one of quality and worth the students' time.

It should also be remembered that the long-standing primary purpose of large-scale testing has been to provide a general assessment as to how groups of students are progressing in a school district. Such information, if it does not become the focus of instruction, can be one piece of information used to contribute to a broad base of information for planning, supporting, and evaluating school- and system-wide curricula and instruction.

This approach strongly suggests that *matrix sampling* be used for large-scale assessment, thus eliminating the need to administer to all students the same test items or tasks. Testing time can be considerably shorter if carefully selected samples of students take different parts of a test instead of the whole thing. Good sampling should yield results similar to those obtained when all students take the entire test. Nothing is lost in reporting, since individual scores are of little concern. In addition, matrix sampling provides a general indication of the progress of groups of students, not a blueprint for instruction of individual students.

Performance Assessments Can Provide the Key Linkage

Figure 3 illustrates the linkages across three general audience types that will be essential to solving the assessment puzzle. Norm-referenced information provides a link between parents and decision makers other than teachers. However, the key linkage across all three general audiences is criterion-referenced performance assessments. Various approaches to performance assessment are being developed and tried out in school district assessment programs. Such assessments can be designed by teachers themselves. In fact, this has been done in several local school districts around the United States by teachers cooperating and interacting in order to meet their assessment needs. The same procedures are being tried at the state level in Maryland, Arizona, California, and Utah, and other states are sure to move in this direction.

The teachers who have been most successful in using this approach have had the support of administrators who could see over the assessment wall. Their support generated public interest and support. In some school systems, published or teacher-created integrated language performance assessment has already become a primary source of information for judging school accountability.

While teachers can create integrated language performance activities on a classroom basis, using them for accountability will require carefully developed or prepared programs that have been made congruent system-wide. This was done in River Forest, Illinois, where teachers developed their own rubrics, anchor papers, and inservice training. This kind of structuring will be necessary if the public, the press, and administrators are to be expected to value these tests as the key indicators of accountability and sources of directions for key decisions, such as curriculum development.

At the same time, of course, these tests can reflect authentic student performance. Not only are they very closely related to instructional activities and thus of high utility to teachers, they are actually instructional activities in and of themselves so the class time they require is doubly well invested.

The Portfolio Is the Flagship of Performance Assessment

Most developers of integrated language assessment programs highly recommend putting the student products into portfolios, a direct acknowledgment that the roots of language performance assessment lie in a portfolio approach to assessment and instruction. Portfolio performance assessment is so integral in good classrooms today that it is vital to note the qualities that make the portfolio approach a successful one.

A successful portfolio approach to assessment must revolve around regular and frequent attention to the portfolio by the student and the teacher. It does minimal good just to store a student's papers in a big folder and let them gather dust for lengthy periods of time. Papers must be added frequently; others can be weeded out in an ongoing rearrangement and selection process; most importantly, the whole process should involve frequent self-analysis by the student and regular conversations between the teacher and the student.

Too many teachers who contend that they are using portfolios do not do these things. Here are a few requirements if portfolios are to provide good assessment:

• The portfolio *belongs* to the student. It is his or her work and property, not some classroom requirement. Students should have choice about what goes in, and they should be encouraged to decorate and personalize their portfolios in unique ways.

• Portfolios are not primarily a display, although students may help arrange them for their parents and administrators to see. They are a shifting, growing repository of developing processes and ideas—a rather personal melting pot that the student uses to reflect on his or her own literacy development and to discuss interesting reading and writing activities with the teacher.

• The teacher's role in portfolio development is that of a consultant who helps convince the student that the work should show a variety of materials reflecting the reading-writing-thinking process as well as examples of responses to common classroom tasks and the student's favorite creations.

• The portfolio should contain numerous and varied pieces written and revised in response to reading. Reading logs reporting ongoing responses to books and articles make valuable contributions to portfolios.

• Portfolios should be reflective collections, revealing genuinely individual and personal responses to classroom activities and to ideas.

• At an absolute minimum, there should be four one-on-one, teacher/student discussions and analyses each semester of a student's developing portfolio. These sessions should not be short and perfunctory. If this requirement is not met, the assessment potential of the portfolio process is forfeited.

• Keeping the portfolio is an ongoing process. Its real value as an assessment tool materializes as the student can analyze his or her progress and development over time.

New Emphases in Assessment Have Common Qualities

Portfolios are part of a group of classroom performance assessments, some of them quite informal, that link the assessment interests of teachers, students, and parents. Portfolios can also be highly revealing to school specialists and administrators who, with the students' permission, take the time to examine them. All of these emerging strategies are both authentic and involve performance assessment. They are:

• Highly individualized, even though they may take place during activities that involve groups of students.

• A part of classroom activities and instruction designed to match an individual student's interests and needs and to use a student's strengths to develop more incisive and creative use of language.

• Activities that integrate several language behaviors.

• Chances to use critical thinking and to express unique and emerging reactions and responses to ideas encountered in text.

• Models that encourage and develop self-assessment by the student, making him or her aware of the language-related strengths that are developing.

How School Districts Can Begin to Solve the Assessment Puzzle

Too often school district testing programs are nothing more than test-and-file procedures. The tests are administered; when the scores are available, they are reported in some way; and teachers are admonished to peruse and use the test results. Yet many educators across the U.S. already embrace the suggestions made here for solving the assessment puzzle. Administrators are aware that testing programs can and do divide educators. Superintendents do not want to abandon their accountability responsibilities, yet they want to support effective ongoing classroom assessment that provides teachers with information that is congruent with current knowledge about reading/writing processes. Teachers want to be more involved in developing an assessment program that serves and matches their instructional needs. They all sense that what is needed is an integrated system that is effective in fostering better teaching and learning.

Many of these school districts need help with developing an assessment program that links audiences instead of dividing them—one that supplies broad-based accountability information yet is customized to the particular system, its teachers, and its students. One way for school districts to begin is to discuss the pieces of the assessment puzzle in their system. Representatives of all the audiences with assessment needs should take part. As this process develops, the discussions need to be recorded in some way and synthesized. Out of all this can come other brainstorming sessions and ultimately inservice workshops to help all teachers understand how a broad-based assessment program can be pulled together. Equally important, many teachers will welcome inservice training on using different types of informal assessments.

These kinds of workshops can be started within school districts right away. For instance, teachers who are exceptionally good observers or use the portfolio approach with great success are almost always easily identified. They could be enlisted and supported by administrators to run workshops that can be conducted while the discussions about broader reading assessment are helping representative groups define the assessment problems and their district's needs.

The assessment puzzle can be solved. The solution, however, is not as simple as identifying a nonexistent test that will do the whole job nor as arbitrary as eliminating most reading assessment. Rather it takes a vision that focuses on what real literacy means and the awareness that various groups have a stake in helping students to develop as literate citizens. Such a vision must not use assessment to isolate. It must respect the complex nature of literacy, it must serve students and help them to become reflective self-assessors, and it must create links that bring instruction and assessment together.

References

Brown, R. (1986). Evaluation and learning. In A.R. Petrosky & D. Bartholomae (Eds.), *The teaching of writing: Eighty-fifth yearbook of the National Society for the Study of Education* (pp. 114–130). Chicago, IL: University of Chicago Press.

Burstall, C. (1986). Innovative forms of assessment: A United Kingdom perspective. *Educational Measurement: Issues and Practice, 5,* 17–22.

Bush, G. (1991). *America 2000: An education strategy.* Washington, DC: U.S. Department of Education.

Cambourne, B., & Turbill, J. (1990). Assessment in whole language classrooms: Theory into practice. *The Elementary School Journal, 90,* 337–349.

Farr, R. (1970). *Reading: What can be measured?* Newark, DE: International Reading Association.

Farr, R., & Carey, R. (1986). *Reading: What can be measured?* (2nd ed.). Newark, DE: International Reading Association.

Farr, R., & Fay, L. (1982). Reading trend data in the United States: A mandate for caveats and caution. In G. Austin & H. Garber (Eds.), *The rise and fall of national test scores* (pp. 83–141). New York: The Academic Press.

Farr, R., Fay, L., Myers, R., & Ginsberg, M. (1987). *Reading achievement in the United States: 1944–45, 1976, and 1986.* Bloomington, IN: Indiana University.

Finn, C.E., Jr. (1992, January 12). Turn on the lights. *The New York Times,* p. D19.

Goodman, Y. (1991). Evaluating language growth: Informal methods of evaluation. In J. Flood, J. Jensen, D. Lapp, & J. Squire (Eds.), *Handbook of research on teaching the English language arts* (pp. 502–509). New York: Macmillan.

Jongsma, K. (1989). Portfolio assessment. *The Reading Teacher, 43,* 264–265.

Madaus, G.F. (1985). Public policy and the testing profession: You've never had it so good? *Educational Measurement: Issues and Practice, 4,* 5–11.

McClellan, M.C. (1988). Testing and reform. *Phi Delta Kappan, 69,* 766–771.

Michigan State Board of Education. (1987). *Blueprint for the new MEAP reading test.* Lansing, MI: Author.

Mullis, V.S., Owen, E.H., & Phillips, G.W. (1990). *Accelerating academic achievement: A summary of the findings from 20 years of NAEP.* Princeton, NJ: Educational Testing Service.

National Commission on Excellence in Education. (1983). *A nation at risk.* Washington, DC: U.S. Department of Education.

Pearson, P.D., & Valencia, S. (1987). *The Illinois State Board of Education census assessment in reading: An historical reflection.* Springfield, IL: Illinois State Department of Education.

Popham, W.J. (1987). The merits of measurement-driven instruction. *Phi Delta Kappan, 68,* 679–682.

Priestley, M. (1982). *Performance assessment in education and training: Alternate techniques.* Englewood Cliffs, NJ: Educational Technology Publications.

Purves, A., & Niles, O. (1984). The challenge to education to produce literate citizens. In A. Purves & O. Niles (Eds.), *Becoming readers in a complex society: Eighty-third yearbook of the National Society for the Study of Education* (pp. 1–15). Chicago, IL: University of Chicago Press.

Resnick, D. (1982). History of educational testing. In A.K. Wigdor & W.R. Garner (Eds.), *Ability testing: Uses, consequences, and controversies, Part 2* (pp. 173–194). Washington, DC: National Academy Press.

Salganik, L.H. (1985). Why testing reforms are so popular and how they are changing education. *Phi Delta Kappan, 66,* 628–634.

Salmon-Cox, L. (1981). Teachers and tests: What's really happening? *Phi Delta Kappan, 62,* 631–634.

Saretsky, G. (1973). The strangely significant case of Peter Doe. *Phi Delta Kappan, 54,* 589–592.

Stedman, L.C., & Kaestle, C.F. (1987). Literacy and reading performance in the United States from 1880 to the present. *Reading Research Quarterly, 22,* 8–46.

Stiggins, R.J., Conklin, N.F., & Bridgeford, N.J. (1986). Classroom assessment: A key to effective education. *Educational Measurement: Issues and Practice, 5,* 5–17.

Valencia, S. (1990). A portfolio approach to classroom reading assessment: The whys, whats, and hows. *The Reading Teacher, 43,* 338–339.

Valencia, S., & Pearson, P. (1987). Reading assessment: Time for a change. *The Reading Teacher, 40,* 726–732.

Wolf, D.P. (1989). Portfolio assessment: Sampling student work. *Educational Leadership, 46,* 35–39.

Report Cards and Reading

Peter Afflerbach

March 1993

Teachers regularly write report cards that are carried home by students, read by parents, signed, and returned by the student to the teacher. Underlying this traditional routine are the assumptions that teachers can share what they know about their students' reading development by writing report cards, and that by reading report cards parents can better understand their children as readers. There are, however, many continuing concerns with report cards. This article examines issues related to reading report cards and provides suggestions for revising them to increase their effectiveness in communicating students' reading achievement. The issues considered in this article follow from my recent and ongoing work with report cards with colleagues in a variety of school districts (Afflerbach & Johnston, in press; Afflerbach & Sammons, 1992).

Continuing Concerns With Report Cards

Many report card formats cannot describe the range of students' achievement and development in reading. Bray (1986) noted that report cards often limited the nature of communication of student progress to a single letter or number grade and sometimes a brief comment. These report cards included generally poor information of little use to parents and students. Freeman and Hatch (1989) examined kindergarten report cards in Ohio and determined that more than 90% of the school districts required teachers to report students' reading achievement in a *strand format*, which breaks reading into discrete skills or ability areas. For example, reading is separated from the other language arts, and might be broken down into phonics, vocabulary, and comprehension components, with separate grades assigned for each. The strand report card presents a fragmented picture of the student as reader and language user (Cambourne & Turbill, 1990). The strand portrait may or may not reflect students and their development within a particular reading or integrated language arts program.

Teacher input into the development of report cards is seldom solicited (Goacher & Reid, 1983), and teachers have at best minor roles in developing the form and content of the report cards they are required to use. Even in districts that encourage teacher participation, there may be considerable numbers of teachers whose values and preferences are not represented (Afflerbach & Sammons, 1992). Because of their lack of input into the development of report cards, teachers face conflicts when they have to fit their personal values and understanding of students' reading development to the format and limited space of the strand report card. Afflerbach and Johnston (in press) asked teachers to think aloud while they composed reading and language arts report cards. As one teacher wrote a strand format report card, she reported,

> There are so many things he is capable of—and growth in all of these areas—but I have this list on the report card, "Reading," "Spelling," "Handwriting," "Composition,"...and then this incredibly tiny space for my written comments.

Afflerbach and Sammons (1992) investigated teachers' training, practices, and values in writing report cards and found that individual teachers in the same schools sometimes wrote for markedly different purposes and audiences. Few of these teachers felt that their report cards were flexible enough to adequately address this wide range of purposes and audiences, and many felt this inflexibility was problematic. Teachers in schools with recently revised report cards indicated that they needed increased time to write report cards, but that no additional time was provided by their schools.

Changing the Report Card: Addressing Key Questions

Given the regular use of reading report cards in most schools and their potential for communicating students' progress, it is important to examine their effectiveness. The appropriateness of currently used reading report cards can be investigated by using feedback from teachers, parents, students, and administrators. The feedback may help determine if the report card is aligned with the reading curriculum, if it reflects teachers' values, if parents receive information that helps them understand their children's strengths and needs, if students themselves use this information, and if admin-

istrators reference the report card as evidence of reading program success. When the existing report card does not help in the effective communication of students' strengths, successes, and areas of need, the school community can take steps to improve it.

In the next section, five questions related to developing effective reading report cards will be examined. Three related assumptions about effective reading report cards guide the consideration of each question. First, the report card development process should include representatives from all groups who read and write report cards. Second, the report card should be useful, both for teachers sharing their knowledge of students' reading development and for parents and students interested in this knowledge. Third, useful report cards are those that achieve a balance of *flexibility* in reporting, allowing teachers to use a variety of means to communicate their knowledge of students' reading development, and *manageability*, presenting the writer and reader of the report card with doable tasks.

1. What Is the Audience and Purpose of the Reading Report Card?

Reading report cards are written to serve different purposes and are read by diverse audiences. Like any form of communication, report cards are most effective when their purposes and audiences are clearly identified. Table 1 contains representative audiences and purposes, and provides suggestions for accommodating each in the reading report card. The Table provides information that might be used by schools considering a report card revision or by teachers seeking to augment an existing reading report card.

Unfortunately, certain report card formats cannot serve particular audiences and purposes, and in some instances those formats may stand in the way of clear communication. For example, a strand format report card may be used by a particular school or district, but many parents

Table 1
Reading report card revisions for addressing different audiences and purposes

Audience	Purpose	Suggested revisions
Parent and students	To provide greater detail on the nature of students' reading development	Checklist of student behaviors; narrative reports of student progress; section for anecdotal records; references to other sources of information
Students	To motivate students	Section acknowledging student effort; section inviting student to set goals in reading
Students	To more effectively involve students in their development as readers	Section that personalizes the report card; allows room for specific references to students' reading choices, challenges, and accomplishments; provides formative feedback; lists expectations for next marking period
Parents	To involve parents; to coordinate school and home efforts	Section that asks parents to work with the school on setting and working toward particular goals; provides specific information on goals, materials, and instruction
Teachers and administrators	To inform fellow teachers and administrators of students' accomplishments in previous or current reading classes	List describing books read by student, classroom projects and activities
Reading teachers	To establish congruence of classroom and remedial reading instruction	Detailed list of student's reading accomplishments and goals; notes on instructional methods and materials
Parents and students	To seek regular feedback to improve the report card	Questions about the usefulness of report card information; requests for suggestions to improve communication

may want more detailed information about their children's growth as readers. Such a situation should signal the need for revising the existing report card. If it does not, a teacher might amend the existing card with a reading checklist. The amended report card tells parents that their child received B, B, and A in decoding, vocabulary, and comprehension respectively, but also pro-

vides relative detail about the student's reading development. An example of a reading checklist is presented in Table 2.

Here, specific information related to a student's engaged reading activities and reading strategy use is provided. The information elaborates on the single letter grades to inform us that the student is an enthusiastic reader who choos-

---
Table 2
Checklist of reading behaviors

Engaged reading activities

✔ ____ Chooses reading during independent class time

____ ____ Reads a variety of texts on a variety of topics

✔ ____ Borrows books from the school library

✔ ____ Shares books with teacher and classmates

____ ____ Understands the value of reading as a tool

____ ____ Understands the value of reading as recreation

✔ ____ Reads with enthusiasm

Strategy use when reading

✔ ____ Sets purposes for reading

____ ____ Adjusts rate of reading to reflect task and goals

✔ ____ Uses flexible strategies to decode unfamiliar words

✔ ____ Predicts and monitors meaning

____ ____ Summarizes text effectively

____ ____ Searches for text information needed to perform specific tasks

____ ____ Exhibits metacognitive ability; reflects on what is read

____ ____ Reads fluently

---

es to read during independent class time, visits the school library to borrow books, and shares what is read with the teacher and classmates. Further, the checklist tells us that the student is capable of using strategies to set purposes for reading, to decode unfamiliar words, and to predict and monitor meaning from the text. Thus, the checklist can enhance the understanding of the reader's development and accomplishments by adding specificity to more general grades.

Another option for addressing different audiences and purposes is the narrative report. Within a narrative report, teachers can provide detail about student development in particular strands (e.g., vocabulary, decoding, and comprehension). Further, teachers can describe the interrelatedness of these strands and their relationship to the other language arts and different content areas. The narrative can include relatively detailed information about a student's strengths and needs, personal challenges and accomplishments, and describe the variety of a student's reading experiences and how reading fits in the larger portrait of the student.

An example of a narrative report of a student's reading development and accomplishment is presented in Table 3. In this example, the narrative report informs us that Aidan uses reading strategies, gives details on the types of strategies, and provides information on the context in which the strategies were used. The narrative also describes the relationship between reading and other language arts and content areas in Aidan's literacy development: how Aidan used reading to gather information for use in his collaborative writing of a play. Finally, the narrative describes Aidan's use of reading to pursue his personal interests and his use of information gathered through reading to advocate saving the environment of lions and tigers.

Note that the narrative report usually offers greater flexibility than a reading checklist, but it may place considerable demands on teacher time and creativity.

2. Who Will Participate in the Design of the Report Card?

Effective reading report cards are created through a process that engages the people who write and read them. Reading report cards involve students, teachers, parents, and administrators, and it is important to examine their needs for, and expectations of, the report card. The inclusion of different perspectives in developing the report card changes the process: It may be more challenging, as different values and perspectives on reading instruction and learning are considered, negotiated, and accommodated. The product of this process may be a reading report card that better represents more of the people who are influenced by it. When the development of the reading report card is a shared responsibility, the rationale underlying the development of the content and format of the report card are better understood by the people who write and read them.

3. What Is the Context of Communicating Reading Assessment?

It is important to consider the relationship of the report card to other means of assessing and communicating students' reading achievement,

---

Table 3
A narrative frame for reports to parents

In the last marking period, your son Aidan demonstrated the following:

Development of reading strategies:
    Aidan regularly set purposes for his reading and adjusted his reading rate to suit these purposes. For example, Aidan needed to locate detailed information about animals in the tropical rain forest to help him develop animal characters for his play. He ably searched a chapter in his science text to locate the information.

Using reading for school projects and assignments:
    Aidan and three classmates worked on a play entitled "Help Save the Forest." While reading to develop characters and settings for the play, Aidan also demonstrated his use of the strategies to set purposes for reading, and to regularly monitor his comprehension.

Reading to pursue personal interests:
    Aidan continues to read any and every book he can find on lions and tigers. He has become the class expert on "big cats," and he regularly shares with his classmates the newest information he has found, as well as his concerns for protecting the environment in which lions and tigers live.

Valuing reading:
    It was clear that Aidan understood the value of reading, as he gathered and synthesized information from selected books on the rain forest to develop descriptions of characters and settings for the play.

Table 4
Contextualizing the reading report card

Dear Parents:

    Our reading report card is one of several sources of information to help describe your child's reading development. Information that may help you further understand and appreciate _____ _Linnae_ _____'s reading development can be found in:

- the reading portfolio
- classroom bulletin board
- statewide performance assessment results
- our parent-teacher meetings
- Linnae's reading log
- reading letters from Linnae's Pen Pals Program
- reading of script, rehearsal, and presentation of class play
- reading related to the integrated unit on living things
- reading the book *Amazing Grace* and using it in the personal challenges group project

---

for this relationship helps define the role, content, and frequency of use of the reading report card. The report card represents a regularly scheduled and standardized form of communication with parents or guardians, whereas the nature and frequency of other communications between teachers and parents vary widely. In some settings, the report card is the only communication between home and school. In others, the report card is part of a regular and frequent series of such communications.

When there is no other formal contact with parents or guardians, the report card is especially important for communicating information about students' reading development. Because this communication is limited, the form, the minimum, essential information to be included, and how parents might interpret the information in the report card should be carefully examined if a report card revision is being considered.

In contrast, when the report card is a part of a reading assessment context that includes students' reading portfolios, written notes, phone conversations, and regular meetings with parents in which students' reading is discussed in depth, parents can build an understanding of students' reading achievement from different sources. Because the report card does not carry the full burden of reporting, the information included may change to best suit the needs of the teachers, parents, and students. In these situations, references to how other measures and indicators may support or elaborate on the information in the report card may be helpful. Table 4 presents a sample reference list that directs parents to complementary sources of information about their child's reading development. The list can include sources of information common to all students in a particular class, and information specific to individual students.

4. What Are the Responsibilities Related to the New Report Card?

Changing the reading report card is often the specific task of a report card committee. There are related responsibilities for those who develop, write, and read the report card—the school, teachers, parents, and students—and attention to these responsibilities is critical for the success of the revised report card.

Report card revision committees and schools. Schools and report card revision committees are responsible for helping the community become familiar with the nature and purpose of the revised report card. For example, a change from a strand format to a narrative reading report card might be most effective when accompanied by explanations of how the new features of the report card allow for a relatively detailed description of students' reading and a discussion of the advantages it offers compared with the previous report card. Informational meetings, brochures, and memos can provide an orientation for parents and students not directly involved with the report card development process. An example of a letter introducing and explaining the revised reading report card to parents is included in Table 5. Since change to writing narratives of students' reading development requires teachers to spend more time with the report card, it is important that schools provide sufficient time to teachers to realize the advantages offered by a new report card.

Teachers. A new report card may provide increased opportunity for teachers to share their knowledge of students' reading development by using narrative accounts of students' reading development, checklists, and descriptions of the context in which classroom reading achievement takes place. Narratives may provide

---

Table 5
Introducing a revised reading report card

Dear Parents,

As you may know, we have been working for the last two years to revise our reading report card. Through our school meetings and parent priority questionnaires, we determined that our new report card would retain the familiar grading system of A, B, C, D, and F. Your feedback indicated that additional, specific information on your child's reading development was a high priority. This information is now included in the narrative section of the report card. In this section, your child's teacher has included a written account of some of the demonstrated strengths and needs of your child as a reader. In addition, we have included a new reading checklist for the K–1 report card, which provides additional information on your child's development.

Many of you expressed a concern that students' efforts in reading were not regularly recognized on the report card. Our revised reading report card includes a section for acknowledging each child's efforts in reading. We feel that this will serve to further encourage our developing readers.

Finally, we have added two other components to the report card. First, we included a section that indicates other sources of information about your child's reading development. Second, we have included a section that invites your feedback on the report card. We would like this section to serve the continued purpose of helping us know your concerns and contributing to the ongoing improvement of our report card.

Thank you for your attention to this memo, and for taking the time to better familiarize yourself with the new report card. We welcome your continuing suggestions and questions.

Sincerely,

Willow Avenue School
Report Card Revision Committee

---

detailed accounts of students' reading achievement, but they also place increased demands on teachers compared with the reporting of a single letter or number grade. Effective narrative writing requires considerable writing ability, and it is important that teachers feel capable of meeting the writing challenges that the narrative report card presents (see Table 3). The task of writing 25 to 35 lucid narrative reports in the last week of the marking period can be overwhelming, and a lengthy time frame for preparing the reports may be needed. Another approach is to stagger the writing and sending home of report cards over a period of a few weeks in an attempt to make the teacher's task more manageable (Johnston, 1992).

Parents and students. The readers of report cards need to familiarize themselves with new or revised formats of reading report cards; this can be accomplished with help from orientation meetings and documents and through conversations with teachers, administrators, and students. Parents and students may habitually read and sign report cards quickly. However, if a revised report card is intended to provide information about coordinating home and school efforts, to encourage reading at home, or to provide specific suggestions for continued progress, readers of the report card should accept more responsibility for reading more carefully and deliberately for particular types of information. In short, parents and students need to become familiar with any and all new roles for the report card.

A final set of responsibilities is related to synthesizing information about students' reading achievement from different sources. When the report card is one of several communications between school and home, readers of report cards should actively seek answers to questions about relationships among different types of information (e.g., a checklist, a narrative, and a set of single letter grades), and about unique and converging sets of information on students' reading development.

5. Will the New Reading Report Cards Be Understood?

When reading report cards go home, they will be interpreted in terms of the readers' personal history with, and prior knowledge of, report cards and reading assessment. Many parents are familiar with the format and information contained in traditional strand format report cards, a familiarity based on their own experiences of getting a single letter or number grade (such as B or 85). Readers of report cards should understand how and why new report cards may differ from those they have encountered previously. A permanent section of the report card that invites parents to raise questions and concerns and to comment on the effectiveness of the report card creates a continual feedback system that can contribute to increased understanding of the reporting system. The section might include questions like "What information is most useful in helping you understand your child's development as a reader?" or "Do you have any questions that are not addressed in this report card?" and "Do you have any suggestions for helping us improve the report card?"

The language spoken at home poses a critical set of concerns for understanding students' reading achievement via the report card. Schools with students from homes in which English is not spoken should regularly seek the assistance of translators, either in writing report cards in the languages used in the students' homes or in reading the report card for persons who do not read English. Alternatives to written report cards may be needed when communicating with parents who do not read.

Conclusions

Reading report cards that accurately reflect the needs and preferences of those who read and write them and that communicate useful information may be critical to students' continued reading development. When report cards do not meet these criteria, they should be changed. Preferences for revised report cards are influenced by the personal values of those who read and write them. No single reading report card will satisfy everyone. Thus, a realistic goal for the development or revision of reading report cards is to produce a report card that provides useful information to the greatest number of people.

Developing or changing the reading report card brings new challenges, but it may also yield several benefits. First, through a systematic consideration of audience and purpose, and a view of the information to be included within the larger context of reading assessment, the role of the report card may be better understood by more members of the school community. The report card may no longer be something inherited from a previous generation, only partly compatible with the current reading curriculum and used without critical examination. Second, by sharing the process of report card development with those who use and who are influenced by report cards, perspectives that previously may have been ignored or underrepresented are included. This contributes to a more balanced representation of values related to reading assessment and to reading report cards that are more easily understood and useful to a majority of report card readers.

Computers can be used to implement many revisions discussed herein. For example, checklists and narrative report formats can be stored in a computer file and tailored to communicate specific information to particular audiences and purposes. Computer files that contain appropriate phrases for describing students' reading development are currently used in some schools, serving to streamline some of the mechanical aspects of writing more descriptive report cards. A caveat for the use of computer programs for helping write report cards, however, is that the formulaic language and limits on descriptive phrases may hinder, rather than help, the communication of student achievement.

In summary, the means by which student achievement, development, and effort in reading are reported should be a focus, rather than an afterthought. Report cards that help teachers communicate effectively to parents, administrators, fellow teachers, and students themselves will help foster increased understandings of students' reading progress.

Author's Notes

The work reported herein is a National Reading Research Center project of the University of Georgia and the University of Maryland. It was supported under the Educational Research and Development Centers Program (PA/AWARD NO. 117A20007) as administered by the Office of Educational Research and Improvement, U.S. Department of Education.

The findings and opinions expressed in this article do not necessarily reflect the position or policies of the National Reading Research Center, the Office of Educational Research and Improvement, or the U.S. Department of Education.

References

Afflerbach, P., & Johnston, P. (in press). Eleven teachers write language arts report cards: Conflicts in knowing and communicating. *The Elementary School Journal*.

Afflerbach, P., & Sammons, R. (1992). Report cards in literacy evaluation: Teachers' training, practices, and values. *Literacy: Issues and Practices*, 9, 10–18.

Bray, E. (1986). Reports to parents. In R. Lloyd-Jones, E. Bray, G. Johnston, & R. Currie (Eds.), *Assessment: From principles to action* (pp. 173–206). London: Macmillan.

Cambourne, B., & Turbill, J. (1990). Assessment in whole language classrooms. *The Elementary School Journal*, 90, 337–349.

Freeman, E., & Hatch, J. (1989). What schools expect young children to know and do: An analysis of kindergarten report cards. *The Elementary School Journal*, 89, 595–605.

Goacher, B., & Reid, M. (1983). *School reports to parents: A study of policy and practice in the secondary school*. Windsor, England: NFER-Nelson.

Johnston, R. (1992). *The constructive evaluation of literacy*. White Plains, NY: Longman.

Section Two

Integrating Assessment and Instruction

Assessing and teaching are interrelated tasks. The articles in this section hold teachers responsible for conducting assessment, and they provide varied examples of assessment tools used by classroom teachers to understand readers and to inform instruction. Although the tools discussed may be familiar to teachers, the articles offer information on more effective implementation of these tools. For example, the article by Rhodes and Natheson-Mejia provides in-depth information on effective use of anecdotal records, which are widely used by teachers to trace observations about student literacy development. Examples of anecdotal records refresh us on what to observe and record, but the authors also model how to analyze and use our notations.

Furthermore, the assessment practices in this section focus on the classroom, but many can be applied to readers in special service programs. For example, an article in this section on the STAIR (System of Teaching and Assessing Interactively and Reflectively) approach may be applied in a variety of contexts. In Chapter 1 programs, various pull-out programs, or in traditional classrooms, teachers of struggling readers can use STAIR to make systematic observations that cause instructional revisions that better meet the needs of learners.

Additional Readings

- Galley, S.M. (1996). Talking their walk: Interviewing fifth graders about their literacy journeys. *Language Arts*, *73*(4), 249–254.
- Remier, K.M., Stephens, D., & Smith, K. (Eds.). (1993). Asking questions/making meaning: Inquiry-based instruction. *Primary Voices K–6*, *1*(1).
- Rhodes, L.K. (Ed.). (1993). *Literacy assessment: A handbook of instruments*. Portsmouth, NH: Heinemann.
- Rhodes, L.K., & Dudley-Marling, C. (1996). *Readers and writers with a difference: A holistic approach to teaching struggling readers and writers*. Portsmouth, NH: Heinemann.

Teachers' Choices in Classroom Assessment

Peter Afflerbach, Editor
Emelie Lowrey Parker, Regla Armengol, Leigh Baxley Brooke,
Kelly Redmond Carper, Sharon M. Cronin, Anne Cooper Denman,
Patricia Irwin, Jennifer McGunnigle, Tess Pardini,
and Nancy P. Kurtz, Guest Authors

April 1995

In this column we will share a variety of assessment practices utilized in our primary classrooms to meet the needs of our diverse student population. Over 80% of our 5- and 6-year-old students are second language learners of English who come from various cultural and economic backgrounds and who have a wide range of literacy experiences for us to build upon.

Our assessment practices are tailored to meet the literacy needs of these children, who range from fluent readers and writers to those with limited or no experience with English. Our goal is to meet students' instructional needs so that we can facilitate their learning. Effective assessment is essential to our instructional program.

We think of assessment as something that permeates every school day. Assessment teaches us not only what our students have learned and are learning, but what they are ready to learn. Information gained through assessment drives our instructional decisions. Long- and short-range planning is based on this information. Lesson content is determined. Questions are answered, such as "What will we teach tomorrow?" and "Who needs to be engaged in what kind of learning activities?" The assessment practices we describe must be continuously refined and modified to meet the ever-changing needs of our students.

Concepts About Print

The beginning of the year presents both a challenge and an opportunity to teachers. One of our first assessments is the child's knowledge of concepts about print, specifically print in books. Our assessment is a modification of the observational survey designed by Marie Clay (1991). This measures the nuts and bolts of print, whether the child knows the front of the book from the back, that print is read rather than illustrations, and that reading is done from left to right and top to bottom. The assessment also measures children's conceptions of word and letter. We work with children individually, using a book selected from our classroom. This 5-minute assessment is invaluable for gauging a beginning point for instruction.

For example, a child who scores low on this assessment needs more exposure to print in various forms. The child probably has not had much experience with print at home, and this alerts the teacher to a potential point of growth for the family. In school the child needs to be surrounded with print, to participate in guided readings and book extensions, and possibly to be paired with another child who has a stronger reading foundation for activities such as buddy reading, listening to books on audio cassette, or writing. On the other hand, a child who already knows print concepts is ready to begin learning other aspects of reading. If the child is able to identify some of the words in the book used for the assessment, similar reading materials could be encouraged. If the child reads the book easily, then more difficult text can be provided, and instruction can center around different types of writing, story structure, or another topic according to the needs of the student. Overall, the concepts about print observation provide an excellent opportunity to assess how a child deals with print and how much the child has been exposed to print in the past. It provides one snapshot of the child that can be combined with other informal assessment results to establish a point to meet the child's literacy needs.

Running Records

Another observational task that we adapted from Marie Clay is the running record. This reading assessment guides our teaching by evaluating students' strengths and needs. We can determine if children are self-monitoring their reading, if their reading material is appropriate, and what strategies the children are using to identify unknown words. When analyzing running records, we look for the intelligence in the child's errors. Based on the type of errors made, we can determine what cues they are using and those that they are neglecting.

Using running records with English as a Second Language (ESL) students has given us a great deal of insight into how they learn to read and speak. We often observe an over-reliance on one or two cueing systems. For example, a child may be using picture and letter sounds to decode text but neglect the use of language structure. Our use of running records with ESL students has helped us understand that as their oral language strengthens, ESL children will transfer this knowledge to reading and begin to rely on all cueing systems simultaneously.

Anecdotal Notes

Children continually change throughout the school year because they are influenced by their observations and interactions with print, their peers, and their family members. They also learn from formal instruction. Anecdotal notes capture student growth as observed by the teacher. We use the notes to demonstrate growth in all areas of instruction, especially reading, writing, and oral language development. Whatever method is used to make anecdotal notes, the goal is the same: to capture the development of the child as it happens and to create a more complete picture of the whole child. Like other assessment tools, anecdotal notes provide information to further tailor each child's individual instruction.

Anecdotal records are as formal or informal as the teacher wants them to be. They look different in every classroom. For example, when dealing with ESL students, an anecdotal note might relate the day that a child began using complete sentences in class, such as saying "May I go to the bathroom?" as opposed to "Bathroom?" Developments such as this may signal that conventions of oral language are being assimilated and applied by the child.

Writing Vocabulary and Word Dictation

The writing vocabulary assessment is administered at the beginning of the school year to gain baseline data on our students. A small group of children are called together and asked to write all the words that they know. Children begin with their names, then write any other words they think that they can write. Some children write only their names or isolated letters, and others write long lists of words. At the end of 10 minutes each child is asked to read the words that were written. Those words that are spelled correctly and that the child reads back accurately are counted. We use the assessment at the end of each academic quarter to show change over time.

Children's responses provide the teacher with valuable information about how they are building a basic writing vocabulary. The assessment also shows the child's knowledge of spelling, sound-symbol relationships, word families, and usage of capital and lower-case letters. It also provides evidence of the child's recall of high-frequency words used in the classroom. This in turn helps the teacher plan for future instruction.

For children to become proficient writers, it is necessary for them to hear the sounds in words and be able to record them. Teachers need to know what children know about spelling in order to guide their instruction. The word dictation assessment provides this information. The first-grade team generated a list of 20 words that required students to demonstrate their spelling progress. Some were chosen because they were high-frequency words (*my*, *and*), some were chosen because they included a particular blend (*jump*, *skip*), vowel sound (*coat*, *game*), or tense (*played*, *looking*); and some words were chosen because of their frequent use in our classroom or in the children's writing (*because*, *then*, *once*) The writing assessment and the word dictation show the progress our children make in recognizing sounds and linking them to symbols, in noticing word patterns, and in understanding that sounds in words may be represented in different ways.

Self-Assessment/ Goal-Setting Interviews

We often use self-assessment/goal-setting interviews in our first-grade classrooms for gaining insight into the child's perspective of writing. The following interview questions help us determine our instructional focus, change the physical environment of the classroom to be more conducive to a writer's needs, and determine expectations: What did you do well as an author/writer? What did/will your audience like best? Why? What do you need to work on/learn next to be a better author/writer? How can I or your friends help you?

Students' answers to these interview questions alert us to stumbling blocks: "I can do the first sound and the last sound. Teach me the middle sounds." The answers are sometimes a humbling assessment of teaching: "You didn't do a good job of teaching us quotation marks. We need to do it again." When we listen to the children, we gather valuable information about guiding and teaching beginning writers. When we use this information to make instructional decisions, the child's writing instruction becomes rich and personalized. Children at all ages can reflect on their learning. Here are questions a kindergarten teacher asks students: How did you learn to read? Which can you do better, read or write? Did writing every day help you to read? How?

The children's responses inform the teacher about their perceptions of literacy. Teachers at our school believe that instruction should lead the children to discover for themselves. Our goal, starting at kindergarten, is to make them a part of the assessment process so that they can take control of their own learning and teachers can facilitate learning.

Nonfiction Journals

Nonfiction journals, learning logs, or "learnals" are a form of assessment that some of us have experimented with in our classrooms. We begin slowly with a lot of modeling and encouragement. First we discuss with the students what to include in their nonfiction journals. We differentiate between fiction and nonfiction and model many nonfiction journal entries. Each entry starts with "I learned about...," I did...," "Today I learned that...." At the end of each day the class brainstorms what they learned that day and makes a list of key words for writing. Next the students choose how to show what they learned: writing, drawings, or diagrams. Finally, the children share and discuss their entries. During this sharing time the first-grade team watches for evidence of higher level thinking, using content-related oral communication, and questioning. Our journal assessment helps us to direct our instruction to the children's needs and interests.

Nonfiction journals are tools for children to express, reflect on, and assess what they have learned. They provide information to the teacher about a child's comprehension of nonfiction reading and of content concepts being studied. The teacher can use this information to further the development and direction of the unit of study, as well as to guide both small and large group lessons.

Scoring Rubrics

Our team has begun to experiment with scoring rubrics in order to provide consistency in assessing student progress and to help us clarify instructional goals. The scoring rubric that we developed last year, for example, focused on assessing the children's understanding of the mathematics and science concepts studied in one of our conceptual units. This interdisciplinary unit, entitled "Connections," is organized around the major concept that cycles occur in nature (the cyclical nature of the four seasons, the growth cycle of plants) as well as in mathematics (geometric and numerical patterns). Throughout the unit students are engaged in many activities: comparing versions of the Johnny Appleseed story, summarizing a nonfiction text, conducting scientific experiments, and engaging in real-world experiences such as planting a garden.

We wanted an assessment that would provide our diverse student population a range of options for demonstrating their learning. A scoring rubric with a numerical scale of 1 to 5 was designed. Students who scored a 5 demonstrated an in-depth understanding of the unit's concepts, and those who scored a 1 showed an emergent understanding of the concepts. We developed a scale that described the characteristics of student performance at each level. The students were rated holistically using teacher observation, anecdotal records, and several performance tasks. This form of alternative assessment afforded all of our students, even those who did not have spoken English competency, ways to demonstrate their learning. A child with very limited oral or written English could demonstrate knowledge through art or drama.

Conclusion

These assessments did not evolve quickly or in sequence. Rather, they are still developing as we continue to tailor our instruction to meet the individual needs of our students. Our assessments are designed to be used primarily by the teacher. However, they are often shared with students to show individual growth over the school year, and we use them with parents to pinpoint areas of children's growth and development.

Assessments prove to be most productive when students are assessed as an integral part of the learning process. Assessing the process as well as the product is important to us. We simultaneously assess what has been learned, how it was learned, and the techniques that we used to teach it. Classroom teachers must formulate assessments based on what is meaningful for them and their students. Assessment should be used as teaching tools to benefit the unique individuals within the classroom.

Reference

Clay, M. (1991). *Becoming literate*. Portsmouth, NH: Heinemann.

Diagnostic Teaching

Sheila W. Valencia, Editor
Karen K. Wixson, Guest Author

February 1991

Diagnostic teaching is a method that integrates assessment and instruction. It permits us to observe the ways in which different reader and contextual factors may be influencing a student's reading and reading acquisition. The term *diagnostic teaching* (Lipson & Wixson, in press) reflects the dual purposes for which the procedure is used. First, the procedure is *diagnostic* because it allows the collection of additional information in order to clarify and test hypotheses about what the reader needs. Second, it is instructional because it provides opportunities to try out methods for working with a student.

Diagnostic teaching is *hypothesis driven*. That is, it assumes that the teacher is intentionally examining one or more of the factors that are suspected to be contributing to or inhibiting reading achievement. Skilled teachers often engage in diagnostic teaching but fail to recognize its value or record the results in any systematic fashion. Consequently, they come to rely more on results of static, formal assessment than on the valuable information gathered during diagnostic teaching.

Diagnostic Teaching Procedures

It is impossible to provide a step-by-step description of how to conduct diagnostic teaching sessions because the procedures vary considerably from situation to situation. However, the *process* of diagnostic teaching can be described in terms of three related tasks: (a) planning, (b) executing, and (c) evaluating.

Planning: Planning for diagnostic teaching involves thinking about the factors we can manipulate in an experimental lesson; we attempt to verify hunches about both the source of the problem and the instructional manipulations that are most likely to foster learning. Most of the problems readers experience lie in the interaction between reader factors (e.g., knowledge, skills, and motivation) and characteristics of the reading context (e.g., settings, methods, and materials). However, because reader factors are difficult to change, it is easier to think about the contextual factors that can or should be altered (see Lipson, *RT* Assessment column, December 1990).

Using the elements of the reading context, the first area we might consider manipulating during diagnostic teaching is the instructional *setting*. For example, we might consider trying to alter the goals for literacy learning that a student has acquired from the instructional context or we might alter the organization of instructional activities and groups (e.g., from lecture to discussion; from a teacher-led group to a cooperative work group or individual instruction).

The *methods* of instruction comprise a second element of the reading context we might consider changing. Within this area, we might consider altering what is being taught (focus) or how it is being taught (approach). For example, we might consider changing the focus of reading lessons from a heavy emphasis on isolated skill instruction to the application of skills in authentic reading materials, or we might shift from a language experience lesson for word identification to a direct instruction lesson.

The third area of the reading context we might consider manipulating in diagnostic teaching consists of *materials and tasks*. The characteristics of texts that are most easily modified include text type, length, readability, familiarity, organization (e.g., temporal sequence, cause-effect), coherence/unity, and structural characteristics (e.g., charts, headings, illustrations, etc.). We might also consider altering the content or the form of the tasks in which a student is asked to engage. This might include changing from recognition tasks to open-ended or discussion tasks, changing from low- to high-level tasks, or altering factors such as the quantity, response mode (e.g., oral, written), or clarity of task directions.

Generally, we should anticipate using multiple settings, methods, materials, and tasks as we engage in diagnostic teaching. We are really attempting to set up the diagnostic teaching to represent or test certain interactions and to test how students learn under a variety of conditions. However, because there are so many possible interactions, only those that appear to be likely candidates for improving a student's reading should be evaluated.

Executing: Once we have planned for the diagnostic teaching session by identifying the factors we want to manipulate or try out, we move into executing the lesson. Among the many ways we might proceed are the *alternative methods* and the *scaffolding* approaches. The alternative methods approach involves conducting diagnostic teaching sessions that try out several distinct alternatives to solving a particular problem. In contrast, the scaffolding approach involves conducting sessions in which an instructional procedure is modified by providing different levels of support to the reader. The procedures employed in both approaches should involve viable instructional techniques for the classroom setting in which they eventually will be used. This ensures that the procedures used for diagnostic teaching are not too specialized or difficult to be used in actual teaching situations.

An alternative methods approach was used in the case of Seth, who was experiencing serious word recognition problems and seemed to have difficulty learning new words. In this case, diagnostic teaching enabled us to try out three distinct instructional approaches: phonics instruction that taught him to break the whole into component parts, phonics instruction that taught him to blend parts into wholes, and sight word instruction. Although Seth learned new words equally well across the three approaches, he learned new words in the part-to-whole phonics and the sight word approaches in a fraction of the time it took him to learn with the whole-to-part phonics approach. These results, combined with Seth's perception that he had learned most easily in the part-to-whole method, led to the implementation of the part-to-whole approach.

The scaffolding approach is a fairly recent innovation that requires the teacher or examiner to present the student with a reading activity, observe the response, and then introduce modifications of the task. These modifications are really hypotheses about what the student requires to become a better reader. The predominant form of these modifications is the layering of prompts. Prompts, or supports, are ordered from least support to most support so that the intervention requiring the least assistance can be identified clearly.

Imagine, for example, that a reader is unable to answer a question or series of questions about a selection. We can add a sequence of prompts such as those that follow and record the point at which the student can respond correctly.

1. What could you do to answer that question?

2. Do you know the answer to the question?

3. Can you figure it out?

4. Is the information you need in the selection?

5. Where in the selection could you find that information?

The next steps would involve actually engaging in instruction designed to help students do whatever is required by the text and task (e.g., locate information, infer connections). In this manner, it is possible to specify how much support is likely to be necessary for the student to perform under the various conditions that have been explored.

Good diagnostic teaching also requires the flexibility to be able to take advantage of opportunities as they arise during the executing of the lesson. Over time we develop a repertoire of both assessment and instruction procedures that can be used to respond to unexpected events. The adjustments will only be useful, however, to the extent that we recognize what is happening when it occurs and are prepared to revise our plans on the spot.

Evaluating: The thrust of evaluating diagnostic teaching is to determine the impact of the interventions on a student's learning, performance, or knowledge. When the alternative methods approach is used, the evaluation involves noting similarities and differences in a student's performance, motivation, or knowledge during and after the administration of the different interventions.

In the case of Seth, this might mean several different types of evaluation. First, we would probably want to test his learning of new words under the different instructional methods to compare the relative effectiveness of them. Second, we would want to observe the extent to which he participated actively in each of the interventions. Other things being equal, Seth's willingness to engage in the instructional activities—that is, the extent to which the techniques made sense to him—is perhaps the most important criterion for future success. No matter how good the instructional technique, it is unlikely to be successful if the reader resists rather than participates actively in its use.

When the scaffolding approach is used, the evaluation will focus on a comparison of the student's learning, performance, knowledge, or motivation at various levels of support. Our purpose is to find an optimal level of support—that is, the level at which the reader is challenged enough to learn but not so much that she or he gives up in frustration or fails to become actively involved. This helps the teacher make decisions about how to structure instruction.

Valuable information can also be gained by interviewing the student during or after either type of intervention. Responses to the following types of questions can reveal a great deal about students' understanding of how to use a new skill or strategy as well as their attitudes and motivation for engaging in particular activities.

1. What do you think we are trying to learn and why? Why am I asking you to do ____?

2. Tell me how you figured out ____?

3. What would you have done differently if I asked you to ____?

4. Which activity did you like best? Why? Which did you think helped you the most? Why?

5. What did you learn, how do you do it, and when would you use it? How would it help you read better?

In conclusion, it is well to think of diagnostic teaching as both cyclical and continuous. Generally, the results of diagnostic teaching are used either to establish a new focus for additional diagnostic teaching or to plan an instructional program.

The purpose of good assessment is to help us make efficient and significant instructional progress with our students. The tremendous advantage of diagnostic teaching is that it melds assessment and instruction.

Reference

Lipson, M.Y., & Wixson, K.K. (in press). *Assessment and instruction of reading disability: An interactive approach*. New York: HarperCollins.

Students' Evaluations Bring Reading and Writing Together

Jane Hansen

October 1992

Reading/writing teachers constantly revise themselves; they never become finished products. These teachers look for mismatches between their authoritarianism and their belief in children as creators of curriculum. Often the words of their students lead the teachers toward change. In this article I write about the teachers in one school who made fundamental changes in their reading/writing program because they listened to their students' plans for themselves as readers and writers.

The Students' Plans for Their Writing and Reading

For 3 years I researched amidst changes in the elementary school in Stratham, New Hampshire, a small upper-middle-class community. During the first semester, I interviewed students to find out what they valued in themselves as readers and writers (Hansen, 1991). We (see endnote) had initiated the research project because we wanted to find out the potential of students as self-evaluators, and I wanted to gather some preliminary data on the students'

ability to view themselves as readers and writers. I asked students from grades 1–5 these questions:

- What have you learned recently in writing?
- What would you like to learn next to become a better writer?
- How do you intend to go about learning how to do that?
- What have you learned recently in reading?
- What would you like to learn next to become a better reader?
- How do you intend to go about learning how to do that?

The answers of two students typify the tone of the other interviews. Abbie, a second grader, said, "I can write a lot of stories and poems. I wrote a poem about a pear.... And I wrote a story about a ghost." To become a better writer, Abbie intended to "Write more stories." She'd learn to write by writing, something she did every day in school.

For reading, Abbie said, "I can read more books," and to become a better reader she planned to "Read more books. My mom's going

77

to teach me. I'm going to learn a lot this year." Similar to writing, she intended to learn to read by reading. However, there was a difference between what she expected from writing versus reading. She knew she would have time to write in school, but that was not true of reading; reading was to be learned at home.

Becky, a fifth grader, said, "I can write a setting." To become a better writer she wanted "to write better settings. This is my first one."

For reading, Becky said, "I want to read better in my brain.... At home I get to pick the books I read. When I pick my books I enjoy them and I read more. You get better because you read more. You practice more."

In both reading and writing, all the students could articulate what they wanted to learn next, and for writing they intended to pursue those goals in school. For reading, however, they felt the school program was so prescribed by the teachers that the only place they could pursue their own goals was at home. In other words, the second question in each set assumes that the learner is in control, which was true in the writing program. The teachers helped the students become aware of options and taught them how to use considerable decision-making power. The students usually chose their own path to follow and felt good about being able to select their own topics and make other decisions.

In reading, however, they were not in control. Since the second of the reading questions did not make sense in regard to their school reading experiences, students placed themselves somewhere else. Without exception, whatever the students wanted to learn next in reading, they intended to go about learning it at home from books of their choice. They did not see the school as the place in which they would become better readers.

I shared my data with the principal, an avowed basal advocate who believed in an authoritarian approach to the teaching of reading. He considered the students' comments for 2 months and decided their comments must receive consideration. He asked me to share my interview data at a special faculty meeting. He supported teachers who had already begun to change their reading instruction and made this statement to his faculty:

> I retract my statement that this will always be a basal school. The students think they are not learning to read here. We have to change the way we teach reading. The students have no confidence in us. You decide how to change, but change.

The teachers, experienced with the teaching of writing, turned to it as the familiar model upon which to base change (as did the teachers in Hansen, 1987). Hallmarks of the new reading program were lots of time for children to read from books of their choice, opportunities for children to talk about books with their classmates, no ability groups, and sessions within which children could plan their growth as readers. These characteristics were modeled after the writing program these students and teachers were accustomed to.

The teachers also observed reading/writing classrooms in other schools. A large percentage of the faculty plus the principal met weekly to share their own reading and writing, and the research team met occasionally. Both kinds of meetings validated the teachers' efforts to teach reading and writing similarly and furthered their thinking, as well as that of their principal.

Their ideas about reading/writing changed as the two programs merged. Reading and writing fed each other. Questions in reading and writing groups started to blur boundaries that had seemed to exist between the two disciplines. Reading groups addressed questions of authorship, such as how various authors created character and plot. In writing, students used favorite authors as models for dialogue and character development.

Thus, the students' answers to the interview question near the beginning of the project, "How do you intend to go about learning how to do that?" initiated changes in the way teachers in this school taught reading. The teachers decided to bring the interview questions into their teaching repertoire, and the students' perceptions of themselves as readers and writers evolved. As students continued to set their own goals, the teachers gave them a stronger voice in the evaluation system.

The Students' Evaluations Within Their Revised Classrooms

By the end of the first year of the project, the limitations of the report card became clear, so a schoolwide committee of teachers revised the report card during the summer (Parsons, 1991). Because they had experienced a new respect for their students' input, the teachers decided to include the students in the report card process at the end of each quarter. In other words, the teachers initiated two changes: First, they changed the design and working of the report card itself, and second, they solicited input from their students when they filled out the cards.

Teachers brought the students into the act of report card evaluation in different ways. Janis Bailey (Bailey et al., 1988), a third-grade teacher, gave her students copies of the report card, talked with them about each item, asked them to fill them out, and asked each student to write two goals for the next quarter on the back of the paper, one for writing and the other for reading. The students' evaluations of themselves, which included their ability to set their goals, impressed Janis; the plans they made for themselves reflected their self-perceived weaknesses.

One child wrote, "*Tiry stekin woth the same bk.*" This student discontinued one book after another and had given himself a low grade for the report card item "Chooses reading material with confidence." Thus he wanted to "try sticking with the same book."

Another child, who always wrote about elves, set the goal, "*Don't use a topic too much.*" She had given herself a low mark for "Chooses writing topics with confidence" and wanted to expand her writing repertoire.

Some teachers solicited their students' plans in interviews rather than in written form. During the third year of the project, Chris Gaudet, a first-grade teacher, decided to allocate 2 weeks for interviews with each child before the end-of-October parent conferences. She had heard the teachers of the older students talk about the plans their students created throughout the entire previous year, and she decided to see what would happen if she opened this door to her young students. The children brought their writing folders to the writing interviews and their reading folders and books to the reading interviews. Chris wondered if the interviews would be worth all the time they took.

They were. She said, "Of all the things I've done during this project, this was the most helpful." Those conferences were the best she had had in 10 years of teaching. She shared the children's words with their parents, and as soon as they heard their child's own words from the half-sheet of paper on which she had recorded each interview, the parents leaned forward and sat on the edge of every word.

The following children's responses to questions during the writing interviews are typical of what the children reported to Chris about what they had learned, what they wanted to learn, and how they planned to go about learning new writing skills:

- "I've learned to make spaces."
- "I can write words and pictures that go together."
- "I want to know more sounds."
- "I'll ask someone—a kid."

The need to know more sounds was a common desire for these young children who wrote daily. They needed to learn sound-symbol correspondences. They learned and practiced their sounds every day as they wrote in clusters with other writers and readers; their invented spellings showed their attempts to match letters to the sounds they heard.

They identified other needs as well. Some children wanted to think of better titles for their writing. Others wanted to learn how to put exciting words in their drafts. The diversity of the children's goals influenced the way their teacher taught.

This classroom, like the other classrooms throughout the school, became a place where students and teacher interacted during writing/reading workshop to help each other with what they wanted to learn next. Chris Gaudet expected the students to get and give help as they worked toward their own varied plans. Responses to the reading questions during the interviews brought answers such as these:

- "I can read *Fantastic Mr. Fox*."
- "I can read *Mr. Fox*!"
- "I want to read *Mr. Gumpy's Outing*."
- "Mark [sixth-grade partner] can help me."

Many children measured their growth by the titles of books they could read, and some children depended on their sixth-grade buddies. In Chris's Grade 1 class, sixth-grade children served as daily helpers, an idea that is receiving increased attention (e.g., Labbo & Teale, 1990). Buddy systems of various kinds sprouted throughout the school. The Stratham children became accustomed to being in classrooms other than their own, and teachers of all grade levels taught their students ways to seek and give help. As a result, many individuals began to share their work in classrooms of older, as well as younger, students.

Over time as the students in the various grade levels continued to share goals and accomplishments, evaluative comments became part of their daily discussions (Levi, 1990). For example, right in the middle of a group a child would say, "That book sounds interesting. Could I read it when you're finished?" Or, when a child had just shared dialogue, another child would say, "Oh! I want to learn quotation marks! That's the next thing I'm gonna learn." Learning environments which encourage assessments of this kind need increased attention in our schools (Brown, 1987).

As the teachers included more and more opportunities for their students to reflect and plan, their initial surprise at their students' ability to evaluate themselves changed to an assumption that their students *could* evaluate their growth. After more than a year of meeting with his students about their report cards, Chip Nelson, a Grade 6 teacher, started filling out the report cards while his students talked rather than at a later time. As they watched him record their suggested grades directly onto the report card, they knew Mr. Nelson took their self-evaluations seriously.

The sixth graders demonstrated their understanding of their report card and what was important in reading and writing. Gordy, a sixth grader, shared his thoughts:

> Now you get to talk to the teacher.... It's not these things you do and you might get marked on them. The way it used to be you might get an A and not deserve it, or you might get a mark that's lower than you deserve because the grade was based on these THINGS you did, tests and things and nothing else. With reading and writing it's better because this has to do with the things you can do well and the things you might work on. It's not ABC or D that you don't know why it's one of those letters.

Gordy and his friends not only appreciated the new role they played in the school's grading system but believed their grades now reflected their reading and writing skills better than in former days when their teachers based their grades on scores from workbooks, worksheets, and other "things." Now the teachers helped the students spend their time directly on reading and writing as the students tried to become better at the skills or strategies they had chosen to "work on." The students' accomplishments, from their own perspectives, became the basis for their grades. With the grading system based on individual goals, the former comparative, rank-order relationships among children faded. The reading/writing program could now become a place where students worked not only for their own welfare but also for that of others.

The Students' Views of Each Other

The students' creation of their own plans also prompted a shift in the school's policy toward students with learning difficulties. In the regular classrooms, all children recognized what they could do and knew of things they wanted to learn. To not know how to do something became expected behavior and opened doors in the school, both classroom and resource room doors. The teachers and students welcomed into the regular classrooms the students who had for years learned to read and write only in the resource room.

The teachers eliminated ability groups (Oakes, 1985) and highlighted strengths of each class member so that everyone became necessary for the classroom interaction patterns to work. The class needed each person. With no one placed in the inferior position of being in a bottom group, each student could be someone with status.

Daily events reinforced the students' positions as people with voices to be heard. Meetings of the new, heterogeneous reading groups became occasions for students to discuss their reading on their terms. A girl shared *Anastasia Again* by Lois Lowry and said, "Anastasia's funny the way she talks to her parents like they're children." The group responded to this comment instead of responding to teacher questions as they had done in previous years. This kind of talk helped the students think about themselves as

they relived the situations of the characters (Bartok, 1985; Greene, 1988), and their contributions carried a different sense of worth.

The teacher trusted them (Kitagawa, 1989) to start the discussion of their books, and rather than using preplanned questions, she based her questions on what they said. The teachers came to the groups with a new perspective. Instead of coming as evaluators to check their students' comprehension (Roller, 1989), teachers came to share what they valued in whatever book they were reading and to honor the children's values about the books they were reading.

This change in the teachers' ability to not only handle diversity in a group but also to actually foster talk about a wide range of books in one session opened possibilities for a new kind of classroom community. Students began to see each other as interesting sources of information, and students with learning difficulties grew alongside their classmates. The story of one particular student highlights this evolution.

Jessica, a fourth grader who had been retained twice (Wansart, 1988), had left her regular classroom for reading and writing for 6 years. She walked around with hunched shoulders and kept her eyes down when you talked to her. Her body language showed that she placed very little value on herself.

Over a period of several months Jessica's teacher, the resource room teacher, and Professor Wansart taught Jessica the skills she needed in order to participate in the classroom reading/ writing workshop. As a result, Jessica's head started to rise. Eventually she stayed in the regular classroom instead of going to the resource room. When she chose an Amelia Bedelia book to learn to read, two other girls brought Amelia Bedelia books and joined Jessica in a corner to help her learn.

When the class received a computer, the resource room teacher taught Jessica how to use it, and she became the class expert. Children sought her expertise. Her head rose higher.

When the class formed a circle, she placed her chair within it instead of three feet back as she had always done. She joined the group. Finally one day in the spring she raised her hand for the first time and asked another student a question after he had read a piece of his writing to the class.

Toward the end of the year, Jane Wiessman, Assistant Director of Special Education for New Hampshire, visited Stratham Memorial School. She spent some time in Jessica's classroom, but no one pointed out Jessica. She was simply a reader/writer blending with the others. Jessica got up from her seat, went to the bookshelf of published books, removed one, and approached Ms. Wiessman with a slight grin inquiring, "May I read my new published book to you?"

This was unprecedented behavior for Jessica. She had now become an integral part of a school in which students share their individual accomplishments, hopes, and frustrations. Teachers and classmates celebrate successes, and help each other achieve their goals. The teachers' overall objective is to help their students see themselves as readers and writers, but the students set their own goals and evaluate themselves. In so doing, they learn to use each other as resources. Readers and writers, as well as reading and writing, work together.

Author's Note

The seven teachers who served on the research team were Christine Gaudet, Grade 1; Nancy Herdecker, Grade 4; Mary Ann Wessells, Grade 5; Chip Nelson and Donna Lee, Grade 6; Mike Quinn, resource room; and Lucinda Wigode, librarian. The principal was also on the team. Several doctoral students from the University of New Hampshire served as researchers at some time during the 3 years: Dan-Ling Fu, Peg Murray, MaryEllen MacMillan, Mary Comstock, Brenda Power, Judy Fueyo, Ann Vibert, and Ruth Hubbard. Besides myself, two other professors from the University of New Hampshire served as researchers: Bill Wansart and Donald Graves. Finally, I wish to thank Peg Murray and Sue Ducharme for considerable help with this manuscript.

References

Bailey, J., Brazee, P., Chiavaroli, S., Herbeck, J., Lechner, T., Lewis, D., McKittrick, A., Redwine, L., Reid, K., Robinson, B., & Spear, H. (1988). Problem solving our way to alternative evaluation procedures. *Language Arts, 65,* 364–374.

Bartoli, J. (1985). The paradox in reading: Has the solution become the problem? *Journal of Reading, 28,* 580–584.

Brown, R. (1987). Literacy and accountability. *The Journal of State Government, 60,* 68–72.

Greene, M. (1988). What are the language arts for? *Language Arts, 65,* 471–478.

Hansen, J. (1987). *When writers read.* Portsmouth, NH: Heinemann.

Hansen, J. (1991). Children evaluate their writing and reading. In J. Roderick (Ed.), *Context-responsive approaches to assessing children's language* (pp. 70–78). Urbana, IL: National Council on Research in English.

Kitagawa, M.M. (1989). Constructing a mosaic in the context of cultural diversity. In J. Jensen (Ed.), *Stories to grow on: Demonstrations of language learning in K–8 classrooms* (pp. 131–146). Portsmouth, NH: Heinemann.

Labbo, L.D., & Teale, W. (1990). Cross-age reading: A strategy for helping poor readers. *The Reading Teacher, 43,* 362–369.

Levi, R. (1990). Assessment and educational vision: Engaging learners and parents. *Language Arts, 67,* 269–273.

Oakes, J. (1985). *Keeping track: How schools structure inequality.* New Haven, CT: Yale University Press.

Parsons, L. (1991). Evaluation: What's really going on? In N. Atwell (Ed.), *Workshop 3: The politics of process* (pp. 58–62). Portsmouth, NH: Heinemann.

Roller, C. (1989). Classroom interaction patterns: Reflections of a stratified society. *Language Arts, 66,* 492–500.

Wansart, W. (1988). The student with learning disabilities in a writing process classroom: A case study. *Reading, Writing, and Learning Disabilities, 4,* 311–319.

Anecdotal Records: A Powerful Tool for Ongoing Literacy Assessment

Lynn K. Rhodes and Sally Nathenson-Mejia

March 1992

A great deal of attention is being paid to the assessment of process in addition to product in reading and writing. Observing a student's process provides the teacher with a window or view on how students arrive at products (that is, a piece of writing or an answer to a comprehension question). This allows the teacher to make good decisions about how he or she might assist during the process or restructure the process in order to best support more effective use of strategies and students' development as readers and writers. Anecdotal records can be written about products or can include information about both process and product. As process assessment, resulting from observation, anecdotal records can be particularly telling.

Observations of students in the process of everyday reading and writing allow teachers to see for themselves the reading, writing, and problem-solving strategies students use and their responses to reading and writing. Genishi and Dyson (1984), Jaggar (1985), Pinnell (1985), Y. Goodman (1985), Galindo (1989), and others discuss the need to observe children while they are involved in language use. Goodman notes:

> Evaluation provides the most significant information if it occurs continuously and simultaneously with the experiences in which the learning is taking place....Teachers who observe the development of language and knowledge in children in different settings become aware of important milestones in children's development that tests cannot reveal. (p. 10)

When teachers have developed a firm knowledge base that they can rely on in observations of students' reading and writing, they usually prefer recording their observations in anecdotal form. This is because the open-ended nature of anecdotal records allows teachers to record the rich detail available in most observations of literacy processes and products. The open-ended nature of anecdotal record taking also allows teachers to determine what details are important to record given the situation in which the student is reading and writing, previous assessment data, and the instructional goals the teacher and student have established. In other words, what is focused on and recorded depends on the teacher, the student, and the context, not on the predetermined items on a checklist.

Taken regularly, anecdotal notes become not only a vehicle for planning instruction and

83

documenting progress, but also a story about an individual. The definition of an anecdote is "a short narrative (or story) concerning a particular incident or event of an interesting or amusing nature" (*The Random House Dictionary of the English Language*, 1966). A story is "a way of knowing and remembering information—a shape or pattern into which information can be arranged....[A story] restructures experiences for the purpose of 'saving' them" (Livo, 1986, p. 5). Anecdotes about events in the reading and writing life of a student tell an ongoing story about how that child responds to the classroom's literacy environment and instruction. Because stories are how we make sense of much of our world, anecdotal records can be a vehicle for helping us make sense of what students do as readers and writers. In addition, teachers find that telling the story accumulated in anecdotal records is a natural and easy way to impart information about students' literacy progress to parents and other caregivers.

In short, anecdotal records are widely acknowledged as being a powerful classroom tool for ongoing literacy assessment (Bird, 1989; Cartwright & Cartwright, 1974; Morrissey, 1989; Thorndike & Hagen, 1977). In this article we will provide information about techniques for collecting and analyzing anecdotal records. In addition, we will review uses of anecdotal records including planning for instruction, informing parents and students, and generating new assessment questions.

Techniques for Writing Anecdotal Records

Reflecting about techniques for writing anecdotal records can positively affect both the content of the records as well as the ease with which they are recorded. Thorndike and Hagen (1977) suggest guidelines for the content of anecdotal records that teachers may find helpful:

1. Describe a specific event or product.
2. Report rather than evaluate or interpret.
3. Relate the material to other facts that are known about the child.

We have found these points particularly helpful if teachers feel that the content of their previous anecdotal records has not been useful to them. Below we have included an example of an anecdotal record for a first grader, Eleanor. Note how Eleanor's teacher uses detailed description to record how Eleanor is starting to understand sound-letter relations, but is still confused about word boundaries and sentences.

> Eleanor
> STRDAIPADENBSNO
> (Yesterday I played in the snow)
> STRDA = yesterday
> I = I
> PAD = played
> EN = in
> B = the (said "du" and thought she was writing "D")
> SNO = snow
>
> Showed her how to stretch her words out like a rubberband—doing it almost on her own by *SNO*. E does have a fairly good grasp of sound/letter relations. However, has a hard time isolating words and tracking words in sentences in her mind. That may hold up progress for awhile. Asked her—at end—what she did in writing today that she hadn't done in previous writing. She said, "I listened to sounds." Told her to do it in her writing again tomorrow.

Instead of recording the descriptive detail found in Eleanor's anecdotal note, the teacher might have written, "Eleanor sounded out words in writing for the first time today and will continue to need lots of help to do so." A general conclusion such as this is not as useful to instructional planning or to documenting progress as the detailed description in the note written by Eleanor's teacher. However, we believe that Thorndike and Hagen's points should be treated as guidelines, not as strict rules. We find that it is sometimes helpful to evaluate or interpret what has been observed. For example, read the sample anecdotal record that follows written about Katie, a fourth grader.

> Katie
>
> I asked if I could read more of the poetry book she had written at home over the last two years. (She had read selected poems to her classmates earlier.) She showed me a poem she didn't want to read to the class "because they wouldn't understand." (It's quite serious and deep.) Poetry doesn't look like poetry though she reads it as poetry—could use a formatting lesson.

The teacher's comment, "could use a formatting lesson," in Katie's note provides useful evaluation and interpretation as long as it is supported by a description of the event or product itself. The comment "Poetry doesn't look like poetry though she reads it as poetry" is the description that supports the interpretive comment.

Observational guides can be valuable complements to anecdotal recording because they serve to remind teachers what might be observed. If teachers find an observation guide helpful, they may want to post for themselves a list of the kinds of observations that might be recorded anecdotally. Figure 1 on the next page illustrates such a guide resulting from teachers' brainstorming. The list is displayed in a place in the classroom where the teachers can easily consult it, especially when they feel they need to improve the content of their notes.

In addition to increasing the content value of anecdotal notes, teachers also are concerned about increasing the ease with which anecdotal notes can be recorded. In part, ease of recording emanates from the classroom environment the teacher has established. Classroom routines that encourage students to be increasingly independent and responsible as readers and writers enable teachers to more easily record anecdotal records than classrooms in which literacy tasks are more teacher directed. Once students are familiar with and secure about the structure and behaviors demanded in routines such as Sustained Silent Reading, Author's Circle, Literature Circles, Writers' Workshop, and Readers' Workshop, teachers can find the time to work with and record observations of individuals or groups.

In addition to encouraging student independence and responsibility in literacy situations, it is easier for teachers to write anecdotal notes as they discover recording techniques that fit their styles and busy classroom lives. Carrying a clipboard to a variety of classroom settings is useful, as is using such complementary recording tools as sticky notes to transfer information to a notebook sectioned off by students' names. Teachers can take notes on a prearranged list of children each day, labeling sticky notes with the date and the names of students to be observed. This technique makes it possible to take notes on every child a minimum of once a week in each curricular area in which notes are taken.

Students can keep records too. Following a conference, the teacher might ask the student to record a summary statement of what they worked on together, what the student learned, or what the student still had questions about or wanted help with. Students also can use sticky notes so that their notes may be placed in the notebook along with the teacher's notes.

Teachers can take notes on groups as well as on individuals. For example, in working with a group of Chapter 1 [U.S. federally funded education program for at-risk children now called Title I] students, one teacher noted that all five students were having difficulty putting the information they were gathering from books into their own words as they took notes. Instead of writing the same information five times, she wrote it once and put the note in a spot in her notebook reserved for notes about the group. When a note is taken in a group, but applies only to selected students in the group, the note can be photocopied for the file of each student to whom it applies.

Figure 1
Teacher-generated observation guide

- functions served in reading and writing
- engagement in reading and writing
- what appears to affect engagement in reading and writing
- what aspects of text student attends to
- interactions with others over reading and writing
- interactions with materials
- insightful or interesting things students say
- hypotheses students are trying out in reading and writing
- misconceptions students have
- miscues students make while reading
- changes students make in writing
- how students use text before, during, and after reading
- how a lesson affects students' reading and writing
- comparisons between what students say and what they do
- plans students make and whether and how plans are amended
- how, where, and with whom students work
- what students are interested in
- what students say they want to work on in their reading and writing
- what students say about reading and writing done outside of school
- how students generate and solve problems in reading and writing
- ideas for reading and writing lessons and materials
- how students "symbol weave" (use multiple symbolic forms)
- how students theorize or talk about reading and writing
- how one reading and writing event relates to another
- how students use a variety of resources in reading and writing

Analyzing Anecdotal Records

Good techniques for recording anecdotal notes must be matched with good techniques for analyzing those notes if the potential for anecdotal records is to be realized. Effective analysis techniques include making inferences from the notes, looking for developmental trends or patterns within individuals and across children, identifying both strengths and weaknesses in learning and teaching, and making time for analysis.

Making Inferences

Teachers continually make inferences about students' reading and writing on the basis of observations. Looking back at the sample anecdotal record on Eleanor, you can see that Eleanor's teacher made one of her inferences explicit: "E does have a fairly good grasp of sound/letter relations." Because the teacher observed that Eleanor was able to consistently produce letters that matched the sounds she heard, she was able to infer that Eleanor had developed knowledge of sound-letter relations.

Katie's teacher does not explicitly infer anything in the first anecdotal record but it is possible for us to hypothesize that Katie may think she is different from many of her classmates with regard to what she thinks and writes. An analysis of other anecdotal records on Katie may lead the teacher to uncover a pattern in Katie's responses that confirms her hypothesis.

Identifying Patterns

Patterns of behavior can be uncovered for individuals and groups by reading and rereading anecdotal records looking for similarities and differences. For example, the following two notes were taken during a reading period in a second-grade classroom in which the majority of the students elect to read in pairs or small groups. What pattern of behavior do you see?

> Brooke & Larry reading a Nate the Great story together—switching off at each paragraph. Brooke jumps in to correct Larry or give him a word at the slightest hesitation.

> Aaron & Shawn reading—switching off after every 2 pgs. Shawn loves the story—keeps telling Aaron the next part will be funny & chuckling as he reads aloud. Shawn is the leader in this situation. He interrupts with immediate help when Aaron hesitates with a word.

In recording and reviewing these notes, the teacher noticed that she had observed the same problem in both pairs of readers; one reader would take over the responsibility for working out words from the other reader. Because she had notes on only two pairs of students, however, the teacher interviewed the class the next day, focusing on what they did to help classmates who encountered difficult words to find out whether the pattern she had uncovered in these two situations was a more general problem. Differing patterns in language use, both oral and written, can be seen through regular anecdotal record keeping.

To illustrate with another example, a second-grade teacher, one of our practicum students, was concerned about Raul, who was new to the United States. She felt he was gaining more control over written and oral English, but she had nothing to document his progress. Moreover, she did not want to push him too hard if he was not ready, or cause him to lag behind. The following are excerpts from anecdotal records Sally took as the practicum supervisor while observing Raul working with his peers, none of whom spoke his native Spanish. These notes demonstrate not only his interaction with print, but also his use of oral language.

> The boys begin reading through the questions. Raul looks at the book and says, "Que es esto?" (What is this?) No one answers him.

> They are sitting next to a chart that has all their names on it. They proceed to copy one anothers' names from the chart. Raul says to the group, "You can get my name from the chart."

> T [the teacher] comes over to see what they are doing. She asks which question they are on. Raul replies, "Where do they live? Water." T reminds them to write the answer in the appropriate square.

Using these and other notes, the teacher was able to see patterns in Raul's use of language on two levels, interacting with print, and interacting with peers. Getting no response when he initiated interaction in Spanish, Raul proceeded to use English to read from the chart, read from the book, speak to his classmates, and respond to his teacher. Together the teacher and Sally were able to plan for how his use of English could continue to be encouraged in context-laden situations without worrying about pushing him too fast.

Identifying Strengths and Weaknesses

Anecdotal records can be analyzed for both strengths and weaknesses in students' reading and writing. Katie's anecdotal record, which we discussed already, reveals that she writes poetry for herself outside of school and that she has a sense of audience. These are strengths. The record also reveals an area in which Katie can grow—formatting the poetry she writes. A look back at Eleanor's note also reveals strengths and weaknesses. For example, the teacher discovered that Eleanor has graphophonic knowledge not previously revealed in their writing and that she could verbalize what she learned during the conference with the teacher. The teacher also discovered that Eleanor previously had been using random strings of letters in her writing because she had such difficulty tracking words in sentences in her mind.

Finding Time for Analysis

Finally, just as it is important to find time to record anecdotal records, it is important to find time to analyze anecdotal records. Some analysis occurs concurrently with recording anecdotal notes and is recorded along with a description of the event that was observed. However, other analysis follows the recording of notes. We recommend that teachers try two things to make time for such analysis. First, use the start of each instructional planning period for an analysis of anecdotal records for individuals and groups. This will serve to focus planning time so that it may be used more efficiently. Second, if teachers meet on a regular basis with other teachers, analyzing anecdotal records can be a fruitful part of the meeting. For example, if a classroom teacher and Chapter 1 teacher both take anecdotal records on the same child, they can analyze both sets of notes together by comparing individual notes and looking for shared patterns and trends. If a group of teachers from the same grade level meets regularly, an analysis of one another's notes may uncover a great deal to talk about, including how best to adapt teaching to students' needs.

Uses of Anecdotal Records

Analysis of anecdotal records allows teachers to find patterns of success and difficulty for both individuals and groups of students. Students who have a need for particular information or for particular kinds of reading and writing opportunities can be grouped together and provided with the information or opportunities meeting their needs. In addition to instructional planning, the records also can be used to inform students and parents about progress and the value of various instruction and learning contexts. Finally, anecdotal records can help teachers generate new assessment questions.

Instructional Planning

To extend what Genishi and Dyson (1984) say about oral language to written language, anecdotal records on children's social behaviors and responses to written language can help teachers plan stimulating situations for the reluctant as well as the enthusiastic reader and writer. Using the set of anecdotal notes taken in the second-grade classroom during buddy reading discussed previously, we will show how the earlier analysis we provided can lead naturally to an instructional plan.

To review, the teacher noted that students in the buddy reading activity were taking reading responsibility away from the classmates when they hesitated or showed any sign of difficulty with reading words. When she interviewed the class the next day to glean more information about why this happened, she found that few students knew any options for helping partners with difficult words except to tell them the words. These assessment data helped the teacher plan lessons to demonstrate how to help readers retain responsibility for figuring out difficult words. For example, she talked to the children about the strategies she used with them—providing plenty of wait time, suggesting that they read on, suggesting that they reread, and so on. Then she demonstrated each of these strategies with a child and made a list of the strategies for the children to refer to. Finally, she ended the next several reading sessions early so that the children could share with her and one another the strategies they used to successfully figure out their own words and to assist peers in figuring out words they did not know. The children also shared problems they encountered and talked about how to solve them.

During the week, as the class focused on improving their strategies, the teacher observed pairs as they read, provided individual coaching for some, recorded more anecdotal notes, and used the notes to couch her lessons in detailed examples. In short, though the original anecdotal records and class interview were the basis of her first lesson, the anecdotal notes taken after the lessons became equally important in planning ongoing instruction to further develop the students' strategies and understanding.

Informing

In addition to using anecdotal records for planning ongoing instruction, teachers also may use them to periodically inform others, including the students themselves, about students' strengths, weaknesses, and progress. Reviewing anecdotal records with students helps them see the growth they have made as readers and writers, and helps them gain a sense of progress over time and learn to pinpoint where improvements need to be made. To illustrate, one Chapter 1 teacher who involved students in generating instructional goals claimed that the process of writing anecdotal records affected the students' attention to the goals they had set: "The children seem to get more focused faster since I started carrying a clipboard and taking notes. It seems to remind them about the goals they decided to work on."

Anecdotal records also can help teachers create support systems for students outside the classroom. Report cards, parent conferences, and staffings are all situations in which instructional planning can take place on the basis of the teacher's analysis of anecdotal records. Specific examples pulled from anecdotal records help parents or other school personnel see the child in the same way as the teacher who has collected the anecdotal records. They can augment the home or test information provided by others and provide clues about what contexts are and are not supportive of the child's learning in school.

Generating New Questions

Analyzing anecdotal records and using them to plan instruction encourages teachers to generate new questions that lead full circle to further assessment of students and of teaching itself. One teacher commented, "As I review kids' notes, sometimes even as I write them, I realize what else I need to find out." Bird (1989) commented that anecdotal records "not only guide [a teacher] in her instructional decision making but also provide her with a frequent opportunity for self-evaluation, enabling her to assess her role as a teacher" (p. 21). We agree, and find that the use of anecdotal records to inform instruction helps teachers become more aware of how their instruction is interpreted by students. Teachers are able to see how they can influence students' interactions with one another as well as with books and other materials through specific instructional practices. To illustrate, the following are some assessment questions generated by the teacher who recorded the anecdotal notes on pairs of students who were reading together in her classroom:

- What effect will the planned lessons have on students' interactions over words during reading?
- What other interactions do students have with one another over ideas in the story when they read together? (Her notes about Shawn led her to wonder this.)

- Do different pairings during reading make a difference in how readers interact with one another? What kinds of pairings are optimal?
- In what other situations is Shawn a leader? What can be done to further encourage that side of him?

The teacher has come full circle. Her original anecdotal notes were analyzed and used to plan instruction. But the notes also led to more focused assessment of individuals as well as assessment of a wider range of students and incidents. Her analysis and instructional planning led her to consider new assessment questions, questions not only about the students' reading but also about the effect of her teaching on their reading. For this teacher and for others who have realized the potential of anecdotal records, these "stories" are the basis from which they assess both their students' learning and their own teaching.

Conclusion

Anecdotal records are a powerful tool for collecting information on an ongoing basis during reading and writing and for evaluating the products of instruction. Keeping anecdotal records on a regular basis can enhance a teacher's classroom observation skills. Teachers report that they see and hear with more clarity when using anecdotal records, by focusing more intensively on how children say things and how they interact with one another. Anecdotal records are advantageous not only for planning instruction but for keeping others informed of children's progress in reading and writing and for focusing future assessment. When teachers discover the value of anecdotal records and figure out techniques to embed them in classroom literacy events and planning, anecdotal record keeping becomes a natural and important part of teaching and learning.

References

Bird, L.B. (1989). The art of teaching: Evaluation and revision. In K. Goodman, Y. Goodman, & W. Hood (Eds.), *The whole language evaluation book* (pp. 15–24). Portsmouth, NH: Heinemann.

Cartwright, C.A., & Cartwright, G.P. (1974). *Developing observational skills*. New York: McGraw-Hill.

Galindo, R. (1989). "Así no se pone, Sí'" (That's not how you write, "sí'"). In K. Goodman, Y. Goodman, & W. Hood (Eds.), *The whole language evaluation book* (pp. 55–67). Portsmouth, NH: Heinemann.

Genishi, C., & Dyson, A.H. (1984). *Language assessment in the early years*. Norwood, NJ: Ablex.

Goodman, Y. (1985). Kidwatching. In A. Jaggar & M.T. Smith-Burke (Eds.), *Observing the language learner* (pp. 9–18). Newark, DE: International Reading Association; Urbana, IL: National Council of Teachers of English.

Jaggar, A. (1985). On observing the language learner: Introduction and overview. In A. Jaggar & M.T. Smith-Burke (Eds.), *Observing the language learner* (pp. 1–7). Newark, DE: International Reading Association.

Livo, N. (1986). *Storytelling: Process and practice*. Littleton, CO: Libraries Unlimited.

Morrissey, M. (1989). When "shut up" is a sign of growth. In K. Goodman, Y. Goodman, & W. Hood (Eds.), *The whole language evaluation book* (pp. 85–97). Portsmouth, NH: Heinemann.

Pinnell, G.S. (1985). Ways to look at the functions of children's language. In A. Jaggar & M.T. Smith-Burke (Eds.), *Observing the language learner* (pp. 57–72). Newark, DE: International Reading Association.

The Random House Dictionary of the English Language. (1966). New York: Random House.

Thorndike, R.L., & Hagen, E.P. (1977). *Measurement and evaluation in psychology and education* (4th ed.). New York: Wiley.

STAIR: A System for Recording and Using What We Observe and Know About Our Students

Peter Afflerbach

November 1993

As teachers, our proximity to the action of literacy allows us to observe students' growth and development in reading. Information gathered from this privileged perspective can inform instruction and help gauge student growth and teaching effectiveness. Although observations can produce much that is valuable, this information may not be put to its best use if it is not carefully recorded, easily accessed, or readily communicated.

I would like to introduce a system for recording and using classroom observations that was developed for elementary and middle school students who have difficulties reading. Often, students are puzzles whose reluctance to read, inconsistency in reading, or seeming inability to read present a challenge that can be met, in part through careful and methodical observation. These students often are from the low groups in traditional classroom groupings and are considered for inclusion in remedial programs such as Chapter 1.

Teachers of these students examine questions related to becoming experts in teaching and assessing reading. The questions include:

• How can I record the information I gather from observation during reading instruction?

• How can my instruction reflect what I know about individual students?

• How do I know I'm doing a good job of teaching and assessing my students?

• How can I develop my assessment voice so that it is heard and valued by different audiences for different purposes?

Recording and using information from teacher observations is central to answering these questions, and STAIR (System for Teaching and Assessing Interactively and Reflectively) is an approach to assessment that was developed for this purpose. STAIR consists of cycles of teacher entries based on classroom observations, related hypotheses about student strengths and needs, and regular checking and revision of the hypotheses. It provides a source of information for planning reading instruction and allows for teacher reflection on the success of instruction. In addition, STAIR may be used to focus on individual concerns that teachers have for students as well as the benchmarks for student reading performance that may be set at the school or district level. The system also provides structure and permanence to teachers' observations, anecdotes, and mental notes so that they can be presented to and used by students, their parents, and other interested people.

The development of STAIR was informed by several strands of the assessment and reading research literature. The system revolves around the teacher as evaluation expert (Johnston, 1987). It is anchored strongly to the beliefs that excellence in teaching is due in part to the ability to reflect on instruction, planning, knowledge, and challenges (Schon, 1983) and that information from classroom observations can be helpful in a variety of situations (Calfee & Hiebert, 1991; Stiggins & Conklin, 1992; Wolf, 1993).

Recording Knowledge of Students' Reading

The STAIR includes information about the text or texts a student reads, the contexts in which reading and reading-related activities take place, and the tasks that students engage in related to reading. To illustrate the different procedures and uses of the STAIR we follow Stan, a fourth-grade teacher and his work with one of his students, John. Early in the school year Stan observes John during independent reading. John gives the outward appearance of being a reader, but Stan notes that he does not turn the pages of his book and is rarely able to discuss what he is reading. In contrast, John sometimes shows that he is a competent and enthusiastic reader. John's unpredictable reading is a puzzle that Stan decides to focus on. Stan hypothesizes that a lack

of motivation prevents John from becoming engaged in the daily reading experiences. Stan's related initial working hypothesis about John's need is illustrated in Figure 1.

Planning Instruction

In his planning for the next reading session, Stan refers to his STAIR hypothesis. He decides that a variety of books on basketball (a favorite topic for John) will serve as a motivation. Stan plans to ask John to choose a book to read and to tell his classmates about it after reading. As the reading block begins, Stan watches John select *Legends of the NBA*. John is enthralled with the book. He perseveres and rereads frequently, intent on understanding the chapter. Despite the challenge that the book represents, John completes the first chapter. John's comprehension is apparent as he retells what he has read to his interested friends—his basketball buddies. John's enthusiasm remains unquenched as he asks to take the book home and continues discussing the book with Stan at the end of the school day. Stan reviews his lesson and decides his original STAIR hypothesis is accurate (see Figure 2).

Reflecting on Instruction and Updating Hypothesis

Stan plans the next week's reading lessons. He believes that continued attention to John's interest in basketball will help him move from an often reluctant reader to an enthusiastic reader. Yet, the next week brings disappointment. John is not eager to read, even with six different books on basketball from which to choose. During the class share time Stan asks students to review the books they are reading, but John only mumbles briefly about his book, *Hoopster Hijinx!* Stan notes that giving John choices for reading on a topic of high interest is not the only ingredient for turning John's reading around.

Figure 1
STAIR (System for Teaching and Assessing Interactively and Reflectively)

Student name: _____John Bagley_____ Date: _4/19_

Hypothesis # ___1___:

John often lacks motivation for reading and this prevents him from becoming engaged in reading class.

Sources of information supporting hypothesis:

Classroom observation of John trying to read _Hatchet_

Classroom observation of John reading chapter in social studies textbook (Chap. 7: The Plains States)

Discussion w/ John about his reading

Instruction to address hypothesis:

My general plan is to find books that are of great interest to John. Basketball is a love of his, as is motorcycle racing. Choice of reading in these two areas will be helpful, I think.

Stan uses this information to update the STAIR. He continues to view motivation as the key to John's success in reading, but notes that book choice alone did not work to this end. Stan notes this in his next entry in the STAIR and revises his hypothesis, as shown in Figure 3.

Revising Instruction

Stan revises his instructional plan while noting that part of his hypothesis seems accurate. John did show an initial interest in the book *Magic!* and he did seem aware of the need to lead a discussion of the book upon completion.

Figure 2
Planning instruction and checking hypothesis

Student name: _____John_____ Date: _4/21_

Context: _____Individual reading / independent reading_____

Text: _____Legends of the NBA_____

Task: _____Share book or story with friends._____

Hypothesis _____ Refined ___✓___ Upheld _____ Abandoned

Sources of information:

I observed John throughout independent reading and he was highly motivated. Knowing that he could finish with a meeting of his friends to describe the book seemed to be extremely motivating. Also, John asked to take the book home, and talked with me at length about the book at the end of the school day.

Instruction to address hypothesis:

Continue to provide motivating texts for John to read. Allowing John to choose from several books on basketball should provide further motivation.

But was this incentive enough for John? Through observation, Stan learns that John perseveres in reading unfamiliar text when he knows he will have the opportunity to share what he has read with a small group of classmates who understand the lingo of the basketball court. Stan uses this information to refine his initial hypothesis. Again, the information gathered through observation and John's work is collected and analyzed. A model of Stan's revised hypothesis and the information he used to revise it are presented in Figure 4.

From these brief sketches we see that Stan builds an understanding of John and his reading

Figure 3
Reflecting on instruction and updating hypothesis

Student name: _____ John _____ Date: 4/22 _____

Context: _____ John chooses one book to read independently _____

Text: _____ Hoopster Hijinx! _____

Task: _____ Oral report to whole class _____

Hypothesis ____✓____ Refined _____ Upheld _____ Abandoned

Sources of information:

Observation of independent reading and subsequent report to whole class.

It appears book is not only factor. Check the social context of reading and demands it places on John.

Instruction to address hypothesis:

Be clear with John about purposes of reading. What are different aspects of motivation to address with John and his reading?

Maybe whole class oral report is a disincentive for John, so try next reading in context of his "basketball buddies".

Figure 4
Reflecting on instruction and updating hypothesis

Student name: _____John_____ Date: _4/23_

Context: _____Independent reading_____

Text: _____Magic!_____

Task: _____Share story with friends_____

Hypothesis _____ Refined _____✓_____ Upheld _____ Abandoned

Sources of information:

Questions for John about his favorite reading, and John's favorite reading tasks.

Observation of John's independent reading and group retelling

Instruction to address hypothesis:

Continue to think of John's motivation for reading as a combination of interesting topic & the social context (s) in which John uses the information he gains from reading.

Remember to question John about his reading and motivation – he appreciates being asked and gives thoughtful answers.

by using information from his observations. STAIR allows Stan to revisit his hypothesis, to reflect on its accuracy, to change it if necessary, and to use his growing knowledge of John to plan appropriate instruction.

Through a cycle of observation, planning, teaching, observing, and reflecting, Stan has learned that John is consistently motivated to read books about basketball when he knows part of the outcome will be giving an elaborate retelling to a certain group of classmates. Stan has also reinforced his belief that understanding students is closely tied to observing them. Finally, Stan has again noted the need to consider his knowledge of each student as an unfinished portrait. He originally considered John's motivation to read as inconsistent. Through careful observation and reflection on his own instruction he learned that John's reading was actually quite consistent, as viewed from an increasingly informed perspective on his uses for reading in the social context of the classroom.

Communicating to Different Audiences

STAIR gives permanence and structure to the rich but often fleeting assessment information that Stan can gather each day in the classroom. It provides a running record of his observations, hypothesis generation and testing, and reflections that can be shared with the different people who care about John's reading and Stan's teaching. Stan shares his STAIR with John and describes how he has observed good reading across the last 3 weeks. John is encouraged when Stan mentions the importance of working with friends and the impressive retellings he has heard John share with his classmates. John is happy to hear about some of his strengths in reading from his teacher, and he is impressed with how well Stan knows him as reader.

At the next parent-teacher conference Stan presents his work to John's parents using STAIR. The use of STAIR provides frequent and detailed documentation of observations of John's growth in reading, demonstrates Stan's careful thinking and planning, and helps John's parents better understand their son's reading strengths and needs. This helps Stan's classroom assessment take center stage—it no longer plays a minor supporting role.

Stan knows that it is not enough to be a competent assessor of his students' growth in reading. People have to trust his information, understand its uses, and find it useful. John's parents are presented with concrete evidence of John's growth in reading. Stan suggests that John's parents continue to take him to the library and provide contexts in which John can share what he has read in discussing, drawing, and acting out scenes from books. Here, the STAIR helps communicate two important messages. First, it describes how John is doing in reading. Second, it demonstrates that Stan's observation is a valid and valuable source of information about John's development as a reader.

Stan's success in using the STAIR revolves around his observations in the classroom and his commitment to reflecting on and updating his knowledge about John. The STAIR requires expertise (or the commitment to developing expertise) in observing students in literate activity and a depth of knowledge of individual students. The system is demanding of time. It requires regular attention, reflection, and updating. Attempting to use the STAIR for every observed behavior of each student will leave little or no time for instruction, or weekends.

STAIR can be a valuable and versatile tool in the assessment process. It can capture the informed observation and hypothesis generation and confirmation that the best teachers do on a regular basis. Teachers' hypotheses about students' needs establish a running record of attention to these needs and students' accomplishments. STAIR provides a means for teachers to reflect on their knowledge of students and to continue their updating of understandings and instructional methods and procedures. Further, STAIR can help communicate increased understandings of students and students' accomplishments in literacy.

Author's Note

I would like to thank the teachers in the University of Maryland Summer Reading Program who provided helpful comments and suggestions related to STAIR.

References

Calfee, R., & Hiebert, E. (1991). Classroom assessment of reading. In R. Barr, M. Kamil, P. Mosenthal, & P.D. Pearson (Eds.), *Handbook of reading research Volume II* (pp. 281–309). White Plains, NY: Longman.

Johnston, P. (1987). Teachers as evaluation experts. *The Reading Teacher, 40*, 744–748.

Schon, D. (1983). *The reflective practitioner: How professionals think in action.* New York: Basic Books.

Stiggins, R., & Conklin, N. (1992). *In teachers' hands: Investigating the practices of classroom assessment.* Albany, NY: State University of New York Press.

Wolf, K. (1993). From informal to informed assessment: Recognizing the role of the classroom teacher. *Journal of Reading, 36*, 518–523.

Section Three

Performance and Portfolio Assessment

While the articles in Section 2 challenge teachers to integrate teaching and assessing, this section takes the notion a step further by suggesting that as teachers integrate the curriculum, new forms of assessment are required. Assessing the performance of learners and developing portfolios as ongoing, tangible records of growth, moves assessment into the realm of collaboration between teachers and students, particularly in setting goals. Possibilities for moving entire districts toward portfolio assessment are described in an article that reports on a professional development project. Two articles on implementing portfolios in primary level classrooms provide inspiration and concrete advice on initiating and managing portfolios with young learners.

Additional Readings

- Campbell-Hill, B., & Ruptic, C. (1994). *Practical aspects of authentic assessment: Putting the pieces together*. Norwood, MA: Christopher-Gordon.
- Fu, Dan-Ling. (1992). One bilingual child talks about his portfolio. In D.H. Graves & B.S. Sunstein (Eds.), *Portfolio portraits* (pp. 171–183). Portsmouth, NH: Heinemann.
- Garcia, G.E. (1994). Assessing the literacy development of second-language students: A focus on authentic assessment. In K. Spangenberg-Urbschat & R. Pritchard (Eds.), *Kids come in all languages: Reading instruction for ESL students* (pp. 180–205). Newark, DE: International Reading Association.
- Jenkins, H., & Hansen, J. (Eds.). (1997). Students and teachers as evaluators. *Primary Voices K–6, 5*(4).
- Valencia, S.W. (1998). *Literacy portfolios in action*. Orlando, FL: Harcourt Brace & Company.

Performance Assessments in Reading and Language Arts

Peter Afflerbach and Barbara Kapinus, Editors
John T. Guthrie, Peggy Van Meter, and Ann Mitchell, Authors

November 1994

Teachers are inventing a wide variety of exciting new ways to integrate reading and writing instruction into the teaching of literature, history, geography, and science. These integrations reflect the view that reading and writing are inextricably linked to knowledge, strategies, and dispositions for learning. Teachers see students as builders and explorers who use resources including texts, peers, and experience to discover meaning and solve self-defined problems. For these teachers, traditional assessments seem incomplete. When instruction is based on trade books, group thinking activities, and projects that may involve the home and community, traditional assessments often fail to capture students' motivational development and higher order competencies. In this column, we discuss a performance assessment designed to reflect a wide spectrum of literacy processes that appear in an integrated curriculum (Grant, Guthrie, Bennett, Rice, & McGough, 1993).

What Is a Performance Assessment in Reading?

Our performance assessment in reading has three fundamental qualities. First, the assessment is instructional, simulating the teaching environment that we maintain in the classroom. As students participate in the assessment, they interact with texts, draw, write, and use their newfound knowledge to solve problems in ways that parallel the typical instructional unit. Consistent with classroom instruction, we expect students to learn, and we record the new concepts they acquire. The assessment is a small unit of instruction for both the students and teachers.

Second, this performance assessment is realistic. It is a mirror of classroom literacy, reflecting authentic and regularly occurring tasks in reading, writing, and problem solving. In integrated curricula, students may write observations from a field trip into a journal, read journals to each other, discuss trade books on topics observed in the field trip, and develop ways to teach what they have learned to other students. Similar connections across learning activities are part of this performance assessment in reading.

Third, this performance assessment provides a public record of tasks students have accomplished. The task in this assessment includes a text (something to read), a response to the text (a way of writing or expressing understanding), and a quality statement (which describes the student performance). This sequence of tasks brings literacy learning to light, enabling students, teachers, and others to observe students as they interact with instruction.

What Does Student Performance Look Like?

This performance assessment accompanies an integrated curriculum, Concept-Oriented Reading Instruction (CORI; Grant et al., 1993), for the third and fifth grades in two schools. Topics used for the assessments include owls, phases of the moon, trees, tides, ponds, and simple machines. To chart growth, we use two topics, one that is closely tied to the curriculum and a second that is less related to it. This permits teachers to see content-based gains as well as generalized gains in reading strategies. Our performance assessments are designed to enable students to perform seven distinct but connected tasks: (1) statement of prior knowledge (stating what they know about the topic), (2) searching (finding resources and ideas about the topic), (3) drawing (expressing what they have learned through drawing), (4) writing (communicating their learning through composition), (5) problem solving (addressing a related problem using conceptual knowledge learned during the unit), (6) informational text comprehension (understanding an expository text related to the theme), and (7) narrative text comprehension

(understanding and responding to a literary text on the theme of the unit).

These assessments are conducted in classrooms as instructional units lasting 4–6 days. One teacher began the performance assessment on owls and how they adapt to their environment by asking the whole class what they knew about owls. Discussion was brief and did not convey new information to students. The teacher then moved the class into Stage 1 and asked students to write down their prior knowledge by responding to the question: "What are the different parts of an owl and how do these parts help it live?" We will follow two third-grade students, Sandra and William, as they perform each of the tasks.

Stage 1: Statement of Prior Knowledge

Sandra recorded her prior knowledge as follows (we have not edited this excerpt): "A owl can eat a lot of food. The owl lives like people. The eat corn. He can live like people. The owl will live good like people."

The quality of the student's performance on each stage is judged using a rubric, which distinguishes lower levels of quality from higher levels of quality. Rubrics enable us to chart student growth, to profile a student's strengths and weaknesses, and to discuss the effectiveness of instruction. Here we present the general rubric for each stage, although specific rubrics for each topic are also needed for complete coding. We created five levels for most rubrics and assigned points to each level.

The rubric for statement of prior knowledge was:

1. No conception (student writes nothing at all or the answer does not contain information relevant to the question).

2. Preconception (student may list objects or parts and their functions may be vaguely described; the answer is scientifically

incorrect but demonstrates an understanding that there are relationships among objects or events relevant to the concept).

3. Partial conception (student answer is scientifically correct and shows a limited understanding of some of the relationships among a few of the relevant objects or events but the statements are vague).

4. Incomplete conception (student answer is scientifically correct, shows an understanding of relationships among many but not all of the relevant objects or events, and the relationships are clear but incomplete).

5. Full conception (student answer is scientifically correct, shows an understanding of relationships among all important objects or events, and the relationships are depicted in clear and complete form).

Sandra's statement of prior knowledge was a Preconception, which we assigned a level of 2. An example of an Incomplete conception (4) was given by William, whose statement was that "the eyes help it see at night to catch its prey and he takes his prey with his clawed feet and he swoops to get it with his giant wings."

William's prior knowledge contained an understanding of several parts of the owl and the survival value of these parts.

Stage 2: Search

Next, we gave students a booklet containing 12 selections of text, which simulated the format of a trade book, containing a table of contents, index, glossary, and chapter headings. Each selection was a 1- to 3-page excerpt from a trade book on the topic of birds. Half of the selections were relevant to the question (What are the different parts of an owl and how do these parts help it live?) and half were not. As the students read through the packets, they maintained a log to record the packet they were reading, why they

chose the packet, and what they learned from it. We gave students a form for their logs, divided into sections 1–8, one for each packet they read, as illustrated here. We did not have 12 sections because we did not expect third graders to read all 12 packets.

Sandra's search log looked like Table 1.

To describe the quality of search for information we coded the logs into 5 levels:

1. No search (no evidence of search or selection of materials).

2. Minimum (students chose at least two relevant packets as well as some irrelevant ones, took good notes from one packet, and gave one clear reason for choosing one of the packets).

3. Moderate (students chose at least three relevant packets and very few irrelevant ones with appropriate reasons for their selections and good notes on two packets).

4. Adequate (students chose at least four relevant packets with few or no irrelevant ones, giving clear reasons for all their selections and clear notes).

5. Proficient (students selected all of the relevant packets with no irrelevant ones and all of their notes were related to the theme. Their reasons for choosing packets were diverse, and their notes showed that they learned during the course of the reading and note-taking activity).

Sandra's log of her activities (rated a 2) contained two packets that were related to the theme. She did not, however, know the difference between a reason for choosing a packet and what she learned from the texts that she chose. Sandra's notes from the first packet clearly stated that owls can "get a quiet mouse and eat the mouse." But her notes from the second packet were not highly elaborated beyond the notion that birds have babies. This was a Minimum search (2).

Table 1
Sandra's search log

A Packet letter	B Why did you pick this packet?	C What did you learn from this packet?
1. D	The owl eat a lot of mouse and can get quiet	I learn the owls can get quiet mouse and eat the mouse to
2.	mouse to Because it is a good	and owls do not miss a thing.
3. B	Birds can fly to trees and some Birds can not fly to a trees.	King Birds, the mother a father will have the baby and Be it will Be Birds.
4.	I put this is about Birds mother has the baby	I put this about the father go get the Baby and get and love.
5.		
6. A	Introducing like to end fish and like to eat Sea birds.	it eat a lot to like and eat fish to like.
7.		
8.		

William used a more well-developed search strategy than Sandra. The log of his activities, which is given in Table 2, was rated Adequate (4).

William chose four packets related to the theme and no irrelevant ones. He showed that he could distinguish the reasons for his choices from what he had learned from the texts. He first learned about how owls see in the dark and turn their heads around. From the next packet he learned that owls use their claws during hunt-

Table 2
William's log of activities

A Packet letter	B Why did you pick this packet?	C What did you learn from this packet?
1. D	I picked it because it tells alot about owls and how they are.	I learned that owls can see in the dark and I learned that they can twist there head all the way around. I also learned that they can twist it.
2. I	I picked it because I shows you how birds get their food.	I learned that birds need their sharp claws to get their food.
3. G	I pick this packet because it tells how birds feed their babies	I learned that birds feed their babies by dropping worms, insects, and bread in their mouth.
4. H	I picked it because it tells (no continuation)	I learned that they need their feet to help them swim.

ing. From the third text he learned that birds feed babies by dropping food into their mouths, and last he discovered that different birds have different types of feet which are adapted to their environments.

Stage 3: Drawing

After students searched for information, we asked them to make a picture that showed everything they knew about owls. These third graders were asked to make a drawing to teach second graders about owls, without using their notes. We described the quality of student drawings with the same rubric used for describing their statements of prior knowledge: No conception, Preconception, Partial conception, Incomplete conception, and Full conception. Sandra's drawing was a Preconception (2) because she presents some of the parts of the owl, but the functions are not described and the relationships among the parts were vague (see Figure). William's drawing was an Incomplete Conception (4). It is scientifically correct and it shows an understanding of relationships among parts of an owl, but his drawing omitted several parts of the owl that were described in the text. Because this part of the assessment focused on students' understanding, we accepted invented spelling and punctuation.

Figure
Students' drawings about owls

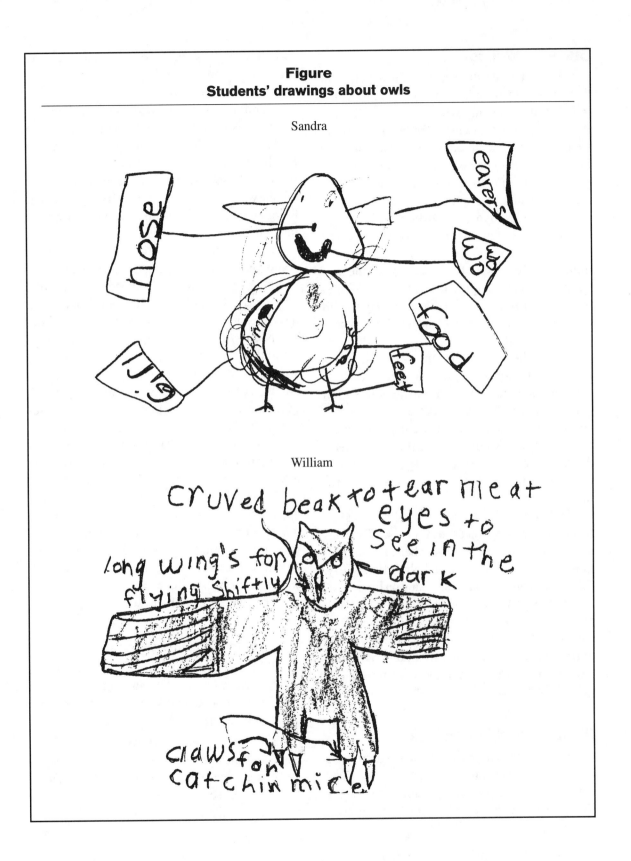

Sandra

William

Stage 4: Writing

We next asked students to write a statement that showed their understanding of the topic using their drawing and what they remembered. As in the Concept-Oriented Reading Instruction, we did not encourage copying or rote learning. Students were expected to construct and reorganize their thoughts continually to express them in writing, without using notes from their search activity. Sandra's written statement of how the parts of an owl help it to live was the following: "The owl can see thing and get the thing and it eat them. Owl like mouse and water and owl can get quite thing. Owl eat a lot to be love and live from food and can fly to and fly to a tree and like tree to and eat thing in tree. I thing owl will like it."

Using the same rubric that we used to describe prior knowledge, we classified Sandra's written understanding as a Partial conception (3). Comparing Sandra's written statement to her prior knowledge, we can see that she gained conceptual knowledge during the assessment. As the notes in her search log indicate, she learned that owls have exceptional eyes for hunting mice.

William's written understanding was an Incomplete conception (4) as follows: "The eyes help it see in the dark. A hooked beak to tear meat in half and a long wing span help it fly swiftly. The claws help catch mice and hang on branches."

Although William understood the owl as a predator more fully than Sandra at the time of the writing task, Sandra learned more new concepts during the assessment than William. William's task performance does not give evidence that he gained conceptual knowledge about owls.

Stage 5: Problem Solving

Students then used their knowledge to write a solution to a new problem: "Suppose you saw a type of owl that was blind. But these owls are living a very good life. What things would these owls have to be good at to be able to keep living? What would the body parts of these owls be like? Please explain your answer."

Sandra wrote: "The owl can hear thing but this is not so good. I will like to know what can do when owl are blind. I will not like to be blind. I will like to know how it is some owl have friend and friend like to help people. Maybe the friend will help her or him see thing and hear thing and eat thing. I think owl will not go out in the day and will be wild."

During her search activity, Sandra learned that owls could see even in the dark and capture "quiet things." In the new problem when the owl was deprived of sight, Sandra could not employ the concept of adaptation to generate newly developed senses for the owl, although she understood that such information was called for. She solved the owl's problem by giving the owl a friend. Although Sandra was aware that the question called for information about the senses and their adaptations, her solution did not illustrate the concepts of adaptation of body parts to the environment. In contrast, William solved the new problem by writing "he will have to hear his prey and then catch it, if it was a great horned owl he would have to keep his tufts of feathers up so that he could signal his family, maybe he would have to use his wings to feel around when he is flying, maybe he could smell where his prey is in the woods."

The rubric for problem solving consisted of the following:

1. No solution (no answer given).

2. Presolution (solution is scientifically incorrect or not relevant to the problem; some conceptual knowledge of the topic is evident).

3. Partial solution (some objects are present but the concepts are not applied to solving the problem; solution is scientifically correct, but the answer is vague or incomplete).

4. Incomplete solution (all objects and/or events are present and the concepts are related to solving the problem, but the answer is incomplete or vague).

5. Full solution (all objects and events are present; the concepts are fully applied and the answer is complete).

In solving the new problem, Sandra's notion that the owl could make friends which would help her see things was not realistic (a Presolution 2), although she showed that serious adjustments would have to take place. William's solution contained the generative concept that adaptations of other senses such as hearing and feeling in the wings would increase to help support the owl in hunting. But his statement was an Incomplete solution (4) because there are many other adaptations that might have been included.

Stage 6: Informational Text Comprehension

During the search stage of the assessment, different students use different text selections and their notes may not reflect their full comprehension of the material. A relatively low level search performance may reflect a low text-selection strategy or low text comprehension ability or both. Because text comprehension is fundamental, we gave students two tasks. One was a short informational text containing related illustrations. The accompanying question required students to integrate information from both the text and the illustration. This informational text explained the development of a bird inside an egg.

The rubric to describe the quality of students' responses to informational text was:

1. No answer (no answer; answer relies on prior knowledge not related to the text; or information is incorrect, nonspecific, or verbatim copy).

2. Accurate (response accurately integrates information from two or more parts of the text).

3. Elaborated (response connects an integrated statement with additional information in the text that elaborates, explains, or contextualizes the statement).

Sandra's response was not related to the text, nor was it very coherent (No answer 1): "I now that egg has a red line on the yolk and the egg will have to get water a food to grow and you can see the hen babyes and the baby can float in the egg."

William's response was based on appropriate segments of text, and he added shape and color (Elaborated 3): "inside of an egg is a baby chick and yolk for the baby to eat. The baby looks like a bird. the yolk is light yellow."

Stage 7: Narrative Text Comprehension

Students read a 350-word excerpt from "Izzard the Lizard," a story in which a girl brings to the classroom a lizard that entertains and distracts the students. Three questions required the students to (a) reproduce a brief portion of text from memory, (b) give an explanation for an important event, and (c) provide a personal reaction to a character, event, or theme. We include narrative because our integrated curriculum contains literary as well as informational books.

Quality of narrative comprehension was judged with a rubric based on responses to all of the questions. Student responses to the reproductive, explanatory, and open-extension questions were rated as appropriate (accurate and text-based) or elaborated (embellished with details and characterizations). The scoring scheme was: 1-no appropriate responses; 2-one appropriate response; 3-two appropriate responses; 4-three appropriate responses; 5-three appropriate responses and at least two elaborated responses. Although all of the responses cannot be given here, Sandra received an overall score of 1 and William received a 4.

To the question, "Why couldn't Izzard go to school anymore?" Sandra wrote, "I thing the Izzard will be good but it will be log and the teacher will be happy."

William said, "Because the class wasn't waching the teacher. they where waching Izzard."

What Are the Advantages of a Performance Assessment and Who Does It Help?

Developing an assessment challenged us to examine our teaching aims and objectives. We clarified what we wanted students to learn and what evidence we would accept as indicators that they had learned. This process helped us to understand where we were going in our teaching as well as where our students had been in their learning (Gaskins et al., in press). Many of these instructional benefits are shared with portfolio assessment (Valencia & Place, 1993). This performance assessment can be placed in a student's portfolio, providing a common task that permits teachers to compare students and to chart growth over time.

Students benefit from this assessment because they can use the tasks as a basis for their own self-appraisal. Students can reflect on whether they used their background knowledge in their search and whether they applied their search findings to their writing and problem solving. We believe that administrators and policy makers may benefit from performance assessments, too, because the assessments reflect the shape of the curriculum and teachers' aspirations for authentic learning. By communicating the outcomes of the assessment to administrators as well as to other teachers, we have been able to make public the higher order accomplishments of our students on a diversity of important and realistic tasks. We believe that a performance assessment that simulates instruction can be a stage where schooling and its appraisal are acted out together.

What Are the Demands on and Responsibilities of Teachers Who Want to Conduct This Performance Assessment?

One teacher can design, administer, and evaluate the results of this performance assessment, but the demands on the teacher's time will be prohibitive. We recommend that a group of teachers with similar curricula and goals at a given grade level, perhaps across several schools, join together to develop a performance assessment. A cluster of teachers within a school or an entire district may design, administer, score, interpret, and report a performance assessment. The assessment presented in this article may be used as a starting point for the development of instructional assessments that are tailored to the curricula, student populations, and cultural contexts of particular schools or districts.

References

Gaskins, I.W., Guthrie, J.T., Satlow, E., Ostertag, J., Six, L., Byrne, J., & Conner, B. (in press). Integrating instruction of science and reading/writing processes: Goals, assessments, and teacher development. *Journal of Research in Science Teaching.*

Grant, R., Guthrie, J., Bennett, L., Rice, M.E., & McGough, K. (1993). Developing engaged readers through concept-oriented reading instruction. *The Reading Teacher, 47*, 338–340.

Valencia, S.W., & Place, N. (1993). Literacy portfolios for teaching, learning and accountability: The Bellevue literacy assessment project. In S.W. Valencia, E.F. Hiebert, & P.P. Afflerbach (Eds.), *Authentic reading assessment* (pp. 134–167). Newark, DE: International Reading Association.

Equity and Performance-Based Assessment: An Insider's View

Marshá Taylor DeLain

February 1995

Equity. Opportunity to learn. Appreciation for diversity. Recently these terms have been tossed about in academia, district offices, schools, and classrooms. What does it all mean? How will our interpretation of these terms, particularly in assessment, impact our children?

I am an African American, but my interests in these issues extend far beyond my personal perspective. It is important to me that all children learn to their highest potential. This simply is not possible if we think of these terms (equity, opportunity to learn, appreciation for diversity) as only having relevance for minorities. Besides, who is the minority? Today we consider minorities to be Hispanics, African Americans, Native Americans, Asians; the list goes on. However, demographic projections tell us that by the year 2000 people of color will be the majority in the United States. But that really shouldn't matter. If our focus is on what's best for children, the definition of "best" shouldn't change when the demographic characteristics of the classroom change.

So what is best for all children? Children should be expected to achieve levels of excellence and afforded the opportunities and environment to do so. This is a critical part of my definition of equity. Expectations for success should not vary dependent upon race, gender, ethnicity, where you live, how many parents you have, or whether your mom went to college. We teach the mix of students who walk through the door—black, white, yellow, tall, short, rich, or poor. Our responsibility does not change. The paths we take to actualizing and evaluating success for our students may vary, but the bottom line stays the same. All children need to be given the tools they need to "be all that they can be." However, for years the definition of what children are and what they can be has been influenced by the results of assessments.

Until recently, assessment has been based upon the validity of breaking reading processes into discrete pieces; the assumption has been that if you know the pieces, you know the whole. Therefore, assessment of the pieces was presumed to provide evaluative information on a student's achievement of the processes. In reading, this meant testing vocabulary knowledge using lists of words or testing comprehension using short, artificially created paragraphs.

109

These assessment methods provided a relatively quick and inexpensive way of testing large numbers of students. However, performance on these assessments was most often reported in terms of how well students measured up against each other, not against clear standards of what the student was supposed to know and be able to do. Ironically, the assessments provided very little information on how well a student could actually read and comprehend real literature.

But what does this have to do with equity, and what does equity mean? For me, equity includes the following:

• equitable access to resources,

• equitable opportunities to learn new and challenging information,

• equitable expectations for outcomes of excellence, and

• sensitivity to and appreciation for diversity and how that diversity can enhance learning for all students.

Performance-based assessment has brought a new slant on these issues, particularly as they relate to evaluating student achievement of the "outcomes of excellence" previously mentioned. Performance-based assessment involves actual demonstrations, which involve integration of several processes, skills, and concepts. Student achievement is assessed by evaluating some type of student product that is planned, constructed, or developed.

Performance assessment in reading and other language arts is not new. For years students have read books and plays, written reports, given oral presentations, and dramatized scenes. Research has been conducted on topics of interest through trips to the library, interviews with experts, and collaboration with peers. All of these "performance" activities take place under the watchful eye of teachers who firmly believe that students must be actively involved in the process of learning. Simply put, students had to

do in order to learn. What is different in this era of reform is the importance of attaching the activities to clearly stated instructional outcomes and evaluating student success on these activities against clearly stated criteria. Also, this type of assessment has gained acceptance because it is more aligned with how students actually learn and more useful for instructional improvement and accountability.

Aspects of performance assessment are provided in the following example, which is adapted from a project generated by an Interstate Teacher Team at the 1991 New Standards Project Workshop in Snowmass, Colorado, USA.

***

West End Elementary is planning a Visitors' Night. Students will give presentations on their favorite authors, the school choir will sing, artwork will be displayed, a science experiment will be done, and a storyteller will be present. The students in Mrs. Edwards' class are asked to (a) prepare presentations based on their favorite authors, (b) create an invitation for Visitors' Night, and (c) write directions or draw a map from their homes to the school.

Performance-based assessment can:

• be aligned with instructional practice. For example, we expect that students will apply what they have learned in school to real-life activities. In the example, reading and using texts in a decision-making process is a real-life activity. The map drawing activity is not only authentic, but it also draws on communication skills, spatial understanding, and reasoning abilities.

• provide students opportunities to express or represent their knowledge in different ways. In the example, students have the opportunity to express what they have learned by writing compositions, oral presentations, drawing, and cutting and pasting. In the activities planned for Visitors' Night, opportunities are broadened even more to include singing, constructing experiments, and retellings.

• provide better indicators of the depth of a student's knowledge. When students supply information or explain their understandings, we develop much richer insight into what they really know. In the example, students are asked to select and give a presentation on their favorite author. In the presentation they are expected to articulate reasons for their choices. This requires the students to have a deep understanding of the materials and identify and translate key elements of that understanding for an audience.

• stretch students' minds by requiring them to construct, design, compose, model, or build their response rather than select it from an array of choices. In the sample above, students are asked to develop a presentation that convinces, invitations that entice and excite, maps and directions that clearly point the way, and an activity schedule that gives the presenters adequate time while keeping things flowing at a nice pace. All of these activities stretch students' minds by requiring them to draw on, integrate, and apply skills from several areas in ways that are creative yet useful to a real audience.

• be aligned with ongoing classroom instruction so that it ceases to become an end in and of itself. Assessment can and should be an ongoing and integral part of classroom activity. The closer assessment is aligned with instruction and curriculum, the better it can inform the teacher and the student, and the less likely it is to become a separate, unrelated activity.

While performance assessment can provide useful information, like all other assessments it has limitations. Performance-based assessment cannot:

• answer all questions about what a child knows and is able to do. As noted above, assessment should be an ongoing, integral part of classroom activity, and performance-based assessment is simply one way to attain evaluative information. There may also be a need for more traditional types of assessments. Once the purpose of the assessment and the type of student behavior to be evaluated are decided, the methods or formats that best accomplish those purposes are chosen.

• be a panacea to all the assessment and instructional ills of the current educational system. If assessment is the only change in the classroom, it simply becomes a fad. Instruction and curriculum within the context of the total school climate must all be evaluated and systematically aligned if change is going to make a difference.

As the stakes attached to all forms of assessment become higher and higher, those who typically have been disenfranchised by normed assessments may ask "Is performance assessment another obstacle that blocks the success of our children?" This question speaks directly to the issue of equity. My response is "yes and no."

I believe that performance-based assessment provides more opportunity for teachers to get a clearer understanding of what their students actually know and more opportunity for students to demonstrate what they know. Some students do not perform well on multiple choice, timed assessments. With performance-based assessment, these same students have the opportunity to show what they know in different formats. Instead of darkening in the bubbles of a machine-scored test, they can write a play, give an oral presentation, build a model, or conduct an experiment.

On the other hand, no assessment or series of assessments, regardless of their validity or usefulness, can compensate for students not being exposed to information; not having the opportunity to participate in hands-on learning; or not being engaged in discussions that force them to expand, reflect upon, critically evaluate, justify, and defend their thinking. Without the appropriate support, performance-based assessment will only emphasize what's not happening in the classroom and the school—what opportunities the student has not had.

So what are the options? How should equity be integrated into a reconceptualization of assessment? We must first have a clear vision of where we are going. Most of our conversations as educators have been based on an oft-repeated premise that "All children can learn." I have to add "All children can learn at high standards." If this is truly believed, then the following must be considered to achieve the goal.

• Everything must reflect the commitment to high standards. "Everything" includes not only a careful conceptualization and use of assessment, but issues pertaining to school climate (e.g., how the classes are organized, how discipline is administered, how instruction is delivered, and how curriculum is determined).

• Change or reform must first be structured and systematic. Changing one part of the system without considering the context of that system often results in failed reform.

• The demands created by equity must be considered when assessments are redesigned.

The design of the assessments (e.g., format, content, language), the development and application of scoring criteria (e.g., who participates in setting standards, or how the criteria may be differentially interpreted based on cultural knowledge), the integration of assessment within curriculum, and the interpretation and use of the assessment results should all reflect the commitment to equity. If these issues are not addressed, performance-based measures have the potential of being one more "No, you can't do it" message to those who can least afford to hear it.

In conclusion, we cannot afford to have differing expectations for success. All children must be provided the opportunity to achieve excellence. This premise should be the cornerstone of our commitment to students. Clearly stated instructional outcomes tied to standards of excellence and performance assessments can provide students with new and engaging ways to demonstrate their knowledge. They can also provide useful information on a student's achievement. Equitable opportunities and equitable success. That's what education should be about.

A Portfolio Approach to Classroom Reading Assessment: The Whys, Whats, and Hows

Sheila Valencia

January 1990

Why Do We Need Portfolios?

Developing artists rely on portfolios to demonstrate their skills and achievements. Within the portfolio, they include samples of their work that exemplify the depth and breadth of their expertise. They may include many different indicators: work in a variety of media to demonstrate their versatility, several works on one particular subject to demonstrate their refined skill and sophistication, and work collected over time to exemplify their growth as artists. With such rich sources of information, it is easier for the critics and the teachers, and most importantly, the artists themselves, to understand the development of expertise and to plan the experiences that will encourage additional progress and showcase achievements. A portfolio approach to the assessment of reading assumes the position that developing readers deserve no less.

A portfolio approach to reading assessment has great intuitive appeal: It resonates with our desire to capture and capitalize on the best each student has to offer; it encourages us to use many different ways to evaluate learning; and it has an integrity and validity that no other type of assessment offers. In addition to its intuitive appeal, there are theoretical and pragmatic reasons for a portfolio approach to reading assessment that are summarized in four guiding principles drawn from both research and instructional practices.

1. Sound assessment is anchored in authenticity—authenticity of tasks, texts, and contexts. Good assessment should grow out of authentic reading instruction and reading tasks. Students read a variety of authentic texts in class and in life; thus, they should be presented with that same diversity of texts during assessment. Students read for a variety of purposes; therefore, they should be presented with various purposes for reading during assessment. Reading assessment must mirror our understanding of reading as an interactive process. Any assessment must consider not only how the reader, the text, and the context influence reading but how

113

they interact and impact the construction of meaning.

Further, because the assessment activities resemble actual classroom and life reading tasks, they can be integrated into ongoing classroom life and instruction. Teachers and students do not have to take time away from real reading for assessment. Real reading is used as an assessment opportunity.

Finally, the principle of authenticity insures that we assess the orchestration, integration, and application of skills in meaningful contexts. We cannot become lost in the mire of subskill assessment because assessment of such isolated skills would not resemble authentic reading.

2. Assessment must be a continuous, ongoing process; it must chronicle development. This is the difference between simply assessing the outcome of learning (the product) and assessing the process of learning over time. When we are positioned to observe and collect information continuously, we send a message to students, parents, and administrators that learning is never completed; instead, it is always evolving, growing, and changing.

3. Because reading is a complex and multifaceted process, valid reading assessment must be multidimensional—committed to sampling a wide range of cognitive processes, affective responses, and literacy activities. In addition to assessing across a range of texts and purposes, we need to consider other important dimensions of reading such as interest and motivation, voluntary reading, and metacognitive knowledge and strategies. If we simply model our assessments on existing reading tests, we accept a constrained definition of reading and ignore many of the aspects that we value and teach.

4. Assessment must provide for active, collaborative reflection by both teacher and student. Historically, teachers and students have viewed assessment as something that must be done to appease others, something to be done for them rather than something to be done for ourselves. Instead, assessment must be viewed as a process within our control that helps us evaluate how well we have learned and what we need to learn next.

As teachers, assessment helps us evaluate our own teaching effectiveness and helps us with our instructional decisions. Similarly, assessment activities in which students are engaged in evaluating their own learning help them reflect on and understand their own strengths and needs, and it instills responsibility for their own learning. It is when students and teachers are collaboratively involved in assessment that the greatest benefit is achieved. Collaborative assessment strengthens the bond between student and teacher and establishes them as partners in learning. Collaboration precipitates meaningful dialogue about the criteria and process we use in evaluation and provides an important model for students as they become self-evaluators.

These four guiding principles provide a powerful rationale for proposing a portfolio approach. No single test, single observation, or single piece of student work could possibly capture the authentic, continuous, multidimensional, interactive requirement of sound assessment.

What Do Portfolios Look Like?

Our rationale for portfolios helps us construct a picture of what such an approach to assessment might look like. Physically, it is larger and more elaborate than a report card. Practically, it must be smaller and more focused than a steamer trunk filled with accumulated artifacts. It is more like a large expandable file folder that holds (a) samples of the student's work selected by the teacher or the student, (b) the teacher's observational notes, (c) the student's own periodic self-evaluations, and (d) progress notes contributed by the student and teacher collaboratively. The range of items to include in a portfolio is almost limitless but may include written responses to reading, reading logs, selected daily work, pieces of writing at various stages of completion, classroom tests, checklists, unit projects, and audio or video tapes, to name a few. The key is to ensure a *variety* of types of indicators of learning so that teachers, parents, students, and administrators can build a complete picture of the student's development.

Logically, portfolios should be kept in a spot in the classroom that is easily accessible to students and teachers. Unlike the secretive grade book or the untouchable permanent records stored in the office, these are working folders. Their location must invite students and teachers to contribute to them on an ongoing basis and to reflect on their contents to plan the next learning steps.

How Is a Portfolio Organized?

There is little doubt that portfolios can be messy business. However, many teachers and school districts committed to more valid and useful assessment procedures are beginning to give portfolios a try. Because the exact nature of the portfolio will vary depending on the curriculum goals and the students, it is difficult to prescribe exactly what should be included and how and when it should be evaluated. But it *is* possible to think of some organizational strategies that might make a portfolio more useful and more manageable.

Planning for a Portfolio

First, it is important to be *selective* about what should be included in the portfolio. Since the decision about what to assess must grow out of curricular and instructional priorities, the critical step is to determine, as a school, grade level, district, or state, the key goals of instruction. Goals of instruction are broad, not overly spe-

cific isolated skills or individual lesson objectives. For example, goals might involve understanding the author's message, learning new information from expository texts, summarizing the plot of a story, using word identification skills flexibly to construct meaning, reading fluently, or exhibiting an interest and desire to read. If the goals of instruction are not specified, portfolios have the potential to become unfocused holding files for odds and ends, or worse, a place to collect more isolated skills tests.

Second, it is helpful to think about what you do *instructionally* to help students progress toward those goals and how you and the students determine progress. This step will help you to identify some of the content and format of the assessment activities. One way to approach this task is to examine existing evaluation strategies and to decide the areas that are being assessed adequately and those that need to be added, adapted, or expanded. There is no need to start from scratch because many good instructional activities currently used in classrooms would be appropriate for portfolios. For example, many teachers use story maps as part of their instruction on understanding story structure. The very same technique could be used to assess students' plot knowledge after they have completed a story. No special test would be required; no special text or passage would be assigned; yet, we would assess an important goal of instruction.

Filling a Portfolio

After planning the focus of the portfolio, it is helpful to organize the contents in two layers: (a) the actual evidence, or raw data, that is included in the portfolio, and (b) a summary sheet or organizing framework to help synthesize that information. Including the first layer enables teachers to examine students' actual work and progress notes rather than relying simply on a number or grade. Including the summary sheet forces teachers to synthesize the information in a way that helps them make decisions and communicate with parents and administrators.

Managing the Contents of a Portfolio

In many ways, a portfolio approach to assessment mirrors what good teachers have been doing intuitively for years. The difference is that now we acknowledge the importance and value of alternative forms of assessment. However, if we are not careful, portfolio information will remain only in the classroom, failing to inform others who are involved with decision making. That is why we must deliberately plan to make portfolio assessments accessible to administrators and parents.

While the flexibility of the portfolio is one of its greatest assets, it may also be one of its greatest problems. One reason this type of classroom assessment has not been more popular is the concern about unreliability, inconsistency, and inequity across classrooms, schools, and districts. However there are several mechanisms to protect against this criticism. First, by engaging in discussions about the goals and priorities for instruction and assessment, we can build a common understanding of expectations and criteria. Second, by assessing in an ongoing way, we collect several indicators for any particular goal; generally, the more measures one has, the greater the reliability of the conclusions or decisions one makes.

A third way to attend to consistency is to include two levels of assessment evidence—required evidence and supporting evidence. The required evidence enables us to look systematically across students as well as within each student. This provides the kind of evidence that administrators desire and expect, thus enhancing the likelihood that they will use the portfolio in *their* decision making. These assessments might be particular activities, checklists, or projects (or a list from which to choose), which are tied to identified goals and included in the portfolios of all students at a grade level. They might be fairly structured (e.g., an emergent literacy checklist, a reading log) or more flexible (e.g., students select their best piece of writing to include every six weeks; an audio tape of a student reading a favorite passage recorded at the beginning and end of the school year).

Supporting evidence is additional documentation of learning to include in the portfolio. The evidence may be selected independently or collaboratively by the student and the teacher. It may be the result of a spontaneous activity (e.g., a letter to an author of a favorite book), or it may be carefully planned (e.g., a semantic map completed before and after reading an informational selection). Supporting evidence is critical to building a *complete* picture of a student's literacy abilities because it adds the depth and variety typically missing in traditional assessments. It provides the opportunity for teachers and students to take advantage of the uniqueness of each classroom and each student by encouraging the inclusion of a variety of indicators of learning.

Using the Portfolio for Classroom Decision Making

A portfolio can be used at planning time for periodic review and reflection of its contents. The teacher and student might plan to collaboratively visit the portfolio every several weeks; in addition, the students might plan to visit it at other times individually or with a friend. During the collaborative visits, the teacher and student might discuss progress, add written notes, and plan for the inclusion of other pieces. At the end of the school year, they might collectively decide which pieces will remain in the portfolio for the next year and which are ready to go home. In addition, portfolios are a valuable source of information during conferences with parents and administrators. While parents might be interested in the raw data, the actual evidence of learning, principals or superintendents might be interested in the condensed information found on the summary sheet. In either case, the assessments would reflect more authentic, continuous information than ever before available.

The intrapersonal and interpersonal dialogue that results from visits to the portfolio is a critical component of both assessment and instruction. And as a way of encouraging and monitoring the use of the portfolio, everyone might be asked to initial and date each visit. This is a sure way to remind us that portfolio evaluation is intended to be used.

Summary

In the coming months and years, there are sure to be many very different, perhaps conflicting, iterations of a portfolio approach to reading assessment. The real value of a portfolio does not lie in its physical appearance, location, or organization; rather, it is in the mindset that it instills in students and teachers. Portfolios represent a philosophy that demands that we view assessment as an integral part of our instruction, providing a process for teachers and students to use to guide learning. It is an expanded definition of assessment in which a wide variety of indicators of learning are gathered across many situations before, during, and after instruction. It is a philosophy that honors both the process and the products of learning as well as the active participation of the teacher and the students in their own evaluation and growth.

For additional information on portfolios see the following:

Au, K.H., Scheu, J.A., Arakaki, A.J., & Herman, P.A. (in press). Assessment and accountability in a whole literacy curriculum. *The Reading Teacher*.

Lucas, C.K. (1988). Toward ecological evaluation, part one and part two. *The Quarterly of the National Writing Project and the Center for the Study of Writing*, *10*(1), 1–7; *10*(2), 4–10.

Valencia, S.W., McGinley, W., & Pearson, P.D. (in press). Assessing reading and writing: Building a more complete picture. In G. Duffy (Ed.), *Reading in the middle school*. Newark, DE: International Reading Association.

Wolf, D.P. (1989). Portfolio assessment: Sampling student work. *Educational Leadership*, *46*(7), 4–10.

Initiating Portfolios Through Shared Learning: Three Perspectives

Bette S. Bergeron, Sarah Wermuth, and Rebecca C. Hammar

April 1997

Today's literacy education is characterized by lively dialogue among professionals with distinct experiences and perspectives. Collaboratively, these perspectives can revitalize current instruction and inform future policies. The purpose in sharing this article is to offer a collaborative model for professional development that recognizes the value inherent in the shared learning that occurs when divergent perspectives are jointly explored. Specifically, we center our discussion on issues related to the implementation of classroom portfolios. This focus is particularly relevant in light of current wide-scale efforts toward mandatory implementation and the subsequent need for teachers to develop a system of support in meeting challenges endemic to these mandates.

Perhaps more than other current assessment issues, portfolios have provided the impetus for discussion across literacy education. As instructional philosophies shift, alternative assessments that include portfolios appear to better align with new child-centered, constructivist curricula (Bergeron, 1994; Salinger & Chittenden, 1994). Assessment reform also reflects new ways participants are viewed within the education process. For example, portfolios empower teachers to make instructional and assessment decisions, provide useful information to facilitate the development of grade reports, and enhance teachers' knowledge about their students (Stewart & Paradis, 1993). The changes in literacy instruction resulting from portfolio implementation can enable teachers to rethink their roles and re-examine conceptions about teaching and children's learning (Gomez, Graue, & Bloch, 1991). In addition, portfolios can encourage students to set their own learning goals (Valencia, 1990). As teachers become more involved in the design and implementation of curriculum and as students assume more responsibility in their own learning, the need for changes in assessment practices becomes a critical issue.

While many educators intuitively appreciate the benefits of portfolio assessment, the realities of practice often thwart successful implementation. For example, teachers may feel uncomfortable with their new role in assessment (Gomez et al., 1991) and with allowing children greater responsibility. An additional impediment to implementation appears to

118

be the daunting task of organization, coupled with issues of time management (e.g., Herman & Winters, 1994). Because literacy educators tend to willingly accept new challenges and programs, they also become quickly overwhelmed by their own reform efforts.

Perhaps the most substantive challenge to portfolio assessment, however, has been efforts at the district and state levels to mandate this reform. Case (1994) contends that mandating portfolios on a large-scale basis may inhibit students from reflecting on and controlling their own learning as well as impede the integration of curriculum. Mandating portfolios is of particular interest to us, because all K through Grade 12 teachers in our state of Indiana are required to implement classroom portfolios by 1998–99. Indiana's portfolios are to be used across any subject area, as determined by individual teachers and/or district policy. The portfolios must contain three parts, which may include test scores, attendance records, and students' work samples. At present, there are no established expectations for assessing the portfolios at either the state or district level.

The ambiguity of the state's mandate, and the lack of direction provided to teachers in its implementation, brought the three of us together to explore how best to involve teachers in productively responding to this assessment mandate. As we worked together in planning and implementing a professional development program, we came to appreciate more fully the potential of shared learning. We define shared learning as the opportunity for educators from varied perspectives and experiences to acknowledge and learn from one another's unique perspectives.

Therefore, through this article, we hope to offer a model of shared learning in which educators jointly explore issues and solutions inherent to the challenge of portfolio implementation. While this model is proposed within the framework of an imposed assessment policy, it can be used as a means for productively responding to

any instructional mandate as teachers directly and jointly determine the direction of the reform. Professional collaboration can assuage fears associated with implementation, support participants' attempts to try a variety of assessments, and stimulate the pursuit of knowledge (Stewart & Paradis, 1993). In the sections that follow, we share our process of collegial sharing so that others who may be overwhelmed by the challenges of portfolio implementation or other policy mandates can be supported in their own journey of discovery and change.

A Model for Shared Collegial Learning

Our collaborative journey was initiated by administrators in a large urban district who were concerned with preparing teachers for the state's upcoming portfolio mandate. Bette was approached by the district's Title I office to develop a professional development program that would extend through the school year. While excited with the opportunity to work with teachers on a long-term basis, Bette, a college professor, felt that she did not have enough practical knowledge to make the sessions most useful to the participants. This led to the involvement of Sarah, who was refining the portfolios used within her developmental K–1 Title I program. The joint collaboration of Bette and Sarah provided a valuable balance of experience, theory, and practice. Added to their perspectives was the input from Becky, a participant in the program, whose unique openness to new ideas and commitment to literacy learning as a holistic process provided both Bette and Sarah with invaluable feedback as the sessions progressed.

Introductions: Initial District Meeting

During the first part of the school year, Bette and Sarah shared a 1-hour presentation with the district's Title I teachers. The purpose of this meeting was to provide teachers with an introduction to portfolios and to solicit both volunteers and suggested topics for the follow-up sessions. To introduce portfolios, Bette shared information regarding the state's anticipated mandates, rationale for using portfolios, and general tips for organization and implementation. Sarah then provided information regarding practical issues of implementation and, most specifically, shared examples of her own evolving portfolio program. For example, Sarah illustrated how she used a table of contents to organize information and the movement toward a more open-ended, narrative format for her Language Development Progress Report, which she included in each child's portfolio. Sarah also showed additional documents, required by the district's Title I guidelines, that she chose to contain in each child's portfolio. These included developmental checklists, parental involvement documents, screening results, and summative reports. Most importantly, Sarah recounted her own frustrations with implementing portfolios—including how to balance her requirements with the need for student choice—and how she was dealing with these obstacles.

Shared Learning: Follow-Up Sessions

Bette and Sarah were both surprised and overwhelmed by the participants' response to the initial presentation, as most indicated the desire to commit to the remaining five follow-up sessions. In order to facilitate change and collaboration, participants attended with three to seven other Title I teachers from their school; a total of eight elementary schools were represented. These teachers realized, perhaps better than Bette and Sarah, that growth and change require the commitment of time that cannot be afforded through a single 1-hour inservice. Each participant was provided with two texts from which suggested readings were drawn (see

Figure 1 for a listing of possible seminar texts). In addition to the readings, participants were provided with suggestions for classroom activities. Participants were also encouraged to keep personal journals in which they recorded and reflected upon the process of portfolio implementation. An overview of session topics, suggested readings, and seminar activities is presented in Figure 2.

Session 1: Introductions

The first session began with the opportunity for participants to jointly brainstorm goals that they wished to set for both themselves and the sessions in general. For example, participants noted in the initial district meeting that they wanted to "lose fear" of the portfolio concept and acquire basic information so that portfolios could be initiated. This was accomplished in part from listening to "The Parable of the House Builder Teachers" (Farr, 1990), which creatively portrayed recent assessment reform. Bette also overviewed the state's literacy proficiencies and their impact on portfolio development. The potential effects of mandating portfolios (e.g., Case, 1994; Herman & Winters, 1994) were jointly debated. Because the participants all worked with Title I literacy programs, concrete examples were provided that demonstrated the use of portfolios with special populations (e.g., Rivera, 1994; Schutt & McCabe, 1994; Yunginger-Gehman, 1991).

Session 2: Initiating Portfolios

Issues of organization and initiation were explored in the second session. Participants had been asked to review related literature to find pieces describing portfolio implementation. Before asking participants to share their findings with the group, Bette and Sarah modeled this process through articles they had reviewed (e.g., Lamme & Hysmith, 1991; Paulson, Paulson, & Meyer, 1991; Valencia & Place, 1994; Vavrus, 1990).

Figure 1
Portfolio booklist

Anthony, R.J., Johnson, T.D., Mickelson, N.I., & Preece, A. (1991). *Evaluating literacy: A perspective for change*. Portsmouth, NH: Heinemann.
This book focuses on the assessment and evaluation of literacy and offers a theoretical model of evaluation that provides the framework for the text's topics. Chapter topics include data gathering, data interpretation, and reporting to parents. [seminar text]

Black, L., Daiker, D.A., Sommers, J., & Stygall, G. (Eds.). (1994). *New directions in portfolio assessment: Reflective practice, critical theory, and large-scale scoring*. Portsmouth, NH: Heinemann.
The essays in this text move beyond introductory information to critical questions of practice and theory. The text is divided into three sections: perspectives, portfolios in the classroom (subdivided into students' voices, teachers' voices, and teacher training), and large-scale portfolio assessment.

Farr, R., & Tone, B. (1994). *Portfolio and performance assessment: Helping students evaluate their progress as readers and writers*. Fort Worth, TX: Harcourt Brace.
As the title suggests, this book focuses on literacy and the use of portfolios as a means for student self-evaluation. Topics include initiating portfolios, conferences, and performance assessments. Tips, suggested activities, and side notes are interspersed throughout the book. Also included are three Appendices: common questions asked about portfolios, related sources, and reproducible tools. [seminar text]

Graves, D.H., & Sunstein, B.S. (Eds.). (1992). *Portfolio portraits*. Portsmouth, NH: Heinemann.
This book offers case studies of portfolio use in a range of contexts, including primary classrooms, middle schools, and college courses, with an emphasis on literacy learning. Also included are administrators' perspectives and the role of portfolios within large-scale assessment.

Jasmine, J. (1993). *Portfolios and other assessments*. Huntington Beach, CA: Teacher Created Materials.
Topics in this resource include rubrics, assigned-tasks assessment, and portfolios. Contains several reproducible assessment tools as well as examples of their use.

Perrone, V. (1991). *Expanding student assessment*. Alexandria, VA: Association for Supervision and Curriculum Development.
The author states that the purpose of this book is to encourage discussion about assessment and provide directions for change, particularly in regard to alternatives to standardized assessment. The book's case studies range in topics from the rhetoric of writing assessment to active assessment within science.

Smith, M.A., & Ylvisaker, M. (Eds.). (1993). *Teachers' voices: Portfolios in the classroom*. Berkeley, CA: National Writing Project.
Included in this book are 12 case studies of portfolio use, ranging from perspectives of a first-grade teacher to a college English department. Other topics include teachers' roles in portfolio assessment, using portfolios in high school biology, and Vermont's statewide writing portfolios.

Student portfolios. (1993). Washington, DC: National Education Association.
This text is part of NEA's "teacher to teacher" book series. Each chapter is written by classroom teachers, ranging from elementary to secondary levels, and includes their implementation of portfolios. Descriptions of school- and statewide portfolios are also included.

Figure 2
Overview of workshop session topics, suggested readings, and seminar activities

	Topic	Suggested readings	Seminar activities
Session 1	Introductions	• Prologue • Chapters 1–2 (Farr & Tone) • Chapters 1–3 (Anthony et al.)	• Invite students to share products of their own literacy learning. • Develop two literacy goals for a child; collect related entries for a future portfolio. • Initiate journal reflections.
Session 2	Initiating portfolios	• Chapter 3 (Farr & Tone) • Chapters 4, 6, 7 (Anthony et al.)	• Develop three literacy goals for a student group; collect possible portfolio entries. • Establish personal goals for the seminars. • Review related professional literature. • Reflect on the process of individual literacy learning. • Continue journal reflections.
Session 3	Conferences	• Chapter 5 (Farr & Tone) • Chapter 11 (Anthony et al.)	• Reflect on progress toward personal goals. • Try a variety of teacher/student conferences; generate a list of conference guidelines. • Tape record teacher/student conference and critique the experience. • Generate tips for successful parent/teacher conferences. • Select additional items for the mock portfolio. • Continue journal reflections.
Session 4	Grading and evaluation	• Chapters 4 & 6 (Farr & Tone) • Chapters 8–10 (Anthony et al.)	• Continue charting personal goals. • Review literature relating to evaluation of portfolios and the role of report cards. • Find examples of alternative reporting systems. • Select additional items for the mock portfolio. • Continue journal reflections.
Session 5	Rubrics, performance-based assessment, and final celebration	• Chapters 7–8 (Farr & Tone)	• Continue charting personal goals. • Brainstorm qualities of effective oral reading. • Try a performance-based assessment strategy with students. • Continue journal reflections.

The most successful component of the session, however, was a hands-on experience with a mock portfolio. The purpose of this activity was to demonstrate that effective portfolios differ from "scrapbook" collections in that they reflect specific assessment and literacy goals. Before the session, Bette and Sarah had collected and photocopied a variety of possible portfolio entries, including samples of students' work and literacy checklists. In order to provide a common framework for discussion, Bette and Sarah developed three literacy goals, which were outlined on a sample table of contents. Participants were given the task of sorting through individual copies of the portfolio and identifying on the table of contents the entries that most closely fit the stated goals (or that should be omitted). Participants then shared their selections and offered rationales for their choices. This activity not only gave participants concrete experience in organizing portfolio materials, but also focused them on the importance of having specific goals to guide the assessment process. While predetermined goals were provided for the purposes of this initial experience, it was emphasized in the session that teachers and students must generate their own goals when implementing actual classroom portfolios.

Session 3: Conferences

The issue of scheduling conferences, particularly in regard to time management, was suggested by participants as an important concern worth exploring. The third session, therefore, began with a whole-group brainstorming of conference tips; these suggestions were later reproduced for the participants. Resources were shared addressing the use of portfolio conferences (e.g., Farr & Tone, 1994; Flood & Lapp, 1989; Glazer, 1995; Kasse, 1994). Participants were then invited to share their own conference experiences, as well as any related entry samples they had chosen to add to their mock portfolios.

A video that Sarah provided, in which she demonstrated portfolio conferences conducted one-on-one with kindergarten students, had the greatest impact during this session. Through these conferences, Sarah invited the children to discuss their entries, review what they had learned to that point in the year, and share their favorite work. These concrete examples provided participants with real faces to put with the information they were gaining.

Session 4: Grading and Evaluation

Once they became more comfortable with portfolio formats and possible avenues for implementation, concerns about evaluation pervaded participants' discussion. In particular, participants wanted to explore whether portfolios themselves should be evaluated and how they might be used with report cards. They were also concerned with the perceived pressures from parents to provide letter grades and anticipated difficulties explaining portfolio procedures with parents. While we recognized that portfolios may be most useful if not encumbered with a grade, we provided examples of the variety of ways state pilot programs had interwoven assessment with portfolios. In addition, Sarah shared how her documentation of students' progress had evolved to include more room for anecdotal narratives to supplement grades; her use of summary sheets for the next year's teacher was also demonstrated. These materials were included in each child's portfolio.

Session 5: Rubrics and Performance-Based Assessment

The final session began with a focus on rubrics and performance-based assessments, as these were some of the tools participants hoped to eventually include in their students' portfolios. A variety of rubric formats was presented, including those developed to assess a single project, the state's use of rubrics to analytically score writing samples, and others that reflected student achievement across the curriculum. Participants also were invited to jointly create a rubric to be used to assess oral reading. In order to prepare for this activity, participants were asked to generate and bring a list of qualities that effective oral readers possess. During the session, these qualities were jointly listed and common categories of traits were suggested. A demonstration was given on how to use these categories and related qualities in the development of an oral reading rubric.

Performance-based assessment tools, the second topic of discussion, were compared to more traditional formats (e.g., Brown, 1994). Sample literacy performance tasks were shared, such as following a recipe or writing directions to a common destination. Participants concluded the session by sharing the portfolios they had initiated in their classrooms. Most portfolios were in progress, as participants realized the importance of time within the process of change—and that their assessment practices would continue to evolve through the coming school year.

Three Perspectives

As we stated in our introduction, each of us approached this journey with different experiences, expectations, and knowledge that have uniquely affected the process of shared learning as the challenges of portfolio mandates were addressed. We would therefore like to add our individual perspectives of this process and then, based on these reflections and those of our participants, offer suggestions for others to consider as they develop their own classroom portfolios.

Bette

As I reflect on this experience, I am struck initially by a series of images. I can see the tight groups that teachers formed during small-group discussions, the laughter and frustration that prevailed in the room, and the stacks of folders and overflowing crates that contained the beginning pieces of portfolios. I also remember my own frustration with a participant who was convinced that portfolios would be only another burden within his already overloaded schedule, and my elation when he took the risk to share his ideas and emerging portfolios with the group. His process of change demonstrated one of the greatest potentials of shared learning.

This experience has also made me more aware of the importance of time within the process of change. I never felt that participants were given enough opportunities for small-group discussion to explore and share issues, and regret that I did not better balance whole-group presentations with the time to reflect. A certain benefit of this experience, however, has been the luxury of time as our sessions spread across the school year. One participant had noted midway through the year that she felt as if the group had finally gone "over the hump," and had stopped worrying about why they had to implement portfolios but instead had started focusing on how. It was at that point, she reflected, that she and her colleagues really got to work. These related issues cause me to rethink my own 1-hour inservices, which I am invited to provide on a variety of topics throughout the school year, and wonder how or if they can really affect change. I suspect that they cannot because they do not allow for the level of reflection and sharing that accompanies effective change.

Through this experience, I have also developed a keen appreciation of others' talents and a deeper regard for the realities and challenges of classroom practice, particularly when those practices are imposed through policy mandates. This has most clearly been a process of sharing, as I have learned as much as—if not more than—the session participants. I am now uncomfortable with the presumption that I may be an "expert" simply because I teach at the university level; we are all experts, and all learners, in a variety of unique ways.

Sarah

When Bette invited me to assist her in presenting to a group of my peers, I was honored and at the same time overwhelmed. I had had 6 years of experience developing portfolios in my classroom, yet doubted the fact that I had any strong hold on what an "authentic" portfolio should look like and what it should achieve. My professional training and philosophy about how children learn have always been the driving forces behind the practices that I use in my classroom. I have also had wonderful experiences in my own childhood where learning was valued, my curiosity was encouraged, and I was viewed as a learner who was allowed to make choices for myself. Therefore, portfolios have been the natural way for me to assess students and let them begin to evaluate themselves as learners.

Although my own experiences have shaped the teacher and person that I am, I toiled over how I was going to share these experiences with my fellow teachers in a nonthreatening and meaningful way. I wanted to make sure that portfolios would make sense within any child-centered classroom, even if teachers had not had my same experiences or training. I also wanted to stress the fact that I had taken several years to develop portfolios with my students, and each year revel in the fact that my portfolios look different with each child and with my ever-evolving curriculum.

It was also extremely important to me that the teacher participants had a voice in the goals and expectations of the learning to take place. As a former classroom teacher myself, I know the frustrations of dealing with children's needs, parents, administration, new teaching ideas, and my own personal life outside the classroom. Many times I have felt the isolation of confronting all of these issues and not being able to collaborate and talk with others about possible solutions. Therefore, from the beginning of our planning sessions, Bette and I always took the perspective that the learners needed to be involved so that real change could take place. I knew that it was important for these teachers to have not only the theory behind portfolios, but also the concrete evidence that portfolios do work. We needed to dispel the fears of even beginning the process of developing portfolios.

A vital part to the sessions' success was the small-group discussions. It was during these times, as I milled from group to group, that I began to hear teachers discussing specific literacy goals implemented in their classrooms, how they initiated portfolios on a small scale, techniques used to convince administrators and other teachers of the importance of portfolios, and the development of time lines for implementation. Most importantly, I heard how teachers were making provisions to allow children to decide what work would be included and how items would be evaluated. These discussions were very important to the group, and I felt that this was where learning was best supported. Teachers began to think in terms of how portfolios would allow them to grow as facilitators of learning and help empower their students to become lifelong learners.

Over the course of this whole learning experience, I not only witnessed growth and reform on the part of the teachers that were present but also grew as a person. Portfolios have given me the courage to allow children to evaluate themselves and be empowered as learners. In my former classroom, children evaluated themselves by reviewing their work four times a year. The children then planned a conference with their parents. At these conferences, children discussed the areas in which they had improved and asked parents for guidance to help them meet future goals. Working in a Title I program with a large caseload of kindergartners at risk has made this task of constructive self-evaluation a tremendous undertaking. While children are given a lot of choice in the hands-on activities in which they engage, I had not translated that same level of choice to portfolios. The experience of collaborating with other teachers struggling with similar challenges has more clearly focused me on the need to help children gain ownership in all facets of their learning, even at very young developmental ages.

The experience has also given me the ability to look more closely at myself as a learner and at the impact of the small-group discussions on my own development. During the sessions, I found myself moving away from my role as a group facilitator and into the circle of participants. This change has lessened my own frustrations and fears of isolation. Being part of the shared learning experience has also renewed my hope and spirit that joint educational reform can happen.

Becky

Eight Title I teachers had the advantage of representing our school at the portfolio workshops. Having this many faculty members attend six formal meetings during a year that coincided with Title I schoolwide planning was a major feat in itself. Added to that was the recognition that my cohorts and I were a skeptical bunch who first had to be convinced of the worth of any new idea to be implemented. The Indiana portfolio mandate made it imperative that all educators within the state have an understanding of portfolios. Bette's original presentation was the impetus needed to get us thinking about the actual implementation of portfolios.

Three topic activities, presented through hands-on demonstration, represented the highlights of the subsequent sessions: the mock portfolio, conference video, and oral reading rubric. The authentic children's papers in the mock portfolios gave teachers their first view of what might go into a portfolio—and again emphasized the need for teachers and students to set literacy

goals. Not only did teachers begin talking about what might be included, they were now more carefully considering why a piece should or should not be selected. Because it underscored the idea that there is no one right way to implement portfolios in the classroom, this activity also gave the teachers at my school more confidence that they had the liberty to choose what entries they and their students wanted. Perhaps because of this renewed confidence, the portfolios that were eventually developed reflected their instruction and grade-level goals. It was an important breakthrough for my school cohort to realize that portfolios are indeed an item of empowerment, and can grant teachers and students the liberty to direct their own curriculum.

The second major highlight was Sarah's conference video. The realistic nature of this video provided teachers with an authentic model of how to conduct a portfolio conference with a child. This video showed how easy it was to implement a conference revolving around a child's collected work; material for discussion was readily at hand. The final session's total-group brainstorming approach for selecting criteria to evaluate the literacy goal of oral reading via a rubric was again an eye-opener. Making teachers comfortable enough to freely participate permitted a wide range of responses and supported many levels of understanding.

As I reflect on the total experience of the inservice sessions, it has become apparent that shared and in-depth understandings of the process and implementation of portfolios have emerged. Long-term association with peers revolving around one aspect of the curriculum kept the topic of discussion fresh. When group members encountered one another in faculty meetings, team meetings, or in the lounge, we found we had common ground for dialogue. Portfolios became our bond; after all, we were struggling through this newly mandated and professionally dynamic topic together, and we considered ourselves at the top of current reform. In a very real sense, we were leading the way for our staff.

Throughout the inservice sessions, we found that we came to rely on one another for support. As professionals, we explored others' opinions regarding why a potential portfolio entry should be included or rejected. This was the first time we actually listened to one another. Our school lives are so harried and hurried that finding time for others is a difficult task. As a group, we learned to respect the thoughts of our peers. This was a difficult step. Too often, teachers become islands and do not request or receive support from their peers. However, support can be gained only after establishing trust as a foundation for a relationship. Trust did develop through the inservice sessions, where each teacher was invited to voice his/her views on a variety of topics. Dialogue created an understanding of one another's problems and beliefs. Listening enabled an appreciation of each individual as a professional to be valued.

Final Reflections

At the final session, participants were invited to reflect on their own accomplishments as well as to evaluate the sessions' success (or failures). Many participants felt that their own professional goals had been accomplished. They noted, for example, that their staff colleagues had started talking and planning together, reading/writing horizons were broadened, and there was concrete evidence of change within their schools. One participant noted, "we're working beyond my original expectations." Many realized that what they were already doing in their classrooms could be translated into a portfolio program, thus lessening their anxiety. While some participants were still apprehensive, they realized that change in assessment was an ongoing learning process.

Shared learning emerged as a specific strength of the sessions. Participants noted that it was beneficial to learn of others' uses of portfolios and exchange ideas through group discussions. Also recognized were the openness of participants and the establishment of a positive and encouraging learning environment. Concrete examples and resources were also noted as beneficial, as were Sarah's firsthand accounts of her practical experiences with portfolios. Based on these perceptions we feel that the development of trust and openness are keys to change as learning and sharing are facilitated through concrete modeling and demonstration.

While trust and collaboration are integral to the sessions' success, it is imperative to consider whether the professional development endeavors actually affected literacy instruction and assessment for the participants. The cohort at Becky's school is currently using portfolios as a means for building more writing experiences into the curriculum. The assessment of students' writing portfolios in Grades 1 to 3 is based on goals developed by teams of grade-level teachers. A writing checklist that focuses on both mechanics and content has been modified for each of these grade levels (see Figure 3). Grade-level teams jointly determine how the checklist could be used and the number of entries to be included in their classes' portfolios. Teachers have chosen to assess the portfolios periodically throughout the year, using comparative samples of children's work.

Although their assessment goals are similar, teachers at different grade levels at Becky's school have developed unique strategies for portfolio implementation. For example, one grade level links entries with genre studies of children's literature, while another includes language experience stories for frequent evaluation. Each team, however, has had a representative at the Title I inservices. The interest generated by the workshops created the need for those teachers to become leaders within their own grade-level cohorts and to subsequently share their knowledge with their peers.

Figure 3
Checklist for portfolio writing entries

Wilson School–desired outcomes
Grade 3 writing inventory

Student: _____ Grade: _____

	Entry 1	Entry 2	Entry 3	Entry 4
Basic skills				
Capitals	_____	_____	_____	_____
Periods	_____	_____	_____	_____
Complete sentences	_____	_____	_____	_____
Relevant title	_____	_____	_____	_____
Punctuation skills				
Use of question marks	_____	_____	_____	_____
Use of exclamation points	_____	_____	_____	_____
Use of commas	_____	_____	_____	_____
Other punctuation	_____	_____	_____	_____
Story skills				
Sequence	_____	_____	_____	_____
Consistent tense	_____	_____	_____	_____
Use of description	_____	_____	_____	_____
Use of referents	_____	_____	_____	_____
Paragraphs	_____	_____	_____	_____
Character description	_____	_____	_____	_____
Plot development	_____	_____	_____	_____
Story structure	_____	_____	_____	_____

Students at Becky's school are also becoming active learners in the portfolio process by conferring with teachers and parents about the portfolio entries and jointly exploring their growth as writers. As they evaluate their work using the writing checklist, students are beginning to look more critically at their own writing and consequently setting personal and specific goals. They also enjoy revisiting their portfolios and the entries they have selected during the year. Becky notes that students are becoming excited about their portfolios and often self-initiate portfolio entry selections.

A focus on portfolios supports literacy learning in the classrooms in which Sarah team-teaches by helping her develop instruction around student choice and concentrate on literacy goals and objectives that are purposeful for students. Her own professional development has also helped Sarah become more organized and given her a common ground for open dialogue when discussing student progress with classroom teachers. It has helped to validate what teachers are already seeing and doing with children. Sarah notes that this process has also guided classroom teachers in focusing on specific learning objectives appropriate for emerging readers and writers. In addition, teachers are currently initiating a schoolwide portfolio proposal, where specific learning goals are identified for each grade level. For example, first-grade portfolios contain journal entries to reflect the goal of writing development through invented spelling.

The level of student involvement in portfolios varies among classrooms at Sarah's school, primarily because many teachers are still learning about portfolios themselves. In some classrooms, however, students reflect on the work in portfolios that include their choices in dictated and original writing. Through informal conferences, children are invited to evaluate their own progress verbally. However, time constraints and the teachers' need for further professional development currently impede a more substantive inclusion of student self-evaluation or goal setting. A commitment to future inservices, direct support from trained individuals, and strong leadership are needed before student empowerment is actualized and the challenges to mandated implementation can be accommodated.

Portfolio initiatives in other schools represented at the inservices involve the use of three-part portfolios and periodic teacher/student conferences. The three sections contained in one first-grade portfolio include documentation of favorite book selections, journal entries, and the students' free choices (or "private papers"). At each grading period, these children meet with either their classroom teacher or Title I specialist to review their portfolio's contents, complete a reading and writing attitude survey, and dictate their reflections regarding the portfolio's implementation (see Figure 4). Third-grade students at another school are developing electronic port-

---

Figure 4
Portfolio reflection prompts

Student: _____ Date: _____

1. What is your favorite piece in your portfolio?

2. Why is this your favorite?

3. What do you like the most about working in your portfolio?

4. What do you like the least about working in your portfolio?

5. Do you think your writing has improved? How?

6. How can you improve your writing?

7. How can teachers help you improve your writing?

folios that emphasize a variety of writing activities and word processing skills. Monthly portfolio entries, generated on the computer and selected by students, are developed and stored on individual disks.

At a recent follow-up session, a participant noted that one positive impact of the state's portfolio mandate has been to compel teachers to make assessment changes. However, we are reminded by Salinger and Chittenden (1994) that portfolios will remain dynamic only when these assessments reflect adaptations to individual classroom needs. This is an especially compelling concern when the consequences of top-down portfolio mandates are considered. In order to resolve the challenges inherent to policy mandates, the personal assessment theories and perspectives of all literacy educators must remain open to reflection and shared dialogue.

References

Bergeron, B.S. (1994). Spelling out success with portfolios. *Writing Teacher, 7*(5), 20–22.

Brown, J.H. (1994). Does your testing match your teaching style? *Instructor, 104*(2), 86–89.

Case, S.H. (1994). Will mandating portfolios undermine their value? *Educational Leadership, 52*(2), 46–47.

Farr, R.C. (1990, May). *Promoting literacy through the use of reading-writing portfolios.* Paper presented at the 35th Annual Convention of the International Reading Association, Atlanta, GA.

Farr, R., & Tone, B. (1994). *Portfolio and performance assessment: Helping students evaluate their progress as readers and writers.* Fort Worth, TX: Harcourt Brace.

Flood, J., & Lapp, D. (1989). Reporting reading progress: A comparison portfolio for parents. *The Reading Teacher, 42*, 508–514.

Glazer, S.M. (1995). Students lead their own parent conferences. *Teaching K–8, 25*(7), 92, 94.

Gomez, M.L., Graue, M.E., & Bloch, M.N. (1991). Reassessing portfolio assessment: Rhetoric and reality. *Language Arts, 68*, 620–628.

Herman, J.L., & Winters, L. (1994). Portfolio research: A slim collection. *Educational Leadership, 52*(2), 48–55.

Kasse, S. (1994). Student/parent conferences: A new generation. *Teaching K–8, 25*(3), 78–79.

Lamme, L.L., & Hysmith, C. (1991). One school's adventure into portfolio assessment. *Language Arts, 68*, 629–640

Paulson, F.L., Paulson, P.R., & Meyer, C.A. (1991). What makes a portfolio a portfolio? *Educational Leadership, 48*, 60–63.

Rivera, D. (1994). Assessment: Portfolio assessment. *LD Forum, 19*(4), 14–16.

Salinger, T., & Chittenden, E. (1994). Analysis of an early literacy portfolio: Consequences for instruction. *Language Arts, 71*, 446–452.

Schutt, P.W., & McCabe, V.M. (1994). Portfolio assessment for students with learning disabilities. *Learning Disabilities, 5*(2), 81–85.

Stewart, R.A., & Paradis, E.E. (1993). Portfolios: Agents of change and empowerment in classrooms. In D.J. Leu & C.K. Kinzer (Eds.), *Examining central issues in literacy research, theory, and practice* (pp. 109–116). Chicago: National Reading Conference.

Valencia, S. (1990). A portfolio approach to classroom reading assessment: The whys, whats, and hows. *The Reading Teacher, 43*, 338–340.

Valencia, S.W., & Place, N. (1994). Portfolios: A process for enhancing teaching and learning. *The Reading Teacher, 47*, 666–669.

Vavrus, L. (1990). Put portfolios to the test. *Instructor, 100*(1), 48–53.

Yunginger-Gehman, J. (1991, May). *Portfolio assessment in a Chapter 1 program.* Paper presented at the 36th Annual Convention of the International Reading Association, Las Vegas, NV.

Portfolio Assessment for Young Readers

Scott G. Paris

May 1991

The overarching goal of new approaches to literacy assessment is to change the ways that teachers and students interact in the classroom. Ideally, new assessments will increase the engagement of students in thoughtful reading and writing activities and will provide more detailed records of students' literacy development over time. Portfolios should also inform teachers about the interactive dimensions of literacy and make them sensitive to processes of learning rather than just the outcomes. Portfolio assessments empower teachers to select and create measures of students' talents and weaknesses so that appropriate instructional opportunities can be provided for different students. Thus, teachers are often enthusiastic but bewildered by the challenge of creating their own portfolio assessments. In this brief essay, I would like to highlight some of the promising avenues to pursue as teachers strive to create alternative literacy assessments.

Valencia (1990) points out that effective portfolios of literacy assessment involve authentic activities that promote collaborative reflection. Developing abilities should also be measured repeatedly with a multidimensional variety of tasks. In this manner, portfolios assess cognitive, motivational, and social processes that underlie literacy development. Assessment is embedded in the curriculum and interwoven with instruction so that strategies can be assessed and improved. Self-perceptions of competence and control can be encouraged, and appropriate individual mastery goals can be set and pursued.

During the past year, several students and I have worked with teachers and administrators to design portfolio assessments for reading in primary grades. We quickly discovered that most published tests were not consistent with the philosophy of the district, so we examined different research tasks used to measure comprehension strategies, metacognition, motivation, and literate environments. We shuffled through tasks around a large table and negotiated an agenda that none of us could have articulated beforehand, a process that was aptly described by Donmoyer (1990) as the "deliberative approach" to curriculum evaluation. After many hours of reviewing, creating, and revising tasks appropriate for young children, we created a battery of different tasks that were administered to children in six different schools. Our experiences and data revealed that some tasks were on target and appropriate while others were fundamentally flawed. We were pleased to find that several of our tasks provided robust measures of young children's strategic reading and metacognition. These seem particularly worthwhile to share because they can be adapted easily to portfolios at any grade level.

Strategic Reading, Comprehension, and Metacognition

We used the Strategy Assessments in *Heath Reading* (1989) as a model for measuring children's understanding of strategies before, during, and after reading. These prototypes include examples of relevant questions to ask students as they read and thus provide a "think aloud" procedure for assessing comprehension and metacognition simultaneously. The procedure avoids asking young children hypothetical questions that often elicit fabricated or socially desirable answers.

We modified the tasks by asking five uniform kinds of questions: identification of the topic from text cues before reading, predictions of the content based on previous passage information, inferences from text, monitoring the meaning of a novel word, and summarizing key information. In addition, children were asked five follow-up questions such as "How did you know that?" or "If you did not know that, how could you find out?" Children's responses to these metacognitive questions were given one point if they explained such things as how they used the titles for identifying the topic, how prior text influenced their predictions, how rereading or skimming might help them make an inference, and how context provides clues about the meaning of an unknown word.

These ten questions, five comprehension and five metacognitive, were woven into a conversation as children read aloud the passages, one narrative and one informational. As children read the passages and answered the questions, we recorded the frequency of strategies observed (e.g., lookbacks, questions, elaborations, rereadings, etc.). Good readers generally exhibited three observable strategies as they read each passage. Children who scored at least 3 of the 5 points for comprehension questions and 3 of the 5 points for their metacognitive explanations were found to be using appropriate strategies and displaying good awareness of their own thinking.

The high correlations among the measures of comprehension, metacognition, and observed strategies indicate that children's abilities to explain how they did answer questions are related to their comprehension. Thus, the task provides useful information about reading comprehension strategies and thinking that has been difficult to obtain for young readers. We also designed tasks suitable for kindergartners and gave the passages as listening rather than reading tasks to children who could not read adequately. The tasks worked equally well as reading or listening comprehension assessments.

There are several distinct advantages to the strategic reading task that make it useful as a prototype for portfolio assessments. First, the strong relations among strategy use, comprehension, and metacognition have been shown empirically. Second, the task can be presented as either a listening or reading task and is therefore suitable for children with different abilities in kindergarten and first grade. Third, the procedures can be modified so that the passages and strategies are taken directly from the classroom curriculum. This means that the assessment is not an added burden to the teacher but is embedded in regular instruction. Fourth, the task can provide cumulative evidence of children's abilities to use reading strategies that have been taught in the classroom.

Additional Measures of Comprehension

Two other tasks seem promising for measuring children's comprehension: cloze procedures and retelling. Cloze tasks are highly correlated with age and awareness of print conventions in our studies of young readers and, additionally, they are consistently correlated with measures of strategic reading in older children (Paris, Cross, & Lipson, 1984). Cloze tasks are particularly well-suited to comprehension assessment for several reasons: They can be designed by teachers with regular curricular materials; they can be made easy or difficult by varying the numbers of options provided for each missing word (in the slots or word banks); they can be given as reading or listening tasks; and they can be given to groups of students and scored quickly.

Retellings are much more labor intensive but can be used flexibly with curricular materials as reading or listening tasks so that they also become embedded in instruction. The *Qualitative Reading Inventory* (Leslie & Caldwell, 1990) provides grade-level passages and guidelines for assessing comprehension using oral retelling (as well as running records and comprehension questions).

Additional Measures of Metacognition

We also created a Book Selection task, based on Kemp (1990), in which children engage in thinking aloud as they identify books that they would like to read. We encouraged children to tell us how they decided if they liked the books. We recorded their comments and checked their use of overt strategies such as skimming the book, making affective statements, or talking about previously read books or prior knowledge about the subject. After chil-

dren had sorted books into two piles, we chose one book from the preferred stack and used it to assess children's concepts about print.

Our interview was modeled after Kemp's (1990) procedures and Clay's (1979) *Sand* and *Stones* tasks. In our pilot study, the children's think-aloud comments and their concepts about print were related to age and comprehension. The virtue of this task is that it provides an assessment of children's conceptual orientation to text that is often not available for young readers. Teachers have flexibility in the materials and concepts they select so that the assessment is developmentally appropriate for children who may not read much.

Motivation

We created a motivation-for-reading questionnaire that included questions such as "Are you a good reader?" and "Do you enjoy reading?" Questions about young children's abilities, interests, and enjoyment were answered with optimism and enthusiasm by nearly all children and, thus, were not related to other aspects of reading behavior. The positive, nondiscriminating attitudes are consistent with developmental research on young children and may be due to optimism, poor self-evaluation, or naiveté. Many other attitude scales reveal similar skewed responses by young children (McKenna & Kear, 1990), which suggests that decontextualized attitude surveys may not provide useful data for young children. We urge teachers to use behavioral descriptions of motivation and attitudes such as effort, challenge seeking, and goal setting, in order to substantiate their judgments about students' motivation.

Literate Environments

We designed several indirect measures of literacy backgrounds of the children. For example, we created two lists of well-known children's books and authors (that also included nonbooks and nonauthors) and then asked children to circle any of the books and authors that they had heard about before. This simple recognition measure (based on research by Stanovich & Cunningham, in press) was highly correlated with children's ages and with comprehension and concepts about print tasks. Our survey of children's literacy habits beyond school was not highly correlated with other measures of reading. Although literacy practices at home may be related to children's reading and writing, surveys of young children may not provide sensitive measures of the quality of their literate environments.

In summary, we believe that portfolios of literacy development offer exciting opportunities for teachers to create assessments that engage students in authentic activities and provide genuine guidance for instruction. Some of our tasks can be adapted easily by teachers to fit their needs and curricula. Here are some simple suggestions: Start slowly. Try two or three new tasks with another teacher. Develop a system for keeping records and sharing the information with students and parents. Use portfolios to stretch your teaching into new areas of literacy, for example, strategic reading, metacognition, or motivation. The new activities may open new horizons for students and teachers alike.

References

Clay, M.M. (1979). *The early detection of reading difficulties*. Auckland, NZ: Heinemann.

Donmoyer, R. (1990) Curricuium evaluation and the negotiation of meaning. *Language Arts, 67,* 74–86.

Heath Reading. (1989). Lexington, MA: Heath.

Kemp, M. (1990). *Watching children read and write.* Portsmouth, NH: Heinemann.

Leslie, L., & Caldwell, J. (1990). *Qualitative reading inventory.* Glenview, IL: Scott, Foresman.

McKenna, M.C., & Kear, D.J. (1990). Measuring attitude toward reading: A new tool for teachers. *The Reading Teacher, 43,* 626–634.

Paris, S.G., Cross, D.R., & Lipson, M.Y. (1984). Informed strategies for learning: A program to improve children's reading awareness and comprehension. *Journal of Educational Psychology, 76,* 1239–1252.

Stanovich, K.E., & Cunningham, A.E. (in press). Assessing print exposure and orthographic processing skill in children: A quick measure of reading experience. *Journal of Educational Psychology.*

Valencia, S. (1990). A portfolio approach to classroom reading assessment. *The Reading Teacher, 43,* 338–340.

Student Portfolios: Building Self-Reflection in a First-Grade Classroom

Lindy Vizyak

December 1994/January 1995

"It is some of my best work. I Xed out words that were wrong and put other words on top. I got the right spelling for Antarctica from the globe. This is fiction and has a summary. Can I read it to you?" Comments from a third or fourth grader? Actually, Aaron is a student in my first-grade classroom. His comments, which were recorded during a portfolio conference, confirmed my belief that young children can reflect upon and evaluate their own learning.

For the past 5 years, I have been using portfolios in my classroom to document student growth and to assess performance. The process has been evolving for me and for my students. During the first 3 years, my time was spent developing a portfolio model, management system, and recording forms which fit my philosophy of assessment. However, as I researched alternative methods of assessment, I became increasingly uncomfortable with a teacher-controlled model. It did not align with current research, which stresses the importance of providing opportunities for students to participate in their assessment and to reflect on their learning.

Last year, I decided to put my research-based knowledge into practice. I provided file folders for each child to collect his or her work. Some students collected work samples; most did not. At the end of the year, in reflecting on this less-than-successful experience, I decided I had not modeled the process, demonstrated possible contents of a portfolio, or discussed reasons for selecting the contents. In addition, I had not provided time for students to work with and share their portfolios. This realization prompted my decision to provide a structure this year that would support my goal of developing collaborative assessment.

I implemented my new plan by introducing the term *portfolio* during the first week of school. To provide a clear visual model, I shared my own portfolio with the class. I had decorated the cover of an 8" × 12" manila folder with my drawing of the cover of *The True Story of the Three Pigs* (Scieszka, 1989; a favorite children's book), a drawing of my family, and a

University of Colorado logo (my son is a recent graduate). I also shared the contents of my portfolio and explained the significance of each entry. Children were given blank folders to decorate and then share with the class. This first step created instant ownership. (See Figures 1 and 2 for examples of student portfolio entries.)

Several times each week, students shared pieces from their portfolios with each other and explained the reasoning behind their selections. At the beginning of the year, students had no previous experience with this process, and most

found it difficult to explain their choices. Ryan shared a story he had written about his dog and said simply, "I put this in my portfolio because it is about my dog and I like my dog."

I wanted to model other possible reasons for Ryan's including the story in his portfolio, so I said, "I know that Ryan loves to write and often writes at home and during his free time. I also see that he has a title for his story." Ryan promptly added, "Oh, yeah. I also have a summary on the back of my story." I asked him where he got the idea, and he said that he

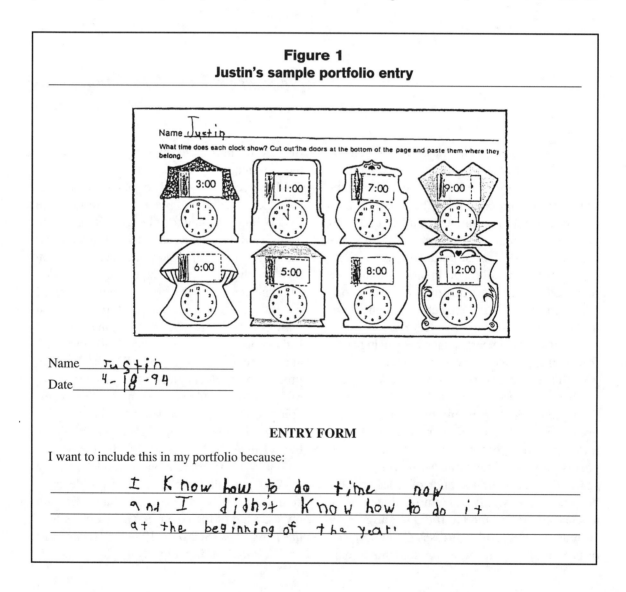

Figure 1
Justin's sample portfolio entry

Name Justin

What time does each clock show? Cut out the doors at the bottom of the page and paste them where they belong.

3:00   11:00   7:00   9:00

6:00   5:00   8:00   12:00

Name Justin
Date 4-18-94

ENTRY FORM

I want to include this in my portfolio because:

I Know how to do time now and I didn't Know how to do it at the beginning of the year.

Figure 2
Ryan's sample portfolio entry

Name _____ Ry 40 _____

Date _____ 4-13-94 _____

ENTRY FORM

I want to include this in my portfolio because:

It's the frist Story I made on my Computer. It even has a titel Page.

noticed many of the books I read to the class had a summary on the back. Ryan clearly had made a connection between reading and writing!

Drawing on my experience with writer's workshop minilessons, I structured portfolio minilessons. I focused on the content of student-managed portfolios and reasons for the selections. These lessons provided the language needed for self-reflection. The majority of the first student selections were examples of best work. As the year progressed, minilessons explored other reasons for selecting portfolio pieces: something you have learned (growth), something that took a long time (effort), something that was challenging (risk taking), and something that showed interests outside of school (holistic learning).

The students have generated a classroom chart that lists "Things That Can Go in a Portfolio." The list includes a story or book, science projects, letters, notes, cards, best work, math papers, artwork, photographs, things from home, challenging things, things that demonstrate improvement, and work from a favorite subject. The list is ongoing and is expanded as students discover new categories of possible portfolio inclusions.

Each Friday, anyone who has a new portfolio entry (including me) is invited to share it with the class. These regular share sessions have resulted in improved metacognition and opportunities for building self-esteem and confidence as students develop a voice in the assessment process.

In addition to the student-managed portfolio, I also have a teacher-student portfolio. Twice a month, students meet with a volunteer and choose one or two pieces from their teacher-student portfolio. They may select assessment data (reading and writing conference notes, miscues, math tasks, content-area unit tests, etc.), student work samples (story maps, responses to literature, projects, writing samples, problem solving, etc.), or parent input (surveys, conference notes, etc.). An entry form slip that explains the student's reason(s) for each choice is attached to the appropriate piece. This process gives students practice in selecting meaningful work and reflecting on those selections. It also provides valuable information for me about each student's ability to self-reflect.

Next year, I will not have an assistant in my classroom, so I have set a realistic goal to confer with each student once every 9-week grading period. I feel confident that our new teacher-student portfolio is a successful marriage of student reflection, self-evaluation, and teacher accountability.

Section Four

Miscue Analysis

Miscue analysis is perhaps the most informative practice developed for the purpose of understanding readers. As an assessment practice it has evolved directly from how reading happens, providing insights into a reader's proficient use of the reading process. Its techniques (charting and analyzing miscues and assessing the retelling) make observable the largely invisible process of reading. Most often, miscue analysis is a procedure used by reading clinicians to understand struggling readers, but can be used to reveal insights about any reader.

Involving readers in examination of their own miscues provides them with opportunities to develop an understanding of themselves as readers and to revalue their developing control over the reading process. Yetta Goodman calls this collaborative discussion between a reader and teacher *retrospective miscue analysis*. This specialized procedure aims to help students reflect on their reading behaviors, recognize their strengths, and identify areas for growth. The two articles on the individualized practice of retrospective miscue analysis included in this section will provide readers of this compilation the basic knowledge to appreciate the Rhodes and Shanklin article that modifies traditional miscue procedures in order to make the process practical for classroom settings.

Additional Readings

- Bloome, D., & Dail, A.R. (1997). Toward (re)defining miscue analysis: Reading as a social and cultural process. *Language Arts*, *74*(8), 610–617.
- Goodman, K. (1996). *On reading: A common-sense look at the nature of language and the science of reading*. Portsmouth, NH: Heinemann.
- Goodman, Y., Watson, D.J., & Burke, C.L. (1987). *Reading miscue inventory: Alternative procedures*. New York: Richard C. Owen.
- Martens, P. (1997). What miscue analysis reveals about word recognition and repeated reading: A view through the miscue window. *Language Arts*, *74*(8), 600–609.
- Martens, P., Goodman, Y., & Flurkey, A.D. (Eds.). (1995). Miscue analysis for classroom teachers. *Primary Voices K–6*, *3*(4).

Revaluing Readers While Readers Revalue Themselves: Retrospective Miscue Analysis

Yetta M. Goodman

May 1996

For the last 10 years I have been re-searching a reading instructional strategy called Retrospective Miscue Analysis (RMA). As I have been writing articles and monographs about RMA (Y. Goodman & Marek, 1989), I have begun to realize how my interest in exploring RMA is built on and grew out of my earlier work in miscue analysis and kidwatching. My involvement in miscue analysis resulted from my interest in understanding how young people learn to read. As part of miscue analysis, I realized that readers' beliefs about themselves as readers often influence their literacy development. As I realized the importance of such observations of students' reading, I coined the term *kidwatching* (Y. Goodman, 1978, 1985).

Although the concept of informed observations of students' learning experiences is not new, I wanted to legitimatize the importance of knowledgeable teachers' ongoing evaluations of their students' learning experiences. Learning from careful observation is basic to all scientific endeavors; learning from our students as we watch them learn is important not only for the planning of curriculum and instruction but also for constantly expanding our knowledge about teaching and learning. Kidwatching is equally necessary for researchers and teacher educators.

One experience during a longitudinal miscue study of my daughter Wendy's reading when she was 7 years old exemplifies the experiences that eventually led me to retrospective miscue analysis. (Wendy is now an experienced teacher in the Tucson Unified School District.) She was reading a realistic fiction account of a group of children visiting a live animal museum called *Let's Go to the Museum*. Wendy read *maximum* for *museum* each of the six times it occurred throughout the text, intoning it as a noun. In her retelling, after the reading, she kept telling me about the live animal maximum that the children had visited as she thoroughly discussed the events and characters in the story. I asked her what she thought a live animal maximum was. She responded quite confidently that she thought the word might be museum and "animals live in museums except, most of the times, when they

140

live in museums, they're dead and stuffed." So she decided the word couldn't be museum and tried maximum instead. It was obvious that she knew that the word wasn't maximum so we talked about how sometimes words are used in unusual ways and that readers have to decide, like she did, whether to use the word they think it is even if it doesn't make sense or to try something else. I remember thinking how confusing it was that the author would write about a live animal museum; I didn't have a schema for it either. Ironically, both Wendy and I have spent almost 20 years in a city with the famous Arizona Sonoran Desert Museum that includes live animals in its displays.

When I revisit my early experiences with miscue analysis research, I realize that Wendy and I both learned more about the reading process during our discussion than we had known previously. We became aware of the importance of the reader's background and experience. We realized that readers make decisions and problem solve as they read. I learned that I could discuss reading and the reading process with a young child. And I gained additional support for the results from miscue analysis research (Allen & Watson, 1977) about the importance of substitutions, even unusual ones, because substitutions act as syntactic or grammatical placeholders that provide support for readers to continue to make sense as they read.

In all kidwatching, including miscue analysis, the observer's beliefs influence what he or she understands from the observation. As Piaget is often quoted as saying, we see what we know, we do not just know what we see. Our perceptions are influenced by our conceptions: our beliefs and our knowledge about the world. So kidwatching is more than merely looking, and miscue analysis and RMA are more than listening to kids read. Both involve seeing based on knowledge and understanding about development and language. Therefore, if teachers and researchers are to fully examine students' mis-

cues and their unique retellings, they need to be aware of the understandings about the reading process that emanate from miscue analysis research and theory (Y. Goodman, Watson, & Burke, 1987). At the same time, examining miscues and asking "what knowledge do these readers have about language and the reading process that causes them to make these miscues" provide information about readers and the reading process that informs the planning of reading instruction and the development of curriculum (Y. Goodman & Burke, 1980; K. Goodman, Bird, & Y. Goodman, 1990, 1992).

Retrospective Miscue Analysis

From the beginnings of my wondering about how kids such as Wendy read, I have observed readers with the belief that everything readers do is caused by their knowledge—their knowledge of the world, their knowledge of language, and what they believe about reading and the reading process.

Miscue analysis, first developed by Kenneth Goodman (1969) helped me construct my views about reading. I have spent years researching miscue analysis with teachers and learning from them how their knowledge about miscue analysis influences their developing understandings about the reading process and their teaching of reading. Teachers often say that once they have participated in doing a complete miscue analysis of one of their own students, they never listen to a kid read in the same way. They become aware that miscues reveal the strategies kids use when they read and the knowledge kids have about language. Miscues show the degree to which readers use the graphophonic (including phonics), syntactic, and semantic/pragmatic language systems. Teachers come to realize that most readers self-correct only those miscues that are disruptive to reading and do not usually self-correct predictions that make sense as the reader is constructing a meaningful text. Miscue analysis provides teachers with a lens through which to observe the reading process. Over time they learn to discover patterns of miscues that reveal readers' linguistic and cognitive strengths as well as those that need support from the teacher. Because of teachers' interest in miscue analysis and discussing their insights with their students, I have become interested in involving students themselves in the miscue analysis process. I call readers' reflection on their own reading process retrospective miscue analysis (RMA).

Over the last decade, with teachers and graduate students, I have been researching strategies that involve readers in evaluating their own reading process (Y. Goodman & Marek, in press). Research into the use of RMA procedures develops understandings about how readers make shifts in their views about the reading process and in themselves as readers as a result of examining the power of their own miscues. Revaluing themselves as readers often leads to greater reading proficiency. We have learned about these processes by engaging in conversations with readers as they examine their miscues and talk about the reading strategies and the language they use.

Many readers, even in graduate classes, have built negative views about themselves as readers. Such readers believe that it is cheating to skip words, that slow reading is evidence of poor reading, and that good readers (something they can never call themselves) know every word and remember everything that they read. Through RMA, readers "demythify" the reading process as they discover that reading isn't a mysterious process about which they "haven't a clue." They come to value themselves as learners with knowledge. They begin to realize that they can question authors and not believe everything that is in print. They become critical of what they are reading and confident to make judgments about the way a published text is written and the quality of the work.

At the same time, they demystify the process as they discover that they already use reading strategies and language cues in ways that can help them become even more proficient as readers, especially as they acknowledge what they can do. They build a more realistic view of how readers read than they held before and become aware that reading is more than calling words accurately and reading fluently. They realize that a mythical perfection and recall of every item in a text is not the goal of reading. They come to understand that reading is a meaning-making, constructive process influenced by their own investment in and control over that process. They learn that all readers miscue and transform the published text as they read, constructing a text parallel to that of the author (K. Goodman, 1994). They are often amazed to discover that proficient readers also skip words, phrases, sentences, paragraphs, and sometimes even pages, not necessarily reading from the first page of a work to the last, and that it is not cheating to do so.

The RMA process helps readers become aware that they are better readers than they think they are. Ken Goodman (in press) has termed this process revaluing. Readers who revalue themselves become confident and willing to take risks.

At the same time that we conduct research on RMA, we are involved in the use of RMA as an instructional strategy since many of the researchers with whom we work are classroom teachers. In this article, I focus on ways to involve readers, especially readers who are considered to be or consider themselves to be troubled readers, to participate in retrospective miscue analysis in classroom settings.

Planned Retrospective Miscue Analysis: An Instructional Tool

I used and researched a number of different instructional settings for retrospective miscue analysis. In this article, I discuss two such settings. In the first, RMA is a planned experience during which students ask questions about their miscues by listening to their own audiotaped readings as they follow a typescript of what they have read. This is done in a face-to-face conference between teacher and student or in small groups usually with the teacher as one member of the group. The second setting is in the classroom when there are specific moments in a school day during a variety of curricular experiences during which RMA is an incidental reading instructional strategy. During these critical teaching or learning moments either the students or the teacher decide to engage in talk about miscues and the reading process.

In order to organize for observational analysis of miscues, a traditional reading miscue inventory (RMI) (Y. Goodman et al., 1987) is collected. In this procedure, a reader reads a whole text orally without any help from others and retells the story or article after the reading. The RMI is tape-recorded. After the RMI has been collected, the teacher/researcher can take two different roads to planned retrospective miscue analysis. If a reader lacks confidence or has a teacher who believes the reader is not successful, the teacher/researcher may decide to preselect the miscues. For readers who generally are considered to be average or better readers, the teacher may involve the reader or readers in an examination of the whole reading from the beginning of the text during the RMA session. The decision about which procedure to follow depends on the teacher's purpose, taking into consideration the age and confidence level of the students. I discuss each of these possibilities separately.

Teacher Selection of Miscues

To preselect miscues, teachers first mark the miscues on a typescript of the material. They then analyze the quality of the miscues, searching for patterns that highlight each reader's abilities in using reading strategies and that reveal the reader's knowledge of the language cueing systems.

The teacher sets up a series of RMA sessions with the student after selecting five to seven miscues for a 40-minute session and planning the sequence of miscue presentation. The student reads a new selection for RMI purposes after each RMA session in order to demonstrate changes in reading strategies over time and to have new miscues for discussion purposes. At these sessions, it is helpful to have two tape recorders. One is used to listen to the recording of the original reading, and the second one is used to record the RMA session in order to keep track of the student's changes in attitudes and beliefs.

The teacher selects miscues initially to demonstrate that the reader is making very good or smart miscues. The initial sessions are planned to help readers realize that they are using strategies that support their meaning construction as they read. For example, teachers initially select high-quality substitution miscues that result in syntactically and semantically acceptable sentences and make little change in the meaning of the text. (The reader in the following examples is Armando, who will be introduced later.)

| Text: | All I have to do is move this stick up and down so the cream will turn into butter. |
| Reader: | All I have to do is move this stick up and down. Soon the cream will turn into butter. |

Or the teacher selects word or phrase omission miscues where the reader has retained the syntactic and semantic acceptability of the sentence.

| Text: | What do you do all day while I am away cutting wood... |
| Reader: | What do you do all day while I'm cutting wood. |

Or the teacher selects miscues that show good predictions followed by self-correction strategies only when necessary.

Text:	The big pig ran around and around the room.
Reader:	The big pig ran out.... (self-corrects to) around and around the room.

During subsequent RMA sessions, the teacher selects more complex miscue patterns that may show disruption to meaning construction. Examples include miscues that the reader unsuccessfully attempts to self-correct at first, but eventually reads as expected. The teacher and student examine each instance and discuss the cues the reader uses and what strategies eventually led to the expected response. During the discussions about the miscues, the teacher helps the reader to explore the reasons for the miscues and to see how knowledge of language and reading strategies can help resolve any problems encountered in the text.

The following questions help guide the discussion with the reader:

Does the miscue make sense? Or sound like language?

Did you correct? Should it have been corrected?

Does the word in the text look like the word substituted? Does it sound like it?

Why did you make the miscue?

Did it affect your understanding of the story/article?

Why do you think so? How do you know?

The following conversations between a teacher and Armando, a seventh-grade student whose miscues were used for the above examples, provide examples of these discussions.

Teacher:	Did what you did make sense?
Armando:	Yes.
Teacher:	Should you have corrected it?
Armando:	Yes.
Teacher:	Why?
Armando:	Because it didn't make sense with around and around.

Teacher:	Why do you think you read *ran out* before you corrected it?
Armando:	Because I thought he ran out of the house, like the woodman scared him out of the house.

Of all the readers with whom we worked in a research study of seventh graders (Y. Goodman & Flurkey, in press), Armando was most reluctant to talk about his strengths and abilities, yet at the same time he was able to discuss issues of language and the reading process with his teacher.

Text:	Then he climbed down from the roof.
Armando:	Then the... (self-corrects) Then he climbed down from the roof.
Teacher:	Did your miscue make sense?
Armando:	No.
Teacher:	Why not?
Armando:	Because it wouldn't say he or she climbed down.
Teacher:	Why did you miscue?
Armando:	I probably thought something else was going to happen.

The teacher's discussions with Armando provide evidence that many readers believe in the efficacy of the text. Through RMA discussions readers have the opportunity to demystify the power of the author and to consider their own roles as active readers. After a number of RMA sessions, Tomás, another seventh grader, begins to understand that he has the right to construct meaning.

Text:	I'm sure somebody left it here because it's boring.
Tomás:	I'm sure somebody let it to be because it's so boring.
Tomás:	It's so boring (commenting on what he heard).
Teacher:	OK. Let's talk about that one.
Tomás:	...It's so boring...there's more expression with so boring. 'Cause if you put, it's boring, you don't know what's boring really.... But if you say so, then he must be really bored, so it sounds better.

Teacher:	Did that miscue change the meaning of the sentence?
Tomás:	No, it made it better, I think.
Teacher:	Now let's listen to something else that happened in the sentence (rewinds the tape and listens again).
Tomás:	Left it to be... I guess I was reading, predicting the words [that] are going to come up. Left it to be (laughs). It's like... I think it makes sense. Left it to be...because to be means like let be...like some older talk, like let the snake be or like let the animal be.
Teacher:	Is that what you were thinking?
Tomás:	Yeah, like let it be. If it was there, don't touch it.
Teacher:	Someone let it be because it was so boring.
Tomás:	Yeah.... And I guess I have a lot of stuff in here in my brain and I guess sometimes some words get mixed up...and then sometimes it sounds OK in a way.

Students select their own miscues for discussion. If students are involved in the total process, including selecting the miscues to be discussed, the teacher doesn't have much preparation prior to the RMA session. This procedure is especially supportive of students revaluing themselves when two or more readers participate (Costello, 1992, in press; Worsnop, in press). In this case, one student volunteers to let the others listen to his or her audiotaped reading and retelling. Students work on their own in groups of up to four for about 30 minutes. After the students become experienced with the procedures, the teacher is involved only during the last few minutes to answer questions or to raise issues that push students to consider aspects of their reading they may not have attended to. Sarah Costello (1992, in press) calls this procedure Collaborative Retrospective Miscue Analysis (CRMA).

Any listener can stop the recorder when he or she hears something that is unexpected. Using the term *unexpected response* is in keeping with the notion that miscues are not mistakes but un-expected responses that occur for a variety of linguistic and cognitive reasons. When the tape recorder stops, students determine whether a miscue has occurred and then talk about the nature of the miscue. Students ask the reader questions similar to the ones asked in the previous procedures: Why did you make the miscue? Did you correct it? Should you have corrected it? Does the miscue make sense and sound like language? If it is a substitution miscue, does it look like the word or phrase for which it is substituted? Sometimes, these questions are on a form the students use. However, if the students participate in the procedure over a period of time, it is important to not allow the form to become formulaic and followed without thoughtful discussion.

If the teacher is not continuously part of the collaborative RMA group, he or she often presents strategy lessons to the whole class during which the students discuss the nature of the reading process (Y. Goodman & Burke, 1980). Through examples of miscue patterns, the teacher helps readers understand that not all miscues need to be corrected. The teacher helps the readers know that there are high-quality miscues that retain the syntactic and semantic acceptability of the text that indicate sophisticated reading. Through analysis and discussion of miscue patterns, the teacher highlights how readers predict and confirm and points out how the miscues reveal the reader's knowledge about the language cueing systems and reading strategies. The teacher engages the class in additional strategy lessons (Y. Goodman, Watson, & Burke, 1996) about the reading process. For example, it is easy to show readers that they are predicting when a strategy lesson is planned by choosing a cohesive section of a text that has an important repeated noun or verb omitted throughout. By using such selected slotting strategy lessons, the teacher explores with the students how they use their knowledge about the world and about language as they read.

The following is a transcript of a group of seventh graders as they focus on one miscue during a collaborative RMA session (Costello, 1992):

Text:	He stood in the hall gasping for breath.
Carolyn:	He stood in the hall gasping for his breath.
Carolyn:	Gasping for his breath instead of air.
Jose:	No, you said gasping for his breath.
Carolyn:	But it's *air*.
Kirb:	Where?
Jose:	You didn't say "air."
Carolyn:	Oh.
Kirb:	Where is *air*? It's supposed to be *breath*.
Carolyn:	OK. Who wants to tell me the answers: This is my miscue.
Terry:	Does it make sense?
Jose:	It does make sense!
Kirb:	It doesn't make sense there. I mean do you gasp for breath?
Carolyn:	Gasping for HIS breath! Does the miscue make sense? Yes, it does. I just added *his*.
Kirb:	It means the same thing.
Carolyn:	No, I shouldn't have changed it.
Kirb:	It would have been a waste of time.
Carolyn:	What I said makes more sense. Why do I think I made this miscue? Because I was predicting.

Carolyn made an additional miscue in listening to herself read. She thinks the text reads "gasping for air" and that she said "gasping for his breath." The group discusses this and then focuses on the acceptability of the miscue in the context of the story.

Involving students in planned sessions during which they become expert at talking about miscues and the reading process works successfully with students in upper elementary grades, middle schools, and secondary schools and with adults who do not value themselves as readers. For all ages, however, it is helpful to recognize the power of discussing miscues and how students read incidentally throughout the school day during appropriate moments.

Retrospective Miscue Analysis and Critical Moment Teaching

The teachers with whom I work in using retrospective miscue analysis are masters at making the most out of the critical moments that emerge whenever students ask serious questions about their reading. Students begin to talk seriously about the process of reading when their responses are treated with respect during discussions. An Australian fifth grader in a classroom where exploring the reading process is a common daily practice discussed his reading with me, showing me how he uses different language cues in order to understand what he is reading. At one point, he said in a confident and serious manner, "If you don't know what it is, you have a go at it."

The RMA critical moment teaching often takes place in a matter of a few minutes as the teacher supports the reader's move toward new understandings. The learner experiences an intuitive leap (Bruner, 1977)—the insightful "aha" moment. Critical learning/teaching moments can happen whenever teachers or students read aloud in the class, whenever the students ask questions about what they are reading or why the author has chosen to write in a certain way as they are struggling with new concepts or challenging language.

I credit teachers, as my colleagues in research and curriculum planning, for having taught me much about involving students in self-reflection of their miscues. I want the role of these teachers/researchers explicit because they have continuously influenced my own professional development and theoretical understandings of the reading process (Y. Goodman & Marek, in press). The most important learnings in classrooms are often the result of a critical teaching moment recognized and supported by a knowledgeable and successful classroom teacher. Teacher educators and researchers in universities and colleges need to help teachers and administrators value the importance of these moments and to document their occurrences.

When Teachers Make Miscues

Don Howard has taught primary grades for many years in southern Arizona and in the Chicago area. Don discovered early in his teaching that it wasn't necessary to pretend to make miscues in order to talk about them with his students. His students noticed most of the miscues he made spontaneously during his daily oral reading to them. As Don realized the teaching potential of the moments in which he made miscues, he began to exploit his miscues whenever they occurred. He talked with his students about how his miscues showed that he was a good reader and that they were his way of always trying to understand what he is reading.

Don believes that kids feel very comfortable when they see adults making mistakes. In an environment where the authority in the class makes mistakes, students can make mistakes as well. Students are willing to take risks because they become aware that mistake making is simply a natural part of learning. Don makes this last statement explicit during appropriate moments in the classroom and encourages his students through open-ended discussions to believe and talk this way themselves.

Don and his students explore the reasons learners make miscues. They decide together that some miscues are good ones and some are not, depending on whether the miscues make sense. The good miscues are celebrated and accepted as helpful to the students' learning. The other miscues need to be fixed, especially if they are important to the reader's comprehension. The reader decides which need to be corrected and which are unimportant. In the latter case, the reader usually decides not to worry because the miscues don't disrupt the meaning construction of the story or article.

Many teachers produce tape recordings for listening centers to accompany books they want kids to read or that are the students' favorites. I know teachers who spend hours re-reading to make the tapes completely accurate. I suggest to them that high-quality miscues be left on the tape and if a student notices, the teacher has another critical moment to explore the significance of a miscue and to reflect on its meaning.

Using Critical Moments During Reading Conferences

Don Howard also uses regularly scheduled reading conferences to help his students reflect on their effective reading strategies. Students bring a book that they are reading and start reading orally where they left off in their silent reading, or they choose from a carefully selected range of books, usually not accessible to the students, that Don sets aside for reading conferences. Don makes notes about their miscues and their reading strategies. When they finish their reading and complete a retelling, Don asks the students to discuss anything they noticed about their reading that they would like to talk about. By focusing on the reasons for their miscues and the range of strategies they use, the students come to appreciate the flexibility they have in selecting appropriate reading strategies. Don says that he and the kids talk about strategies and the role of making miscues daily.

Reading Instructional Episodes

Wendy Hood, a primary teacher in Tucson, Arizona, uses critical moment teaching when she leads a reading strategy group of second graders. She noticed one day, as the group was reading a story silently together, that none of the students knew the word *mirror* when they came to the sentence *He looked into the mirror* at the bottom of the page toward the end of *Nick's Glasses*. The story is a take-off on a folk tale of a wise man looking for his glasses and using logical elimination to find them—on his forehead. Nick is involved in a similar search in this story. Wendy noticed that when Eli came to the bottom of the page, he hesitated for a few seconds and then turned to the next page, which showed the main character's face centered within a frame. Eli looked back at the word on the previous page and said aloud, "That says mirror."

"How did you figure that out?" Wendy asked. Wendy queries kids' responses regardless of whether the responses are the expected ones or not. That way students don't conclude that she only questions them when their responses are wrong and they consider all of their answers thoughtfully.

Eli said, "I sounded it out. See…mmm-iiii-rrroooaaarrr." Wendy responded by saying, "You don't call that mirroar, do you? Take another minute and think about what you did."

Then Eli reported, "I knew he was going to find them. I wondered where he could be looking that started with an *m*. I then looked at the next page and saw him looking in the mirror and then looked back at the word and I knew it was *mirror*."

After the other kids discussed whether they agreed or disagreed with Eli's explanation and why, Wendy summarized the literacy lesson they all shared: "You did a lot of good things as you were reading. You knew that you wanted the story to make sense and knew he had to find his glasses. You knew that it would be in a place so you were looking for a place word; we call that a noun. You also used what you know about the sounds of the language because you looked at the first letter of the word. You used the illustration to help you and decided the word was mirror, and then you checked yourself by looking back at the word to see if all your thinking about it was right. You did a lot of hard work on that; you used a lot of good strategies and it worked for you."

When Wendy teaches kindergarten, she often discovers that a few children read conventionally but aren't aware of their own abilities. She helps such children think of themselves as readers by involving them in talking about their reading. In order to plan for such an experience, Wendy carefully selects the written text to suit the purpose of her interactions with the student. In order to work with Robin, for example, she selected a predictable book that had high correlation between text and illustration but that had an ending that shifted in a different way than the more common predictable books do.

Wendy chose "Eek, A Monster," a story from an out-of-print basal reader, in which boys and girls are chased by a monster. The language of the text builds on and repeats common phrases such as: *Boys. Boys run. Boys run up. Boys run down.* Toward the end there is a page where the pattern changes, eliminating the noun: *Jump up.* While reading, Robin demonstrates a number of things that he knows about reading. He knows how to handle a book in terms of directionality and moving continuously through the text page by page. He makes good use of the illustrations. But he also knows that the printed language that he reads as *Boys run* is different than what he says when he looks at the picture: "the boys are running." In other words, he knows that what he sees in the illustration and the written language do not match in any simplistic way.

Retrospective miscue analysis helps Robin discover his power over print. When Robin got to the page that says *Jump up*, he read, "Boys jump up." He looked closer at the print and read, "Boys." With his index finger, he touched the word *jump*, and again read, "boys"; he touched the word *up* and read, "jump." He picked up his finger, moved his head closer to the print, sat up triumphantly, and read, "jumped up."

Wendy used this critical moment to get this 5-year-old to reflect on his reading. "Tell me about what you just did."

Robin replied, "It was supposed to say *Boys* but there weren't enough words and that word is *jump* (pointing again to jump in the text). It has the *j*."

And Wendy said, probing a bit, "How did you know that wasn't *boys*?"

And he said, "It's *jump* like on the other page," and he turned back to a previous point in the text where the word *jump* was first introduced.

Wendy said, "That's a good thing to do when you read. You thought about what it would be and when it didn't match what you saw, you thought about it again."

And Robin responded, "I could read" and proceeded to finish reading the story.

Over the Back of a Chair

When Alan Flurkey moved to teaching first grade, he was surprised that first graders could talk about the reading process. He had used RMA with upper grade special education students and knew that they could engage in retrospective miscue analysis, but he didn't expect first graders to discuss reading with such sophistication. Alan often walked around the room when the students were reading independently, stopped at a child's desk, and asked him or her to keep reading but to read aloud so he could hear. One day, early in the school year, he stopped at Maureen's table, peering over her shoulder. Maureen produced a miscue, regressed to the beginning of the sentence, self-corrected, and read on:

> Text: As he turned the corner he saw the lion.
> Maureen: As he turned the corner he was…(regresses to beginning of sentence and rereads) As he turned the corner he saw the lion.

Alan wanted to help Maureen see the importance of the predicting and confirming strategy she was using. He waited until she came to the end of the page where there was a shift in the plot, and the following conversation took place.

Alan:	I noticed that near the top of the page you stopped, backed up and then continued to read, and I'm just wondering what you were thinking about. Why did you do that?
Maureen:	(pointing) You mean up here?
Alan:	Yes.
Maureen:	Well, when I got to the middle of the sentence, it didn't make sense so I just started over.
Alan:	What didn't make sense?
Maureen:	Well, I thought it was going to say, like, "…he was scared…," was scared of what was there…
Alan:	So then what did you do?
Maureen:	It didn't say that so I just started over.

Alan summarized for Maureen that she was employing predicting, confirming, and self-correcting strategies; that she was clearly aware of how and when she was using these strategies; and that she was able to discuss her reading strategies with confidence.

Critical moment teaching provides powerful learning experiences for teachers and kids and needs to be legitimatized in planning for reading instruction. Critical teaching moments not only document what knowledge students use as they read but also reveal the knowledge and capabilities of teachers. These important moments show what teachers know about the reading process, about language, and about learning. They show what teachers know about their students' reading and how to select materials to meet their students' needs.

Students who engage in retrospective miscue analysis become articulate about the reading process and their abilities as readers. In order to use language with confidence, students need to feel comfortable to make mistakes, to ask "silly" questions, to experiment in ways that are not always considered conventional. Readers who are confident, who develop a curiosity about how reading works, and who are willing to take risks in employing "keep going" strategies are most likely to become avid readers. They are willing to risk struggling with a text at times because they are confident that eventually their meaning construction will be successful. In addition, I have discovered that RMA provides an environment in which students become capable of talking and thinking about the reading process. When they are in environments where what they have to say about their reading and the reading of others is taken seriously, the language that is necessary to discuss the issues emerges. Through kidwatching using miscue analysis and RMA such insights into readers' abilities are readily available to every teacher/researcher.

Retrospective miscue analysis is not necessarily an easy strategy to put into practice because the procedure often means shifts in both teachers' and students' views about readers and the reading process. It means revaluing and learning to trust the learning process and to respect the learner. But I know of no experience that provides teachers/researchers with greater insights into the reader and the reading process. There is much left to learn about how readers of a range of ages talk and think about the reading process. I know that planned RMA sessions work well with middle school and older readers. I believe that, for the most part, younger readers are best served through more spontaneous conversations as reflected in critical moment teaching. All readers, including teachers, benefit from critical moment teaching, which most often turns into critical moment learning. There is no doubt in my mind that the teacher is the essential element in organizing classrooms that invite readers to think seriously and talk openly about reading and the reading process.

In closing I must make it clear that retrospective miscue analysis is a small part of a reading program. The procedures that I have described take place no longer than 40 minutes a few times a week for middle school children and older and much less than that for younger children. The heart of a reading program is using reading as a tool to enrich literacy experiences.

As students read and write to get in touch with their world, to discover worlds beyond theirs, to solve important problems, and to inquire into significant questions, RMA and related reading strategy instruction used selectively by knowledgeable teachers can support the development of lifelong readers.

Author Notes

The concepts of *demythify* and *demystify* are from Barbara Flores in personal conversation and presentations at conferences.

I use teacher/researcher to recognize the growing involvement of teachers in classroom research as well as to denote that either teachers or researchers may be engaged in RMA.

References

Allen, P., & Watson, D. (Eds.). (1977). *Findings of research in miscue analysis: Classroom implications*. Urbana, IL: ERIC and National Council of Teachers of English.

Bruner, J. (1977). *The process of education*. Cambridge, MA: Cambridge University Press.

Costello, S. (1992). *Collaborative retrospective miscue analysis with middle grade students*. Unpublished doctoral dissertation, University of Arizona, Tucson.

Costello, S. (in press). The emergence of an RMA teacher/researcher in retrospective miscue analysis. In Y. Goodman & A. Marek (Eds.), *Retrospective miscue analysis: Revaluing readers and reading*. Katonah, NY: Richard C. Owen.

Goodman, K. (1969). Analysis of oral reading miscues: Applied psycholinguistics. *International Reading Association, V*, 9–29.

Goodman, K. (1994). Reading, writing and written texts: A transactional sociopsycholinguistic view. In R.B. Ruddell, M.R. Ruddell, & H. Singer (Eds.), *Theoretical models and processes of reading* (4th ed., pp. 1093–1130). Newark, DE: International Reading Association.

Goodman, K. (in press). Revaluing. In Y. Goodman & A. Marek (Eds.), *Retrospective miscue analysis: Revaluing readers and reading*. Katonah, NY: Richard C. Owen.

Goodman, K., Bird, L., & Goodman, Y. (1990). *The whole language catalog*. Santa Rosa, CA: American School Publishers.

Goodman, K., Bird, L., & Goodman, Y. (1992). *The assessment supplement to the whole language catalog*. Santa Rosa, CA: American School Publishers.

Goodman, Y. (1978). Kidwatching: An alternative to testing. *National Elementary Principal*, *57*(4), 41–45.

Goodman, Y. (1985). Kidwatching: Observing children in the classroom. In A. Jagger & M. Trika Smith-Burke (Eds.), *Observing the language learner* (pp. 9–18). Newark, DE: International Reading Association.

Goodman, Y., & Burke, C. (1980). *Reading strategies: Focus on comprehension*. Katonah, NY: Richard C. Owen.

Goodman, Y., & Flurkey, A. (in press). Adapting retrospective miscue analysis for middle school readers. In Y. Goodman & A. Marek (Eds.), *Retrospective miscue analysis: Revaluing readers and reading*. Katonah, NY: Richard C. Owen.

Goodman, Y., & Marek, A. (1989). *Retrospective miscue analysis: Two papers* (Occasional Paper #19). Tucson, AZ: University of Arizona, Program in Language and Literacy.

Goodman, Y., & Marek, A. (Eds.). (in press). *Retrospective miscue analysis: Revaluing readers and reading*. Katonah, NY: Richard C. Owen.

Goodman, Y., Watson, D., & Burke, C. (1987). *Reading miscue inventory: Alternative procedures*. Katonah, NY: Richard C. Owen.

Goodman, Y., Watson, D., & Burke, C. (1996). *Reading strategies: Focus on comprehension* (2nd ed.). Katonah, NY: Richard C. Owen.

Worsnop, C. (in press). Using miscue analysis as a teaching tool: The beginnings of Retrospective Miscue Analysis. In Y. Goodman & A. Marek (Eds.), *Retrospective miscue analysis: Revaluing readers and reading*. Katonah, NY: Richard C. Owen.

Using Retrospective Miscue Analysis to Inquire: Learning From Michael

Patricia Tefft Cousin, Beth Berghoff, and Prisca Martens, Editors
Prisca Martens, Author

October 1998

I t was April. Michael, a third-grade student with learning disabilities (LD), and I had been working together on his reading twice a week since September. As part of our Retrospective Miscue Analysis (RMA) session, Michael listened to his audiotaped reading of the sentence in Figure 1 from *The One in the Middle Is the Green Kangaroo* (Blume, 1981).

After listening, Michael said that he heard himself substitute *over* for *around* and that he inserted *big*. He confidently explained that these were good miscues that made sense and showed he was predicting and thinking about the story. Michael's comments and responses demonstrated that he understood that reading is not about recognizing words to accurately reproduce the printed text but about constructing meaning. He valued his miscues as evidence that he was thinking and making sense of the text for himself as he read. This conversation with Michael about miscues and reading was very different than the talks we had had when we first began working together.

Michael and I first met when I asked the principal of his school if she could suggest the names of a few children having trouble with reading with whom I could work for a year. I wanted to understand more about why some children have difficulties with reading and how they can be better supported in becoming more proficient. This has been a driving inquiry for me, first as an elementary classroom teacher and now as a researcher working with children and as a teacher educator concerned with helping preservice teachers develop strategies to use with struggling readers in their own classrooms. On my journey of inquiry, I had already learned about miscue analysis and RMA. I had come to understand how readers' beliefs about reading, the reading process, and themselves as readers either constrain or liberate them. I realized that readers' beliefs about what reading is and how it is accomplished focus them on either predicting and constructing a meaningful text for themselves or on accurately reproducing the printed text in order to understand.

RMA had been used very successfully with older students and adults, helping them revalue reading as a transactive process of constructing meaning and revalue themselves as readers, learners, and language users (Y. Goodman, 1996; Goodman & Marek, 1996). I wondered if RMA could be used successfully with younger children. What did Michael believe about the reading process? Were those beliefs affecting his reading? Could I use RMA to help Michael revalue his own reading process and himself and become a more proficient reader?

In this column, I describe one inquiry journey Michael and I took together. After providing a brief background on RMA and Michael, I explain how I used RMA in my sessions with Michael and the learning and revaluing the happened for each of us.

Retrospective Miscue Analysis

Miscues are unexpected responses a reader makes to a text (K. Goodman, 1996). Research (Brown, Goodman, & Marek, 1996) documents that miscues are not random, capricious, or evidence of carelessness but reveal the logical predictions readers make based on their background knowledge, experience, and what they know about language and how language works. In miscue analysis, a teacher/researcher has a "window" (Goodman, 1970) into a reader's use of language systems (semantic/pragmatic, syntactic, and graphophonic) and reading strategies (sampling, inferring, predicting, con-

firming/disconfirming, and correcting) and into how proficiently the reader integrates these systems and cues to construct meaning in a text. (For more information on miscue analysis, see Goodman, Watson, & Burke, 1987, 1996.)

In retrospective miscue analysis (RMA), readers are invited to look through that window with the teacher/researcher to examine their own reading process and to evaluate, understand, and learn from it (Y. Goodman, 1996; Goodman & Marek, 1996). To prepare for RMA, the reader is first audiotaped reading and retelling a text following standard miscue analysis procedures. In the next session, the reader listens to him/herself read while following along in the original text and discusses selected miscues with the teacher/researcher. They discuss why a particular miscue was made, if it made sense, how much it resembles the printed text, if it was corrected, and if it needed to be corrected. Through these discussions over time, readers develop and more regularly use strategies for constructing the meaning of a text. The reading process is demystified, and readers revalue reading and themselves as readers.

Before working with Michael, I preselected high-quality miscues for us to consider in order to focus our time primarily on emphasizing his strengths. After listening to the tape and marking his miscues on the typescript, I examined the typescript asking, "Where is there evidence of Michael using strategies proficiently that I can

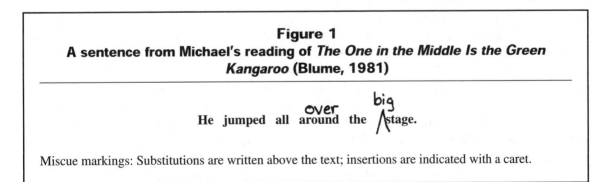

Figure 1
A sentence from Michael's reading of *The One in the Middle Is the Green Kangaroo* (Blume, 1981)

He jumped all ~~around~~ over the ^big stage.

Miscue markings: Substitutions are written above the text; insertions are indicated with a caret.

use to highlight strengths and help him understand and revalue the reading process and himself as a reader?" The miscues I chose included (a) uncorrected high-quality substitutions, omissions, and insertions that retained the meaning of the text and (b) self-corrections he made when his predictions did not make sense.

In our session, Michael listened to himself read the sentences with these selected miscues. Then we evaluated them and discussed how proficient readers use these same strategies to construct meaning. Just like proficient readers, he had self-corrected when his predictions didn't make sense and didn't correct when his substitutions, insertions, and omissions did make sense. The tape provided indisputable evidence of that. Gradually, the revaluing happened for Michael.

Michael's Story

On our meeting days, Michael was usually waiting or looking for me when I arrived at the school. Our sessions began with our sharing what was new in our lives. As an avid sports fan, Michael eagerly provided play-by-play descriptions of the football game he played in over the weekend and commented on professional games that he watched on television. He talked about his mom, other family members, his neighborhood friends, the latest escapades of his 1-year-old brother, and his church activities. Michael talked about school, projects he was working on, and reports he had to research and write. He was polite, friendly, cooperative, and cheerful, but he lacked confidence as a reader and learner.

Michael's difficulties with reading began when he entered kindergarten. His mother, Karen, related that she read to Michael regularly when he was a young child, but he had not shown a real interest in reading. Michael's kindergarten teacher described him as having difficulty focusing on letters and sounds. The following year he repeated kindergarten in an all-day program at a different school. Michael's difficulties with reading continued in first grade, and in second grade he was tested. The test results asserted Michael had learning disabilities in reading (decoding and comprehension), and spelling, and that he had Attention Deficit Disorder. He was put on medication in the spring of second grade. When there were no major changes in his behavior or achievement, Karen stopped the medication. I began working with Michael at the beginning of third grade. At that time, he received support from an aide in the classroom; twice a week he left the classroom to work on word meanings and associations and to see a reading specialist for additional help.

Michael's Beliefs About Reading and Himself as a Reader

To understand Michael as a reader and gain insight into the reasons for his difficulties with reading, I needed to know how he perceived reading and himself as a reader, the strategies he used, his view of good readers, and how he believed he could be a better reader. His answers to questions in the reading interview (Goodman & Marek, 1996; Goodman et al., 1987), comments during our conversations, and his reading of texts in our first sessions revealed those beliefs. The two strategies Michael named for dealing with something he didn't know when reading were to "sound it out" and to "ask the teacher." He thought that good readers usually read without difficulty and that when they do encounter difficulties, they sound out and always solve their problems. To help someone having trouble with reading, Michael said that he would get a friend to sound out the problem for the person. He thought his teacher would also help the person by sounding out. The most important thing about reading to Michael was remembering the words. When asked what he would like to do better as a reader, he stated he wanted to read the words better. I was not surprised that, when asked, he did not feel good about himself as a reader.

Figure 2
A portion of Michael's reading of "Strange Bumps" (Lobel, 1975a)

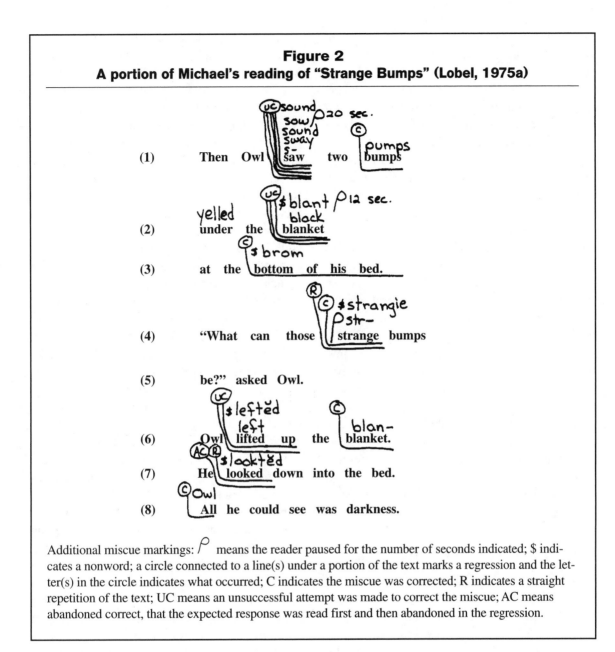

Additional miscue markings: ⌒ means the reader paused for the number of seconds indicated; $ indicates a nonword; a circle connected to a line(s) under a portion of the text marks a regression and the letter(s) in the circle indicates what occurred; C indicates the miscue was corrected; R indicates a straight repetition of the text; UC means an unsuccessful attempt was made to correct the miscue; AC means abandoned correct, that the expected response was read first and then abandoned in the regression.

Michael's perception of reading as remembering words and sounding out was confirmed in an analysis of his reading. One of the first stories he read was "Strange Bumps" (Lobel, 1975a), a portion of which is shown in Figure 2. Michael's miscues showed that his primary focus seemed to be on reproducing the printed text word by word, not on reading a meaningful story. He paused for extended periods of time to sound out (see lines 1 and 2), continued reading when his substitutions (nonwords or real words) didn't make sense and didn't sound like language (lines 1, 2, and 6), and abandoned a correct response for a nonword to produce something that

Using Retrospective Miscue Analysis to Inquire   155

graphically resembled the text more closely (see line 7). His reading was slow and labored; he seemed to be more concerned with working on small segments of text than constructing a coherent whole. He sometimes covered an unknown word with his finger and moved it back letter by letter as he tried to sound it out.

Even with these inefficient strategies, Michael's strengths were evident. His retellings of this and other stories were usually strong. (In this story, he told about Owl thinking his feet under the blanket were strange bumps, not being able to get rid of them, and going downstairs to sleep in his chair.) He sometimes corrected predictions or substitutions that didn't make sense (see lines 1, 3, 4, and 8) and solved problems as he read on and gathered more information in the text (see blanket in lines 2 and 6). While not shown in this portion, Michael also made some high-quality substitutions that he didn't correct.

Although Michael understood what he read, he did not construct meaning efficiently (Goodman, 1994). He needed to refine his understanding and comprehension of stories and greatly increase his use of efficient strategies. RMA provided opportunities to emphasize and affirm Michael's strengths for him and to build on them.

Supporting Michael Through RMA and Strategy Lessons

In our first RMA session, Michael and I explored high-quality miscues he made while reading *The Three Little Pigs* (Madden, 1971). One such miscue is seen in Figure 3. Michael's concern with remembering the words and reproducing the text was again apparent in our discussion. On several occasions Michael substituted *called* for *cried* or *cried* for *called*. Although he recognized the similarity in their meanings, he insisted that his substitution of *cried* for *called* was not good because he believed it did not make sense. From my perspec-

tive, predicting and substituting *cried* for *called* was a high-quality miscue and evidence of Michael's strength as a reader. He integrated his knowledge that he needed a past tense verb (syntactic cueing system), his understanding of what was happening in the story (semantic/pragmatic cueing system), and his awareness of the graphic cues in the text (graphophonic cueing system), all without creating a major change in the story meaning. For Michael, however, his miscue didn't make sense because it wasn't an accurate reproduction of the printed text. He couldn't appreciate the high quality of the miscue and his strength and knowledge in making it because it wasn't the word in the text.

This discussion was typical of those in our first several RMA sessions. It didn't matter to Michael what the quality of his miscues were; if his reading wasn't accurate, it didn't make sense. He was very resistant to the idea that he could still make sense if he changed the text, and that meaningful changes were evidence of his strength and knowledge of the story and language. To further help him understand this, I talked about the miscues I made while reading to him and used other strategy lessons such as selected deletions (Goodman et al., 1996). Sometimes I even covered a difficult text portion and talked him through what was happening in the story to encourage him to predict meaning using other available cues.

Then, in October, Michael read "Upstairs and Downstairs" (Lobel, 1975b). In our next session, Michael listened to the tape of the sentence in Figure 4 and identified his miscues. After we discussed how his miscues were meaningful and made sense, Michael asked why the author, Arnold Lobel, didn't phrase the sentence "'I am up,' said Owl" the way he had. Michael also suggested that Lobel could have written upstairs instead of up. Throughout this discussion it was clear that Michael was beginning to think about text differently. He was understanding that just as authors make decisions on how to create

---

Figure 3
A sentence from Michael's reading of _The Three Little Pigs_ (Madden, 1971)

---

          cried
The   wolf   called,   "Little   pig,   little   pig,   let   me   in."

Figure 4
A sentence from Michael's reading of "Upstairs and Downstairs" (Lobel, 1975b)

---

              said Owl
"I   am   up,"   he   said.

---

meaning in their stories, readers make those decisions too for themselves. He was seeing that as a reader, he had the responsibility of constructing a meaningful text that made sense to him. He was pushing the boundaries of his beliefs. The revaluing was beginning.

Our sessions continued through the fall and winter. We had conversations about the strategies of proficient readers and his strategies, miscues, and strengths. We talked about how the tape showed he knew how to use strategies like proficient readers do and that he just needed to do that more often. Michael began talking freely about these meaning-making strategies before there was evidence that he applied them to his reading. Gradually, though, he internalized his knowledge, and by November his reading and miscues showed that he was consciously beginning to monitor himself for meaning more closely. His long pauses, nonwords, and multiple attempts on unknown words decreased. And there was an increase in his meaningful substitutions, in his searching for and integrating cues in addition to graphic cues, and in his complex miscues showing less focus on remembering the words and more focus on constructing a meaningful text. He was more confident and articu-late about reading and strategies; he began referring to himself as a good reader. The revaluing was growing.

Michael's Growth

By spring, when asked what good readers do when they read, Michael named a variety of strategies, such as skip ahead and come back, substitute something that makes sense, and self-correct if reading is not making sense. In our RMA discussions about his miscues, he described his high-quality uncorrected substitutions as good because they made sense and explained his self-corrections as necessary for meaning. He pointed out how his miscues showed he was predicting and thinking.

During our final sessions together Michael read _The One in the Middle Is the Green Kangaroo_ (Blume, 1981). While there were still places where he used inefficient strategies, he was much more focused on making sense and constructing meaning as he read than he had been in September, as the excerpt in Figure 5 shows. Michael usually corrected when his miscues didn't make sense (see lines, 2, 4, 5, 7, and 8) and didn't correct when they did (see lines, 2,

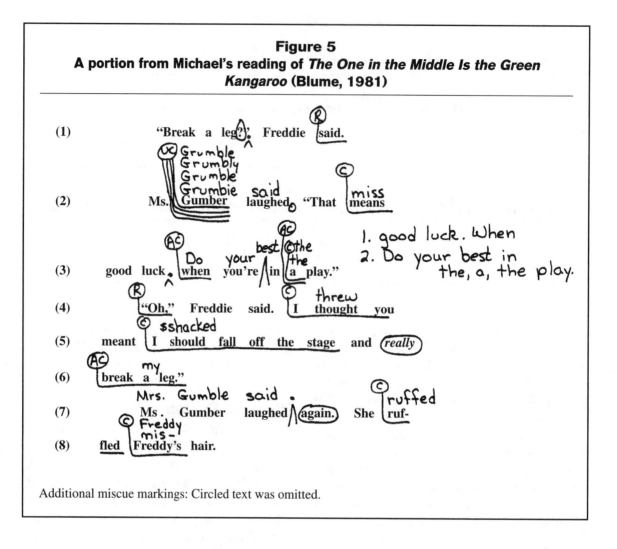

Figure 5
A portion from Michael's reading of *The One in the Middle Is the Green Kangaroo* (Blume, 1981)

(1) "Break a leg?" Freddie said.

(2) Ms. Gumber laughed, "That miss means

(3) good luck. when you're in a play."

1. good luck. When
2. Do your best in the, a, the play.

(4) "Oh," Freddie said. I thought you

(5) meant I should fall off the stage and really

(6) break a leg."
Mrs. Gumble said.

(7) Ms. Gumber laughed again. She ruffed

(8) fled Freddy's hair.

Additional miscue markings: Circled text was omitted.

3, and 5). He inefficiently made multiple attempts on Gumber in line 2 but later (line 7) efficiently made a name substitution and continued reading (the latter is what he usually did with this name). Twice he read the text correctly and abandoned that response for one that made more sense to him (see lines 3 and 6). (He, like Freddy in the story, was unfamiliar with the phrase "break a leg.") He transformed the syntactic structures in line 2 and line 3 to construct a parallel structure and text that made sense to him and didn't change the meaning of the story. His retelling was rich. Michael understood that his reading had to make sense to him and confidently took that challenge. The revaluing continued.

Conclusion

My experiences with Michael ended when the school year did. Michael's original view of the reading process as one of remembering the words had constrained and limited his ability to focus on meaning as he read. Understanding how central meaning is in reading and seeing his own strengths and building on them liberated him to use strategies flexibly with a goal of constructing a text that was meaningful and made sense to him. Michael was revaluing reading and himself as a reader.

When I reflected on our year together, I realized that although I had started this inquiry journey alone, Michael had joined me along the way. Through RMA Michael had become an inquirer too. Our discussions about reading and his miscues had caused him to wonder about (and revalue) reading and readers. And, just as importantly, RMA had helped him see reading as a process of inquiry, one in which he continually asked himself questions such as "Does what I am reading make sense?" and "Does what I am reading sound like language?" and, if the answers were "No," "What are my options for changing that?" By becoming an inquirer, asking questions and seeking answers, Michael had taken control of and responsibility for his reading and become a more empowered reader. While we didn't completely solve all of his difficulties, assuming responsibility for and control of his reading with a focus on constructing meaning was a step in the direction of being a proficient reader.

I learned and grew a lot through Michael that year. He helped me revalue RMA as a tool to support readers in becoming more proficient. RMA is a powerful process, one I hope others will use to invite struggling readers to inquire, learn, and grow in understanding the reading process.

References

Brown, J., Goodman, K., & Marek, A. (1996). *Studies in miscue analysis: An annotated bibliog-raphy*. Newark, DE: International Reading Association.

Goodman, K. (1970). Behind the eye: What happens in reading. In K. Goodman & O. Niles (Eds.), *Reading: Process and program* (pp. 3–38). Urbana, IL: National Council of Teachers of English.

Goodman, K. (1994). Reading, writing, and written texts: A transactional socio-psycholinguistic view. In R.B. Ruddell, M.R. Ruddell, & H. Singer (Eds.), *Theoretical models and processes of reading* (4th ed., pp. 1093–1130). Newark, DE: International Reading Association.

Goodman, K. (1996). *On reading*. Portsmouth, NH: Heinemann.

Goodman, Y. (1996). Revaluing readers while readers revalue themselves: Retrospective Miscue Analysis. *The Reading Teacher, 49*, 600–609.

Goodman, Y., & Marek, A. (1996). *Retrospective miscue analysis: Revaluing readers and reading*. Katonah, NY: Richard C. Owen.

Goodman, Y., Watson, D., & Burke, C. (1987). *Reading miscue inventory: Alternative procedures*. Katonah, NY: Richard C. Owen.

Goodman, Y., Watson, D., & Burke, C. (1996). *Reading strategies: Focus on comprehension*. Katonah, NY: Richard C. Owen.

Children's Books Cited

Blume, J. (1981). *The one in the middle is the green kangaroo*. New York: Dell.

Lobel, A. (1975a). Strange bumps. In *Owl at home* (pp. 19–29). New York: Harper & Row.

Lobel, A. (1975b). Upstairs and downstairs. In *Owl at home* (pp. 41–49). New York: Harper & Row.

Madden, D. (1971). *The three little pigs*. Glenview, IL: Scott, Foresman.

Miscue Analysis in the Classroom

Sheila W. Valencia, Editor
Lynn K. Rhodes and Nancy L. Shanklin, Authors

November 1990

Miscue analysis examines students' use of language cues and strategies, permitting a powerful "window onto the reading process" (Goodman, 1965). When strategies and cues are used ineffectively, comprehension is affected. With this in mind, Denver area Coordinators/Consultants Applying Whole Language (CAWLs) developed an instrument to help teachers efficiently gather miscue data. This instrument, the Classroom Reading Miscue Assessment (CRMA), has been successfully used in several Denver area school districts for four purposes: (a) to provide teachers with a framework for understanding the reading process, (b) to aid teachers in instructional planning, (c) to help students evaluate their own reading progress, and (d) to provide information to parents and policy makers about students' reading progress. (CAWLs consists of Chapter 1, language arts, and reading coordinators from area school districts and university consultants. The group has met monthly for the last 5 years.)

As CAWLs worked on developing the instrument, we tried to keep administration time to a minimum by trusting in trained teacher judgment. As a result, we chose to use Likert scales as part of the instrument. We decided to

trade off the depth, detail, and extensive quantification of data available from elaborate, formalized miscue analysis procedures for a more manageable, yet still informative, version of miscue analysis. The group believed this was necessary if the benefits of miscue analysis were to be realized in more classrooms.

Procedures

It takes about 10–15 minutes to administer the CRMA to an individual student. (See the sample CRMA on the next page.) Many teachers collect data on one or two students per day, using time allocated for sustained silent reading, Readers' Workshop, special classes, recess, or planning periods.

A key difference between the CRMA and most miscue analysis procedures is that CRMA miscue data are obtained without audiotaping the student's reading. Instead, the teacher records observations about the data heard "live" in the process of reading.

When selecting a passage for the CRMA, choose a whole text that has a sense of completeness such as a chapter, section of a content book, or whole story. The text should be one that the student has not read previously. The

160

Classroom Reading Miscue Assessment
Developed by Coordinators/Consultants Applying Whole Language

Readers' name _____   Date _____

Grade level assignment _____   Teacher _____

Selection read: _____

I.   What percent of the sentences read make sense?

_____ Number of semantically acceptable sentences

_____ Number of semantically unacceptable sentences

Sentence by sentence tally	Total

_____ % Comprehending score: $\dfrac{\text{Number of semantically acceptable sentences}}{\text{Total number of sentences read}} \times 100$ TOTAL_____

	Seldom	Sometimes	Often	Usually	Always
II. In what ways is reader constructing meaning?					
A. Recognizes when miscues have disrupted meaning	1	2	3	4	5
B. Logically substitutes	1	2	3	4	5
C. Self-corrects errors that disrupt meaning	1	2	3	4	5
D. Uses picture and/or other visual clues	1	2	3	4	5
In what ways is reader disrupting meaning?					
A. Substitutes words that don't make sense	1	2	3	4	5
B. Makes omissions that disrupt meaning	1	2	3	4	5
C. Relies too heavily on graphic clues	1	2	3	4	5

III. If narrative text is used:

	No		Partial		Yes
A. Character recall	1	2	3	4	5
B. Character development	1	2	3	4	5
C. Setting	1	2	3	4	5
D. Relationship of events	1	2	3	4	5
E. Plot	1	2	3	4	5
F. Theme	1	2	3	4	5
G. Overall retelling	1	2	3	4	5

If expository text is used:

	No		Partial		Yes
A. Major concepts	1	2	3	4	5
B. Generalizations	1	2	3	4	5
C. Specific information	1	2	3	4	5
D. Logical structuring	1	2	3	4	5
E. Overall retelling	1	2	3	4	5

passage should be about 300–500 words long. Passages that use natural language patterns, have strong narrative or expository structures, and contain pictures or diagrams are best. The text should be challenging enough that the student will make miscues that allow the teacher to observe the student's reading strategies but not so difficult that it causes the student to be frustrated. A reasonable rule of thumb is that the reader should not make more than one meaning-disrupting miscue in every 10 words.

Begin the assessment session with a statement like the following: "I would like you to read this passage aloud. If you come to a word you don't understand, do what you would normally do if you were reading alone. When you finish reading, I'll ask you to retell all you can remember. When we are all finished, I'll share with you what I found out about your reading."

If a student asks for assistance during the reading, the teacher should gently remind the student "Remember, do what you would if you were by yourself" or "Remember, we are pretending that I'm not here." The teacher should not help unless absolutely necessary to keep the reader involved because it is important for the teacher to uncover the student's repertoire of strategies used during independent reading. This information is invaluable for planning instruction.

As the student reads the text, the teacher determines each sentence to be semantically acceptable or unacceptable. To accomplish this, the teacher considers whether each sentence makes sense after self-corrections are taken into account. For example, if a student read the sentence *Marie decided to paint her new home* as *Marie decided to paint her new house*, it would be semantically acceptable. On the other hand, if the child read the sentence as *Marie decided to paint her new horse*, it would be semantically unacceptable.

By dividing the number of semantically acceptable sentences by the total number of sentences read, a comprehension (in-process comprehension) score may be figured. This provides an index of the degree to which the student constructs meaning effectively while reading. These data are recorded in Part I of the CRMA assessment form. Proficient readers will have a comprehension score of approximately 80% or above, adequate readers 60–80%, and poor readers 60% or below. These procedures and scoring guides are the same as those found in the Goodman, Watson, and Burke (1987) *Reading Miscue Inventory: Alternative Procedures*.

While tallying semantic acceptability, a teacher can also make general observations about the student's strategy and cue use. After the student finishes reading the text, record these observations in Part II of the CRMA form.

Next, the teacher listens to the student's unaided retelling of the story. Once the student is finished, ask "Is there anything else you can remember?" Finally, the teacher can use question probes to assess information not recalled spontaneously. Record observations about the retelling in Part III of the CRMA form, using the appropriate narrative or expository descriptors.

For the purpose of instructional planning, it is sufficient for the teacher to be internally consistent in determining ratings. If the instrument is to be used across classrooms or aggregated for policy making purposes, practice scoring sessions need to be held. In these sessions, teachers listen to tapes of a variety of readers, carefully rating and discussing a student's reading and retelling in order to achieve a common understanding of criteria and consistency across teachers.

Collecting and Analyzing Data for Different Purposes

To inform instruction. The primary purpose of the CRMA is to inform instruction by providing data which allow a teacher to make instructional decisions for specific students. Thus, the CRMA may be used to observe a student's reading at any time in the year when more specific information is needed. For example, a teacher could use the CRMA with those students whose progress is of most concern, to observe students reading various types of text, or to check students' progress at particular intervals (e.g., at the end of each grading period).

To communicate progress to parents. CRMA data allow a teacher to communicate to parents specific information regarding their child's reading progress. Teachers might also choose to audiotape students' reading of the same text at intervals throughout the year and let parents listen to the tape. Then the teacher and parents can witness the development of the effective use of reading strategies and text cues.

To respond to policy makers' requests for data. Educators are increasingly interested in performance data to supplement or replace norm-referenced tests. CRMA data may be aggregated to provide administrators with information to help make policy decisions such as the focus of staff development, allocation of resources, and special program needs.

The CRMA helps teachers gather important instructional information by providing a framework for observing students' oral reading and their ability to construct meaning. It is an alternative assessment tool many have found to be informative and easy to use.

Refer to the following resources for more information about miscue analysis procedures:

Allen, P.D., & Watson, D.J. (Eds.). (1976). *Findings of research in miscue analysis: Classroom implications.* Urbana, IL: ERIC/National Council of Teachers of English.

Goodman, K.S. (1965). A linguistic study of cues and miscues in reading. *Elementary English, 42,* 639–643.

Goodman, Y., Watson, D., & Burke, C. (1980). *Reading strategies: Focus on comprehension.* New York: Richard C. Owen.

Goodman, Y., Watson, D., & Burke, C. (1987). *Reading miscue inventory: Alternative procedures.* New York: Richard C. Owen.

Section Five

Formal Assessment Instruments

Over the past 10 years, numerous excellent formal assessment tools have been published in *The Reading Teacher*. This section includes six formal protocols on varied topics: phonemic awareness, phonics knowledge, knowledge of strategic reading processes, primary and intermediate motivation-to-read tools, and a reader self-perception scale. Each of these instruments can be used to reveal consequential information about large groups or individual readers, to inform instruction, and to provide information to parents and policy makers. The completed assessments also can be included in readers' portfolios.

Additional Readings

- Dole, J.A., Duffy, G.G., Roehler, L.R., & Pearson, P.D. (1991). Moving from the old to the new: Research on reading comprehension instruction. *Review of Educational Research*, *61*(2), 239–264.
- Falk-Ross, F. (1997). Developing metacognitive awareness in children with language difficulties: Challenging the typical pull-out system. *Language Arts*, *74*(3), 206–216.
- Freppon, P.A., & Dahl, K.L. (1991). Learning about phonics in a whole language classroom. *Language Arts*, *68*(3), 190–197.
- Mills, H., O'Keefe, T., & Stephens, D. (1992). *Looking closely: Exploring the role of phonics in one whole language classroom*. Urbana, IL: National Council of Teachers of English.
- Stahl, S.A., Duffy-Hester, A.M., Stahl, K.A.D. (1998). Theory and research into practice: Everything you wanted to know about phonics (but were afraid to ask). *Reading Research Quarterly*, *33*(3), 338–355.
- Wood, J.M. & Duke, N.K. (1997). Inside "Reading Rainbow": A spectrum of strategies for promoting literacy. *Language Arts*, *74*(2), 95–106.

A Test for Assessing Phonemic Awareness in Young Children

Hallie Kay Yopp

September 1995

Two decades ago few educational researchers and practitioners were familiar with the concept of phonemic awareness. In the last several years, however, phonemic awareness has captured the attention of many individuals in both the research community and elementary classrooms, and this interest is likely to continue for some time. What is this concept that has attracted so much attention? Phonemic awareness, as the term suggests, is the awareness of phonemes, or sounds, in the speech stream. It is the awareness that speech consists of a series of sounds.

Most youngsters enter kindergarten lacking phonemic awareness. Indeed, few are conscious that sentences are made up of individual words, let alone that words can be segmented into phonemes.

By the end of first grade, however, many (but not all) children have gained this awareness and can manipulate phonemes in their speech. For example, they can break spoken words into their constituent sounds, saying "/d/-/i/-/g/" when presented with *dig*; they can remove a sound from a spoken word, saying "rake" when asked to take the /b/ off the beginning of the word *break*; and they can isolate the sound they hear at the beginning, middle, or end of a word. [Parallel lines surrounding a letter (e.g., /z/) are used to represent the sound rather than the name of the letter. For the ease of the reader, typical spellings of sounds will be used within these lines rather than the symbols used in phonetic transcriptions.]

Research has demonstrated that phonemic awareness is a very important ability. There is substantial evidence that phonemic awareness is strongly related to success in reading and spelling acquisition (Ball & Blachman, 1991; Liberman, Shankweiler, Fischer, & Carter, 1974; Perfetti, Beck, Bell, & Hughes, 1987; Share, Jorm, Maclean, & Matthews, 1984; Treiman & Baron, 1983; Yopp, 1992a). In a review of the research, Stanovich (1986) concluded that phonemic awareness is a more potent predictor of reading achievement than nonverbal intelligence, vocabulary, and listening comprehension, and that it often correlates more highly with reading acquisition than tests of general intelligence or reading readiness. He restated this conclusion recently in the pages of *The Reading Teacher*: "Most importantly, [phonemic awareness tasks] are the best predictors of the ease of early reading acquisition—better than anything else that we know of, including IQ" (Stanovich, 1994, p. 284).

A growing number of studies indicate that phonemic awareness is not simply a strong predictor, but that it is a necessary prerequisite for success in learning to read (Bradley & Bryant, 1983, 1985; Tunmer, Herriman, & Nesdale, 1988; see also Stanovich's 1994 discussion). For instance, Juel and Leavell (1988) determined that children who enter first grade lacking phonemic awareness are unable to induce spelling-sound correspondences from print exposure or to benefit from phonics instruction. Likewise, in her comprehensive survey of the research on learning to read, Adams (1990) concluded that children who fail to acquire phonemic awareness "are severely handicapped in their ability to master print" (p. 412).

The importance of phonemic awareness appears to cut across instructional approaches, as evidenced by the work of Griffith, Klesius, and Kromrey (1992), who found that phonemic awareness is a significant variable in both whole language and traditional classrooms. Few now would argue with the claim that this ability is essential for reading progress.

Given the evidence that phonemic awareness is necessary for success in reading development, many researchers are sounding the call for teachers of young children to include experiences in their curriculum that facilitate the development of phonemic awareness (Griffith & Olson, 1992; Juel, 1988; Lundberg, Frost, & Petersen, 1988; Mattingly, 1984). Particular attention needs to be given to those children lacking this ability. How, then, can teachers determine which students have this critical ability?

Any assessment instrument used to identify those students needing more activities that facilitate phonemic awareness must be both reliable and valid. The purpose of this article is to provide teachers with a tool for assessing phonemic awareness, and to offer evidence of its reliability and validity. The Yopp-Singer Test of Phoneme Segmentation is easy to administer, score, and interpret.

The Instrument

The Yopp-Singer Test of Phoneme Segmentation measures a child's ability to separately articulate the sounds of a spoken word in order. For example, given the orally presented word *sat*, the child should respond with three separate sounds: /s/-/a/-/t/. Note that sounds, not letter names, are the appropriate response. Thus, given the four-letter word *fish*, the child should respond with three sounds: /f/-/i/-/sh/ (see the 22-item Test on the next page). Words were selected for inclusion on the basis of feature analysis and word familiarity. (For a complete discussion of the word list rationale, see Yopp, 1988.) The test is administered individually and requires about 5 to 10 minutes per child.

Children are given the following directions upon administration of the test:

Today we're going to play a word game. I'm going to say a word and I want you to break the word apart. You are going to tell me each sound in the word in order. For example, if I say "old," you should say "/o/-/l/-/d/" (The administrator says the sounds, not the letters.) Let's try a few words together.

The practice items are *ride*, *go*, and *man*. The examiner should help the child with each sample item—segmenting the item for the child if necessary and encouraging the child to repeat the segmented sounds. Then the child is given the 22-item test. Feedback is given to the child as he or she progresses through the list. If the child responds correctly, the examiner nods or says, "That's right." If the child gives an incorrect response, he or she is corrected. The examiner provides the appropriate response.

A child's score is the number of items correctly segmented into all constituent phonemes.

Yopp-Singer Test of Phoneme Segmentation

Student's name _____ Date _____

Score (number correct) _____

Directions: Today we're going to play a word game. I'm going to say a word and I want you to break the word apart. You are going to tell me each sound in the word in order. For example, if I say "old," you should say "/o/-/l/-/d/." (*Administrator: Be sure to say the sounds, not the letters, in the word.*) Let's try a few together.

Practice items: (*Assist the child in segmenting these items as necessary.*) ride, go, man

Test items: (*Circle those items that the student correctly segments; incorrect responses may be recorded on the blank line following the item.*)

1. dog	_____		12. lay	_____
2. keep	_____		13. race	_____
3. fine	_____		14. zoo	_____
4. no	_____		15. three	_____
5. she	_____		16. job	_____
6. wave	_____		17. in	_____
7. grew	_____		18. ice	_____
8. that	_____		19. at	_____
9. red	_____		20. top	_____
10. me	_____		21. by	_____
11. sat	_____		22. do	_____

The author, Hallie Kay Yopp, California State University, Fullerton, grants permission for this test to be reproduced. The author acknowledges the contribution of the late Harry Singer to the development of this test.

No partial credit is given. For instance, if a child says "/c/-/at/" instead of "/c/-/a/-/t/," the response may be noted on the blank line following the item but is considered incorrect for purposes of scoring. Correct responses are only those that involve articulation of each phoneme in the target word.

A blend contains two or three phonemes and each of these should be articulated separately. Hence, item 7 on the test, *grew*, has three phonemes: /g/-/r/-/ew/. Digraphs, such as /sh/ in item 5, *she*, and /th/ in item 15, *three*, are single phonemes. Item 5, therefore, has two phonemes and item 15 has three phonemes. If a child responds with letter names instead of sounds, the response is coded as incorrect, and the type of error is noted on the test.

Teachers of young children should expect a wide range of performance on this test. A sample of kindergartners drawn from the public schools in a West Coast city in the United States obtained scores ranging from 0 to 22 correct (0% to 100%) during their second semester. The mean (average) score was 11.78, with a standard deviation of 7.66 (Yopp, 1988, see below). Similar findings from a sample of kindergartners on the East Coast of the United States were reported by Spector (1992): the mean score was 11.39 with a standard deviation of 8.18.

Students who obtain high scores (segmenting all or nearly all of the items correctly) may be considered phonemically aware. Students who correctly segment some items are displaying emerging phonemic awareness. Students who are able to segment only a few items or none at all lack appropriate levels of phonemic awareness. Without intervention, those students scoring very low on the test are likely to experience difficulty with reading and spelling.

Teachers' notes on the blank lines of the test will be helpful in understanding each child. Some children may partially segment—perhaps dividing words into chunks larger than phonemes. These children are beginning to have an insight into the nature of speech. Others may simply repeat the stimulus item or provide nonsense responses regardless of the amount of feedback and practice given. They have very little insight into the phonemic basis of their speech. Still others may simply offer letter names.

If the letter names are random (e.g., given *red* the child responds "n-b-d-o"), the teacher learns that the child lacks phonemic awareness but knows some letter names. If the letter names are close approximations to the conventional spelling of the words (e.g., given *red* the child responds "r-a-d"), the teacher knows that either the child has memorized the spellings of some words or that he or she is phonemically aware and has mentally segmented the items, then verbally provided the examiner with the letters corresponding to those sounds—an impressive feat! The examiner should repeat the instructions in this case to make sure the child fully understands the task.

Data on the Instrument

A number of years ago I undertook a study to compare tests of phonemic awareness that appeared in the literature and to examine the reliability and validity of each (Yopp, 1988). Nearly 100 second-semester kindergarten youngsters drawn from three public elementary schools in a southern California school district that serves children from a lower middle to an upper middle class population were each administered 10 different phonemic awareness tests over a period of several weeks. Children ranged in age from 64 to 80 months with an average age of 70 months, and were predominantly white, with 1% black, 2% Asian, and 15% with Spanish surnames. All children were fluent English speakers.

Performance on the phonemic awareness tests was compared, the reliability of each test was calculated, and a factor analysis was conducted to determine validity. One of the tests in the battery, the Yopp-Singer Test of Phoneme Segmentation, had a reliability score (Cronbach's alpha) of .95, indicating that it can be appropriately used in the assessment of individuals. Experts in tests and measurement tell us that instruments should have reliability coefficients above .85 (Hills, 1981) or even .90 (Jensen, 1980) if they are to be used to make decisions about individuals.

Analyses also indicated that the Yopp-Singer Test is a valid measure of phonemic awareness. Construct validity was determined through a factor analysis (for details see Yopp, 1988). Predictive validity was determined by collecting data on the reading achievement of the same students each year beginning in kindergarten and concluding when the students were in sixth grade;

spelling achievement data were obtained in Grades 2 to 6. Thus, 7 years of longitudinal data are available. (See Yopp, 1992a for details on this study.) A test of nonword decoding was administered in kindergarten. In order to determine reading and spelling achievement in Grades 1 through 6, records of the students' performance on the Comprehensive Test of Basic Skills (CTBS, 1973), a timed, norm-referenced, objectives based test, were obtained. This standardized test, widely used by school districts as part of their regular testing program, includes word attack, vocabulary, comprehension, and spelling subtests in the reading and spelling achievement battery. These tests are described in Table 1.

Table 1
Descriptions of reading and spelling tests used to determine predictive validity

Nonword Reading Test
> The nonword reading test was administered for the purpose of determining each child's ability to use sound-symbol correspondences to decode nonwords. Children were assessed on their ability to sound and blend printed nonwords such as *paz* and *kov*.
> Administered in kindergarten.

CTBS Word Attack Subtest
> The word attack section requires students to identify letters corresponding to the initial or final single consonant, cluster, or digraph sounds or the medial vowels heard in orally presented words. Recognition of sight words is also measured in this subtest.
> Administered during Grades 1 through 3.

CTBS Vocabulary Subtest*
> The vocabulary section measures children's ability to identify a word associated with an orally presented category or definition, in addition to identifying same-meaning words or unfamiliar words in context.
> Administered during Grades 1 through 6.

CTBS Reading Comprehension Subtest*
> The reading comprehension section is used to measure children's comprehension of both sentences and stories. Children are asked to respond to objective questions after reading each selection.
> Administered during Grades 1 through 6.

CTBS Spelling Subtest
> The spelling section measures children's ability to recognize correctly spelled words.
> Administered during Grades 2 through 6.

*A "total" reading score is generated for each child that combines the vocabulary and comprehension subtests.

Table 2
Correlation of performance on phonemic awareness task administered in Grade K with performance on reading and spelling subtests, Grades K–6

Grade level			Subtests			
	Nonword	Word attack	Vocabulary	Comprehension	Total	Spelling
K	.67**					
1		.46**	.66**	.38**	.62**	
2		.62**	.72**	.55**	.67**	.53**
3		.56**	.66**	.62**	.67**	.44**
4			.51**	.62**	.58**	.60**
5			.56**	.57**	.59**	.55**
6			.78**	.66**	.74**	.46**

*$p<.05$ **$p<.01$

Table 2 presents the correlation between performance on the Yopp-Singer Test of Phoneme Segmentation administered in kindergarten and all subtests on the reading and spelling achievement battery throughout the grade levels as well as the kindergarten nonword reading measure. Each correlation is significant: Performance on the Yopp-Singer Test of Phoneme Segmentation has a moderate to strong relationship with performance on the nonword reading test given in kindergarten and with the subtests of the CTBS—word attack, vocabulary, comprehension, and spelling (and the total score)—through Grade 6. Thus, the phonemic awareness test has significant predictive validity.

Because reading and spelling achievement are related to phonemic awareness and to future reading and spelling achievement, these impressive correlations (as high as .78) do not address the question of whether a measure of phonemic awareness truly contributes to the prediction of reading and spelling performance years later, independent of previous reading and spelling achievement. For instance, a significant correlation between phonemic awareness in kinder-

garten and reading in Grade 1 might be obtained because reading performance in kindergarten and Grade 1 are highly correlated, and reading performance in kindergarten and phonemic awareness in kindergarten are highly correlated.

Thus, the relationship between phonemic awareness in kindergarten and reading in first grade might simply be a byproduct of these other relationships. We want to know whether a measure of phonemic awareness obtained in kindergarten contributes to the prediction of future reading and spelling achievement above and beyond the contribution that past reading and spelling achievement makes on future achievement in reading and spelling. Does performance on a measure of phonemic awareness offer us any unique insights into future performance in reading and spelling?

In order to rule out the effect of reading and spelling achievement over the years on subsequent reading and spelling performance, partial time-lag correlations were also conducted. These correlations are "partial" in that they partial out, or eliminate, the effects of one variable (in this case, past reading or spelling perfor-

Table 3
Partial time-lag correlation of performance on phonemic awareness task administered in Grade K with performance on reading and spelling subtests, Grades 1–6, controlling for performance on reading and spelling subtests administered the previous year

Grade level	Subtests				
	Word attack	Vocabulary	Comprehension	Total	Spelling
1	.33**	.55**	.08	.43**	
2	.51**	.36**	.43**	.32**	
3	.20	.19	.43**	.33**	.11
4		−.05	.38**	.10	.43**
5		.54**	.18	.36*	.26
6		.51**	.45**	.47**	−.05

*p < .05   **p < .01

mance) on another (in this case, later reading or spelling performance); they are "time-lag" in that they examine the relationship between two variables over time (earlier phonemic awareness performance and later reading or spelling achievement). The partial time-lag correlations are presented in Table 3.

Each correlation coefficient indicates the strength of the relationship between performance on the phonemic awareness test in kindergarten and performance on reading and spelling subtests in Grades 1–6 when the previous year's achievement in these areas has been controlled. Thus, the .54 correlation found in Table 3 between phonemic awareness in kindergarten and vocabulary in Grade 5 is the strength of the relationship after fourth-grade vocabulary performance has been accounted for.

Table 3 reveals that most of the correlations remain significant, some as high as .51, .54, and .55. Thus, they reveal that scores on the Yopp-Singer Test of Phoneme Segmentation make a unique contribution to predicting students' read-

ing and spelling achievement above and beyond their previous achievement in these areas.

The power of a 5- to 10-minute, 22-item test administered in kindergarten to predict students' performance in reading and spelling achievement years later, even after controlling for previous reading and spelling achievement, is quite surprising. In his review of the research on phonemic awareness, Stanovich (1994) noted the strong relationship between performance on a number of simple, short phonemic awareness tasks and reading acquisition and suggests that the power of such simple tasks to predict reading acquisition is one of the reasons for the tremendous research energy currently devoted to this line of inquiry.

Implications

What do these findings mean for teachers? They mean that we now have a tool—one that is both valid and reliable as well as simple and quick to administer—that can be used to determine a child's phonemic awareness, and we have the knowledge that performance on this measure is significantly related to a child's achievement in reading and spelling for years to come.

What can we do with this information? We can identify children quite early who are likely to experience difficulty in reading and spelling and give them appropriate instructional support. Fortunately, a growing body of evidence indicates that training of phonemic awareness is possible and that it can result in significant gains in subsequent reading and spelling achievement (Ball & Blachman, 1991; Bradley & Bryant, 1983; Cunningham, 1990; Lie, 1991; Lundberg et al., 1988). Thus, a child need not be labeled "phonemically unaware" and therefore inevitably a "poor" reader. Phonemic awareness is an ability that teachers and reading/language arts specialists can develop in many students.

Some researchers have argued that systematic training in phonemic awareness should be part of every youngster's education before the onset of formal reading instruction (Mattingly, 1984; Tunmer et al., 1988). The need for this, of course, depends upon the abilities of the individual children in the classroom. Further, in many classrooms the onset of formal reading will be difficult to identify—there is no onset of "formal" instruction and reading is not differentiated from prereading.

A growing number of teachers hold an emergent literacy perspective, viewing literacy as an evolving process that begins during infancy and they provide a wealth of valuable literacy experiences for children very early on. Certainly these experiences should not be withheld until children become phonemically aware!

However, it is important for teachers and other practitioners to appreciate that children will likely make little sense of the alphabetic principle without phonemic awareness, and so phonemic awareness should be developed as part of the larger literacy program for many children. Fortunately, phonemic awareness activities can be readily incorporated into preschool, kindergarten, and early primary grade classrooms. Recent articles in *The Reading Teacher* (Griffith & Olson, 1992; Yopp, 1992b) have provided suggestions for helping young children focus on the sounds of language through stories, songs, and games. A few suggestions will be highlighted here.

Griffith and Olson (1992) and I (Yopp, 1995) suggest that one simple means to draw children's attention to the sound structure of language is through the use of read-aloud books. Many children's books emphasize speech sounds through rhyme, alliteration, assonance, phoneme substitution, or segmentation and offer play with language as a dominant feature. For instance, P. Cameron's *"I Can't," Said the Ant* (1961) makes use of a simple rhyme scheme, Seuss's *Dr. Seuss's ABC* (1963) uses alliteration as each letter of the alphabet is introduced, and his *There's a Wocket in My Pocket* (1974) incorporates initial phoneme substitution to create a household of humorous nonsense creatures.

I have suggested (Yopp, 1995) that such books can be read and reread, their language can be enjoyed and explored in class discussions, predictions that focus on language can be encouraged, and additional verses or alternate versions of the texts can be created using the language patterns provided. (See Yopp, 1995, for an annotated bibliography of books to develop phonemic awareness.)

A guessing game that I have used successfully both with groups of children and in individualized settings is "What am I thinking of?" (Yopp, 1992b). This game encourages children to blend orally spoken sounds together. The teacher tells the children a category and then speaks in a segmented fashion the sounds of a particular item in that category. For instance, given the category "article of clothing," the teacher might say the following three sounds: "/h/-/a/-/t/." Children's attempts to blend the sounds together to say "hat" are applauded and the game continues. Eventually, children may become the leaders and take turns providing their peers with segmented words for blending.

Categories may be selected to relate to curriculum areas under investigation (e.g., "I'm thinking of one of the types of sea animals we have been learning about—it is a /c/-/r/-/a/-/b/") or as an extension of integrated literacy experiences. When teaching about bears and their habitats, teachers may encourage children to write about bears, listen to stories about bears, view films about bears, create art projects involving bears, and learn poems and songs about bears. After singing the song, "The bear went over the mountain," children may play the guessing game to hypothesize the kinds of things seen by the bear on his outing (A Treasury of Literature, 1995)—"he saw a /t/-/r/-/ee/."

Common children's songs can be easily altered to emphasize the sounds of language. For instance, the initial sounds of words can be substituted. Instead of "merrily, merrily, merrily, merrily" in "Row, Row, Row Your Boat," children can suggest other sounds to insert in the initial position—"jerrily, jerrily, jerrily, jerrily" or "terrily, terrily, terrily, terrily." Young children often find such manipulations of sounds amusing and are likely to be heard singing nonsensical lyrics on the playground.

Concrete objects may help children attend to the sounds in speech. Elkonin boxes have been used in Reading Recovery to help low achieving readers focus on the sounds in words (Clay, 1985). A series of connected boxes are drawn across a page. The number of boxes corresponds to the number of sounds in a target word. The word chick, for example, is represented by three boxes. As the teacher slowly says the word, he or she models moving an object such as a chip into each box (from left to right) as each sound is articulated. The child eventually takes over the process of articulating the word and moving the objects into place.

Ultimately, the moving of chips into the boxes is replaced by the writing of letters in the boxes. (In the case of chick two letters are written in the first box because two letters spell the first sound: ch. Likewise, two letters are written in the third and final box: ck.) This activity is purposeful in the larger context of literacy acquisition when used to support children as they attempt to record thoughts or communicate in writing. (For a similar activity to facilitate phonemic awareness and support invented spelling, see Cunningham & Cunningham, 1992.)

Note that these activities fit into a meaning-based framework. Phonemic awareness should not be addressed as an abstract isolated skill to be acquired through drill type activities. It can be a natural, functional part of literacy experiences throughout the day.

Use of the Test

The Yopp-Singer Test of Phoneme Segmentation was designed for use with English speaking kindergartners. It may be used as a general assessment tool in order for teachers to learn more about their students and so develop suitable experiences; or it may be used selectively as teachers observe individual children experiencing difficulty with literacy-related tasks. Certainly, it need not be administered to the child who is already reading. Independent reading implies the existence of phonemic awareness. Further, phonemic awareness is not an end to itself—rather, it is one aspect of literacy development.

First-grade teachers, too, may wish to administer the test to students at the beginning of the school year in order to determine the phonemic awareness needs of the children in the classroom. Reading/language arts specialists or clinicians who work with children experiencing difficulty in literacy acquisition may also wish to assess their students' phonemic awareness as part of a larger diagnostic survey. And, although there are currently no data regarding the use of this particular test with older populations, we know that often older nonreaders lack phonemic awareness.

This instrument may be helpful to teachers of older individuals, including adult emerging readers, as they begin to build a profile of the strengths and needs of the individuals with whom they work. If phonemic awareness is poor, then it is appropriate to include activities that support its development in the larger picture of literacy experiences.

Should students who are limited in English proficiency be given this test? There are no data on using this test with an EL (English learner) population. Further, the issue is problematic since not only is there a potential problem with understanding task directions and familiarity with vocabulary (recall that the items on the test were selected, in part, on the basis of word familiarity), but there is also the possibility that performance on the test could be influenced by the fact that some speech sounds that exist in the English language may not exist in a student's dominant language.

Research does indicate that phonemic awareness is a critical variable in languages that have an alphabetic orthography (i.e., ones that map speech at the level of the phoneme rather than larger units). Therefore, the ideas presented in this article apply to children learning to read in an alphabetic script. The next step for educational researchers, therefore, is to develop reliable, valid assessment tools in other alphabetic languages to help teachers working with populations of children who are reading in languages other than English.

Conclusion

One of many insights that individuals must gain along the path to literacy is phonemic awareness. Research has shown that phonemic awareness is a more potent predictor of success in reading than IQ or measures of vocabulary and listening comprehension, and that if it is lacking,

emergent readers are unlikely to gain mastery over print. However, teachers can provide activities that facilitate the acquisition of phonemic awareness. With an assessment device readily available, practitioners can quickly identify those children who may benefit most from phonemic awareness activities and reduce the role that one factor—phonemic awareness—plays in inhibiting their success in reading and spelling.

References

Adams, M.J. (1990). *Beginning to read: Thinking and learning about print*. Cambridge, MA: MIT Press.

Ball, E.W., & Blachman, B.A. (1991). Does phoneme segmentation training in kindergarten make a difference in early word recognition and developmental spelling? *Reading Research Quarterly, 26*, 49–66.

Bradley, L., & Bryant, P. (1983). Categorizing sounds and learning to read: A causal connection. *Nature, 301*, 419–421.

Bradley, L., & Bryant, P. (1985). *Rhyme and reason in reading and spelling*. Ann Arbor, MI: University of Michigan Press.

Cameron, P. (1961). *"I can't," said the ant*. New York: Coward-McCann.

Clay, M.M. (1985). *The early detection of reading difficulties* (3rd ed.). Portsmouth, NH: Heinemann.

Cunningham, A.E. (1990). Explicit versus implicit instruction in phonemic awareness. *Journal of Experimental Child Psychology, 50*, 429–444.

Cunningham, P.E., & Cunningham, J.W. (1992). Making Words: Enhancing the invented spelling-decoding connection. *The Reading Teacher, 46*, 106–115.

Griffith, P.L., Klesius, J.P., & Kromrey, J.D. (1992). The effect of phonemic awareness on the literacy development of first grade children in a traditional or a whole language classroom. *Journal of Research in Childhood Education, 6*, 86–92.

Griffith, P.L., & Olson, M.W. (1992). Phonemic awareness helps beginning readers break the code. *The Reading Teacher, 45*, 516–523.

Hills, J.R. (1981). *Measurement and evaluation in the classroom* (2nd ed.). Columbus, OH: Charles E. Merrill.

Jensen, A.R. (1980). *Bias in mental testing*. New York: Free Press.

Juel, C. (1988). Learning to read and write: A longitudinal study of 54 children from first through fourth grades. *Journal of Educational Psychology, 80,* 437–447.

Juel, C., & Leavell, J.A. (1988). Retention and non-retention of at-risk readers in first grade and their subsequent reading achievement. *Journal of Learning Disabilities, 21,* 571–580.

Liberman, I.Y., Shankweiler, D., Fischer, F.W., & Carter, B. (1974). Explicit syllable and phoneme segmentation in the young child. *Journal of Experimental Child Psychology, 18,* 201–212.

Lie, A. (1991). Effects of a training program for stimulating skills in word analysis in first-grade children. *Reading Research Quarterly, 23,* 263–284.

Lundberg, I., Frost, J., & Petersen, O. (1988). Effects of an extensive program for stimulating phonological awareness in preschool children. *Reading Research Quarterly, 23,* 263–285.

Mattingly, I.G. (1984). Reading, linguistic awareness, and language acquisition. In J. Downing & R. Valtin (Eds.), *Language awareness and learning to read* (pp. 9–25). New York: Springer-Verlag.

Perfetti, C., Beck, I., Bell, L., & Hughes, C. (1987). Phonemic knowledge and learning to read are reciprocal: A longitudinal study of first grade children. *Merrill-Palmer Quarterly, 33,* 283–319.

Seuss, Dr. (1963). *Dr. Seuss's ABC*. New York: Random House.

Seuss, Dr. (1974). *There's a wocket in my pocket*. New York: Random House.

Share, D., Jorm, A., Maclean, R., & Matthews, R. (1984). Sources of individual differences in reading acquisition. *Journal of Educational Psychology, 76,* 1309–1324.

Spector, J.E. (1992). Predicting progress in beginning reading: Dynamic assessment of phonemic awareness. *Journal of Educational Psychology, 84,* 353–363.

Stanovich, K.E. (1986). Matthew effects in reading: Some consequences of individual differences in the acquisition of literacy. *Reading Research Quarterly, 21,* 360–407.

Stanovich, K.E. (1994). Romance and reason. *The Reading Teacher, 47,* 280–291.

A treasury of literature. (1995). Orlando, FL: Harcourt Brace.

Treiman, R., & Baron, J. (1983). Phonemic-analysis training helps children benefit from spelling-sound rules. *Memory and Cognition, 11,* 382–389.

Tunmer, W., Herriman, M., & Nesdale, A. (1988). Metalinguistic abilities and beginning reading. *Reading Research Quarterly, 23,* 134–158.

Yopp, H.K. (1988). The validity and reliability of phonemic awareness tests. *Reading Research Quarterly, 23,* 159–177.

Yopp, H.K. (1992a). *A longitudinal study of the relationships between phonemic awareness and reading and spelling achievement*. Paper presented at the annual meeting of the American Educational Research Association, San Francisco, CA.

Yopp, H.K. (1992b). Developing phonemic awareness in young children. *The Reading Teacher, 45,* 696–703.

Yopp, H.K. (1995). Read-aloud books for developing phonemic awareness: An annotated bibliography. *The Reading Teacher, 48,* 538–542.

Further Validation and Enhancement of the Names Test

Frederick A. Duffelmeyer, Anne E. Kruse,
Donna J. Merkley, and Stephen A. Fyfe

October 1994

To become proficient readers, students must develop and successfully apply strategies for decoding unfamiliar words. Among the three major strategies for deciphering new words—knowledge of letter-sound correspondences, word structure clues, and context clues—knowledge of letter-sound correspondences, or phonics, appears to be the most crucial (Adams, 1990; Perfetti, 1991). Although many children induce letter-sound correspondences on their own, others are dependent upon direct, systematic instruction (Adams, 1990; Ehri & Wilce, 1985; Stahl, 1992). Thus, at any given grade there will exist among students a wide range in phonics ability. This underscores the importance of assessing students prior to implementing phonics instruction, regardless of the overall nature of the reading program (e.g., basal, whole language).

It appears, however, that the assessment-prior-to-instruction practice is seldom followed, due mainly to the absence of an easy-to-administer, reliable, and valid test of students' phonics ability (Groff, 1986). The validity requirement is particularly important. Most phonics tests are group paper-and-pencil tests which require students to select from among several options the letter, letter combination, or word that corresponds to either a picture or to a word spoken by the examiner. A task of this sort does reveal something about students' knowledge of letter-sound correspondences. As Pikulski and Shanahan (1980) have pointed out, however, it is the exact opposite of the task students face in reading: When reading, students convert written symbols into spoken sounds, whereas in group paper-and-pencil tests, it is the other way around. In other words, group paper-and-pencil tests assess encoding (converting sound to print) rather than decoding (converting print to sound).

A more valid way to assess phonics ability is to have students attempt to read printed words. This is not as easy as it sounds, however. If high frequency (common) words are used, students may know them at sight, in which case one is assessing whole word recognition rather than the ability to apply knowledge of letter-sound correspondences. On the other hand, if low frequency (uncommon) words are used, they may not be in the students' listening vocabulary, in which case students are deprived of the positive reinforcement of arriving at a pronunciation of a word they know. (The latter disadvantage also applies to the use of nonsense words).

To sidestep this high/low frequency problem, Cunningham (1990) developed an easy to administer phonics assessment, called the Names Test, which requires decoding rather than encoding. As Cunningham states:

> There is one type of word that is not often seen in print but can be found in most children's listening vocabularies: persons' names. As children watch television and movies and interact with peers and adults in their neighborhoods and schools, they are constantly hearing first and last names they don't see in print. As a result, most children have many more names in their listening vocabularies than in their reading vocabularies. This provides an ideal source of words for use in assessing decoding skills. (p. 125)

Briefly, Cunningham's test (see top half of Table 1) consists of 25 pairs of first and last names selected to meet four criteria: (a) they are not some of the most common names; (b) they are fully decodable (i.e., they sound the way they are spelled); (c) they represent a sampling of the most common phonics elements (e.g., consonant blends, short vowels); and (d) they represent a balance of shorter and longer namers. Admittedly, several of the names (e.g., Jay, Tim, Chuck, Glen) could be sight words for many students, older children in particular. Therefore, the previously mentioned high frequency problem is not avoided altogether. However, it would appear that a large majority of the names would not be in most students' sight vocabulary, and are therefore appropriate for their intended use.

The Names Test is administered individually. As the student reads the names aloud, the examiner records a check mark on a scoring sheet (protocol) for each name read correctly (i.e., according to English spelling rules) and phonetic spellings for names which are mispronounced. Afterward, the examiner analyzes the results to determine the student's strengths and weaknesses in phonics. For example, a student may experience little or no difficulty with consonant blends, but moderate to serious difficulty with short vowels.

Cunningham's rationale for employing the Names Test and the ease with which it can be administered are appealing qualities. However, to truly be useful a test must be valid and reliable. Validity refers to how well a test measures what it claims to measure. One method of determining validity is to compare the results of the test under study with a second established instrument believed to measure the same ability. Reliability refers to how consistently a test measures the ability being evaluated. If a test is reliable, a person would receive the same (or nearly the same) score on repeated testings. A test's reliability can be estimated with a statistic called a reliability coefficient. One method of obtaining a reliability coefficient is to divide the test into odd-numbered and even-numbered items after it is administered, and then correlate the two sets of scores. This procedure is called a split-half reliability estimate.

To gain information about its validity and reliability, Cunningham field tested the Names Test with 120 randomly selected students in Grades 2 through 5 (30 per grade). With respect to validity, Cunningham reported that second graders obtained an average score of 22.6, compared to an average score of 47.3 for fifth graders. This provided initial evidence that the Names Test is valid, since phonics ability has been shown to develop rather quickly in second grade and to peak in later grades. The Kuder-Richardson 20, a type of split-half reliability, yielded a reliability coefficient of .98, a very high reliability estimate.

After careful consideration of its rationale, development, and the results of the field testing, we concluded that the Names Test has the potential to become a useful diagnostic tool for classroom teachers as well as teachers who work in a remedial setting. At the same time, we felt

Table 1
Original and augmented versions of the Names Test

Original version (25 pairs of first and last names)

Jay Conway	Cindy Sampson	Flo Thornton
Tim Cornell	Chester Wright	Dee Skidmore
Chuck Hoke	Ginger Yale	Grace Brewster
Yolanda Clark	Patrick Tweed	Ned Westmoreland
Kimberly Blake	Stanley Shaw	Ron Smitherman
Roberta Slade	Wendy Swain	Troy Whitlock
Homer Preston	Glen Spencer	Vance Middleton
Gus Quincy	Fred Sherwood	Zane Anderson
		Bernard Pendergraph

Augmented version (35 pairs of first and last names)*

Jay Conway	Stanley Shaw	Bernard Pendergraph
Tim Cornell	Wendy Swain	*Shane Fletcher*
Chuck Hoke	Glen Spencer	*Floyd Sheldon*
Yolanda Clark	Fred Sherwood	*Dean Bateman*
Kimberly Blake	Flo Thornton	*Austin Shepherd*
Roberta Slade	Dee Skidmore	*Bertha Dale*
Homer Preston	Grace Brewster	*Neal Wade*
Gus Quincy	Ned Westmoreland	*Jake Murphy*
Cindy Sampson	Ron Smitherman	*Joan Brooks*
Chester Wright	Troy Whitlock	*Gene Loomis*
Ginger Yale	Vance Middleton	*Thelma Rinehart*
Patrick Tweed	Zane Anderson	

*Added names are in italics.

that it could be strengthened in two areas: category reliability and usability. We also felt that it warranted further investigation concerning its validity. The remainder of this article describes what we did to increase category reliability, to further examine the test's validity, and to enhance its usability.

Category Reliability

One of Cunningham's selection criteria was that the names represent a sampling of the most common English spelling patterns. More specifically, the intent was to include sufficient in-

stances of a given phonics category, or subscale, so that a student's performance in relation to it could be considered reliable. Category reliability, then, refers to the reliability of a test's subscale scores. Generally, the more items there are on a test or within a subscale, the more reliable the test or subscale becomes.

The question is: How many instances of a phonics category should there be? Although there is no hard and fast rule, Schell and Hanna (1981) have proposed a ballpark figure of 20 for subscale scores in general. Our analysis of the 50 items that comprised the Names Test revealed that five phonics categories fell considerably short of that figure: consonant digraphs 8, long vowels 9, vowel consonant final-e 6, vowel digraphs 8, and the schwa 9.

We recognize that Cunningham intended the Names Test to enable a quick assessment of phonics ability, and that it was therefore desirable to keep the number of names to a minimum. On the other hand, since one of the stated features of the Names Test is that it can provide teachers with diagnostic information based on error patterns, we increased the number of examples in the aforementioned categories to a minimum of 15. This entailed adding 10 pairs of first and last names to Cunningham's list of 25 (see bottom half of Table 1). Although this results in a less quick assessment of phonics ability (70 items versus 50), it seemed to us an acceptable trade-off for increased category reliability. The additional 20 items were obtained in the same manner as the original 50 (refer to pp. 125–126 in Cunningham's article).

The augmented version of the Names Test, which yielded a Kuder-Richardson 20 reliability coefficient of .93, resulted in the following breakdown:

Phonics category	Instances
Initial consonants (InCon)	37
Initial consonant blends (InConBl)	19
Consonant digraphs (ConDgr)	15
Short vowels (ShVow)	36
Long vowels/VC-final e (LV/VC-e)	23
Vowel digraphs (VowDgr)	15
Controlled vowels (CtrVow)	25
Schwa	15

The two categories LV and VC-e were combined because even after the new names were added, neither category alone met the criterion of 15 instances: long vowels had 10 instances, while VC-final e had 13.

Validity

As mentioned earlier, Cunningham obtained initial evidence that the Names Test is valid in

that the average score for fifth grade (47.3) approached the highest possible score (50), and was considerably higher than the average score for second grade (22.6). We sought further evidence of its validity through three methods.

First, we analyzed the performance of students in Grades 2 through 5 in each of the eight phonics categories as well as the entire test. We reasoned that a valid phonics test should yield minimal between-grade-level variation relative to phonics elements that typically are introduced early in a phonics curriculum, and greater variation relative to phonics elements that tend to be introduced later on.

Second, we kept a record of how long it took the students to read the names. Automaticity theory (LaBerge & Samuels, 1974; Samuels, 1979) predicts that older students, on average, will read the names not only with greater accuracy than younger students, but more rapidly; we investigated whether this hypothesis was borne out by our results.

Finally, we compared the students' performance on the Names Test with their performance on an established test of reading ability, in this case the Reading subtest of the Iowa Test of Basic Skills. Using reading comprehension as a criterion variable was deemed justifiable in that decoding ability is positively associated with comprehension performance (e.g., Byrne, Freebody, & Gates, 1992; Freebody & Byrne, 1988).

Procedure

Our sample consisted of 142 students in Grades 2 through 5 from a single building in a Midwestern school district. The breakdown by grade level was as follows: second 34, third 34, fourth 33, and fifth 41. Prior to administering the augmented version of the Names Test in October, we analyzed all 70 names, reached consensus, with the aid of several phonics books (e.g., Baer, 1991; Cunningham, 1991; Heilman,

1993), on what phonics elements each name assessed, and organized this material into a matrix for scoring purposes.

In Cunningham's field testing, the 25 pairs of first and last names that the students read were arranged in two columns on a single sheet of paper. For our study, one of us (Fyfe) designed a computer program that automated the presentation of the names one pair at a time in 12 pt. boldface type on a Macintosh SE series microcomputer. After entering the student's name and grade level into the computer, the examiner said,

> I want you to pretend that you are a teacher who is taking attendance on the first day of school. But instead of reading your students' names from a list, you will read them from a computer screen. As you read the names, I will be taking notes to help me remember what you say.
>
> Here is how it works: When you press this key that has an orange circle on it [the RETURN key], you will see one of your student's names. After you read it out loud, press the key with the orange circle on it and another name will soon appear. Keep doing this until there are no more names to read.
>
> Some of the names may be hard for you to read. I won't be able to help you read them. But even if you're not sure what a name is, try to make a guess. It doesn't matter if you don't get all of the names right.
>
> Remember, after you read a name, press the key with the orange circle on it and another name will appear. Do you have any questions? All right, press the key with the orange circle on it and begin.

While the examiner kept track of the student's oral reading performance on a protocol sheet, the computer program timed to the nearest 100th of a second the elapsed time between the presentation of a name pair and the key press executed by the students after it was read. One might anticipate that students would occasionally pause between the oral production of a word and the keying of the next one, thereby artificially affecting the rate at which the students read the names. However, we observed no such delays; furthermore, the quickness of the key pressing response itself did not appear to vary as a function of grade level.

Although the examiners (Duffelmeyer, Kruse, and Merkley) were prepared to discontinue testing if a student showed obvious signs of frustration with the name-reading task, testing had to be terminated with only one student; the remainder of the students stayed on task and completed the entire test, for which there was no time limit.

After the testing phase of the study was completed, the protocols were randomly divided into three sets; each set was then randomly assigned to and scored by one of the three examiners. Scoring involved counting and recording the number of names read correctly, and indicating for each name misread which phonics elements were mispronounced. For example, the last name *Brewster* was scored for the initial consonant blend Br and two controlled vowels, ew and er. One student misread Brewster as Brownster; thus, the student received credit for the initial blend and the second controlled vowel, but not for the first controlled vowel or the name as a whole. Interrater reliability was .99 and .93 for the names and the phonics elements, respectively. Each protocol was then scored a second time by a different examiner; any disagreements were resolved by the two examiners in question.

Results

For the 70 first and last names, the mean scores ranged from a low of 63% correct for second grade to a high of 92% for fifth grade; the mean scores for the third and fourth grades fell in between these two extremes at 73% and 89%, respectively. These results demonstrate that (a) the higher the grade level, the higher the score; and (b) the smallest grade level difference (3%) occurred between fourth and fifth grade, which is consistent with the observation that phonics ability peaks in later grades. Both results tend to validate the enhanced version of the Names Test.

The phonics category results provided further evidence of the test's validity. First, the mean scores increased as grade level increased for each phonics category. Second, there was very little between-grade-level variation for phonics elements that typically are introduced early in a phonics curriculum. For example, the mean percent correct scores for initial consonants ranged from 91% (second grade) to 98% (fifth grade), a difference of only 7%. Third, there was greater between-grade-level variation for phonics elements that typically are introduced later on. For example, the mean scores for vowel digraphs ranged from 74% (second grade) to 97% (fifth grade), a difference of 23%.

Next we analyzed the rate at which the students read the names. Recall that the computer program timed the interval between the onset of a first-name-last-name pair and the key press executed by the student immediately after the same pair was read aloud; thus, 35 time intervals were recorded for each student. Once all of the pairs had been presented, the program calculated the mean and standard deviation for the entire set of names. The means were later sorted by grade level and ranked from highest to lowest within each level. The mean rates in the top and bottom 10% of each grade level distribution were then discarded, leaving the middle 80%. This "trimming" procedure (Wainer, 1976) was employed to eliminate the contaminating effect of extreme scores on the grade level rate means. The mean of the remaining middle 80% in each distribution, called the "midmean" (Tukey, 1977), was then selected as being representative of the rate performance at each of the four grade levels.

The midmeans ranged from a high of 8.2 seconds per name pair for second grade to a low of 3.1 seconds per pair for fifth grade; the results for Grades 3 and 4 fell between these two extremes at 5.4 and 3.9 seconds, respectively. In other words, the higher the grade level, the faster the names were read. Furthermore, the largest grade level difference occurred between Grades 2 and 3 (2.8 seconds), and the smallest between Grades 4 and 5 (.8 seconds), which is consistent with the well-documented observation that older students are more proficient at word recognition than younger students. The fact that the Names Test was sensitive to this phenomenon provides additional evidence of its validity.

To further investigate the validity of the Names Test, we compared students' total raw score performance on it with their stanine performance (local norms) on the Reading subtest of the Iowa Test of Basic Skills, which was administered 2 weeks following the administration of the Names Test in all grades except Grade 2 as part of the school district's ongoing assessment of student achievement. To effect this comparison, we first divided the students at each of the three grade levels into upper, middle, and lower thirds based on their raw scores on the Names Test. Then we determined the percentage of students in each third of the three grade level distributions that fell in the Iowa Test of Basic Skills stanine ranges of 1–3, 4–6, and 7–9.

The results of this comparison are shown in Table 2. One approach to analyzing these data is to examine the pattern of results in the upper (7–9) stanine range. If the Names Test is valid, one should expect the upper third to be better represented than the middle third, and the middle third to be better represented than the lower third. Indeed, this pattern was evident at each grade level: Grade 3 (100%–45%–9%); Grade 4 (82%–55%–27%); and Grade 5 (100%–71%–21%). Similar patterns of performance were found for the middle (4–6) and lower (1–3) stanine ranges. Thus, students' performance on the Names Test proved to be a reasonably good predictor of their performance on an established measure of reading ability, which provides additional evidence of the Names Test's validity.

Table 2
Comparison of children's performance on the ITBS Reading subtest and on the Names Test

Score category on Names Test	Percentage of students, by grade and ITBS stanine score band								
	Grade 3			Grade 4			Grade 5		
	1–3	4–6	7–9	1–3	4–6	7–9	1–3	4–6	7–9
Upper third	-	-	100	-	18	82	-	-	100
Middle third	-	55	45	9	36	55	-	29	71
Lower third	9	82	9	18	55	27	-	79	21

ITBS = Iowa Test of Basic Skills.

Usability

In conjunction with our study, we developed two forms that should make the Names Test more convenient for teachers to use: A Protocol Sheet and a Scoring Matrix.

For a Protocol Sheet, Cunningham suggested typing the list of names in a column and following each name with a blank line to be used for recording a student's responses. While not finding specific fault with this suggestion, we decided that arranging the names in rows, leaving sufficient space between the rows for recording students' responses above the names, would be an improvement (see Table 3). This format makes it easier for the examiner to keep his or her place, particularly when it is necessary to write a phonetic spelling for a word that the student has mispronounced. It also makes it easier to compare a student's mispronunciation with the stimulus word, and then to identify the phonics element(s) on which the student erred.

Notice also that the Protocol Sheet includes a section for tabulating the test results. To facilitate tabulation, we developed the reproducible Scoring Matrix shown in Table 4. Below the space for the student's names, all 70 names are listed alphabetically along the left side; the eight phonics categories appear across the top. The phonics elements for which the names are scored appear in the cells. For example, the Scoring Matrix indicates that Anderson is scored for a short vowel A, a controlled vowel er, and a schwa o; Austin for a vowel digraph Au and a schwa i.

The scoring procedure is as follows: The teacher locates on the Protocol Sheet each name that the student mispronounced, circles on the Scoring Matrix which phonics elements were mispronounced, sums the number of circled elements for each phonics category, and transfers the error scores to the Protocol Sheet.

A Protocol Sheet for a hypothetical third-grade student is shown in Table 5. The bottom section reveals that Jimmy experienced difficulty with long vowel patterns, vowel digraphs, and controlled vowels. It would appear that Jimmy is in need of direct and systematic instruction in the aforementioned phonics areas. Lest our readers misunderstand us, we are not advocating "skilling and drilling," but rather phonics instruction that focuses on the internal structure of words rather than rule learning, and that is integrated into text reading (see Stahl, 1992).

Table 3
Protocol sheet for the Names Test

Name_____ Grade _____ Teacher _____ Date _____

Jay Conway	Tim Cornell	Chuck Hoke	Yolanda Clark
Kimberly Blake	Roberta Slade	Homer Preston	Gus Quincy
Cindy Sampson	Chester Wright	Ginger Yale	Patrick Tweed
Stanley Shaw	Wendy Swain	Glen Spencer	Fred Sherwood
Flo Thornton	Dee Skidmore	Grace Brewster	Ned Westmoreland
Ron Smitherman	Troy Whitlock	Vance Middleton	Zane Anderson
Bernard Pendergraph	Shane Fletcher	Floyd Sheldon	Dean Bateman
Austin Shepherd	Bertha Dale	Neal Wade	Jake Murphy
Joan Brooks	Gene Loomis	Thelma Rinehart	

Phonics category	*Errors*
Initial consonants	_/37
Initial consonant blends	_/19
Consonant digraphs	_/15
Short vowels	_/36
Long vowels/VC-final *e*	_/23
Vowel digraphs	_/15
Controlled vowels	_/25
Schwa	_/15

Conclusion

At the outset, we expressed our belief that the Names Test has the potential to become a useful diagnostic tool. Having improved its category reliability by increasing the number of first-name-last-name pairs from 25 to 35, having obtained additional evidence of its validity via scores by grade level, the rate data, and stanine comparisons with the Iowa Test of Basic Skills, and having enhanced its usability with the creation of a revised Protocol Sheet and a Scoring Matrix, we are even more confident of its potential than before.

An often leveled criticism of phonics instruction is that a number of children are taught phonics skills/patterns that they already seem to know. Consequently, as Groff (1986) has noted,

Table 4
Scoring matrix for the Names Test

Name_____   Date_____

Name	InCon	InConBl	ConDgr	ShVow	LngVow/VC-e	VowDgr	CtrVow	Schwa
Anderson				A			er	o
Austin						Au		i
Bateman	B				ate			a
Bernard	B						er, ar	
Bertha	B		th				er	a
Blake		Bl			ake			
Brewster		Br					ew, er	
Brooks		Br				oo		
Chester			Ch	e			er	
Chuck			Ch	u				
Cindy	C			i	y			
Clark		Cl					ar	
Conway	C			o		ay		
Cornell	C			e			or	
Dale	D				ale			
Dean	D					ea		
Dee	D					ee		
Fletcher		Fl	ch	e			er	
Flo		Fl			o			
Floyd		Fl				oy		
Fred		Fr		e				
Gene	G				ene			
Ginger	G			i			er	
Glen		Gl		e				
Grace		Gr			ace			
Gus	G			u				
Hoke	H				oke			
Homer	H				o		er	
Jake	J				ake			
Jay	J					ay		
Joan	J					oa		
Kimberly	K			i	y		er	
Loomis	L					oo		i
Middleton	M			i				o
Murphy	M		ph		y		ur	

(continued)

Table 4
Scoring matrix for the Names Test (continued)

Name_____   Date_____

Name	InCon	InConBl	ConDgr	ShVow	LngVow/VC-*e*	VowDig	Contr r	Schwa
Neal	N					ea		
Ned	N			e				
Patrick	P			a, i				
Pendergraph	P		ph	e, a			er	
Preston		Pr		e				o
Quincy				i	y			
Rinehart	R				ine		ar	
Roberta	R				o		er	a
Ron	R			o				
Sampson	S			a				o
Shane			Sh		ane			
Shaw			Sh				aw	
Sheldon			Sh	e				o
Shepherd			Sh	e			er	
Sherwood			Sh			oo	er	
Skidmore		Sk		i			or	
Slade		Sl			ade			
Smitherman		Sm	th	i			er	a
Spencer		Sp		e			er	
Stanley		St		a		ey		
Swain		Sw				ai		
Thelma			Th	e				a
Thornton			Th				or	o
Tim	T			i				
Troy		Tr				oy		
Tweed		Tw				ee		
Vance	V			a				
Wade	W				ade			
Wendy	W			e	y			
Westmoreland	W			e			or	a
Whitlock			Wh	i, o				
Wright					i			
Yale	Y				ale			
Yolanda	Y			a	o			a
Zane	Z				ane			

Table 5
Sample protocol for a third-grade student

Name *Jimmy Smith*   Grade 3   Teacher *Ms. Brown* Date *10-9-93*

✔ *Conver* Jay Conway	✔ *Carnell* Tim Cornell	✔ ✔ Chuck Hoke	*Yondolada* ✔ Yolanda Clark
✔ ✔ Kimberly Blake	✔ ✔ Roberta Slade	✔ ✔ Homer Preston	✔ *Quancy* Gus Quincy
Kindy ✔ Cindy Sampson	✔ ✔ Chester Wright	*Ging Yell* Ginger Yale	✔ ✔ Patrick Tweed
Standly ✔ Stanley Shaw	*Wendell Swan* Wendy Swain	✔ ✔ Glen Spencer	✔ *Steward* Fred Sherwood
Floy Thonton Flo Thornton	✔ ✔ Dee Skidmore	✔ *Bowster* Grace Brewster	✔✔ Ned Westmoreland
✔ ✔ Ron Smitherman	✔ ✔ Troy Whitlock	✔ ✔ Vance Middleton	*Zan* ✔ Zane Anderson
Barnid Pedugraph Bernard Pendergraph	✔ ✔ Shane Fletcher	✔ ✔ Floyd Sheldon	✔ *Batmin* Dean Bateman
Astin ✔ Austin Shepherd	*Betha* ✔ Bertha Dale	*Ned* ✔ Neal Wade	✔ ✔ Jake Murphy
Jane ✔ Joan Brooks	*Glen* ✔ Gene Loomis	*Clemitha Rainhart* Thelma Rinehart	

Phonics category	*Errors*
Initial consonants	2 /37
Initial consonant blends	1 /19
Consonant digraphs	2 /15
Short vowels	1 /36
Long vowels/VC-final *e*	8 /23
Vowel digraphs	6 /15
Controlled vowels	9 /25
Schwa	1 /15

the time spent needlessly reteaching and relearning them reduces the time available for reading itself. Groff goes on to state, "The inadequacy of this procedure reminds us that phonics teaching is desperately in need of a reliable and valid, quick-scoring test of children's [phonics] knowledge..." (p. 922). It is our belief that the augmented version of Cunningham's Names Test can satisfy this need.

Authors' Notes

This project was supported by the Research Institute for Studies in Education, College of Education, Iowa State University. We would also like to acknowledge the staff and students at East Elementary School in Ankeny, Iowa.

References

Adams, M.J. (1990). *Beginning to read: Thinking and learning about print*. Cambridge, MA: MIT Press.

Baer, G.T. (1991). *Self-paced phonics: A text for education*. New York: Merrill.

Byrne, B., Freebody, P., & Gates, A. (1992). Longitudinal data on the relations of word-reading strategies to comprehension, reading time, and phonemic awareness. *Reading Research Quarterly, 27*, 140–151.

Cunningham, P.M. (1990). The Names Test: A quick assessment of decoding ability. *The Reading Teacher, 44*, 124–129.

Cunningham, P.M. (1991). *Phonics they use: Words for reading and writing*. New York: HarperCollins.

Ehri, L.C., & Wilce, L.S. (1985). Movement into reading: Is the first stage of printed word learning visual or phonetic? *Reading Research Quarterly, 20*, 163–179.

Freebody, P., & Byrne, B. (1988). Word-reading strategies in elementary school children: Relations to comprehension, reading time, and phonemic awareness. *Reading Research Quarterly, 23*, 441–453.

Groff, P. (1986). The maturing of phonics instruction. *The Reading Teacher, 39*, 919–923.

Heilman, A.W. (1993). *Phonics in proper perspective*. New York: Merrill.

LaBerge, D., & Samuels, S.J. (1974). Toward a theory of automatic information processing in reading. *Cognitive Psychology, 6*, 293–323.

Perfetti, C.A. (1991). The psychology, pedagogy, and politics of reading. *Psychological Science, 2*, 70–76.

Pikulski, J., & Shanahan, T. (1980). A comparison of various approaches to evaluating phonics. *The Reading Teacher, 33*, 692–702.

Samuels, S.J. (1979). The method of repeated readings. *The Reading Teacher, 32*, 403–408.

Schell, L.M., & Hanna, G.S. (1981). Can informal reading inventories reveal strengths and weaknesses in comprehension subskills? *The Reading Teacher, 35*, 263–268.

Stahl, S.A. (1992). Saying the "p" word: Nine guidelines for exemplary phonics instruction. *The Reading Teacher, 45*, 618–625.

Tukey, J.W. (1977). *Exploratory data analysis*. Reading, MA: Addison-Wesley.

Wainer, H. (1976). Robust statistics: A survey and some prescriptions. *Journal of Educational Statistics, 1*, 285–312.

A Questionnaire to Measure Children's Awareness of Strategic Reading Processes

Maribeth Cassidy Schmitt

March 1990

Good readers are actively involved in the comprehension process. They select and use appropriate strategies and monitor their comprehension as they read to help them understand and remember information. Some of the strategies good readers employ include previewing the text, hypothesizing about the content, generating questions, and summarizing periodically.

Several studies have shown that children can be taught metacomprehension strategies. For example, Paris, Cross, and Lipson (1984) taught children how and when to set purposes for reading, activate background knowledge, attend to main ideas, draw inferences, and monitor comprehension. Also, Baumann, Seifert-Kessell, and Jones (1987) used a think-aloud technique to help children monitor their comprehension during reading.

Because it has been shown that awareness of metacomprehension strategies is characteristic of good comprehenders (e.g., Paris & Jacobs, 1984; Schmitt, 1988), it would be useful for teachers to evaluate their students' aware-

ness of those strategies. Such knowledge could be used informally to design a reading program that includes explicit instruction in metacomprehension skills (e.g., Paris et al., 1984) or is structured so that it fosters the development of such skills (e.g., Duffy et al., 1987; Schmitt, 1988; Schmitt & Baumann, 1986).

This article describes a multiple-choice questionnaire—the Metacomprehension Strategy Index (MSI)—that teachers can use to evaluate middle and upper elementary students' knowledge of strategic reading processes. The questionnaire was originally developed to measure strategic awareness of students who participated in a metacomprehension training study (Schmitt, 1988), and adaptations of the index have been used in several additional studies (e.g., Baumann et al., 1987; Lonberger, 1988). It is currently being used at the Benchmark School in Pennsylvania in a 3-year research and development study funded by the McDonnell Foundation. This article describes the MSI and supporting validity and reliability data. Also discussed are suggestions on how teachers can

189

interpret and use the information derived from the MSI.

Description of the MSI

The MSI is a 25-item, 4-option, multiple-choice questionnaire (see the Appendix at the end of this article) that asks students about the strategies they could use before, during, and after reading a narrative selection. The MSI assesses students' awareness of a variety of metacomprehension behaviors that fit within six broad categories: (a) predicting and verifying, (b) previewing, (c) purpose setting, (d) self-questioning, (e) drawing from background knowledge, and (f) summarizing and applying fix-up strategies. The response for each item that is indicative of metacomprehension strategy awareness is underlined in the Appendix.

Table 1 correlates individual MSI items to the six categories. For example, option C in item 1—"Make some guesses about what I think will happen in the story"—is a prediction. The strategies assessed by the MSI are consistent with those taught in several metacomprehension instructional studies (e.g., Braun, Rennie, & Labercane, 1986; Palincsar & Brown, 1984; Paris et al., 1984; Risko & Feldman, 1986).

Reliability and Validity of the MSI

The MSI has been shown to be a reliable measure of metacomprehension strategy awareness. Lonberger (1988) reported an MSI internal consistency value of .87 using the Kuder-Richardson Formula 20. To increase overall reliability of the MSI, it was designed to have several questions address each strategy cluster.

Validity data for the MSI come from several sources. I (Schmitt, 1988) compared it with The Index of Reading Awareness (IRA), a self-report measure of awareness of the need to eval-

uate, plan, and regulate reading processes (Paris et al., 1984; Paris & Jacobs, 1984). A statistically significant correlation was found between the MSI and the IRA ($r = .48$, $p < .001$), suggesting both instruments are measuring similar constructs. In addition, I found that in my experimental study (Schmitt, 1988), students who received training in metacomprehension strategies scored significantly higher on the MSI than students in an instructed control group. I also found statistically significant correlations between the MSI and two comprehension measures, an error detection task ($r = .50$, $p < .001$) and a cloze task ($r = .49$, $p < .001$). These data provide further evidence of the relationship between performance on the MSI and tasks (error detection, cloze) commonly used to measure students' metacomprehension ability.

Classroom Use and Interpretation of the MSI

Using and Adapting the MSI

The MSI can be administered in two ways: (a) teachers may choose to read the questions and possible answers aloud to the students, or (b) they may allow the students to read and answer the questionnaire silently. I recommend the former procedure if it is a teacher's judgment that students' limited decoding ability or slow reading rate would interfere with their ability to perform on the questionnaire.

The MSI is designed to measure strategies specific to *narrative* text comprehension only. Because previewing, predicting, summarizing, questioning, etc. are strategies that can be used for both narrative and expository text, the MSI can be adapted easily to measure expository text strategies or content-specific strategies. Following is an example of an item (#2) that has been rewritten to be appropriate for use with a content textbook:

Table 1
Strategies measured by the MSI

Predicting and verifying

Predicting the content of a story promotes active comprehension by giving readers a purpose for reading (i.e., to verify predictions). Evaluating predictions and generating new ones as necessary enhances the constructive nature of the reading process.

Item nos. 1, 4, 13, 15, 16, 18, 23

Previewing

Previewing the text facilitates comprehension by activating background knowledge and providing information for making predictions.

Item nos. 2, 3

Purpose setting

Reading with a purpose promotes active, strategic reading.

Item nos. 5, 7, 21

Self-questioning

Generating questions to be answered promotes active comprehension by giving readers a purpose for reading (i.e., to answer the questions).

Item nos. 6, 14, 17

Drawing from background knowledge

Activating and incorporating information from background knowledge contributes to comprehension by helping readers make inferences and generate predictions.

Item nos. 8, 9, 10, 19, 24, 25

Summarizing and applying fix-up strategies

Summarizing the content at various points in the story serves as a form of comprehension monitoring. Rereading or suspending judgment and reading on when comprehension breaks down represents strategic reading.

Item nos. 11, 12, 20, 22

Before I begin reading, it's a good idea to:

a. Look at the illustrations to see what the chapter will be about.

b. Decide how long it will take me to read the chapter.

c. Sound out the words I don't know.

d. Check to see if the information is making sense.

Interpreting the MSI

The results of the MSI can be used to help teachers design programs of reading comprehension instruction for individual students. Table 2 presents a portion of a teacher-constructed class record for the MSI for a hypothetical fourth-grade class. On the record are the students' performance on each of the six clusters of items, a total MSI score, and, for comparison purposes, the national percentile rank for the comprehension subtest of a recently administered standardized achievement test. MSI results can be interpreted both quantitatively and qualitatively. Following are descriptions of the

Table 2
Class record for fourth graders' performance on the MSI

| | MSI Data | | | | | | | | Teacher |
	P / V (7)	Pre (2)	Pur (3)	Que (3)	B/K (6)	S/FU (4)	Total (25)	%ile	observations
Linda A.	6	2	2	3	5	4	22	89	A strong, competent reader performing at a high level on all reading comprehension tasks.
Emily B.	2	0	1	1	1	1	6	12	Struggles with most reading tasks; tends to over rely on the graphophonic cue system.
Dwayne B.	6	2	2	2	4	3	19	17	A capable student and a good decoder, but he has difficulty in many comprehension tasks; does not always seem to apply skills well.
Constance C.	3	0	1	2	1	2	9	67	A good reader with no apparent problems in reading comprehension.

Key: P/V = Predicting and verifying; Pre = Previewing; Pur = Purpose setting; Que = Self-questioning; B/K = Drawing from background knowledge; S/FU = Summarizing and applying fix-up strategies; %ile = comprehension score from a standardized test. Number of items within each metacomprehension category is indicated by parentheses.

decision-making processes for several students in this fourth-grade class.

Linda A.

Linda performed at a high level on the MSI, selecting 22 out of 25 responses that are indicative of metacomprehension awareness. Further, her standardized test score suggests that she is a skilled comprehender, and her teacher's opinion of Linda's abilities was consistent with both of these findings. Thus, the MSI served to affirm the teacher's belief that Linda was a competent, strategic reader.

Emily B.

Emily's performance on the MSI suggests low strategic awareness, and her performance on the standardized test suggests a low general performance in reading comprehension. Emily's teacher sees her struggling with reading comprehension and also notes that Emily tends to focus on accurate word pronunciation during reading rather than reading for meaning. As a result, Emily's miscues tend to be semantically unacceptable, though they are good phonic representations of the words she attempts to pronounce. Consistent with this finding is Emily's tendency to select responses on the MSI that were related to word identification (e.g., she chose "Sound out words I don't know, "Check to see if the words have long or short vowels in them").

In addition, Emily tended to select responses that were inappropriate with the phase of reading. For example, for item 6, which probed for a *before* reading behavior, Emily selected "Retell all of the main points that have happened so far," a *during* or *after* reading behavior. This suggests that she is unaware of when to select specific strategies for use. Emily's teacher concludes that she would benefit from a program of instruction that involves explicit teaching of metacomprehension strategies and when to apply those strategies; the program of instruction should also enable Emily to achieve a balance in drawing from graphophonic and meaning clues.

Dwayne B.

Dwayne performed at an acceptable level on the MSI, selecting 19 of 25 items that indicate strategy awareness. However, his overall comprehension performance on the standardized test was in the low range, and his teacher also observes Dwayne having comprehension problems. She notes further that Dwayne does not always seem to apply comprehension strategies well; he tends to perform acceptably during the skill lessons, but he has difficulty calling up strategies that he presumably has learned. Dwayne's teacher concludes that although he seems to know what he should be doing strategically during reading, he has difficulty actually implementing reading strategies. Therefore, she has decided that Dwayne would benefit from instruction that involves teacher modeling and guided practice of strategy application. Further, she plans to arrange for some one-on-one instruction with Dwayne, so he can receive on-the-spot instruction and application of comprehension strategies as he is actually reading stories.

Constance C.

Constance achieved a high average score on the standardized comprehension test, and her teacher observes that she has no difficulty understanding what she reads. However, Constance's performance on the MSI is relatively low (9 of 25 expected responses). Therefore, Constance's teacher is in a quandary about what to do. After some thought, she has decided not to engage in any special intervention for Constance, as she believes that Constance is a student whose strategic knowledge is tacit information; that is, she has the strategic abilities but is not consciously aware of them or their use. The teacher will observe Constance carefully, however, and provide instruction as required if she begins to demonstrate difficulties in reading comprehension.

Cautions About Interpreting the MSI

It should be understood that although there is support for the reliability and validity of the MSI, it is a self-report instrument, and, as such, has the limitations associated with such instruments. For example, one cannot tell from the instrument alone whether or not children actually *do* the behaviors they say they do (as is the case for Dwayne). Teacher observation is required to verify the say/do relationship.

Also, while the overall reliability of the MSI is good, one should be cautious when interpreting individual item clusters, as they can be highly unreliable. For example, just because a student may have answered both previewing items with the strategic response and failed to do so for all three purpose setting items, it does not mean that the student is able to preview text but is unable to establish purposes for reading. There are too few items to make these kinds of sweeping statements.

Finally, as with any assessment instrument, the MSI should not be used in isolation. Rather, teachers should consider it as one source of information about students' reading abilities that must be viewed in conjunction with other sources of information.

Instructional Techniques

Methods for promoting awareness and use of metacomprehension activities abound in the professional literature (e.g., see Irwin & Baker,

1989; McNeil, 1987; Wilson & Gambrell, 1988). A few techniques will be mentioned here as possible options for teachers wanting to increase students' strategic reading skills.

Students can benefit from observing teachers modeling the thinking processes they are using to make sense of text (e.g., Baumann et al., 1987; Bereiter & Bird, 1985; Davey, 1983). These processes should include previewing, predicting, questioning, using fix-up strategies for comprehension breakdowns, and summarizing as a monitoring strategy.

Comprehension skill instruction should focus on teaching the skills as *strategies* for getting meaning. Including conditional knowledge about the skills (i.e., *when* they should be used and *why* they are important or relevant) will promote use of them in a strategic manner (Baumann & Schmitt, 1986; Duffy et al., 1987). For example, instruction in how to identify implicit main ideas should include the information that it is most useful as a strategy when the text is expository and that it is an important skill to learn because it will help students learn and remember the information more easily.

Directed reading activities can be conducted in a manner that promotes metacomprehension skills and fosters independent, strategic reading. For example, an elaborated directed reading activity involves allowing students to activate their own background, set purposes for reading, generate prequestions, hypothesize, verify or reject hypotheses, and summarize where appropriate (Schmitt, 1988; Schmitt & Baumann, 1986).

Conclusion

The MSI provides one means to evaluate elementary school students' awareness of pre-reading, during reading, and postreading metacomprehension strategies for reading narrative prose. The information gleaned from the instrument may be used to identify students' levels of awareness of metacomprehension. It also can be used to interpret qualitatively the kinds of strategies students consider to be important, and to evaluate their awareness of the need to match strategies to the appropriate reading phase (before, during or after reading). This information may be useful to teachers in designing a comprehensive reading program that fosters metacomprehension strategy awareness and competence.

References

Baumann, J.F., Seifert-Kessell, N., & Jones, L. (1987, December). *Effects of think-aloud instruction on elementary students' ability to monitor their comprehension*. Paper presented at the National Reading Conference, St. Petersburg, FL.

Baumann, J.F., & Schmitt, M.C. (1986). The what, why, how, and when of comprehension instruction. *The Reading Teacher*, *39*, 640–646.

Bereiter, C., & Bird, M. (1985). Use of thinking aloud in identification and teaching of reading comprehension strategies. *Cognition and Instruction*, *2*, 131–156.

Braun, C., Rennie, B.J., & Labercane, G.D. (1986). A conference approach to the development of metacognitive strategies. *Solving problems in literacy: Learners, teachers, and researchers*. The 35th Yearbook of the National Reading Conference, 204–209.

Davey, B. (1983). Think aloud—Modeling the cognitive processes of reading comprehension. *Journal of Reading*, *27*, 44–47.

Duffy, G., Roehler, L.R., Sivan, E., Rackliffe, G., Book, C., Meloth, M.M., Vavrus, L.G., Wesselman, R., Putnam, J., & Bassiri, D. (1987). Effects of explaining the reasoning associated with using reading strategies. *Reading Research Quarterly*, *22*, 347–368.

Irwin, J.W., & Baker, I. (1989). *Promoting active reading comprehension strategies: A resource book for teachers*. Englewood Cliffs, NJ: Prentice Hall.

Lonberger, R. (1988, February). *Effects of training in a self-generated learning strategy on the prose processing abilities of 4th and 6th graders*. Paper presented at the annual meeting of the Eastern Education Association, Savannah, GA.

McNeil, J.D. (1987). *Reading comprehension: New dimensions for classroom practice* (2nd ed.). Glenview, IL: Scott, Foresman.

Palincsar, A.S., & Brown, A.L. (1984). Reciprocal teaching of comprehension fostering and monitoring activities. *Cognition and Instruction, 1,* 117–175.

Paris, S.G., Cross, D.R., & Lipson, M.Y. (1984). Informed strategies for learning: A program to improve children's reading awareness and comprehension. *Journal of Educational Psychology, 76,* 1239–1252.

Paris, S.G., & Jacobs, J.E. (1984). The benefits of informed instruction for children's reading awareness and comprehension skills. *Child Development, 55,* 2083–2093.

Risko, V.J., & Feldman, N. (1986). Teaching young remedial readers to generate questions as they read. *Reading Psychology, 23,* 54–64.

Schmitt, M.C. (1988). The effects of an elaborated directed activity on the metacomprehension skills of third graders. *Dialogues in literacy research.* The 37th Yearbook of the National Reading Conference, 167–181.

Schmitt, M.C., & Baumann, J.F. (1986). How to incorporate comprehension monitoring strategies into basal reader instruction. *The Reading Teacher, 40,* 28–31.

Wilson, R.M., & Gambrell, L.B. (1988). *Reading comprehension in the elementary school: A teacher's practical guide.* Newton, MA: Allyn & Bacon.

Appendix
Metacomprehension Strategy Index

Directions: Think about what kinds of things you can do to help you understand a story better before, during, and after you read it. Read each of the lists of four statements and decide which one of them would help *you* the most. *There are no right answers.* It is just what *you* think would help the most. Circle the letter of the statement you choose.

I. In each set of four, choose the one statement which tells a good thing to do to help you understand a story better *before* you read it.

1. Before I begin reading, it's a good idea to:
   A. See how many pages are in the story.
   B. Look up all of the big words in the dictionary.
   C. Make some guesses about what I think will happen in the story.
   D. Think about what has happened so far in the story.

2. Before I begin reading, it's a good idea to:
   A. Look at the pictures to see what the story is about.
   B. Decide how long it will take me to read the story.
   C. Sound out the words I don't know.
   D. Check to see if the story is making sense.

3. Before I begin reading, it's a good idea to:
   A. Ask someone to read the story to me.
   B. Read the title to see what the story is about.
   C. Check to see if most of the words have long or short vowels in them.
   D. Check to see if the pictures are in order and make sense.

4. Before I begin reading, it's a good idea to:
   A. Check to see that no pages are missing.
   B. Make a list of the words I'm not sure about.
   C. Use the title and pictures to help me make guesses about what will happen in the story.
   D. Read the last sentence so I will know how the story ends.

5. Before I begin reading, it's a good idea to:
   A. Decide on why I am going to read the story.
   B. Use the difficult words to help me make guesses about what will happen in the story.
   C. Reread some parts to see if I can figure out what is happening if things aren't making sense.
   D. Ask for help with the difficult words.

6. Before I begin reading, it's a good idea to:
   A. Retell all of the main points that have happened so far.
   B. Ask myself questions that I would like to have answered in the story.
   C. Think about the meanings of the words which have more than one meaning.
   D. Look through the story to find all of the words with three or more syllables.

7. Before I begin reading, it's a good idea to:
   A. Check to see if I have read this story before.
   B. Use my questions and guesses as a reason for reading the story.
   C. Make sure I can pronounce all of the words before I start.
   D. Think of a better title for the story.

8. Before I begin reading, it's a good idea to:
   A. Think of what I already know about the things I see in the pictures.
   B. See how many pages are in the story.
   C. Choose the best part of the story to read again.
   D. Read the story aloud to someone.

9. Before I begin reading, it's a good idea to:
   A. Practice reading the story aloud.
   B. Retell all of the main points to make sure I can remember the story.
   C. Think of what the people in the story might be like.
   D. Decide if I have enough time to read the story.

(continued)

---

* Underlined responses indicate metacomprehension strategy awareness.

10. Before I begin reading, it's a good idea to:
    A. Check to see if I am understanding the story so far.
    B. Check to see if the words have more than one meaning.
    C. Think about where the story might be taking place.
    D. List all of the important details.

II. In each set of four, choose the one statement which tells a good thing to do to help you understand a story better *while* you are reading it.

11. While I'm reading, it's a good idea to:
    A. Read the story very slowly so that I will not miss any important parts.
    B. Read the title to see what the story is about.
    C. Check to see if the pictures have anything missing.
    D. Check to see if the story is making sense by seeing if I can tell what's happened so far.

12. While I'm reading, it's a good idea to:
    A. Stop to retell the main points to see if I am understanding what has happened so far.
    B. Read the story quickly so that I can find out what happened.
    C. Read only the beginning and the end of the story to find out what it is about.
    D. Skip the parts that are too difficult for me.

13. While I'm reading, it's a good idea to:
    A. Look up all of the big words in the dictionary.
    B. Put the book away and find another one if things aren't making sense.
    C. Keep thinking about the title and the pictures to help me decide what is going to happen next.
    D. Keep track of how many pages I have left to read.

14. While I'm reading, it's a good idea to:
    A. Keep track of how long it is taking me to read the story.
    B. Check to see if I can answer any of the questions I asked before I started reading.
    C. Read the title to see what the story is going to be about.
    D. Add the missing details to the pictures.

15. While I'm reading, it's a good idea to:
    A. Have someone read the story aloud to me.
    B. Keep track of how many pages I have read.
    C. List the story's main characters.
    D. Check to see if my guesses are right or wrong.

16. While I'm reading, it's a good idea to:
    A. Check to see that the characters are real.
    B. Make a lot of guesses about what is going to happen next.
    C. Not look at the pictures because they might confuse me.
    D. Read the story aloud to someone.

17. While I'm reading, it's a good idea to:
    A. Try to answer the questions I asked myself.
    B. Try not to confuse what I already know with what I'm reading about.
    C. Read the story silently.
    D. Check to see if I am saying the new vocabulary words correctly.

18. While I'm reading, it's a good idea to:
    A. Try to see if my guesses are going to be right or wrong.
    B. Reread to be sure I haven't missed any of the words.
    C. Decide on why I am reading the story.
    D. List what happened first, second, third, and so on.

(continued)

* Underlined responses indicate metacomprehension strategy awareness.

19. While I'm reading, it's a good idea to:
    A. See if I can recognize the new vocabulary words.
    B. Be careful not to skip any parts of the story.
    C. Check to see how many of the words I already know.
    <u>D</u>. Keep thinking of what I already know about the things and ideas in the story to help me decide what is going to happen.

20. While I'm reading, it's a good idea to:
    <u>A</u>. Reread some parts or read ahead to see if I can figure out what is happening if things aren't making sense.
    B. Take my time reading so that I can be sure I understand what is happening.
    C. Change the ending so that it makes sense.
    D. Check to see if there are enough pictures to help make the story ideas clear.

III. In each set of four, choose the one statement which tells a good thing to do to help you understand a story better *after* you have read it.

21. After I've read a story it's a good idea to:
    A. Count how many pages I read with no mistakes.
    B. Check to see if there were enough pictures to go with the story to make it interesting.
    <u>C</u>. Check to see if I met my purpose for reading the story.
    D. Underline the causes and effects.

22. After I've read a story it's a good idea to:
    A. Underline the main idea.

B. Retell the main points of the whole story so that I can check to see if I understood it.
    C. Read the story again to be sure I said all of the words right.
    D. Practice reading the story aloud.

23. After I've read a story it's a good idea to:
    A. Read the title and look over the story to see what it is about.
    B. Check to see if I skipped any of the vocabulary words.
    <u>C</u>. Think about what made me make good or bad predictions.
    D. Make a guess about what will happen next in the story.

24. After I've read a story it's a good idea to:
    A. Look up all of the big words in the dictionary.
    B. Read the best parts aloud.
    C. Have someone read the story aloud to me.
    <u>D</u>. Think about how the story was like things I already knew about before I started reading.

25. After I've read a story it's a good idea to:
    <u>A</u>. Think about how I would have acted if I were the main character in the story.
    B. Practice reading the story silently for practice of good reading.
    C. Look over the story title and pictures to see what will happen.
    D. Make a list of the things I understood the most.

* Underlined responses indicate metacomprehension strategy awareness.

Measuring Attitude Toward Reading: A New Tool for Teachers

Michael C. McKenna and Dennis J. Kear

May 1990

In 1762, the philosopher Rousseau speculated that any method of teaching reading would suffice given adequate motivation on the part of the learner. While present-day educators might resist such a sweeping pronouncement, the importance of attitude is nevertheless widely recognized. The Commission on Reading in its summary of research (Anderson, Hiebert, Scott, & Wilkinson, 1985) concluded that "becoming a skilled reader requires...learning that written material can be interesting" (p. 18). Smith (1988) observed that "the emotional response to reading...is the primary reason most readers read, and probably the primary reason most nonreaders do not read" (p. 177). Wixson and Lipson (in press) acknowledge that "the student's attitude toward reading is a central factor affecting reading performance." These conclusions are based on a long history of research in which attitude and achievement have been consistently linked (e.g., Purves & Beach, 1972; Walberg & Tsai, 1985).

The recent emphasis on enhanced reading proficiency has often ignored the important role played by children's attitudes in the process of becoming literate. Athey (1985) suggested that one reason for this tendency is that the affective aspects of reading tend to be ill-defined and to involve "shadowy variables" (p. 527) difficult to conceptualize, measure, and address instructionally.

The focus of recent research and development in assessment has been comprehension rather than attitude. Some progress has been made in the development of individually administered, qualitative instruments, but quantitative group surveys, which form a natural complement to qualitative approaches, are often poorly documented in terms of desirable psychometric attributes, such as normative frames of reference and evidence of reliability and validity. Our purpose was to produce a public-domain instrument that would remedy these shortcomings and enable teachers to estimate attitude levels efficiently and reliably. This article presents that instrument along with a discussion of its development and suggestions for its use.

Development of the Scale

Several important criteria were established to guide the development of the instrument. The authors agreed that the survey must (a) have a large-scale normative frame of reference; (b) comprise a set of items selected on the basis of desirable psychometric properties; (c) have empirically documented reliability and validity; (d) be applicable to all elementary students, Grades 1 through 6; (e) possess a meaningful, attention-getting, student-friendly response format; (f) be suitable for brief group administration; and (g) comprise separate subscales for recreational and academic reading. We knew of no instrument that possessed all of these characteristics.

A pictorial format was elected because of its natural appeal for children and because of its comprehensibility by the very young. An informal survey of more than 30 elementary teachers indicated that the comic strip character Garfield was more apt to be recognized by children in Grades 1 through 6 than any other. Jim Davis, who is the creator of Garfield, and United Features, his publisher, agreed to supply four black-line, camera-ready poses of Garfield, ranging from very happy to very upset, and to permit the resulting instrument to be copied and used by educators. (See the Elementary Reading Attitude Survey and scoring sheet prior to the Appendix at the end of this article.)

An even number of scale points avoids a neutral, central category which respondents often select in order to avoid committing themselves even when clear opinions exist (Nunnally, 1967). The use of four points was based on a substantial body of research suggesting that young children typically can discriminate among no more than five discrete bits of information simultaneously (e.g., Case & Khanna, 1981; Chi, 1978; Chi & Klahr, 1975; Nitko, 1983).

Several earlier surveys were used as models in the creation of an item pool from which the final set of items would be constructed (e.g., Estes, 1971; Heathington, 1979; Right to Read, 1976; Robinson & Good, 1987). A total of 39 items were developed, each related to one of two aspects of attitude: (a) attitude toward recreational reading (24 items) or (b) attitude toward academic reading (15 items). To establish a consistent, appropriate expectation on the part of the students, each item was worded with a uniform beginning: "How do you feel.…"

This prototype instrument was then administered to 499 elementary students in a middle-sized midwestern U.S. school district. For each of the two item sets (recreational and academic), final sets of 10 items each were selected on the basis of inter-item correlation coefficients. The revised instrument was then administered at midyear to a national sample of over 18,000 children in Grades 1–6. Estimates of reliability, as well as evidence of validity, were based on this national sample. A complete description of the technical aspects of the survey appears in the Appendix.

Administering and Scoring the Survey

The Elementary Reading Attitude Survey (ERAS) can be given to an entire class in a matter of minutes, but, as with any normed instrument, it is important that the administration reflect as closely as possible the procedure used with the norming group. The administration procedures are presented in the "Directions for Use" information that accompanies the instrument itself. This process involves first familiarizing students with the instrument and with the purposes for giving it. The teacher next reads the items aloud twice as the students mark their responses.

Each item is then assigned 1, 2, 3, or 4 points, a "4" indicating the happiest (leftmost) Garfield. The scoring sheet that follows the instrument can be used to organize this process and record recreational, academic, and total scores, along with the percentile rank of each. The results are then ready for use.

Using the Survey

Collecting data about students is an empty exercise unless the information is used to plan instruction. Scores on the ERAS can be helpful in this process, but it is important to understand what they can and cannot do as well as how they relate to other sources of information.

Strengths and limitations. This survey provides quantitative estimates of two important aspects of children's attitudes toward reading. Like global measures of achievement, however, they can do little in themselves to identify the causes of poor attitude or to suggest instructional techniques likely to improve it. On the other hand, the instrument can be used to (a) make possible initial conjecture about the attitudes of specific students, (b) provide a convenient group profile of a class (or a larger unit), or (c) serve as a means of monitoring the attitudinal impact of instructional programs.

A classroom plan. A teacher might begin by administering the ERAS during the first few weeks of the school year. Class averages for recreational and academic reading attitude will enable the teacher to characterize the class generally on these two dimensions. Scores for individual students may suggest the need to further explore the nature, strength, and origins of their values and beliefs. This goal could be pursued through the use of individually conducted strategies such as structured interviews, open-ended sentence instruments, or interest inventories. Reed (1979) suggested using nonreactive measures as well, such as recorded teacher observations following reading instruction and reading-related activities. The combination of these techniques provides a variety of useful information that can be collected in portfolio fashion for individual students.

Survey results can be very useful in deciding what sorts of additional information to pursue. Four general response patterns are especially notable, and we will depict each of them with hypothetical students who are, in fact, composites of many with whom we have worked.

Two profiles involve sizable differences (5 points or more) between recreational and academic scores. Jimmy, a third grader, has a recreational score of 29 and an academic score of 21. The difference suggests a stronger attitude toward reading for fun than for academic purposes. To an extent, this pattern is typical of third graders (compare the means in Table 2 in the Appendix), but not to the degree exhibited in Jimmy's case. Had both scores been higher, Jimmy's teacher might have been justified in disregarding the difference, but a score of 21 is low both in the criterial sense (it is close to the slightly frowning Garfield) and in a normative one (18th percentile rank). Examining the last 10 items of the survey one-by-one might prove helpful in forming hypotheses about which aspects are troublesome. These can then be tested by carefully observing Jimmy during reading instruction.

For Katy, a fifth grader, assume that the two scores are reversed. By virtue of her stronger attitude toward academic reading, Katy is somewhat atypical. Her academic score of 29 is quite strong in both a criterial sense (it is near the slightly smiling Garfield) and a normative sense (71st percentile rank). Her score of 21 in recreational reading attitude is cause for concern (13th percentile rank), but the strong academic score suggests that her disdain is not total and may be traceable to causes subject to intervention. Because items 1–10 are somewhat global in nature, it is unlikely that scrutinizing her responses will be very helpful. A nonthreatening chat about reading habits may be much more productive in helping her teacher identify Katy's areas of interest and even suggest a book or two. Katy may not have been exposed to a variety of interesting trade books.

Two other profiles involve differences between attitude and ability. These are very real possibilities that require careful attention

(Roettger, 1980). Consider Patrick, a second grader whose academic attitude score is 28 and who has been placed in a low-ability group by his teacher. Patrick's relatively positive score (near the smiling Garfield) may encourage his teacher, for it is apt to be higher than others in his reading group. However, more than half of his second-grade peers across the country have stronger attitudes toward reading in school. Data from this study document a widening attitudinal gap between low- and high-ability children as they move through school. Patrick's teacher should be concerned about the likely effects of another frustrating year on his attitude toward instruction. Teaching methods and instructional materials should be scrutinized.

Ironically, the same conclusion might be reached for Deborah, a sixth-grade student of extraordinary ability. Her academic attitude score, however, is only 17, which is quite negative, whether one looks to its position among the pictures or notes that it represents a percentile rank of 11. If Deborah's recreational score were substantially higher, her teacher would be correct in wondering whether the instruction she is receiving is adequately engaging. As with Jimmy, an inspection of her responses to items 11–20 could be helpful, followed by a nonintrusive reading interview and tactful observation. On the other hand, suppose that Deborah's recreational score were also 17. This would place her total score (34) at the 5th percentile rank and suggest a strong disinclination to read despite the ability to do so. This would warrant action on the part of an insightful teacher who is willing to make instructional and leisure reading attractive.

Examples of this nature illustrate how the Elementary Reading Attitude Survey can enter into the process of instructional planning, especially near the beginning of a school year. As the year draws to a close, the survey can again be given, this time to monitor any attitudinal changes of the class as a whole. By comparing class averages from the beginning and end of the year, a teacher can gauge the movement of a class relative both to its own earlier position and to a national midyear average. Estimating year-long changes for individual students is a less reliable process and should only be attempted with regard to the standard error of measurement for a given subscale and grade level (see Table 2 in the Appendix). We recommend using twice the standard error to construct an adequate confidence interval. In other words, the pre/post difference would, in general, need to be 5 points or more on either the academic or recreational subscale before *any* real change could be assumed. On the total score, the pre/post change would need to be 7 or 8 points.

Conclusion

The instrument presented here builds on the strengths of its predecessors and, it is hoped, remedies some of their psychometric shortcomings. Its placement into the public domain by means of this article provides teachers with a tool that can be used with relative confidence to estimate the attitude levels of their students and initiate informal assessment efforts into the role attitude plays in students' development as readers.

Authors' Note

The authors wish to express their sincere thanks to Jim Davis for his Garfield illustrations and for his concern for children's literacy abilities.

References

Anderson, R.C., Hiebert, E.H., Scott, J.A., & Wilkinson, I.A.G. (1985). *Becoming a nation of readers: The report of the Commission on Reading.* Washington, DC: National Institute of Education.

Athey, I.J. (1985). Reading research in the affective domain. In H. Singer & R.B. Ruddell (Eds.), *Theoretical models and processes of reading* (3rd ed., pp. 527–557). Newark, DE: International Reading Association.

Case, R., & Khanna, F. (1981). The missing links: Stages in children's progression from sensorimotor to logical thought. In K.W. Fischer (Ed.), *Cognitive development (New directions for child development, No. 12)*. San Francisco: Jossey-Bass.

Chi, M.T. (1978). Knowledge structures and memory development. In R.S. Siegler (Ed.), *Children's thinking: What develops?* Hillsdale, NJ: Erlbaum.

Chi, M.T., & Klahr, D. (1975). Span and rate of apprehension in children and adults. *Journal of Experimental Psychology, 19*, 434–439.

Cronbach, L.J. (1951). Coefficient alpha and the internal structure of tests. *Psychometrika, 16*, 297–334.

Estes, T.H. (1971). A scale to measure attitudes toward reading. *Journal of Reading, 15*, 135–138.

Heathington, B.S. (1979). What to do about reading motivation in the middle school. *Journal of Reading, 22*, 709–713.

Nitko, A.J. (1983). *Educational tests and measurement: An introduction*. New York: Harcourt Brace Jovanovich.

Nunnally, J.C. (1967). *Psychometric theory*. New York: McGraw-Hill.

Purves, A.C., & Beach, R. (1972). *Literature and the reader: Research in response to literature, reading interests, and the teaching of literature*.

Urbana, IL: National Council of Teachers of English.

Reed, K. (1979). Assessing affective responses to reading: A multi-measurement model. *Reading World, 19*, 149–156.

Right to Read Office. (1976). *Reading interest/attitude scale*. Washington, DC: United States Office of Education.

Robinson, R., & Good, T.L. (1987). *Becoming an effective reading teacher*. New York: Harper & Row.

Roettger, D. (1980). Elementary students' attitudes toward reading. *The Reading Teacher, 33*, 451–453.

Rousseau, J-J. (1762/1979). *Emile, or on education* (trans. A. Bloom). New York: Basic Books.

Smith, F. (1988). *Understanding reading: A psycholinguistic analysis of reading and learning to read* (4th ed.). Hillsdale, NJ: Erlbaum.

Statistical abstract of the United States. (1989). Washington, DC: Bureau of Census, Department of Commerce.

Walberg, H.J., & Tsai, S. (1985). Correlates of reading achievement and attitude: A national assessment study. *Journal of Educational Research, 78*, 159–167.

Wixson, K.K., & Lipson, M.Y. (in press). *Reading diagnosis and remediation*. Glenview, IL: Scott, Foresman.

Elementary Reading Attitude Survey
Directions for use

The Elementary Reading Attitude Survey provides a quick indication of student attitudes toward reading. It consists of 20 items and can be administered to an entire classroom in about 10 minutes. Each item presents a brief, simply worded statement about reading, followed by four pictures of Garfield. Each pose is designed to depict a different emotional state, ranging from very positive to very negative.

Administration

Begin by telling students that you wish to find out how they feel about reading. Emphasize that this is *not* a test and that there are no "right" answers. Encourage sincerity.

Distribute the survey forms and, if you wish to monitor the attitudes of specific students, ask them to write their names in the space at the top. Hold up a copy of the survey so that the students can see the first page. Point to the picture of Garfield at the far left of the first item. Ask the students to look at this same picture on their own survey form. Discuss with them the mood Garfield seems to be in (very happy). Then move to the next picture and again discuss Garfield's mood (this time, a *little* happy). In the same way, move to the third and fourth pictures and talk about Garfield's moods—a little upset and very upset. It is helpful to point out the position of Garfield's *mouth*, especially in the middle two figures.

Explain that together you will read some statements about reading and that the students should think about how they feel about each statement. They should then circle the picture of Garfield that is closest to their own feelings. (Emphasize that the students should respond according to their own feelings, not as Garfield might respond!) Read each item aloud slowly and distinctly; then read it a second time while students are thinking. Be sure to read the item *number* and to remind students of page numbers when new pages are reached.

Scoring

To score the survey, count four points for each leftmost (happiest) Garfield circled, three for each slightly smiling Garfield, two for each mildly upset Garfield, and one point for each very upset (rightmost) Garfield. Three scores for each student can be obtained: the total for the first 10 items, the total for the second 10, and a composite total. The first half of the survey relates to attitude toward recreational reading; the second half relates to attitude toward academic aspects of reading.

Interpretation

You can interpret scores in two ways. One is to note informally where the score falls in regard to the four nodes of the scale. A total score of 50, for example, would fall about mid-way on the scale, between the slightly happy and slightly upset figures, therefore indicating a relatively indifferent overall attitude toward reading. The other approach is more formal. It involves converting the raw scores into percentile ranks by means of Table 1. Be sure to use the norms for the right grade level and to note the column headings (Rec = recreational reading, Aca = academic reading, Tot = total score). If you wish to determine the average percentile rank for your class, average the raw scores first; then use the table to locate the percentile rank corresponding to the raw score mean. Percentile ranks cannot be averaged directly.

Elementary Reading Attitude Survey

School _____ Grade_____ Name _____

1. How do you feel when you read a book on a rainy Saturday?

2. How do you feel when you read a book in school during free time?

3. How do you feel about reading for fun at home?

4. How do you feel about getting a book for a present?

(continued)

5. How do you feel about spending free time reading?

6. How do you feel about starting a new book?

7. How do you feel about reading during summer vacation?

8. How do you feel about reading instead of playing?

GARFIELD: © 1978 United Feature Syndicate, Inc.

(continued)

GARFIELD: © 1978 United Feature Syndicate, Inc.

9. How do you feel about going to a bookstore?

10. How do you feel about reading different kinds of books?

11. How do you feel when the teacher asks you questions about what you read?

12. How do you feel about doing reading workbook pages and worksheets?

(continued)

GARFIELD: © 1978 United Feature Syndicate, Inc.

13. How do you feel about reading in school?

14. How do you feel about reading your school books?

15. How do you feel about learning from a book?

16. How do you feel when it's time for reading class?

(continued)

17. How do you feel about the stories you read in reading class?

18. How do you feel when you read out loud in class?

19. How do you feel about using a dictionary?

20. How do you feel about taking a reading test?

GARFIELD: © 1978 United Feature Syndicate, Inc.

Elementary Reading Attitude Survey scoring sheet

Student name _____

Teacher_____

Grade _____ Administration date _____

Scoring guide

4 points	Happiest Garfield
3 points	Slightly smiling Garfield
2 points	Mildly upset Garfield
1 point	Very upset Garfield

Recreational reading

1. _____
2. _____
3. _____
4. _____
5. _____
6. _____
7. _____
8. _____
9. _____
10. _____

Raw score: _____

Academic reading

11. _____
12. _____
13. _____
14. _____
15. _____
16. _____
17. _____
18. _____
19. _____
20. _____

Raw score: _____

Full scale raw score (Recreational + Academic): _____

Percentile ranks

Recreational

Academic

Full scale

Appendix
Technical Aspects of the Elementary Reading Attitude Survey

The norming project

To create norms for the interpretation of scores, a large-scale study was conducted in late January 1989, at which time the survey was administered to 18,138 students in Grades 1–6. A number of steps were taken to achieve a sample that was sufficiently stratified (i.e., reflective of the American population) to allow confident generalizations. Children were drawn from 95 school districts in 38 U.S. states. The number of girls exceeded by only 5 the number of boys. Ethnic distribution of the sample was also close to that of the U.S. population (*Statistical abstract of the United States*, 1989). The proportion of blacks (9.5%) was within 3% of the national proportion, while the proportion of Hispanics (6.2%) was within 2%.

Percentile ranks at each grade for both subscales and the full scale are presented in Table 1. These data can be used to compare individual students' scores with the national sample and they can be interpreted like achievement-test percentile ranks.

Table 1
Mid-year percentile ranks by grade and scale

Raw Scr	Grade 1 Rec	Grade 1 Aca	Grade 1 Tot	Grade 2 Rec	Grade 2 Aca	Grade 2 Tot	Grade 3 Rec	Grade 3 Aca	Grade 3 Tot	Grade 4 Rec	Grade 4 Aca	Grade 4 Tot	Grade 5 Rec	Grade 5 Aca	Grade 5 Tot	Grade 6 Rec	Grade 6 Aca	Grade 6 Tot
80			99			99			99			99			99			99
79			95			96			98			99			99			99
78			93			95			97			98			99			99
77			92			94			97			98			99			99
76			90			93			96			97			98			99
75			88			92			95			96			98			99
74			86			90			94			95			97			99
73			84			88			92			94			97			98
72			82			86			91			93			96			98
71			80			84			89			91			95			97
70			78			82			86			89			94			96
69			75			79			84			88			92			95
68			72			77			81			86			91			93
67			69			74			79			83			89			92
66			66			71			76			80			87			90
65			62			69			73			78			84			88
64			59			66			70			75			82			86
63			55			63			67			72			79			84
62			52			60			64			69			76			82
61			49			57			61			66			73			79
60			46			54			58			62			70			76
59			43			51			55			59			67			73
58			40			47			51			56			64			69
57			37			45			48			53			61			66
56			34			41			44			48			57			62
55			31			38			41			45			53			58
54			28			35			38			41			50			55

Table 1
Mid-year percentile ranks by grade and scale (continued)

Raw Scr	Grade 1 Rec	Aca	Tot	Grade 2 Rec	Aca	Tot	Grade 3 Rec	Aca	Tot	Grade 4 Rec	Aca	Tot	Grade 5 Rec	Aca	Tot	Grade 6 Rec	Aca	Tot
53			25			32			34			38			46			52
52			22			29			31			35			42			48
51			20			26			28			32			39			44
50			18			23			25			28			36			40
49			15			20			23			26			33			37
48			13			18			20			23			29			33
47			12			15			17			20			26			30
46			10			13			15			18			23			27
45			8			11			13			16			20			25
44			7			9			11			13			17			22
43			6			8			9			12			15			20
42			5			7			8			10			13			17
41			5			6			7			9			12			15
40	99	99	4	99	99	5	99	99	6	99	99	7	99	99	10	99	99	13
39	92	91	3	94	94	4	96	97	6	97	98	6	98	99	9	99	99	12
38	89	88	3	92	92	3	94	95	4	95	97	5	96	98	8	97	99	10
37	86	85	2	88	89	2	90	93	3	92	95	4	94	98	7	95	99	8
36	81	79	2	84	85	2	87	91	2	88	93	3	91	96	6	92	98	7
35	77	75	1	79	81	1	81	88	2	84	90	3	87	95	4	88	97	6
34	72	69	1	74	78	1	75	83	2	78	87	2	82	93	4	83	95	5
33	65	63	1	68	73	1	69	79	1	72	83	2	77	90	3	79	93	4
32	58	58	1	62	67	1	63	74	1	66	79	1	71	86	3	74	91	3
31	52	53	1	56	62	1	57	69	0	60	75	1	65	82	2	69	87	2
30	44	49	1	50	57	0	51	63	0	54	70	1	59	77	1	63	82	2
29	38	44	0	44	51	0	45	58	0	47	64	1	53	71	1	58	78	1
28	32	39	0	37	46	0	38	52	0	41	58	1	48	66	1	51	73	1
27	26	34	0	31	41	0	33	47	0	35	52	1	42	60	1	46	67	1
26	21	30	0	25	37	0	26	41	0	29	46	0	36	54	0	39	60	1
25	17	25	0	20	32	0	21	36	0	23	40	0	30	49	0	34	54	0
24	12	21	0	15	27	0	17	31	0	19	35	0	25	42	0	29	49	0
23	9	18	0	11	23	0	13	26	0	14	29	0	20	37	0	24	42	0
22	7	14	0	8	18	0	9	22	0	11	25	0	16	31	0	19	36	0
21	5	11	0	6	15	0	6	18	0	9	20	0	13	26	0	15	30	0
20	4	9	0	4	11	0	5	14	0	6	16	0	10	21	0	12	24	0
19	2	7		2	8		3	11		5	13		7	17		10	20	
18	2	5		2	6		2	8		3	9		6	13		5	18	
17	1	4		1	5		1	5		2	7		4	9		6	11	
16	1	3		1	3		1	4		2	5		3	6		4	8	
15	0	2		0	2		0	3		1	3		2	4		3	6	
14	0	2		0	1		0	1		1	2		1	2		1	3	
13	0	1		0	1		0	1		0	1		1	2		1	2	
12	0	1		0	0		0	0		0	1		0	1		0	1	
11	0	0		0	0		0	0		0	0		0	0		0	0	
10	0	0		0	0		0	0		0	0		0	0		0	0	

Appendix
Technical Aspects of the Elementary Reading Attitude Survey (continued)

Reliability

Cronbach's alpha, a statistic developed primarily to measure the internal consistency of attitude scales (Cronbach, 1951), was calculated at each grade level for both subscales and for the composite score. These coefficients ranged from .74 to .89 and are presented in Table 2.

It is interesting that with only two exceptions, coefficients were .80 or higher. These were for the recreational subscale at Grades 1 and 2. It is possible that the stability of young children's attitudes toward leisure reading grows with their decoding ability and familiarity with reading as a pastime.

Table 2
Descriptive statistics and internal consistency measures

Grade	N	Recreational Subscale				Academic Subscale				Full Scale (Total)			
		M	SD	S_eM	Alpha[a]	M	SD	S_eM	Alpha	M	SD	S_eM	Alpha
1	2,518	31.0	5.7	2.9	.74	30.1	6.8	3.0	.81	61.0	11.4	4.1	.87
2	2,974	30.3	5.7	2.7	.78	28.8	6.7	2.9	.81	59.1	11.4	3.9	.88
3	3,151	30.0	5.6	2.5	.80	27.8	6.4	2.8	.81	57.8	10.9	3.8	.88
4	3,679	29.5	5.8	2.4	.83	26.9	6.3	2.6	.83	56.5	11.0	3.6	.89
5	3,374	28.5	6.1	2.3	.86	25.6	6.0	2.5	.82	54.1	10.8	3.6	.89
6	2,442	27.9	6.2	2.2	.87	24.7	5.8	2.5	.81	52.5	10.6	3.5	.89
All	18,138	29.5	5.9	2.5	.82	27.3	6.6	2.7	.83	56.8	11.3	3.7	.89

[a] Cronbach's alpha (Cronbach, 1951).

Validity

Evidence of construct validity was gathered by several means. For the recreational subscale, students in the national norming group were asked (a) whether a public library was available to them and (b) whether they currently had a library card. Those to whom libraries were available were separated into two groups (those with and without cards) and their recreational scores were compared. Cardholders had significantly higher ($p < .001$) recreational scores ($M = 30.0$) than noncardholders ($M = 28.9$), evidence of the subscale's validity in that scores varied predictably with an outside criterion.

A second test compared students who presently had books checked out from their school library versus students who did not. The comparison was limited to children whose teachers reported not requiring them to check out books. The means of the two groups varied significantly ($p < .001$), and children with books checked out scored higher ($M = 29.2$) than those who had no books checked out ($M = 27.3$).

A further test of the recreational subscale compared students who reported watching an average of less than 1 hour of television per night with students who reported watching more than 2 hours per night. The recreational mean for the low televiewing group (31.5) significantly exceeded ($p < .001$) the mean of the heavy televiewing group (28.6). Thus, the amount of television watched varied inversely with children's attitudes toward recreational reading.

The validity of the academic subscale was tested by examining the relationship of scores to reading ability. Teachers categorized norm-group children as having low, average, or high overall reading ability. Mean subscale scores of the high-ability readers ($M = 27.7$) significantly exceeded the mean of low-ability readers ($M = 27.0$, p < .001), evidence that scores were reflective of how the students truly felt about reading for academic purposes.

The relationship between the subscales was also investigated. It was hypothesized that children's attitudes toward recreational and academic reading would be moderately but not highly correlated. Facility with reading is likely to affect these two areas similarly, resulting in similar attitude scores. Nevertheless, it is easy to imagine children prone to read for pleasure but disenchanted with assigned reading and children academically engaged but without interest in reading outside of school. The inter-subscale correlation coefficient was .64, which meant that just 41% of the variance in one set of scores could be accounted for by the other. It is reasonable to suggest that the two subscales, while related, also reflect dissimilar factors—a desired outcome.

To tell more precisely whether the traits measured by the survey corresponded to the two sub-scales, factor analyses were conducted. Both used the unweighted least squares method of extraction and a varimax rotation. The first analysis permitted factors to be identified liberally (using a limit equal to the smallest eigenvalue greater than 1). Three factors were identified. Of the 10 items comprising the academic subscale, 9 loaded predominantly on a single factor while the 10th (item 13) loaded nearly equally on all three factors. A second factor was dominated by 7 items of the recreational subscale, while 3 of the recreational items (6, 9, and 10) loaded principally on a third factor. These items did, however, load more heavily on the second (recreational) factor than on the first (academic). A second analysis constrained the identification of factors to two. This time, with one exception, all items loaded cleanly on factors associated with the two subscales. The exception was item 13, which could have been interpreted as a recreational item and thus apparently involved a slight ambiguity. Taken together, the factor analyses produced evidence extremely supportive of the claim that the survey's two subscales reflect discrete aspects of reading attitude.

Assessing Motivation to Read

Linda B. Gambrell, Barbara Martin Palmer,
Rose Marie Codling, and Susan Anders Mazzoni

April 1996

Teachers have long recognized that motivation is at the heart of many of the pervasive problems we face in teaching young children to read. In a study conducted by Veenman (1984), teachers ranked motivating students as one of their primary and overriding concerns. A more recent national survey of teachers also revealed that "creating interest in reading" was rated as the most important area for future research (O'Flahavan, Gambrell, Guthrie, Stahl, & Alvermann, 1992). The value teachers place on motivation is supported by a robust research literature that documents the link between motivation and achievement (Elley, 1992; Gambrell & Morrow, in press; Guthrie, Schafer, Wang, & Afflerbach, 1993; Purves & Beach, 1972; Walberg & Tsai, 1985; Wixson & Lipson, 1991). The results of these studies clearly indicate the need to increase our understanding of how children acquire the motivation to develop into active, engaged readers.

Highly motivated readers are self-determining and generate their own reading opportunities. They want to read and choose to read for a wide range of personal reasons such as curiosity, involvement, social interchange, and emotional satisfaction. According to Guthrie (1996), highly motivated readers generate their own literacy learning opportunities, and, in doing so, they begin to determine their own destiny as literacy learners.

Research supports the notion that literacy learning is influenced by a variety of motivational factors (Deci & Ryan, 1985; Eccles, 1983; Ford, 1992; Kuhl, 1986; Lepper, 1988; Maehr, 1976; McCombs, 1991; Wigfield, 1994). A number of current theories suggest that self-perceived competence and task value are major determinants of motivation and task engagement. For example, Eccles (1983) advanced an "expectancy-value" theory of motivation, which states that motivation is strongly influenced by one's expectation of success or failure at a task as well as the "value" or relative attractiveness the individual places on the task. The expectancy component of Eccles's theory is supported by a number of research studies that suggest that students who believe they are capable and competent readers are more likely to outperform those who do not hold such beliefs (Paris & Oka, 1986; Schunk, 1985). In addition, students who perceive reading as valuable and important and who have personally relevant reasons for reading will engage in reading in a more planned and effortful manner (Ames &

215

Archer, 1988; Dweck & Elliott, 1983; Paris & Oka, 1986).

The work of other motivational theorists, such as Ford (1992) and Winne (1985), has been grounded in the expectancy-value theory. Ford's (1992) motivational systems theory maintains that people will attempt to attain goals they value and perceive as achievable. Similarly, Winne (1985) views the "idealized reader" as one who feels competent and perceives reading as being of personal value and practical importance. Within this theoretical framework, reading motivation is defined by an individual's self-concept and the value the individual places on reading. Evidence from theory and research supports the notion that high motivation to read is associated with positive self-concept and high value assignment, while low motivation to read is associated with poor self-concept as a reader and low value assignment (Ford, 1992; Henk & Melnick, 1995; Wigfield, 1994). Given the emphasis on self-concept and task value in motivation theory, it seems important that teachers have resources for assessing both of these factors.

A review of current instruments designed to assess reading motivation revealed a number of instruments for measuring students' general attitude toward reading (e.g., McKenna & Kear, 1990; Tunnell, Calder, Justen, & Phaup, 1988), as well as several that measure the specific dimension of self-concept (Harter, 1981; Henk & Melnick, 1995; Pintrich & DeGroot, 1990). Henk and Melnick's (1995) instrument, The Reader Self-Perception Scale, was "developed in response to calls in the professional literature for self-evaluation instruments that measure the way readers appraise themselves" (p. 471). The instrument described in this article extends the work of Henk and Melnick by assessing two fundamental components of motivation suggested by motivational theory: self-concept and task value. In addition, none of the existing instruments combine quantitative and qualitative approaches for assessing reading motivation. Our purpose was to develop a public-domain instrument that would provide teachers with an efficient and reliable way to quantitatively and qualitatively assess reading motivation by evaluating students' self-concept as readers and the value they place on reading. This article presents the Motivation to Read Profile (MRP), along with a discussion of its development and suggestions for its use with elementary students.

Description of the Motivation to Read Profile

The MRP consists of two basic instruments: the Reading Survey and the Conversational Interview. The Reading Survey is a self-report, group-administered instrument, and the Conversational Interview is designed for individual administration. The survey assesses two specific dimensions of reading motivation, self-concept as a reader and value of reading; the interview provides information about the individual nature of students' reading motivation, such as what books and stories are most interesting, favorite authors, and where and how children locate reading materials that interest them most. Figure 1 profiles the two instruments.

Because the MRP combines information from a group-administered survey instrument with an individual interview, it provides a useful tool for exploring more fully the personal dimensions of students' reading motivation. The MRP is highly individualized, which makes it particularly appropriate for inclusion in portfolio assessment.

The Reading Survey. This instrument consists of 20 items and uses a 4-point response scale (see Figure 2). The survey assesses two specific dimensions of reading motivation: self-concept as a reader (10 items) and value of reading (10 items). The items that focus on self-concept as a reader are designed to elicit information about students' self-perceived com-

Figure 1
Motivation to Read Profile

Reading Survey	Conversational Interview
• Group administration	• Individual administration
• 15–20 minutes to administer	• 15–20 minutes to administer
• 20 items	• 14 scripted items
• Cued response	• Open-ended free response

• Subscales:
    Self-Concept as a Reader
    Value of Reading
	• Sections:
	    Narrative reading
	    Informational reading
	    General reading

petence in reading and self-perceived performance relative to peers. The value of reading items are designed to elicit information about the value students place on reading tasks and activities, particularly in terms of frequency of engagement and reading-related activities.

The Conversational Interview. The interview is made up of three sections (see Figure 3). The first section probes motivational factors related to the reading of narrative text (3 questions); the second section elicits information about informational reading (3 questions); and the final section focuses on more general factors related to reading motivation (8 questions).

The interview is designed to initiate an informal, conversational exchange between the teacher and student. According to Burgess (1980), conversational interviews are social events that can provide greater depth of understanding than more rigid interview techniques. Although conversational interviews are scripted, deviations from the script are anticipated and expected (Baker, 1984). The teacher is encouraged to deviate from the basic script in order to glean information that might otherwise be missed or omitted in a more formal, standardized interview approach. Teachers need to keep

in mind that the primary purpose of the conversational interview is to generate information that will provide authentic insights into students' reading experiences. Participating in a conversational interview allows children to use their unique ways of describing their reading motivation and experiences and to raise ideas and issues related to personal motivation that may not be reflected in the scripted interview items (Denzin, 1970).

How Was the MRP Developed?

Item selection for the MRP was based on a review of research and theories related to motivation and included an analysis of existing instruments designed to assess motivation and attitude toward reading. A number of instruments were examined in order to gather ideas for the development of an initial pool of MRP items (Gottfried, 1986; Harter, 1981; Johnson & Gaskins, 1991; McKenna & Kear, 1990; Pintrich & DeGroot, 1990; Raynor & Nochajski, 1986; Schell, 1992; Tunnell et al., 1988).

Figure 2
Reading Survey

Name_____ Date_____

Sample 1: I am in _____.
  ☐ Second grade ☐ Fifth grade
  ☐ Third grade   ☐ Sixth grade
  ☐ Fourth grade

Sample 2: I am a _____.
  ☐ boy
  ☐ girl

1. My friends think I am _____.
  ☐ a very good reader
  ☐ a good reader
  ☐ an OK reader
  ☐ a poor reader

2. Reading a book is something I like to do.
  ☐ Never
  ☐ Not very often
  ☐ Sometimes
  ☐ Often

3. I read _____.
  ☐ not as well as my friends
  ☐ about the same as my friends
  ☐ a little better than my friends
  ☐ a lot better than my friends

4. My best friends think reading is _____.
  ☐ really fun
  ☐ fun
  ☐ OK to do
  ☐ no fun at all

5. When I come to a word I don't know, I can _____.
  ☐ almost always figure it out
  ☐ sometimes figure it out
  ☐ almost never figure it out
  ☐ never figure it out

6. I tell my friends about good books I read.
  ☐ I never do this.
  ☐ I almost never do this.
  ☐ I do this some of the time.
  ☐ I do this a lot.

(continued)

Figure 2
Reading Survey (continued)

7. When I am reading by myself, I understand _____.
- [ ] almost everything I read
- [ ] some of what I read
- [ ] almost none of what I read
- [ ] none of what I read

8. People who read a lot are _____.
- [ ] very interesting
- [ ] interesting
- [ ] not very interesting
- [ ] boring

9. I am _____.
- [ ] a poor reader
- [ ] an OK reader
- [ ] a good reader
- [ ] a very good reader

10. I think libraries are _____.
- [ ] a great place to spend time
- [ ] an interesting place to spend time
- [ ] an OK place to spend time
- [ ] a boring place to spend time

11. I worry about what other kids think about my reading _____.
- [ ] every day
- [ ] almost every day
- [ ] once in a while
- [ ] never

12. Knowing how to read well is _____.
- [ ] not very important
- [ ] sort of important
- [ ] important
- [ ] very important

13. When my teacher asks me a question about what I have read, I _____.
- [ ] can never think of an answer
- [ ] have trouble thinking of an answer
- [ ] sometimes think of an answer
- [ ] always think of an answer

(continued)

Figure 2
Reading Survey (continued)

14. I think reading is _____.
- ☐ a boring way to spend time
- ☐ an OK way to spend time
- ☐ an interesting way to spend time
- ☐ a great way to spend time

15. Reading is _____.
- ☐ very easy for me
- ☐ kind of easy for me
- ☐ kind of hard for me
- ☐ very hard for me

16. When I grow up I will spend _____.
- ☐ none of my time reading
- ☐ very little of my time reading
- ☐ some of my time reading
- ☐ a lot of my time reading

17. When I am in a group talking about stories, I _____.
- ☐ almost never talk about my ideas
- ☐ sometimes talk about my ideas
- ☐ almost always talk about my ideas
- ☐ always talk about my ideas

18. I would like for my teacher to read books out loud to the class _____.
- ☐ every day
- ☐ almost every day
- ☐ once in a while
- ☐ never

19. When I read out loud I am a _____.
- ☐ poor reader
- ☐ OK reader
- ☐ good reader
- ☐ very good reader

20. When someone gives me a book for a present, I feel _____.
- ☐ very happy
- ☐ sort of happy
- ☐ sort of unhappy
- ☐ unhappy

Figure 3
Conversational Interview

Name _____   Date _____

A. Emphasis: Narrative text

Suggested prompt (designed to engage student in a natural conversation): I have been reading a good book…I was talking with…about it last night. I enjoy talking about good stories and books that I've been reading. Today I'd like to hear about what you have been reading.

1. Tell me about the most interesting story or book you have read this week (or even last week). Take a few minutes to think about it. (Wait time.) Now, tell me about the book or story.

Probes: What else can you tell me? Is there anything else? _____
_____
_____
_____
_____

2. How did you know or find out about this story? _____
_____
_____

     ☐ assigned   ☐ in school
     ☐ chosen   ☐ out of school

3. Why was this story interesting to you? _____
_____
_____

B. Emphasis: Informational text

Suggested prompt (designed to engage student in a natural conversation): Often we read to find out about something or to learn about something. We read for information. For example, I remember a student of mine…who read a lot of books about…to find out as much as he/she could about…. Now, I'd like to hear about some of the informational reading you have been doing.

1. Think about something important that you learned recently, not from your teacher and not from television, but from a book or some other reading material. What did you read about? (Wait time.) Tell me about what you learned.

Probes: What else could you tell me? Is there anything else? _____
_____
_____

2. How did you know or find out about this book/article? _____
_____
_____

     ☐ assigned   ☐ in school
     ☐ chosen   ☐ out of school

(continued)

Figure 3
Conversational Interview (continued)

3. Why was this book (or article) important to you? _____

_____

_____

_____

C. Emphasis: General reading

1. Did you read anything at home yesterday? _____ What?

_____

_____

2. Do you have any books at school (in your desk/storage area/locker/book bag) today that you are reading? _____ Tell me about them.

_____

_____

3. Tell me about your favorite author.

_____

_____

_____

4. What do you think you have to learn to be a better reader?

_____

_____

_____

5. Do you know about any books right now that you'd like to read? Tell me about them.

_____

_____

_____

6. How did you find out about these books?

_____

_____

7. What are some things that get you really excited about reading books?

_____

_____

Tell me about…

_____

_____

8. Who gets you really interested and excited about reading books?

_____

_____

Tell me more about what they do.

_____

_____

An assessment instrument is useful only if it is valid and reliable. Validity refers to the instrument's ability to measure the trait it purports to measure, and reliability refers to the ability of the instrument to consistently measure that trait. To gain information about the validity and reliability of the MRP, the Reading Survey and the Conversational Interview were field tested.

Development and Field Testing of the Reading Survey

The criteria for item selection and development for the survey instrument included (a) applicability to Grades 2 through 6, (b) applicability to all teaching approaches and materials, (c) suitability for group administration, and (d) accuracy in reflecting the appropriate dimension of motivation, i.e., self-concept or value. All survey items employ a 4-point response scale to avoid neutral, central response patterns. A 4-point scale also seemed more appropriate for elementary students as there is some evidence to suggest that young children have difficulty simultaneously discriminating among more than five discrete categories (Case & Khanna, 1981; Nitko, 1983). In order to avoid repetition in the presentation of the response alternatives and to control for the threat of "response set" (i.e., children selecting the same responses for each item), some response alternatives proceed from most positive to least positive while others are ordered in the opposite way.

An initial pool of survey items was developed based on the criteria described above. Three experienced classroom teachers, who were also graduate students in reading, critiqued over 100 items for their construct validity in assessing students' self-concept or value of reading. We compiled the items that received 100% agreement. These items were then submitted to four classroom teachers who were asked to sort the items into three categories: measures self-concept, measures value of reading, not sure or questionable. Only those items that received 100% trait agreement were selected for inclusion on the Reading Survey instrument used in the field testing.

The final version of the Reading Survey instrument was administered in the late fall and early spring with 330 third- and fifth-grade students in 27 classrooms in 4 schools from 2 school districts in an eastern U.S. state. To determine whether the traits measured by the Reading Survey (Self-Concept as a Reader and Value of Reading) corresponded to the two subscales, factor analyses were conducted using the unweighted least squares method and a varimax rotation. Only items that loaded cleanly on the two traits were included in the final instrument. To assess the internal consistency of the Reading Survey, Cronbach's (1951) alpha statistic was calculated, which revealed a moderately high reliability for both subscales (self-concept = .75; value = .82). In addition, pre- and posttest reliability coefficients were calculated for the subscales (self-concept = .68; value = .70), which confirmed the moderately high reliability of the instrument.

Development and Field Testing of the Conversational Interview

Approximately 60 open-ended questions regarding narrative and informational reading, general and specific reading experiences, and home and school reading practices were developed for the initial pool of interview items. These items were field tested in the spring with a stratified random sample of 48 students (24 third graders and 24 fifth graders). Classroom teachers identified students as at grade level, above grade level, or below grade level. The teachers were then asked to identify, within each of the three ability level lists, the two most "highly motivated readers" and the two "least motivated readers." Twenty-four students from the list of most highly motivated readers and 24 students from the list of least motivated readers participated in the field testing of the 60 interview items. Two graduate students, who were former classroom teachers, analyzed the 48 student protocols and selected 14 questions that revealed the most useful information about students' motivation to read. These 14 questions were used for the final version of the Conversational Interview.

Validity and Reliability of the MRP

Additional steps were taken to validate the final version of the MRP. Responses to the survey and conversational interview were examined for consistency of information across the two instruments. The survey and interview responses of 2 highly motivated and 2 less motivated readers were randomly selected for analysis. Two independent raters compared each student's responses on the survey instrument and the interview. For example, one item on the survey asks the students to indicate whether they think they are a "very good reader," "good reader," "OK reader," or "poor reader." Comments made during the conversational interview were analyzed to determine if students provided any confirming evidence about their self-perceived competence in reading.

Two raters independently compared each student's responses to items on the survey with information provided during the interview, with an interrater agreement of .87. There was consistent, supporting information in the interview responses for approximately 70% of the information tapped in the survey instrument. The results of these data analyses support the notion that the children responded consistently on both types of assessment instruments (survey, interview) and across time (fall, spring).

A further test of the validity of the Reading Survey explored the relationship between level of motivation and reading achievement. Motivational theory and research indicate a positive correlation between motivation and achievement (Ford, 1992; McKenna & Kear, 1990). Teachers categorized students as having low, average, or high reading performance. Statistically significant differences were found among the mean scores on the self-concept measure for high, middle, and low reading achievement groups, revealing that scores were positively associated with level of reading achievement. In addition, statistically significant differences were found between mean scores of third- and fifth-grade students on the value measure, with younger students scoring more positively than older students. This finding is in keeping with the work of other researchers, who have found that attitude toward reading decreases as children progress through the elementary grades (e.g., McKenna & Kear, 1990).

Administering the MRP

The MRP combines group and individual assessment procedures. The Reading Survey instrument can be administered to an entire class, small group, or individual, while the Conversational Interview is designed to be conducted on an individual basis.

Administration and Scoring of the Reading Survey

The administration of the Reading Survey instrument takes approximately 15–20 minutes (see Figure 4). Teachers should consider grade level and attention span when deciding how and when to administer it. For example, teachers of young children may decide to administer the first 10 items in one session and the final 10 during a second session.

The survey is designed to be read aloud to students. One of the problems inherent in much of the motivational research is that reading ability often confounds the results so that proficient, higher ability readers are typically identified as

Figure 4
Teacher directions: MRP Reading Survey

Distribute copies of the Reading Survey. Ask students to write their names on the space provided.

Say:

   I am going to read some sentences to you. I want to know how you feel about your reading. There are no right or wrong answers. I really want to know how you honestly feel about reading.

   I will read each sentence twice. Do not mark your answer until I tell you to. The first time I read the sentence I want you to think about the best answer for you. The second time I read the sentence I want you to fill in the space beside your best answer. Mark only one answer. Remember: Do not mark your answer until I tell you to. OK, let's begin.

Read the first sample item. Say:
Sample 1: I am in (pause) first grade, (pause) second grade, (pause) third grade, (pause) fourth grade, (pause) fifth grade, (pause) sixth grade.

Read the first sample again. Say:
This time as I read the sentence, mark the answer that is right for you. I am in (pause) first grade, (pause) second grade, (pause) third grade, (pause) fourth grade, (pause) fifth grade, (pause) sixth grade.

Read the second sample item. Say:
Sample 2: I am a (pause) boy, (pause) girl.

Say:
Now, get ready to mark your answer.
I am a (pause) boy, (pause) girl.

Read the remaining items in the same way (e.g., number ____, sentence stem followed by a pause, each option followed by a pause, and then give specific directions for students to mark their answers while you repeat the entire item).

"motivated," while less proficient, lower ability readers are identified as "unmotivated." This characterization is inaccurate; there are proficient readers who are not highly motivated to read, just as there are less proficient readers who are highly motivated to read (McCombs, 1991; Roettger, 1980). When students are instructed to independently read and respond to survey items, the results for the less proficient, lower ability readers may not be reliable due to their frustration when reading the items. For these reasons, the Reading Survey is designed to be read aloud by the teacher to help ensure the veracity of student responses.

Students must understand that their responses to the survey items will not be graded. They should be told that the results of the survey will provide information that the teacher can use to make reading more interesting for them and that the information will be helpful only if they provide their most honest responses.

Directions for scoring the Reading Survey (see Figure 5) and a scoring sheet (see Figure 6) are provided. When scoring the survey, the most positive response is assigned the highest number (4) while the least positive response is assigned the lowest number (1). For example, if a student reported that he/she is a "good" reader,

Figure 5
Scoring directions: MRP Reading Survey

The survey has 20 items based on a 4-point scale. The highest total score possible is 80 points. On some items the response options are ordered least positive to most positive (see item 2 below), with the least positive response option having a value of 1 point and the most positive option having a point value of 4. On other items, however, the response options are reversed (see item 1 below). In those cases it will be necessary to *recode* the response options. Items where recoding is required are starred on the scoring sheet.

Example: Here is how Maria completed items 1 and 2 on the Reading Survey.

    1. My friends think I am _____.
    ☐ a very good reader
    ■ a good reader
    ☐ an OK reader
    ☐ a poor reader

    2. Reading a book is something I like to do.
    ☐ Never
    ☐ Not very often
    ☐ Sometimes
    ■ Often

To score item 1 it is first necessary to recode the response options so that
    a poor reader equals 1 point,
    an OK reader equals 2 points,
    a good reader equals 3 points, and
    a very good reader equals 4 points.

Since Maria answered that she is *a good reader* the point value for that item, 3, is entered on the first line of the Self-Concept column on the scoring sheet. See below.

    The response options for item 2 are ordered least positive (1 point) to most positive (4 points), so scoring item 2 is easy. Simply enter the point value associated with Maria's response. Because Maria selected the fourth option, a 4 is entered for item 2 under the Value of Reading column on the scoring sheet. See below.

Scoring sheet

Self-Concept as a Reader	Value of Reading
*recode 1. <u>3</u>	2. <u>4</u>

To calculate the Self-Concept raw score and Value raw score add all student responses in the respective column. The Full Survey raw score is obtained by combining the column raw scores. To convert the raw scores to percentage scores, divide student raw scores by the total possible score (40 for each subscale, 80 for the full survey).

Figure 6
MRP Reading Survey scoring sheet

Student name _____

Grade _____ Teacher _____

Administration date _____

Recoding scale

1=4
2=3
3=2
4=1

Self-Concept as a Reader

*recode   1.____
           3.____
*recode   5.____
*recode   7.____
           9.____
         11.____
         13.____
*recode   15.____
         17.____
         19.____

SC raw score: ____ /40

Value of Reading

           2.____
*recode   4.____
           6.____
*recode   8.____
*recode   10.____
         12.____
         14.____
         16.____
*recode   18.____
*recode   20.____

V raw score: ____ /40

Full survey raw score (Self-Concept & Value): ____ /80

Percentage scores   Self-Concept   [ ]
                        Value   [ ]
                        Full Survey   [ ]

Comments: _____

_____

_____

a "3" would be recorded. Teachers can compute percentage scores on the entire Reading Survey or on the two subscales (Self-Concept as a Reader and Value of Reading). Space is also provided at the bottom of the scoring sheet for the teacher to note any interesting or unusual responses that might be probed later during the conversational interview.

Administration of the Conversational Interview. The Conversational Interview is designed to elicit information that will help the teacher gain a deeper understanding of a student's reading motivation in an informal, conversational manner (see Figure 7). The entire interview takes approximately 15–20 minutes, but it can easily be conducted in three 5- to 7-minute sessions, one for each of the three sections of the interview (narrative, informational, and general reading). Individual portfolio conferences are an ideal time to conduct the interview.

We suggest that teachers review student responses on the Reading Survey prior to conducting the Conversational Interview so that they may contemplate and anticipate possible topics to explore. During a conversational interview, some children will talk enthusiastically without probing, but others may need support and encouragement. Children who are shy or who tend to reply in short, quick answers can be encouraged to elaborate upon their responses through nonthreatening phrases like "Tell me more about that…," "What else can you tell me…," and "Why do you think that…." Probing of brief responses from children is often necessary in order to reveal important and relevant information.

Teachers are also encouraged to extend, modify, and adapt the 14 questions outlined in the Conversational Interview, especially during conversations with individual students. Follow-up questions based on students' comments often provide the most significant information in such an interview.

Using the Results of the MRP to Make Instructional Decisions

Information from the results of the MRP can be used to plan instructional activities that will support students' reading development. The following list provides some ideas for ways in which the results can be used to enhance literacy learning. First, specific recommendations are present-

---

Figure 7
Teacher directions: MRP Conversational Interview

1. Duplicate the Conversational Interview so that you have a form for each child.

2. Choose in advance the section(s) or specific questions you want to ask from the Conversational Interview. Reviewing the information on students' Reading Surveys may provide information about additional questions that could be added to the interview.

3. Familiarize yourself with the basic questions provided in the interview prior to the interview session in order to establish a more conversational setting.

4. Select a quiet corner of the room and a calm period of the day for the interview.

5. Allow ample time for conducting the Conversational Interview.

6. Follow up on interesting comments and responses to gain a fuller understanding of students' reading experiences.

7. Record students' responses in as much detail as possible. If time and resources permit you may want to audiotape answers to A1 and B1 to be transcribed after the interview for more in-depth analysis.

8. Enjoy this special time with each student!

ed for using the results of the Reading Survey and the Conversational Interview. Then, general recommendations for using the MRP are provided.

Using the Results of the Reading Survey

Because of the highly individualized nature of motivation, careful examination of an individual's responses may provide valuable insights that can be used to create more meaningful, motivational contexts for reading instruction. For example, if a child indicates on the survey form that "reading is very hard" and that "reading is boring," the teacher can suggest books of particular interest to the child that the child can read with ease.

A total score and scores on the two subscales of the Reading Survey (Self-Concept as a Reader and Value of Reading) can be computed for each student. Teachers can then identify those children who have lower scores in these areas. These students may be the ones who are in need of additional support in developing motivation to read and may benefit from interventions to promote reading engagement.

Students who have lower subscores on the Self-Concept as a Reader scale may benefit from experiences that highlight successful reading. For example, to build feelings of competence, the teacher can arrange for the child to read books to children in lower grades.

Students who have lower subscores on the Value of Reading scale may benefit from experiences that emphasize meaningful purposes for reading. For example, the teacher can ask the child to read about how to care for a class pet or involve the child in class plays or skits.

If many children score low on the Value of Reading scale, the teacher can implement meaningful cooperative group activities where children teach one another about what they have read regarding a particular topic. The teacher can also involve the class in projects that require reading instructions, e.g., preparing a recipe, creating a crafts project, or performing a science experiment.

Class averages for the total score and subscores on the Reading Survey can be computed. This information may be helpful in obtaining an overview of the classroom level of motivation at various points throughout the school year.

Teachers may also analyze class responses to an individual item on the Reading Survey. For example, if many children indicate that they seldom read at home, the teacher may decide to implement a home reading program, or the teacher might discuss the importance of home reading and parent involvement during Parent Night. Another survey item asks children to complete the following statement: "I think libraries are…." If many students report a negative response toward libraries, the teacher can probe the class for further information in order to identify reasons, which can then be addressed.

Using the Results of the Conversational Interview

The primary purpose of the Conversational Interview is to gain insight into what motivates the student to engage in reading. Therefore, the interview questions focus on reading that students find most interesting. This information can inform the teacher about specific topics, books, and authors that the individual student finds engaging and motivating.

The Conversational Interview might also reveal particular activities related to reading that the child enjoys. For example, one child in our field study mentioned his father several times during the interview—reading to his father, telling his father about something interesting he had read, and selecting and buying books with his father. In such a situation, a teacher can suggest home activities or even specific books that the father and child might enjoy reading at home.

Class responses to items on the Conversational Interview may also reveal useful information. For example, if many children express interest in a particular topic, the teacher may find ways to include reading activities regarding the topic. If children express interest in a particular instructional activity, such as inviting guest readers into the classroom or "Young Authors' Night" where children present their stories to parents and guests, this information can then be taken into account for future planning.

General Recommendations for Using the MRP

The MRP can provide a means of assessing, monitoring, and documenting student responses to innovations in the classroom that are designed to promote reading motivation. For example, the teacher might collect information using the MRP prior to and following the implementation of a reading motivational intervention, such as a sustained silent reading program or involvement in a classroom or a schoolwide reading motivational program.

The MRP can be given at the beginning of the year to provide the teacher with profiles of each child. This information can be placed in children's reading portfolios. Teachers may decide to administer the MRP several times throughout the school year so that changes in the child's attitudes and interests about reading can be documented and compared.

The MRP can be administered at each grade level and the assessment data retained so that teachers can compare changes in a child's self-concept as a reader and value of reading as he/she progresses from grade to grade.

These are only a sampling of ideas of the ways in which the MRP can be used in the classroom. Each teacher will have his/her own particular insights about ways in which the MRP information can best be applied to meet students' needs.

Cautions About Interpreting Responses to the MRP

Although there is support for the reliability and validity of the MRP, it is a self-report instrument, and it has limitations that are commonly associated with such instruments. For example, it is impossible to determine from self-report instruments alone whether or not students actually feel, believe, or do the things they report. Even though the elaborate, descriptive information gleaned from the interview can substantiate survey responses to some extent, only careful observation can verify information derived from the MRP.

Also, one should be cautious when interpreting responses to individual items due to the contextual nature of reading motivation. For example, a student might feel highly competent as a reader when reading high-interest, self-selected narrative materials and yet feel far less competent when reading content area materials. It is more important to look across the survey and interview responses to determine patterns that reveal factors that are relevant to the student's reading motivation.

Finally, as with any assessment, the MRP should be used in conjunction with other assessment instruments, techniques, and procedures. Teachers should consider the MRP as one source of information about reading motivation.

Summary

Motivation is an integral component of reading instruction. In addition, a number of studies suggest a connection between motivation and achievement. Current motivational theory emphasizes the role of self-perceived competence and task value as determinants of motivation and task engagement. The Motivation to Read Profile was developed to provide teachers with an efficient and reliable instrument for assessing reading motivation by evaluating students' self-concept as readers and the value they place on reading. In addition, the assessment instrument provides both quantitative and qualitative information by combining the use of a survey instrument and an individual interview.

There are a number of ways in which the MRP can be used to make instructional decisions, and teachers are in the best position to decide how they will apply the information gleaned from the MRP in their classrooms. Ideally, the MRP will help teachers acquire insights about individual students, particularly those students whom teachers worry most about in terms of their reading motivation and development. The individualized nature of the information derived from the MRP makes this instrument particularly appropriate for inclusion in portfolio assessment. Careful scrutiny of the responses to the Reading Survey and the Conversational Interview, coupled with teacher observations of student behaviors in various classroom reading contexts, can help teachers plan for meaningful instruction that will support students in becoming highly motivated readers.

Authors' Notes

We would like to thank the students, teachers, and principals in Charles and Frederick Counties, Maryland, USA, for their support and assistance in the piloting and development of the instruments described in this article.

The work reported here is a National Reading Research Project of the University of Georgia and University of Maryland. It was supported under the Educational Research and Development Centers Program (PR/AWARD NO. 117A20007) as administered by the Office of Educational Research and Improvement, U.S. Department of Education. The findings and opinions expressed here do not necessarily reflect the position or policies of the National Reading Research Center, the Office of Educational Research and Improvement, or the U.S. Department of Education.

References

Ames, C., & Archer, J. (1988). Achievement goals in the classroom: Students' learning strategies and motivation processes. *Journal of Educational Psychology, 80*, 260–267.

Baker, C.D. (1984). The search for adultness: Membership work in adolescent-adult talk. *Human Studies, 7*, 301–323.

Burgess, R. (1980). *Field research: A sourcebook and field manual*. London: Allen & Uwin.

Case, R., & Khanna, F. (1981). The missing links: Stages in children's progression from sensorimotor to logical thought. In K.W. Fischer (Ed.), *Cognitive development: New directions for child development* (pp. 21–32). San Francisco: Jossey-Bass.

Cronbach, L.J. (1951). Coefficient alpha and the internal structure of tests. *Psychometrika, 16*, 297–334.

Deci, E., & Ryan, R. (1985). *Intrinsic motivation and self-determination in human behavior*. New York: Plenum.

Denzin, N. (1970). *The research act in sociology*. London: Butterworth.

Dweck, C., & Elliott, E. (1983). Achievement motivation. In E.M. Heatherington (Ed.), *Handbook of child psychology: Vol. 4. Socialization, personality, and social development* (pp. 643–691). New York: Wiley.

Eccles, J. (1983). Expectancies, values and academic behaviors. In J.T. Spence (Ed.), *Achievement and achievement motives* (pp. 75–146). San Francisco: Freeman.

Elley, W.B. (1992). *How in the world do students read?* Hamburg, Germany: International Association for the Evaluation of Educational Achievement.

Ford, M.E. (1992). *Motivating humans*. Newbury Park, CA: Sage.

Gambrell, L.B., & Morrow, L.M. (in press). Creating motivating contexts for literacy learning. In L. Baker, P. Afflerbach, & D. Reinking (Eds.), *Developing engaged readers in home and school communities*. Hillsdale, NJ: Erlbaum.

Gottfried, A.E. (1986). *Children's academic intrinsic motivation inventory*. Odessa, FL: Psychological Assessment Resources.

Guthrie, J.T. (1996). Educational contexts for engagement in literacy. *The Reading Teacher, 49,* 432–445.

Guthrie, J.T., Schafer, W., Wang, Y., & Afflerbach, P. (1993). *Influences of instruction on reading engagement: An empirical exploration of a social-cognitive framework of reading activity* (Research Report No. 3). Athens, GA: National Reading Research Center.

Harter, S. (1981). A new self-report scale of intrinsic versus extrinsic orientation in the classroom: Motivational and informational components. *Developmental Psychology, 17,* 300–312.

Henk, W., & Melnick, S.A. (1995). The Reader Self-Perception Scale (RSPS): A new tool for measuring how children feel about themselves as readers. *The Reading Teacher, 48,* 470–482.

Johnson, C.S., & Gaskins, J. (1991). Reading attitude: Types of materials and specific strategies. *Reading Improvement, 28,* 237–242.

Kuhl, J. (1986). Introduction. In J. Kuhl & J.W. Atkinson (Eds.), *Motivation, thought, and action* (pp. 1–16). New York: Praeger.

Lepper, M.R. (1988). Motivational considerations in the study of instruction. *Cognition and Instruction, 5,* 289–309.

Maehr, M.L. (1976). Continuing motivation: An analysis of a seldom considered educational outcome. *Review of Educational Research, 46,* 443–462.

McCombs, B.L. (1991). Unraveling motivation: New perspectives from research and practice. *Journal of Experimental Education, 60,* 3–88.

McKenna, M.C., & Kear, D.J. (1990). Measuring attitude toward reading: A new tool for teachers. *The Reading Teacher, 43,* 626–639.

Nitko, A.J. (1983). *Educational tests and measurement: An introduction.* New York: Harcourt Brace Jovanovich.

O'Flahavan, J., Gambrell, L.B., Guthrie, J., Stahl, S., & Alvermann, D. (1992). Poll results guide activities of research center. *Reading Today, 10,* p. 12.

Paris, S.G., & Oka, E.R. (1986). Self-regulated learning among exceptional children. *Exceptional Children, 53,* 103–108.

Pintrich, P.R., & DeGroot, E.V. (1990). Motivational and self-regulated learning components of classroom academic performance. *Journal of Educational Psychology, 82,* 33–40.

Purves, A., & Beach, R. (1972). *Literature and the reader: Research on response to literature, reading interests, and teaching of literature.* Urbana, IL: National Council of Teachers of English.

Raynor, J.O., & Nochajski, T.H. (1986). Development of the motivation for particular activity scale. In D.R. Brown & I. Vernoff (Eds.), *Frontiers of motivational psychology* (pp. 1–25). New York: Springer-Verlag.

Roettger, D. (1980). Elementary students' attitudes toward reading. *The Reading Teacher, 33,* 451–453.

Schell, L.M. (1992). Student perceptions of good and poor readers. *Reading Improvement, 29,* 50–55.

Schunk, D. (1985). Self-efficacy and school learning. *Psychology in the Schools, 22,* 208–223.

Tunnell, M.O., Calder, J.E., Justen, J.E., & Phaup, E.S. (1988). Attitudes of young readers. *Reading Improvement, 25,* 237–242.

Veenman, S. (1984). Perceived problems of beginning teachers. *Review of Educational Research, 54,* 143–178.

Walberg, H.J., & Tsai, S. (1985). Correlates of reading achievement and attitude: A national assessment study. *Journal of Educational Research, 78,* 159–167.

Wigfield, A. (1994). Expectancy-value theory of achievement motivation: A developmental perspective. *Educational Psychology Review, 6*(1), 48–78.

Winne, P. (1985). Steps toward promoting cognitive achievements. *The Elementary School Journal, 85,* 673–693.

Wixson, K.K., & Lipson, M.Y. (1991). *Reading diagnosis and remediation.* Glenview, IL: Scott, Foresman.

The Reader Self-Perception Scale (RSPS): A New Tool for Measuring How Children Feel About Themselves as Readers

William A. Henk and Steven A. Melnick

March 1995

Recently, reading educators and researchers have shown renewed interest in how affective factors influence children's academic achievement and behavior (Alvermann & Guthrie, 1993). As a result, our longheld intuitions about the powerful impact that attitudes, values, beliefs, desires, and motivations exert on literacy learning have begun to receive the focused attention they deserve.

Because of research in the affective domain, we now know with greater certainty that children who have made positive associations with reading tend to read more often, for longer periods of time, and with greater intensity. This deeper engagement translates into superior reading achievement (Anderson, Fielding, & Wilson, 1988; Foertsch, 1992). At the same time, we know that when children feel negatively about reading, their achievement tends to suffer. These children will either avoid reading altogether or read with little real involvement. Perhaps this is why, in a recent national poll, teachers ranked motivating students and creating an interest in reading as their first priority (O'Flavahan et al., 1992).

The movement toward greater consideration of affective influences on reading achievement is long overdue but somewhat understandable (Athey, 1985; Mathewson, 1985). Educators and researchers have recognized for some time the importance of knowing as much as possible about the many affective elements that shape readers' engagement (Morrow & Weinstein, 1986). Unfortunately, because affect tends to be difficult to measure, the tools necessary to make truly valid appraisals have not been available (Henk, 1993). Consequently, teachers have been hindered in adjusting classroom learning climates to foster maximum literacy growth.

To help teachers better address the role of affect in reading, we describe an important psychological construct, reader self-efficacy, and introduce a new scale to measure this aspect of literacy. The new scale can be administered to groups of students for the purposes of instruction, assessment, and research, and it provides data on affect that make individual reading evaluations more complete.

Reader Attitudes and Self-Perceptions

Fortunately, educators have made some important strides in measuring affective elements in recent years. For instance, McKenna and Kear (1990) have developed the Elementary Reading Attitude Survey (ERAS), a public domain instrument that measures elementary students' attitudes toward both school-based and recreational forms of reading. The ERAS has been used extensively by primary and intermediate level teachers to determine the overall attitude levels of classes, and it has also provided insights into the reading habits and achievement levels of individual children. Besides its inviting response format that makes use of the comic strip character Garfield the cat, a major advantage of the ERAS has been its extensive norming. Unlike many affective scales, the ERAS exhibits solid validity and reliability characteristics, two critical attributes given the potential importance of attitudinal indicators.

Following in this tradition of instrument development, we created the Reader Self-Perception Scale (RSPS) to measure how intermediate-level children feel about themselves as readers (Henk & Melnick, 1992). The RSPS was developed in response to calls in the professional literature for instruments that measure the way readers appraise themselves (Winograd & Paris, 1988; Wixson, Peters, Weber, & Roeber, 1987). Valencia (1990) refers to this notion of reader self-evaluation as "perception of self as reader," a concept important in both statewide and individual portfolio assessment contexts.

Like the Elementary Reading Attitude Survey, the RSPS has been validated systematically and measures a dimension of affect that almost certainly influences attitudes toward reading. At the same time, the construct tapped by the Reader Self-Perception Scale is different enough from reading attitude to warrant special consideration. The two instruments also differ in terms of grade-level appropriateness. While the ERAS can be used in the primary grades through Grade 6, the RSPS purposely focuses on intermediate-level readers. This targeting stems from developmental research that has consistently indicated that prior to fourth grade, children do not estimate their academic performance accurately, nor attribute its causes properly (Blumenfeld, Pintrich, Meece, & Wessels, 1982; Nicholls, 1978; Stipek, 1981). By contrast, children in the intermediate grades are less likely to attribute their achievement to luck or effort and more likely to attribute performance to ability (Nicholls, 1979; Ruble, Boggiano, Feldman, & Loebl, 1980).

Self-Efficacy and Reading

The Reader Self-Perception Scale is based on Bandura's (1977, 1982) theory of perceived self-efficacy. Bandura defines self-efficacy as a person's judgments of her or his ability to perform an activity, and the effect this perception has on the ongoing and future conduct of the activity. In short, self-perceptions are likely to either motivate or inhibit learning (Schunk, 1982, 1983a, 1983b; Zimmerman & Ringle, 1981). Self-efficacy judgments are thought to affect achievement by influencing an individual's choice of activities, task avoidance, effort expenditure, and goal persistence (Bandura & Schunk, 1981; Schunk, 1984).

In reading, self-perceptions can impact upon an individual's overall orientation toward the process itself. Children who believe they are good readers probably enjoy a rich history of reader engagement and exhibit a strong likelihood of continued positive interactions with text. By contrast, children who perceive themselves as poor readers probably have not experienced much in the way of reading success. They almost surely will not look toward reading as a source of gratification. In this sense, it is not hard to imagine direct links between readers' self-perceptions and their subsequent reading behavior, habits, and attitudes. That is, how an individual feels about herself or himself as a reader could clearly influence whether reading would be sought or avoided, the amount of effort that would occur during reading, and how persistently comprehension would be pursued (Henk & Melnick, 1992).

The basic self-efficacy model (Bandura, 1977, 1982; Schunk, 1984) predicts that individuals take four basic factors into account when estimating their capabilities as a reader: Performance (a very broad category that includes past success, amount of effort necessary, the need for assistance, patterns of progress, task difficulty, task persistence, and belief in the effectiveness of instruction), Observational Comparison, Social Feedback, and Physiological States.

Overall, our previous research into the sources of information that children in the intermediate grades use to make reader self-perception judgments (Henk & Melnick, 1992, 1993) supports this four-factor model. However, as we indicate in the later section on Validation, we found it necessary to redefine the Performance category more narrowly. Consequently, our first source is Progress (PR). We define this scale as how one's perception of present reading performance compares with past performance. The second source, Observational Comparison (OC), deals with how a child perceives her or his reading performance to compare with the performance of classmates. The third source, Social Feedback (SF), includes direct or indirect input about reading from teachers, classmates, and people in the child's family.

Finally, the Physiological States (PS) source refers to internal feelings that the child experiences during reading. The entire Reader Self-Perception Scale is reproduced in Appendix A with items coded by scale to illustrate various item types.

It is important to understand that the four sources of information used in making reader self-perception judgments do not operate in isolation from one another (Marshall & Weinstein, 1984). A very natural overlap exists between the categories. For instance, personal perceptions of progress (PR) will be based, in part, not only upon children's observations of how their performance compares with classmates' performance (OC), but also upon the kinds of positive social feedback (SF) they receive, and their internal comfort while reading (PS). In fact, the scales relate so much to one another that interactions among them are inescapable.

These interactions confirm the idea that literacy learning is both complex and socially situated (Alvermann & Guthrie, 1993). In making reader self-perceptions, individual children may value one or more sources over the others. Much of this valuing process will be related to the social context in which the literacy learning occurs. Of course, observational comparison and social feedback are, by their very nature, socially situated. Even aspects of the physiological states category possess social dimensions, especially in the case of internal feelings experienced during oral reading (Filby & Barnett, 1982). Viewed in this social perspective, the classroom, the home, and anywhere else that reading occurs represent contexts for learning about oneself as a reader.

Why the RSPS?

Somewhat surprisingly, there have been very few attempts to develop instruments for measuring reader self-perceptions. The few scales that do exist definitely have their merits, but all possess some notable limitations (Boersma, Chapman, & MacGuire, 1979; Cohen, McDonell, & Osborn, 1989; Mitman & Lash, 1988). For instance, some scales measure self-perceptions of general achievement or language arts proficiency, but do not focus on reading achievement specifically. Others have very few items, and these items tend to measure reader self-efficacy indirectly at best. Often, major elements of reading such as word recognition, word analysis, fluency, and comprehension are not represented in the item pool as they are in the Reader Self-Perception Scale.

Another major problem with many of the scales is that they have not undergone adequate norming. Some are based on small samples, and others have not considered possible scales. A further major concern is that none of the existing reader self-perception instruments appear to be grounded in learning theory. By contrast, the RSPS takes its lead from a well regarded learning-theory framework and is steeped in a solid tradition of supportive research in the affective domain (Athey, 1985; Mathewson, 1985).

Although previous quantitative scales have fallen short of the mark, several useful structured interview formats are available for qualitative assessment of individual readers' self-perceptions (see Blumenfeld, Pintrich, Meece, & Wessels, 1982; Borko & Eisenhart, 1986; Canney & Winograd, 1979; Filby & Barnett, 1982; Gordon, 1990; Nicholls, 1979; Stipek & Weisz, 1981). Individual data collections can be extremely informative, but they tend to be time consuming and therefore of somewhat less practical value. To date, only the group-administered Reader Self-Perception Scale accounts adequately for concerns related to focus, norming, theoretical grounding, and practicality. Beyond these advantages, the RSPS offers a wide range of assessment, instructional, and research applications that are outlined in later sections.

Description of the Instrument

The Reader Self-Perception Scale consists of 1 general item and 32 subsequent items that represent the four scales (Progress, Observational Comparison, Social Feedback, and Physiological States). (See Table 1 for the number of items and internal consistency reliabilites for each scale.) The general item was used simply to prompt the children to think about their reading ability. The remaining items deal with overall reading ability as well as aspects of word recognition, word analysis, fluency, and comprehension. Wording of the items was kept simple so that reading ability itself would not confound the assessment. In addition, all items were stated positively to foster straightforward decision-making.

Brief written directions to the children appear directly on the instrument. The possible responses and their respective abbreviations are also included. The introductory material also contains a sample item and an accompanying explanation. Before duplicating the instrument for student use, the codes to the left of the items should be covered or removed.

In taking the RSPS, children are asked to read each item and to rate how much they agree or disagree with the statement. They make their ratings using a 5-point Likert system (1 = Strongly Disagree, 2 = Disagree, 3 = Undecided, 4 = Agree, and 5 = Strongly Agree). Because the number of items varies according to the scale (PR = 9; OC = 6; SF = 9; PS = 8), the maximum possible scores will differ for each scale (PR = 45; OC = 30; SF = 45; PS = 40).

Administration and Scoring

The RSPS takes approximately 15 to 20 minutes to complete. The teacher is asked to explain the purpose of the assessment to the children and to work through the example so that

Table 1
Number of items and internal consistency reliabilities for each scale

Scale	Number of items	Alpha reliabilities
Progress	9	.84
Observational Comparison	6	.82
Social Feedback	9	.81
Physiological States	8	.84

The RSPS consists of 33 items with 32 items representing the four scales shown here plus 1 general item ("I think I am a good reader"). $n = 1,525$.

all children understand what they are to do. Children are encouraged to ask questions about any aspect of the instrument they don't understand. The teacher should emphasize that the children should be as honest as possible and that there are no right answers. Specific directions to the teacher are provided in Appendix B.

Scoring of the RSPS is accomplished by summing the raw scores for each of the four scales. The scoring sheet in Appendix C has been provided to help compute scores for the Progress, Observational Comparison, Social Feedback, and Physiological States scales. To calculate the scores, the child's completed RSPS is placed alongside a scoring sheet. With the exception of item 1, the scorer transfers the child's responses to each item on the RSPS to the answer sheet using the numerical scoring key (e.g., SA = 5; SD = 1). After all responses are recorded, the scorer simply adds the number in each column to get a raw score for each scale.

The child's scores can then be compared with the norming data in Table 2. Any score for a scale that is slightly below, equal to, or slightly greater than the mean indicates that the child's self-perceptions are in the normal range. On the other hand, scores that are a good deal lower than the scale's mean would be a cause for concern. When the difference exceeds the size of the standard deviation, the child's scores are in the low range. Rough low range cut-off points

for the scales would be: Progress (34), Observational Comparison (16), Social Feedback (27), and Physiological States (25). By the same token, scores that exceed the mean by an amount equal to or greater than the standard deviation would indicate high reader self-perceptions (i.e., PR = 44+; OC = 26+; SF = 38+; PS = 37+).

Assessment and Instructional Uses

Information obtained from the Reader Self-Perception Scale can be used for both whole group and individual assessments and interventions. Teachers can gain a sense of how the general classroom climate affects children's self-efficacy judgments in reading. These conclusions can be drawn by examining group performance on the total scale and on the four individual scales. For example, after results of the RSPS are available for interpretation, teachers might feel the need to (a) devise more meaningful and considerate ways to communicate reading progress to their students, (b) modify their current classroom oral reading practices, (c) revise their grouping techniques, (d) pay closer attention to the reading materials they assign, (e) become more sensitive to indirect signals they send to children regarding their reading performance, (f) counsel the class and

Table 2
Descriptive statistics by scale and grade level

Grade level	n	Progress			Observational Comparison			Social Feedback			Physiological States		
		Mean	SD	SE	Mean	SD	SE	Mean	SD	SE	Mean	SD	SE
4	506	39.6	4.8	.21	20.7	4.7	.21	33.2	5.3	.24	31.8	5.9	.26
5	571	39.5	5.2	.22	21.0	4.8	.20	32.7	5.4	.22	31.0	6.4	.27
6	402	39.0	5.1	.25	21.3	4.6	.23	32.0	5.5	.27	30.5	6.2	.31
Total	1,479	39.4	5.0	.13	20.9	4.7	.12	32.7	5.4	.14	31.2	6.2	.16

Total possible raw scores are Progress (45), Observational Comparison (30), Social Feedback (45), and Physiological States (40).

the parents about constructive feedback, or (g) strive to make the children more physically and mentally comfortable during the act of reading.

Data from the RSPS can also be useful for monitoring individual children. For instance, scores for the total scale and for the four subscales might be maintained in portfolios to demonstrate changes in self-perceptions over time. A child's results from the beginning of the school year could be compared with those obtained at the midpoint or at the end of the year. Likewise, RSPS results for a child could be compared from year to year. Regardless of timeline, individual instructional adjustments could flow naturally from the findings.

Besides a portfolio application, the scale could help teachers to detect and assist children whose self-perceptions are somewhat below the norm. Depending upon their individual profiles, these children might require one or more of the following instructional adjustments: (a) more frequent and concrete illustrations of their progress; (b) opportunities to read in situations where their performance compares favorably with the performance of peers; (c) increased positive reinforcement from the teacher, parents, and classmates; and (d) modeling of the enjoyment, appreciation, relaxation, and gratification

that can be gained from reading. For example, low scores on the Physiological States scale could signal that the teacher needs to be especially enthusiastic with a particular child, to strive to make her or his reading engagements consistently pleasurable, and to provide the child with a rich array of engaging literature.

Many of these adjustments can be accomplished by carefully estimating and orchestrating the interest, familiarity, and readability of texts. Self-perceptions can also be enhanced when teachers prepare children well for all reading assignments and group them wisely and flexibly. Children with low reader self-perceptions will function best in classrooms where patience is the rule and individual differences are not only tolerated but respected and valued. Additional encouragement and assistance can go a long way in building positive reader self-perceptions.

The Reader Self-Perception Scale can also be used to help identify children who are at risk due to a severe lack of confidence in their reading ability. These children need to be assessed more thoroughly and treated more intensively. When a child's RSPS profile departs markedly from the norm, the teacher can follow up with a personalized, structured interview like those cited previously. Insights gained from the scale itself and from the interview can be applied in counseling the child. In extreme cases, however, the results may be indicative of a deep-rooted or broader self-esteem problem that demands the expertise of a counselor or school psychologist.

One Teacher's Use

Near the beginning of the school year, Ms. Hogan decided to administer the RSPS to her entire class of fourth graders. Since the children came to her from a building that houses only primary students, she knew very little about them. Ms. Hogan recognized that the children would do a great deal more "reading to learn" in fourth grade, and so she wanted to learn how they felt about themselves as readers because this would influence their response to literacy instruction. Ms. Hogan planned to make adjustments that would benefit the whole class as well as individual children. She also planned to administer the RSPS again at the end of the year to determine if her instruction produced affective growth.

After the children's papers had been scored, she looked closely at the scores and was pleased to note that most of the students felt very good about their reading ability. As a group, the children's mean scores on the Progress, Observational Comparison, and Physiological States scales were quite high (42, 23, and 34, respectively), but the mean score for Social Feedback was only 24. Because this score was well below the average range, Ms. Hogan became concerned. In response, she planned to provide the children with reading materials that would allow her to make frequent use of praise. In addition, she decided to monitor her body language closely to make sure that she sent her students positive messages about their reading performance. She would also work hard to create a more supportive climate for literacy by encouraging the children to praise one another and by advising parents how to offer constructive feedback at home.

One of the children, Patti, scored extremely well on all four scales. It was clear that she had a solid appreciation of her own reading ability. On the other hand, the RSPS profile of another student, Bob, showed average scores for Progress, slightly below average for Physiological States, and well below average for Observational Comparison and Social Feedback. Ms. Hogan wondered if Bob felt fine about his silent reading but lacked confidence when reading aloud. She thought that he might have noticed his oral reading didn't compare well with the other children's, and she wondered if the signals he had received in the past from teachers, classmates, and parents had confirmed his doubts. Ms. Hogan believed that his nearly average score on the Physiological States scale might be the result of Bob's feelings about his silent and oral reading offsetting one another. She decided to monitor the situation carefully during the year, to speak with Bob's previous teachers, and to check his permanent record to see if his oral reading had lagged consistently behind his silent reading.

Ms. Hogan was most concerned about Norm. All of his RSPS scores were very low, and his previous achievement test scores indicated a serious reading problem. Norm was new to the district, and Ms. Hogan suspected that the children in her class might read much better than those at his old school. At first, his progress had been slow because the reading materials were much too difficult for him. Also, from listening to the other children read, he learned very quickly that his reading ability didn't compare well. Other children were impatient when Norm read aloud, and she noticed his discomfort with almost any reading task. Because his reading ability was so limited, Ms. Hogan realized that his low reader self-image had probably been shaped over a long time, but she knew that his recent difficulties had made matters worse. She intended to interview Norm individually to gain insights into his reader self-perceptions; to share her results and concerns with the guidance counselor, school psychologist, and principal; and to make as many appropriate instructional adjustments as possible.

A Final Word

Due to its uniqueness and timeliness, the Reader Self-Perception Scale might be immediately useful in a wide array of literacy contexts. The norming of the instrument has been quite extensive, and the scale provides meaningful data for teachers, administrators, parents, and perhaps the students themselves. For the time being, the scale should only be used in fourth through sixth grades, although with additional norming it might prove to be functional at higher grade levels. We would also caution against using the RSPS below fourth grade, even if the items are read aloud to the students. The instrument has not been tested at lower levels and, as we noted previously, research suggests that children in earlier grades tend not to appraise their reading ability accurately, nor attribute the causes of their achievement properly.

Users of the RSPS and the various stakeholders will ultimately need to decide how the instrument ought to be applied and interpreted. The scale yields a general indication of a child's self-perceptions of reading ability. This indicator should not be confused with more specific self-evaluations of reading skills and strategies that students might make as part of regular classroom instruction. Neither does the scale address self-appraisals of specific word analysis techniques or comprehension abilities such as prediction, imagery, self-regulated learning, retelling proficiency, or critical reflection. Whether the scale's major function is for assessment and instruction or for research, our hope is that with additional norming, the instrument will become a routine reading-related assessment on a par with well-known cognitive and affective measures.

Authors' Note

The development of the RSPS was supported in part by the Office of Research and Graduate Studies at Penn State University-Harrisburg.

References

Alvermann, D.E., & Guthrie, J.T. (1993). Themes and directions of the National Reading Research Center. *Perspectives in Reading Research, 1,* 1–11.

Anderson, R.C., Fielding, L.G., & Wilson, P.T. (1988). Growth in reading and how children spend their time outside of school. *Reading Research Quarterly, 23,* 285–303.

Athey, I. (1985). Reading research in the affective domain. In H. Singer & R.B. Ruddell (Eds.), *Theoretical models and processes of reading* (3rd ed., pp. 527–557). Newark, DE: International Reading Association.

Bandura, A. (1977). Self-efficacy: Toward a unifying theory of behavioral change. *Psychological Review, 84,* 191–215.

Bandura, A. (1982). Self-efficacy mechanism and human agency. *American Psychologist, 37,* 122–147.

Bandura, A., & Schunk, D.H. (1981). Cultivating competence, self-efficacy, and intrinsic interest through proximal self-motivation. *Journal of Personality and Social Psychology, 41,* 586–598.

Blumenfeld, P.C., Pintrich, P.R., Meece, J., & Wessels, K. (1982). The formation and role of self-perceptions of ability in elementary classrooms. *The Elementary School Journal, 82,* 401–420.

Boersma, F.J., Chapman, J.W., & MacGuire, T.O. (1979). The student perception of ability scale: An instrument for measuring academic self-concept in elementary school children. *Educational and Psychological Measurement, 39,* 135–141.

Borko, H., & Eisenhart, M. (1986). Students' conceptions of reading and their reading experiences in school. *The Elementary School Journal, 86,* 589–611.

Canney, G., & Winograd, P. (1979). *Schemata for reading and reading comprehension performance* (Tech. Rep. No. 120). Urbana, IL: University of Illinois, Center for the Study of Reading. (ERIC

Document Reproduction Service No. ED 169 520)

Cohen, S.G., McDonell, G., & Osborn, B. (1989). Self-perceptions of "at risk" and high achieving readers: Beyond Reading Recovery achievement data. In S. McCormick & J. Zutell (Eds.), *Cognitive and social perspectives for literacy research and instruction* (pp. 117–122). Chicago: National Reading Conference.

Filby, N.N., & Barnett, B.G. (1982). Student perceptions of "better readers" in elementary classrooms. *The Elementary School Journal, 5,* 435–449.

Foertsch, M.A. (1992). *Reading in and out of school: Factors influencing the literacy achievement of American students in grades 4, 8, and 12 in 1988 and 1990* (Vol. 2). Washington, DC: National Center for Education Statistics.

Gable, R.K. (1986). *Instrument development in the affective domain.* Boston: Kluwer-Nijhoff.

Gordon, C. (1990). Changes in readers' and writers' metacognitive knowledge: Some observations. *Reading Research and Instruction, 30,* 1–14.

Henk, W.A. (1993). New directions in reading assessment. *Reading and Writing Quarterly, 9,* 103–120.

Henk, W.A., & Melnick, S.A. (1992). The initial development of a scale to measure "perception of self as reader." In C.K. Kinzer & D.J. Leu (Eds.), *Literacy research, theory, and practice: Views from many perspectives. 41st Yearbook of the National Reading Conference* (pp. 111–117). Chicago: National Reading Conference.

Henk, W.A., & Melnick, S.A. (1993, December). *Quantitative and qualitative validation of the Reader Self-Perception Scale.* Paper presented at the annual meeting of the National Reading Conference, Charleston, SC.

Marshall, H.H., & Weinstein, R.S. (1984). Classroom factors affecting students' self-evaluation: An interactional model. *Review of Educational Research, 54,* 301–325.

Mathewson, G.C. (1985). Toward a comprehensive model of affect in the reading process. In H. Singer & R.B. Ruddell (Eds.), *Theoretical models and processes of reading* (3rd ed., pp. 841–856). Newark, DE: International Reading Association.

McKenna, M.C., & Kear, D.J. (1990). Measuring attitude toward reading: A new tool for teachers. *The Reading Teacher, 43,* 626–639.

Mitman, A.L., & Lash, A.A. (1988). Students' perceptions of their academic standing and classroom behavior. *The Elementary School Journal, 89,* 55–68.

Morrow, L.M., & Weinstein, C.S. (1986). Encouraging voluntary reading: The impact of a literature program on children's use of library centers. *Reading Research Quarterly, 21,* 330–346.

Nicholls, J.G. (1978). The development of the concepts of effort and ability, perception of academic attainment, and the understanding that difficult tasks require more ability. *Child Development, 49,* 800–814.

Nicholls, J.G. (1979). Development of perception of own attainment and causal attribution for success and failure in reading. *Journal of Educational Psychology, 71,* 94–99.

O'Flahavan, J., Gambrell, L.B., Guthrie, J., Stahl, S., Baumann, J.F., & Alvermann, D.A. (August/September, 1992). Poll results guide activities of research center. *Reading Today, 10,* p. 12.

Ruble, D.N., Boggiano, A.K., Feldman, N.S., & Loebl, J.H. (1980). Developmental analysis of the role of social comparison in self-evaluation. *Developmental Psychology, 12,* 191–197.

Schunk, D.H. (1982). Effects of effort attributional feedback on children's perceived self-efficacy and achievement. *Journal of Educational Psychology, 74,* 548–556.

Schunk, D.H. (1983a). Ability versus effort attributional feedback: Differential effects on self-efficacy and achievement. *Journal of Educational Psychology, 75,* 848–856.

Schunk, D.H. (1983b). Developing children's self-efficacy and skills: The roles of social comparative information and goal setting. *Contemporary Educational Psychology, 8,* 76–86.

Schunk, D.H. (1984). Self-efficacy perspective on achievement behavior. *Educational Psychologist, 19,* 48–58.

Stipek, D. (1981). Children's perceptions of their own and their classmates' ability. *Journal of Educational Psychology, 73,* 404–410.

Stipek, D., & Weisz, J. (1981). Perceived personal control and academic achievement. *Review of Educational Research, 51,* 101–137.

Valencia, S.W. (1990). A portfolio approach to classroom reading assessment: The whys, whats, and hows. *The Reading Teacher, 43,* 338–340.

Winograd, P., & Paris, S.G. (1988). *Improving reading assessment. Writings in reading and language arts.* Lexington, MA: D.C. Heath.

Wixson, K., Peters, C., Weber, E., & Roeber, E. (1987). New directions in statewide reading assessment. *The Reading Teacher, 40,* 749–754.

Zimmerman, B.J., & Ringle, J. (1981). Effects of model persistence and statements of confidence on children's self-efficacy and problem solving. *Journal of Educational Psychology, 73,* 485–493.

Appendix A
The Reader Self-Perception Scale

Listed below are statements about reading. Please read each statement carefully. Then circle the letters that show how much you agree or disagree with the statement. Use the following:

SA = Strongly Agree
A = Agree
U = Undecided
D = Disagree
SD = Strongly Disagree

Example: **I think pizza with pepperoni is the best.** SA A U D SD

If you are *really positive* that pepperoni pizza is best, circle SA (Strongly Agree).
If you *think* that is good but maybe not great, circle A (Agree).
If you *can't decide* whether or not it is best, circle U (undecided).
If you *think* that pepperoni pizza is not all that good, circle D (Disagree).
If you are *really positive* that pepperoni pizza is not very good, circle SD (Strongly Disagree).

	1. I think I am a good reader.	SA	A	U	D	SD
[SF]	2. I can tell that my teacher likes to listen to me read.	SA	A	U	D	SD
[SF]	3. My teacher thinks that my reading is fine.	SA	A	U	D	SD
[OC]	4. I read faster than other kids.	SA	A	U	D	SD
[PS]	5. I like to read aloud.	SA	A	U	D	SD
[OC]	6. When I read, I can figure out words better than other kids.	SA	A	U	D	SD
[SF]	7. My classmates like to listen to me read.	SA	A	U	D	SD
[PS]	8. I feel good inside when I read.	SA	A	U	D	SD
[SF]	9. My classmates think that I read pretty well.	SA	A	U	D	SD
[PR]	10. When I read, I don't have to try as hard as I used to.	SA	A	U	D	SD
[OC]	11. I seem to know more words than other kids when I read.	SA	A	U	D	SD
[SF]	12. People in my family think I am a good reader.	SA	A	U	D	SD
[PR]	13. I am getting better at reading.	SA	A	U	D	SD

(continued)

[OC]	14. I understand what I read as well as other kids do.	SA	A	U	D	SD
[PR]	15. When I read, I need less help than I used to.	SA	A	U	D	SD
[PS]	16. Reading makes me feel happy inside.	SA	A	U	D	SD
[SF]	17. My teacher thinks I am a good reader.	SA	A	U	D	SD
[PR]	18. Reading is easier for me than it used to be.	SA	A	U	D	SD
[PR]	19. I read faster than I could before.	SA	A	U	D	SD
[OC]	20. I read better than other kids in my class.	SA	A	U	D	SD
[PS]	21. I feel calm when I read.	SA	A	U	D	SD
[OC]	22. I read more than other kids.	SA	A	U	D	SD
[PR]	23. I understand what I read better than I could before.	SA	A	U	D	SD
[PR]	24. I can figure out words better than I could before.	SA	A	U	D	SD
[PS]	25. I feel comfortable when I read.	SA	A	U	D	SD
[PS]	26. I think reading is relaxing.	SA	A	U	D	SD
[PR]	27. I read better now than I could before.	SA	A	U	D	SD
[PR]	28. When I read, I recognize more words than I used to.	SA	A	U	D	SD
[PS]	29. Reading makes me feel good.	SA	A	U	D	SD
[SF]	30. Other kids think I'm a good reader.	SA	A	U	D	SD
[SF]	31. People in my family think I read pretty well.	SA	A	U	D	SD
[PS]	32. I enjoy reading.	SA	A	U	D	SD
[SF]	33. People in my family like to listen to me read.	SA	A	U	D	SD

Appendix B
The Reader Self-Perception Scale
Directions for Administration, Scoring, and Interpretation

The Reader Self-Perception Scale (RSPS) is intended to provide an assessment of how children feel about themselves as readers. The scale consists of 33 items that assess self-perceptions along four dimensions of self-efficacy (Progress, Observational Comparison, Social Feedback, and Physiological States). Children are asked to indicate how strongly they agree or disagree with each statement on a 5-point scale (5 = Strongly Agree, 1 = Strongly Disagree). The information gained from this scale can be used to devise ways to enhance children's self-esteem in reading and, ideally, to increase their motivation to read. The following directions explain specifically what you are to do.

Administration

For the results to be of any use, the children must (a) understand exactly what they are to do, (b) have sufficient time to complete all items, and (c) respond honestly and thoughtfully. Briefly explain to the children that they are being asked to complete a questionnaire about reading. Emphasize that this is not a *test* and that there are no *right* answers. Tell them that they should be as honest as possible because their responses will be confidential. Ask the children to fill in their names, grade levels, and classrooms as appropriate. Read the directions aloud and work through the example with the students as a group. Discuss the response options and make sure that all children understand the rating scale before moving on. It is important that children know that they may raise their hands to ask questions about any words or ideas they do not understand.

The children should then read each item and circle their response for the item. They should work at their own pace. Remind the children that they should be sure to respond to all items. When all items are completed, the children should stop, put their pencils down, and wait for further instructions. Care should be taken that children who work more slowly are not disturbed by children who have already finished.

Scoring

To score the RSPS, enter the following point values for each response on the RSPS scoring sheet (Strongly Agree = 5, Agree = 4, Undecided = 3, Disagree = 2, Strongly Disagree = 1) for each item number under the appropriate scale. Sum each column to obtain a raw score for each of the four specific scales.

Interpretation

Each scale is interpreted in relation to its total possible score. For example, because the RSPS uses a 5-point scale and the Progress scale consists of 9 items, the highest total score for Progress is 45 ($9 \times 5 = 45$). Therefore, a score that would fall approximately in the middle of the range (22–23) would indicate a child's somewhat indifferent perception of her or himself as a reader with respect to Progress. Note that each scale has a different possible total raw score (Progress = 45, Observational Comparison = 30, Social Feedback = 45, and Physiological States = 40) and should be interpreted accordingly.

As a further aid to interpretation, Table 2 presents the descriptive statistics by grade level for each scale. The raw score of a group or individual can be compared to that of the pilot study group at each grade level.

Appendix C
The Reader Self-Perception Scale Scoring Sheet

Student name _____

Teacher _____

Grade _____ Date _____

Scoring key: 5 = Strongly Agree (SA)
4 = Agree (A)
3 = Undecided (U)
2 = Disagree (D)
1 = Strongly Disagree (SD)

Scales

General Perception	Progress	Observational Comparison	Social Feedback	Physiological States
1. ____	10. ____	4. ____	2. ____	5. ____
	13. ____	6. ____	3. ____	8. ____
	15. ____	11. ____	7. ____	16. ____
	18. ____	14. ____	9. ____	21. ____
	19. ____	20. ____	12. ____	25. ____
	23. ____	22. ____	17. ____	26. ____
	24. ____		30. ____	29. ____
	27. ____		31. ____	32. ____
	28. ____		33. ____	

Raw score	____ of 45	____ of 30	____ of 45	____ of 40
Score interpretation				
High	44+	26+	38+	37+
Average	39	21	33	31
Low	34	16	27	25

Appendix D
Validation

A pool of initial items was developed that reflected each of Bandura's (1977) four factors (Performance, Observational Comparison, Social Feedback, and Physiological States). Thirty graduate students in reading were presented the pool of items in random order as well as the conceptual definitions for each of the four factor categories. The graduate students were asked to place each item in the category it seemed to fit best. Based upon feedback received in this judgmental process, modifications were made to the item pool.

The instrument was then administered to 625 students in Grades four, five, and six in two different school districts. Preliminary alpha reliabilities for each scale measured in mid 70s. Although alpha reliabilities in this range are quite acceptable for an affective measure (Gable, 1986), the analysis identified some items that did not seem to fit well with the rest of the scale. In addition, an exploratory factor analysis indicated clear scales for Observational Comparison, Social Feedback and Physiological States, but not for the Performance scale. Since the items were not clustering as a single construct, the operational definition of the scale was reexamined. A panel of eight experts (consisting of both university faculty and graduate students enrolled in reading and affective instrument development courses) examined the data more closely and made recommendations. The panel concluded that it was more meaningful to use perceptions of personal progress as the one concrete way readers might be able to make ability judgments apart from the other scales. It was also felt that the progress construct subsumed the majority of the dimensions of the original Performance scale. Thus, the original scale was operationally redefined, and only those items that reflected personal progress were retained. For this reason, the scale was renamed Progress.

After the revisions indicated by the first pilot had been made, an additional 1,479 fourth, fifth and sixth grade children in several urban, suburban, and rural school districts were asked to respond. Further reliability analyses indicated scale alphas ranging from .81 to .84 with all items contributing to the overall scale reliability. Table 1 (p. 237) displays the internal consistency reliabilities for each scale. A factor analysis indicated the existence of each of the expected categories and, as hoped, moderate yet significant relationships were indicated between RSPS scores (total and individual scale) and both the Elementary Reading Attitude Survey (McKenna & Kear, 1990) and a variety of standardized reading achievement measures (Henk & Melnick, 1992, 1993).

Moreover, as Table 2 (p. 238) indicates, the mean scores and standard deviations for each scale were extremely similar across grades, and the corresponding standard errors were desirably low. Children reported the highest relative reader self-perceptions on the Progress scale (39.4 of the maximum possible 45) followed by Physiological States (31.2 of 40), Social Feedback (32.7 of 45), and Observational Comparison (20.9 of 30). Overall, these scores indicate that children tended to think of themselves as capable readers.

High-Stakes Assessments in Reading: Consequences, Concerns, and Common Sense

James V. Hoffman, Kathryn H. Au, Colin Harrison,
Scott G. Paris, P. David Pearson, Carol Minnick Santa,
Sarah H. Silver, and Sheila W. Valencia

Testing, getting ready for tests, and teaching to tests have become commonplace in public education. These activities occupy our attention, consume our resources, and dominate our professional conversations. Educational accountability has become all but synonymous with large-scale testing. This test-ridden educational environment is not a tradition in our public schools. The large-scale testing movement has expanded exponentially over the past 20 years, with reading as a primary focal point. Indeed, students in U.S. public schools have been described as the "most tested in the world" (Resnick & Resnick, 1985, p. 17).

This commentary reflects the strong feelings of many researchers and teachers who are alarmed about the potentially harmful effects of excessive achievement testing under the guise of accountability. We offer this commentary as a call for evaluation of the impact of current types and levels of testing on the quality of teaching, on student motivation, on policy decisions, and on the public's understanding of the quality of schooling. Our concerns are that testing has become a tool to control instruction as opposed to a reference point for making the best decisions about learner needs, and this has the potential to damage the academic growth and emotional health of students. The needs of the learner must be the primary concern in making instructional decisions. Tests and other forms of assessment must be used as tools to help us see student needs more clearly, not as weapons in a struggle between policy makers and professional educators for control of the curriculum, with students caught in the middle.

To guide all educators who use tests as a key element for making decisions about the progress of individual children and the quality of instructional programs, we offer this "learner-first" perspective in the form of a question-answer dialogue, to ensure that important conceptual, practical, and ethical issues are considered by those who bear the responsibility for designing and implementing assessment programs.

Is testing an important part of good educational design?

Yes, testing students' skills and knowledge is certainly an important part of education, but it is only a part of educational assessment. Assessment involves the systematic and purposeful collection of data to inform actions. It provides teachers with useful information about students and guides our instructional decision making. Teachers are the internal audience for assessment. Assessment plays an important role in decision making beyond the classroom level as well. The external audience (for example, administrators, school board members, policy makers, and parents) makes significant decisions that impact students. These decisions are informed by the results of student assessments. The needs of both the internal and external audiences must be considered in building a quality assessment plan.

Testing is a form of assessment that involves the systematic sampling of behavior under controlled conditions. Testing can provide quick, reliable data on student performance that is useful to teachers, administrators, and the public in making decisions. It is, however, only one form of assessment. Other forms might include focused interviews, classroom observations and anecdotal records, analysis of work samples, and work inventories. These forms of assessment are often viewed by classroom teachers as more informative for instructional decision making than traditional tests. They frequently rely on direct measures of students' performance rather than indirect measures, such as filling in ovals on multiple choice items, and they offer the advantage of being available for use on an ongoing basis in the classroom. In addition, these teacher-controlled assessments can be adapted to individual students' needs and can

provide useful information about students' strengths and weaknesses.

Many standardized tests, in contrast, are rooted in a different set of purposes than informing teachers about individual students and their needs. Indeed, standardized tests were designed originally to make normative comparisons across large numbers of students, not to diagnose the skills of individuals. The format of the tests was designed to be economical rather than typical of everyday reading situations. Reading many small paragraphs, answering multiple choice test items, and machine scored answer sheets made testing quick and cheap, not necessarily like typical reading or representative of classroom curricula. In fact, standardized tests were constructed to be insensitive to variations across classrooms in types of teaching practices and educational materials. It is ironic that these same tests are not being used to diagnose individual students and to evaluate teachers and curricula; we feel this is an inappropriate use of standardized tests.

If alternative assessments are so much better than standardized tests, then why do we have standardized tests?

The popularity of standardized tests rests on a number of factors. Traditional forms of standardized reading tests (that is, multiple choice response items) are easy to administer and score. Standardized tests also provide data that aggregate much more directly and efficiently than the data from alternative assessments. This feature makes the data easier to interpret when comparing performance across groups of students or across time. When the focus for assessment moves beyond the individual to the group (such as a class, school, or district) then the results of alternative assessments become more difficult to analyze and interpret.

Some puzzling findings emerge when we look at the uses and valuing of standardized test results. Generally, the public views standardized testing as informative. Gallup polls have suggested that more than 80% of the public view them as useful or somewhat useful (Lerner, 1980). Interestingly, the majority of school administrators view standardized test results as minimally important to them. Administrators justify their tests in terms of their utility at the school and classroom level. Yet the data from the school level reveal that teachers find the results from standardized tests minimally useful to them in instructional decision making. In fact, research surveys of teachers have found that an overwhelming majority believe that standardized tests are inappropriate assessments of many students, that the tests take too much time away from their curriculum, and that test results are often misinterpreted and misused (Sproull & Zubrow, 1981).

We suspect that there is something more basic and troubling in the disregard and devaluing of classroom performance assessments. Performance assessments are regarded by many of those outside the classroom as subjective and impressionistic. Standardized tests are viewed as more rigorous, objective, and scientific. This is an unfortunate comparison of these two data sources. Recent advancements in the area of performance assessment (for example, the use of holistic scoring techniques) have led to levels of reliability and validity that match and even exceed the characteristics of traditional standardized tests (Hoffman et al., 1998). And, as teachers become more effective at using classroom assessments, reliability and validity improve. At the same time, we have come to realize how subjective a typical standardized test can be (note, for example, the setting of criterion scores). Traditional forms of standardized tests are no more inherently scientific or objective than performance assessments. Furthermore, we have come to understand that different assessments are useful for different purposes. If we want to gather information to assist with classroom instruction, we must use classroom assessments that are appropriate in content and method. If we want to know how well a group of students performs globally in comparison to nationally, we use standardized tests. One type of assessment cannot serve all purposes.

Why is it that teachers find the results of standardized tests minimally useful?

Part of the problem is timing. Typically standardized tests are given late in the school year. By the time the teachers receive the results, there is no time to act on them. Part of the problem is in the nature of the information provided. Most norm-referenced tests provide information related to general achievement expressed in terms of a comparison of student performance to a grade level or same-aged peers. This is not new information to the teacher. Most teachers have a fairly accurate estimate of students' relative achievement levels in the basic skill areas based on their own informal assessments. They know who is above, at, and below grade-level performance. They can rank their students from most to least skilled in an area—which is what a norm-referenced test does. Norm-referenced test results do not offer the teacher much guidance on students' specific strengths or instructional needs. At best, they provide some independent confirmation for teachers' judgments. At worst, in particular for the low-performing students, such tests shape expectations, become the basis for labeling and tracking students, and fail to reveal much about the full range of reader abilities.

Standardized tests also provide a limited view of student abilities in reading. Typically, standardized reading tests are restricted in their format to single-item response patterns to closed questions (for example, multiple choice questions in response to a paragraph that has been read). Reading performance is sampled within the limitations of the testing format, and generalizations about reading are derived. Teachers are suspicious of these limitations of tests and what they can reveal about the full range of reader capabilities.

The situation is changing regarding teachers' use of and responsiveness to standardized test results. Tests and test results are becoming not only important to teachers in the decisions they make about instruction, but paramount. Two factors are contributing to this change in connectedness between standardized test results and teaching. The first factor is in the changing nature of the tests themselves. *Criterion-referenced* standardized tests are becoming much more popular—even to the point of displacing norm-referenced tests. Criterion-referenced tests are typically "standardized" in their administration and scoring. At the surface level, they may look very much like a traditional norm-referenced test with multiple-choice test items. Criterion-referenced tests, however, focus on measuring the individual student's ability to perform at a "mastery" or "basic competency" level. There is less interest in comparing a student's performance with his or her peers (the goal of norm-referenced tests) than on calculating the student's ability to perform a particular type of task (for example, recognize a particular letter, perform a particular arithmetic procedure, compose in a particular writing mode). Because criterion-referenced tests are more closely tied to the curriculum (that is, what the students are supposed to learn in the various subject areas), the link to instructional decision making is stronger.

The second factor influencing change has come with a shift in the "consequences" associated with performance on standardized tests. We are seeing an increased use of standardized tests for "high-stakes" assessment in schools across the United States.

"High-stakes" sounds like something out of a gambling hall. What makes testing high-stakes?

The gambling metaphor is not totally inappropriate for the high-stakes testing movement. There are elements of risk, chance, control, and skill involved in both. High-stakes simply means that the consequences for good (high) or poor (low) performance are substantial. Popham (1987) describes high-stakes testing as an assessment device employed to make important decisions about examinees or whose results indicate the effectiveness of instruction. The student's score is high-stakes in the sense that significant contingencies are riding on the test's results.

High-stakes assessments have been a part of education for some time. Perhaps the most conspicuous form of such assessment, historically speaking, has been in the British educational system. National exams in England, and in other countries who adopted the British system of education, have been used in the past to assign students to various educational tracks. Although standardized testing and tracking are linked closely in U.S. public education, the relation is less explicit. The types of high-stakes assessments that are directly comparable in the United States are the MCAT and the LSAT tests used for admissions decisions into medical and law schools, respectively, as well as professional certification examinations (for example, state bar examinations, medical board examinations).

High-stakes assessments have become prominent in grades K–12 in the United States as a result of activity at the state level. States agencies, in an effort to monitor the quality of education in U.S. public schools, have designed state-wide assessments for use. In 1972, only one state had implemented a minimum competency testing program; by 1985, 34 states had implemented such testing. By 1990, every state had mandated the use of some standardized test, and many states have created their own test (Madaus & Tan, 1993). The specific criteria for these tests are drawn directly from the state's curriculum framework and tend to focus on the basic skill areas of reading, writing, and mathematics. Although the patterns are different for different states, most assessments are administered annually to all students at several grade levels within the system. In most cases there are no direct consequences for the students at the early grade levels. In fact, some states do not report results at the individual student level. The focus, for accountability purposes, is on performance aggregated across larger units such as schools or districts.

Why are these state basic skill assessments considered high-stakes?

The high-stakes consequences for many state assessment programs fall on the teachers, administrators, schools, and districts. Some states use the results of these tests to assess the quality of educational programs. Student data are aggregated at the school, district, and state levels and reported to the public. Penalties for low performance may be applied to schools and districts. These penalties can be as severe as loss of accreditation or the state taking control of the school from the district—or taking control of the district itself. The consequences can also apply to the administrators or teachers in the schools. Low levels of student performance may lead to low teaching evaluations and even dismissal. Various systems for rewarding high levels of performance are also in place. For instance, in some states, schools are rewarded with monetary bonuses for high levels of student performance.

Tests are becoming more high-stakes for students as well. More and more states are providing individual student performance reports. A number of states already require students to achieve a certain minimum score before they can receive a high school diploma. Some states are now considering implementing plans for the basic skills test to be used as a criterion for passing on to higher grade levels.

It seems that this kind of system could spur teachers to teach better and students to work harder. This would lead, in turn, to enhanced performance. Right?

This would seem to be the case, but the situation is much more complicated. For low-performing students who do not see themselves as capable, the high stakes become a disincentive for effort. These students become discouraged and give up. Furthermore, because these tests measure minimum competency, the motivation for the high-performing students is also low. They are not challenged by the content, not at risk of failing, and not the focus of attention, so the high stakes become a disincentive for these students as well.

The effects on teachers and teaching is just as complex. Teachers are concerned with all their students in terms of a broad range of learning needs, not just the subject areas that may be covered on a particular test or the specific kind of learning required for a particular test. As the consequences for low performance are raised, teachers are forced to abandon their focus on the total child and the total curriculum, and eventually they "teach to the test." In addition, attention may be diverted from all the students to only those who are in need of attention and have the potential to be brought up to passing levels. Thus teachers who teach to the test may not be teaching the regular curriculum nor motivating all their students to become engaged in reading. Scores on the tests may increase, but this may not be proof of better teaching or more motivated students.

How do you teach to the test when you don't know what is going to be on the test?

Teaching to the test can occur at many different levels and in many different ways. At the most basic level, the teacher can teach the format of the test to the students so they are familiar with the kinds of item responses required. For example, practice with multiple choice formats and tips on how to approach selecting the best answer can enhance performance significantly if that is the format of the test. Even on the more holistic forms of assessment (for example, extended writing in response to a prompt), teacher instruction and guided practice using scoring rubrics can lead to enhanced student performance of students on examinations that adopt this format. Students learn what features of their writing will yield higher scores, and they adapt their writing accordingly. Students who spend extensive amounts of time in learning the format and scoring of the tests will tend to score higher than those who do not (Madaus, 1985).

Teaching to the test also can occur in the form of curriculum adaptations. Teachers who want to improve their students' test scores will focus the curriculum on areas that are tested at the expense of other curricular areas. Most state assessments tend to focus on reading, writing, and mathematics. Students who spend more time engaged in these areas of the curriculum are likely to achieve higher test scores than if they had not. The fine arts, physical education, social studies, the sciences, and other subjects are in danger of being displaced from the "actual" curriculum. The focus of instruction on the areas of reading, writing, and mathematics is even further restricted by the focus of the tests and the limitations of the testing formats. Reading instruction that emphasizes developing a value for reading will be given less emphasis than attention to the word recognition or decoding skills targeted on the test. Writing instruction that emphasizes developing of a writing piece over time will be given less emphasis than writing to a prompt within a short period of time.

Teaching to the test also can occur at the level of targeting students. The scores from a criterion-based test simply reflect which objectives have been mastered and which have not. There is no implied comparison with how other students have done. Teachers who are inclined to teach to the test will focus not only on the objectives included on the test but will tend to focus greatest attention on those students who have not mastered these objectives but who might show improvement with practice. Students who have already mastered these skills are not the focus of instruction because their performance is already assured; students whose test scores are so low that they are perceived to have no hope of performing at a minimum level are ignored as well. We end up with a case of testing triage—find those students who can benefit from short-term, intensive help, and focus energy on them rather than on the students who are most at risk of failure.

What's to prevent teachers and students from just cheating? This sounds like a lot less work for those who don't value the test anyway.

Cheating on tests is not something educators like to talk about—we are an ethical profession. There are reports each year, however, of teachers engaged in unethical testing practices. The pressure to have high test scores is so great that some teachers and administrators feel compelled to cheat on standardized tests. Teachers may rationalize cheating by saying that they are trying to relieve the pressure on students. Cheating is not always as blatant as changing answers or giving answers. Consider the teacher who does nothing to discourage conversations while the test is taking place. What about the teacher who elaborates on the directions to remind students in detail about the particular kind of writing they are to do and what the raters will be looking for?

Concerns about ethical issues reach beyond the classroom and the teacher to institutional and organizational issues. For example, research has demonstrated that as the stakes have increased, more and more students are being labeled as "disabled" and therefore exempted from testing. As the low-performing students are exempted from the testing, scores appear to rise. The same kinds of strategies are being used to exempt students for whom English is a second language. The mandates for high-stakes assessment no doubt accelerate the number of minority students labeled as learning disabled (Allington & McGill-Franzen, 1993). Cheating on tests may also occur after the scores have been transferred from the teacher to the administration. This is not just a teacher problem, but one that can affect actions at all levels as pressures to score well intensify.

What are the effects of high-stakes testing on classroom instruction?

The evidence is clear: Students in classes in which teachers teach to the test will perform better than students in classes that do not. Teachers who teach to their students and not to the test face enormous penalties. A recent survey in one state that relies on high-stakes assessments found that 75% of the classroom teachers contacted regarded the state assessment as having a negative impact on the quality of their teaching (Hoffman et al., in press). Are teachers complaining because of the pressure and work, or are they sounding an alarm that should awaken us to a problem?

The problems with highly centralized control have been demonstrated in practically every field, from political systems, to business, to social services. Teaching is no exception. The further decision making is removed from the level of implementation, the less adaptive the system is to individual needs. Eliminate the decision making of teachers and you destroy their ability to be responsive to the learning needs of students. The quality of service declines. High-stakes testing that puts extreme pressure to teach to the test disempowers teachers.

Test scores in the states that have implemented high-stakes testing plans continue to show growth. The interpretation offered by politicians is that the quality of instruction has improved and, therefore, student learning is improving; the alternative interpretation is that teaching to the test yields better test scores. Analyses of norm-referenced scores do not support the assertion that there have been substantial gains claimed for the state assessments (Texas Education Agency, 1997). Studies of norm-referenced tests in states with sustained patterns of growth in state skill assessments (for example, Texas and Kentucky) show no comparable patterns of gain. In fact, there is evidence that performance on norm-referenced measures may be declining. This may be the result of the fact that high-stakes assessments of basic skills tend to narrow the curriculum and "the minimum becomes the maximum" (National Commission on Excellence in Education, 1983, p. 20).

Interpreting gains in scores over time poses a problem. Those who control the test can directly manipulate the difficulty of the items from one year to the next and adjust the passing score. This direct manipulation of test scores (increasing or decreasing the number of students passing) is much easier to achieve in a criterion-referenced test as compared to a norm-referenced model.

A rising area of concern with respect to high-stakes assessment is the trend toward using the results of these tests for promotion and retention decisions at the elementary level, as shown in a recent case in Waco, Texas. The school board in this district approved a policy that students who failed to pass the state mandated minimum competency test would not be promoted to the next grade level. When 20% of the students failed to pass the test, a crisis emerged. Summer school classes, extra tutorials, transition classes, and other strategies were arranged to address the problem (Johnston, 1998).

Why should students be promoted if they can't do the basics? What's wrong with the policy? The additional instruction may help.

The issues of retention and promotion are complex. Mandates like the one in Waco do not solve the problem; they only complicate the issue. Most school districts attempt to work within a set of general guidelines on retention and promotion decisions, then act on a case-by-case basis. The principle is that each child needs to be considered as an individual and that the best decisions are reached in a collaborative, responsive environment. A school district with a sound assessment plan does not need to wait for the results of a state minimum skills assessment to become aware of student progress. Appropriate interventions, like those that suddenly appeared in Waco, should be ongoing. This is a case of an assessment plan developed for one purpose—monitoring the quality of educational services—being used for a different purpose: student promotion.

The case of Waco is not an isolated one. The popular notion that all students should be able to read before the end of third grade is about to be turned into a high-stakes context for students in many states. In other words, students who cannot achieve the minimum score will not pass on to fourth grade.

A major area of concern is that such tests discriminate unfairly against minorities. Legal challenges to state assessments are pending in Texas and North Carolina. The legal and the underlying moral issues are complex, but the simple fact is that a disproportionate number of minority students are failing such tests and are being retained and/or failing to graduate.

Is retention the only consequence for students who don't pass?

Retaining students who do not pass standardized tests may have more pitfalls than benefits. One problem with retention is that it lowers a student's self-esteem and motivation because it confirms a message of low ability and failure to the student. A second problem is that retention displaces students from their friends and peers of the same age and often does not result in remedial instruction and "catching up." Instead, retention often becomes the first step toward alienation and frustration with school and is the single best predictor of subsequent dropping out of school.

Retention is not the only issue here. Even students who are not retained are affected by the repeated results of low achievement on standardized tests. Remember, half of all students will score below average on a norm-referenced test, and criterion-referenced tests set the passing score so that many students will fail. Usually the same students fail or score poorly on these tests, and neither the students nor the teachers need the test results to know who is having difficulty learning in the classroom. Instead, standardized tests have a cumulative and negative impact on students that erodes their motivation for the testing and perhaps even for school. What low-performing students need is more instruction, not more testing.

Why has high-stakes testing increased so much?

Standardized tests have been around a long time, but their use expanded dramatically in the late 1960s and continues to expand to this day.

During the 1980s states launched major efforts at educational reform, and standardized tests were a key component in the implementation plan. Madaus (1985) believes that these kinds of tests are used to "make things happen, automatically and mechanically to individual teachers, schools, and school districts...." This increased interest in controlling instruction can be linked to the increased financial contributions to local education by state legislators. Resnick and Resnick (1985), in commenting on this trend, argue that the focus in assessment has shifted in the 1990s from pedagogy to politics.

Studies continue to show that the tests control what teachers actually teach in their classrooms. Wise (1990) has argued:

> He who measures the outcomes calls the tune. With high-stakes testing raised to an unprecedented level of visibility, I would anticipate that the degrees of freedom at the local level would ultimately be very few, as all eyes would focus on how well students perform on standardized examinations. As more and more emphasis is placed on standardized tests, less and less will be given to teaching students real skills like writing, thinking, and creating.

Why don't we just quit the high-stakes assessment game?

There are likely many reasons why abandoning high-stakes assessment is difficult. Policy makers have discovered that through the use of high-stakes assessments, they can affect classroom teaching. They have created an accountability mechanism for the mandates from a centralized power base.

It is unlikely that states who are using these assessments will abandon them. Indeed, the most likely scenario is for an increasing number of states to develop and adopt similar plans for assessment. The problem for many states is that the resource commitment to develop these kinds of assessment plans is enormous.

Politics is the main issue in high-stakes assessment. Who has control over the schools, the curriculum, and instructional decision making? Within a high-stakes assessment context, the answer is politicians, bureaucrats, and test publishers. Teachers and reading educators, however, also should have input about assessment practices, and we argue for broader representation in decision making about large-scale testing.

There are classroom teachers, administrators, and other educators who support the high-stakes movement based on a "means-ends" argument. There are those who reason that using these tests draws attention and eventually resources to education and to students in need. Supporters of the high-stakes movement are willing to set aside concerns about the "means" (the high-stakes assessments) in the hope of achieving the "ends" (increased resources). There are also educators who argue that schools are rooted in a structure that will never achieve necessary change from the bottom up. They argue that state-imposed standards and associated high-stakes assessment can be catalysts for reform within the entire system. Unfortunately, this position may yield more resources for those students with needs, but it ignores many liabilities with the high-stakes tests that cannot be ignored.

Can't the U.S. federal government step in and provide a solution to this problem?

The U.S. federal government currently sponsors a national testing program for reading, mathematics, and other subject areas: the National Assessment of Educational Progress (NAEP). But these tests are not high-stakes assessments—at least not yet. The tests are not given every year. They are directed toward the fourth-, ninth-, and twelfth-grade levels only. There is a national sampling procedure used, so a very small proportion of the students in schools actually participate in testing. The tests are designed to give a "national report card" on general achievement levels in the basic subject areas over time. The content of the NAEP in reading is directed toward assessing basic comprehension of grade-level appropriate texts. It is not tied to a national curriculum, nor does it consider mastery of specific component objectives in reading.

Many aspects of the NAEP assessment in reading are commendable. Relative to the concerns raised here, the NAEP sampling strategy has been very useful in keeping efficiency high and maintaining a focus on the questions that the national assessment is supposed to address. Sampling also has provided the NAEP with an opportunity to experiment with a wide variety of testing formats and conditions.

It seems reasonable that states should have a mechanism for monitoring student success in the curriculum that is set forth. Is there a way to provide for this kind of assessment without the undesirable effects on classroom instruction?

The key to unraveling the complexities of high-stakes testing rests in grappling with a concept that those in the field of measurement and assessment have come to label "consequential validity." The broad construct of validity in testing addresses the question, "Does the test (or any assessment) measure what it says it measures?" For example, does a test that purports to measure reading achievement do just that? There are techniques for assessing validity. Educators can look at the content of a test and map its features onto the components of reading, and they can look at students' performance on the test under consideration in comparison to the same students' performance on a well-established measure of reading.

The concept of consequential validity requires that we consider the uses, applications, outcomes, and effects as they relate to the "in-tents" of the instrument. It includes not just the qualities of the test itself, but the procedures used to collect, aggregate, interpret, and communicate the results. If the intent of state assessments is to measure how well students are learning the outcomes identified in the state curriculum framework, then this can be done following the NAEP model, with selective sampling across student populations and across content areas on a systematic basis. Such a strategy would avoid most of the problems associated with the teaching-to-the-test phenomenon described earlier. Such a plan would reflect sound principles of instructional design and assessment.

Sadly, we expect that the intent of these assessments is not limited to gathering information, but that the effects observed on teachers and the curriculum are exactly what is intended—political control of teachers and schools. This is an unfortunate situation that compels a response.

What action can be taken to stem the tide of high-stakes assessments?

We are deeply concerned with the amount of large-scale testing in U.S. schools and the negative impact this testing is having on the quality of teaching. Increasingly, teachers are being forced to teach to tests and to disregard the full range of student needs. The time given over to preparing for tests and taking tests is time taken away from good instruction. The consequences, for low-performing students in particular, are far too great a price to pay for information that is available through other sources.

In framing our recommendations, we wish to stress two points. First, we recognize accountability is a necessary part of education. Our concerns over high-stakes assessment should not be interpreted as a fear or disregard of professional accountability. Second, our intent here is not to blame policy makers for the current dilemma with respect to high-stakes assessment. While policy makers are a central factor in the spread of high-stakes testing, we must all play a key role if we are to affect a change in either direction. Therefore, we address our recommendations to four audiences, recognizing that many of us wear multiple hats.

We begin our recommendations with a consideration of teachers and their responsibility to create rich assessment environments in their classrooms and schools. We move next to researchers who must continue to help us see, through careful study, how assessment can better serve our educational goals. Then, we speak to parents and the members of the community, who we feel may be the most crucial in terms of bringing some balance to the assessment playing field. Finally, we speak directly to policy makers in suggesting a plan of action.

To teachers:
- Construct more systematic and rigorous assessments in classrooms. In this way, the external audiences will gain confidence in the measures that are being used and their inherent value to inform decisions.
- Take responsibility to educate parents and policy makers regarding the tests being used in classrooms.

To researchers:
- Conduct ongoing evaluations of high-stakes assessments that examine issues of consequential validity. These studies should include, but not be limited to: teacher use of results, impact on curriculum focus, time spent in testing and test preparation, the costs of the tests (both direct and hidden), parent and community communication, and effects on teacher and student motivations.

It is remarkable how little data we collect on the impact of tests on instruction. Good base-line data and follow-up studies will help in monitoring the situation. Further, as Nolan, Haladyna, and Haas (1992) have pointed out, these studies should not be left to those who design, develop and implement the tests, but by independent groups and oversight agencies.

- Find ways to better link performance assessment alternatives to the kinds of questions that the external audiences must address on a regular basis. We must continue to offer demonstrations of ways that data from performance assessments can be aggregated in meaningful ways. This strategy allows us to build trust relationships in informal assessments.

To parents, parent groups, and child advocacy groups:
- Be vigilant regarding the costs of high-stakes assessments on the students in schools. Parents must be prepared to ask difficult, direct questions regarding the assessment methods being used in schools today and not simply accept the "we're just holding schools accountable" response as satisfactory. At what cost and with what benefits are these data being collected? Are there alternatives that meet the "need to know" demands and reduce the negative impact on students? The answer to this last question is yes, and parents must demand that schools and policy makers be responsive. Of all the groups who have a role to play, parents and the community leaders are most important for turning the corner toward reasonable assessment plans for schools.

To policy makers:
- Design an assessment plan that is considerate of the complexity of reading, learning to read, and the teaching of reading. A strong assessment plan is the best ally of teachers and administrators because it supports good instructional decision making and good instructional design. Consider the features of a good assessment as out-

lined in IRA's *Standards for the Assessment of Reading and Writing* (1994) when designing your plan for assessment.

- When decisions about students must be made that involve high-stakes outcomes (for example, graduation, matriculation, awards), rely on multiple measures rather than just the performance on a single test. The experiences in England with high-stakes assessment are instructive here. England has moved to a system that values teacher informal assessments, ongoing performance assessments, portfolios, teacher recommendations, and standardized testing. The triangulation of data sources leads to more valid decision making.

- When assessments do not involve decisions related to the performance of individual students (such as program evaluation), use sampling strategies. Sampling is less intrusive, less costly, and just as reliable as full-scale assessment plans. Sampling strategies also provide an opportunity to design alternate forms and types of assessments. Such a variety of assessments encourages careful inspection of validity and reliability issues.

- Do not use incentives, resources, money, and recognition of test scores to reward or punish schools or teachers. Neither the awards (for example, "blue ribbon schools") or the punishing labels (for example, "low performing schools") are in the interest of students or teachers. The consequences of achieving or not achieving in schools are real enough. Well-intentioned efforts to recognize achievement often become disincentives to those who need the most help.

- Do not attempt to manipulate instruction through assessments. In other words, do not initiate, design, or implement high-stakes assessments when the primary goal is to affect instructional practices. Start with the question, Is the primary goal of the assessment to collect data that will be used to make better decisions that impact the individual students taking the test? If the answer is no, seek an alternative.

There is among some educators a sense of fatalism about the high-stakes assessment movement. They reflect a view that this movement cannot be stopped, or that it is something we must learn to live with. The authors of this commentary sense a reluctant acceptance of high-stakes assessment because it has the potential to bring more resources to education (for example, increased funding for remedial programs based on low-performance patterns) or because there is the illusion of better instruction as a result of the tests (for example, more writing). We caution against both stances. Reading educators can and must act forcefully as a profession to keep good assessment at the forefront of educational practice. We cannot succumb to the temptation of allowing the ends to justify the means.

The pattern of testing as the preferred tool to manipulate teaching continues to expand despite past resolutions raising similar concerns. We call on educators, policy makers, community leaders, and parents everywhere to take a common-sense look at the testing that is going on in schools today. Visit classrooms. Talk to teachers. Listen to how the teachers talk about the curriculum and the decisions they are making. Talk to the teachers about the types of assessments they use in the classroom and how they use the data generated. To be opposed to large-scale, high-stakes testing is not to be opposed to assessment or accountability. It is a call to align our purposes and our goals with our methods.

References

Allington, R., & McGill-Franzen, A. (1993). Flunk 'em or get them classified: The contamination of primary grade accountability data. *Educational Researcher, 22*(1), 19–22.

Hoffman, J., Paris, S., Patterson, E.U., Pennington, J., & Assaf, L.C. (in press). High-stakes assessment in the language arts: The piper plays, the players dance, but who pays the price? *Handbook of Research in the Language Arts*.

Hoffman, J., Worthy, J., Roser, N., & Rutherford, W. (1998). Performance assessment in reading: Implications for teacher education. In J. Osborn & F. Lehr (Eds.), *Literacy for all* (pp. 289–302). New York: Guilford.

Johnston, R.C. (1998, August 5). Waco gets tough with summer school efforts. *Education Week*, p. 3.

Lerner, B. (1980). The war on testing: David, Goliath, and Gallup. *The Public Interest*, 121.

Madaus, G.F. (1985) Test scores as administrative mechanisms in educational policy. *Phi Beta Kappan*, 66(9), 611–617.

Madaus, G.F., & Tan, A.G.A. (1993). The growth of assessment. In G. Cawalti (Ed.), *Challenges and achievements of American education* (pp. 53–79). Alexandria, VA: Association of Supervision and Curriculum Development.

National Commission on Excellence in Education. (1983). *A nation at risk: The imperative for educational reform*. Washington, DC: Department of Health, Education, and Welfare.

Nolan, S.B., Haladyna, T.M., & Haas, N.S. (1992). Uses and abuses of achievement test scores. *Educational Measurement: Issues and Practice*, 11(2), 9–15.

Resnick, D.P., & Resnick, L.B. (1985). Standards, curriculum and performance: A historical and comparative perspective. *Educational Researcher*, 14(4), 5–20.

Sproull, L., & Zubrow, D. (1981). Standardized testing from the administrative perspective. *Phi Beta Kappan*, 62(9), 628–631.

Texas Education Agency. (1997). *Texas student assessment program: Student performance results, 1995–1996*. Austin, TX: Author.

Wise, A.E. (1990, January 10). A look ahead: Education and the new decade. *Education Week*, p. 30.

Suggested Readings

Corbett, H.D., & Wilson, B.L. (1991). *Testing reform and rebellion. Research for better schools*. Norwood, NJ: Ablex.

Downing, S., & Haladyna, T. (1996). A model for evaluation of high-stakes testing programs: Why the fox should not guard the chicken coop. *Educational Measurement: Issues and Practice*, 5(1), 5–12.

Green, D.R. (1997, March). *Consequential aspects of the validity of achievement tests: A publisher's point of view*. Paper presented at the annual meeting of the American Educational Research Association, Chicago, IL.

Gutloff, K. (1999). High stakes tests. *NEA Today*, 17(6), 4.

International Reading Association. (1995). *Reading assessment in practice*. Newark, DE: Author.

Linn, R.L. (1993). Educational assessment: Expanded expectations and challenges. *Education Evaluation & Policy Analysis*, 15(1), 1–16.

Madaus, G. (1991, June). *The effects of important tests on students: Implications for a national examination or system of examinations*. Paper presented at the AERA Conference on Accountability as a State Reform Instrument, Washington, DC.

Mathison, S. (1989). *The perceived effects of standardized testing on teaching and curriculum*. Paper presented at the annual meeting of the American Education Research Association, San Francisco, CA.

Moss, P. (1998). The role of consequences in validity theory. *Educational Measurement: Issues and Practice*, 17(2), 6–12.

National Research Council Committee on Appropriate Test Use. (1999). *High stakes: Testing for tracking, promotion, and graduation* (J.P. Heubert & R.M. Hauser, Eds.). Washington, DC: National Academy Press.

Paris, S.G. (1998). Why learner-centered assessment is better than high-stakes testing. In N. Lambert & B. McCombs (Eds.), *Issues in school reform: A sampler of psychological perspectives on learner-centered schools* (pp. 189–209). Washington, DC: American Psychological Association.

Paris, S.G., & Ayers, L.R. (in press). *Becoming reflective students and teachers with authentic assessment*. Washington, DC: American Psychological Association.

Paris, S.G., Lawton, T.A., Turner, J.C., & Roth, J.L. (1991). A developmental perspective on standardized achievement testing. *Educational Researcher, 20*(5), 12–20.

Pipho, C., & Hadley, C. (1985). *State activity: Minimum competence testing as of January 1985 (Clearinghouse Notes)*. Denver, CO: Education Commission of the States.

Popham, W. (1987). Can high-stakes tests be developed at the local level? *NASSP Bulletin, 71*(496), 77–84.

Subject Index

Page references followed by *t* or *f* indicate tables or figures, respectively.

Word Attack Subtest, 170, 170*t*–171*t*, 171–172, 172*t*

CONCEPT-ORIENTED READING INSTRUCTION (CORI), 101

CONFERENCES: portfolio, 123; reading, 147

CONNECTEDNESS: of curriculum, 38*t*

CONSEQUENTIAL VALIDITY, 256

CONTEXTUALIZING REPORT CARDS, 62, 62*t*

CONVERSATIONAL INTERVIEW (MOTIVATION TO READ PROFILE, MRP), 217, 217*f*, 221*f*–222*f*; administration of, 227–228; development and field testing, 223–224; teacher directions, 228*f*; using results, 229–230

COOPERATION, 50–52; among peers, 37*t*

COORDINATORS/CONSULTANTS APPLYING WHOLE LANGUAGE (CAWLs), 160; Classroom Reading Miscue Assessment (CRMA), 160–163, 161*f*

CORI. *See* Concept-Oriented Reading Instruction

CRITERION-REFERENCED PERFORMANCE ASSESSMENTS, 50, 51*f*

CRITICAL MOMENT TEACHING: over chair backs, 149–150; Retrospective Miscue Analysis and, 146–150

CRITICAL MOMENTS: during reading conferences, 147

CRMA. *See* Classroom Reading Miscue Assessment; Collaborative Retrospective Miscue Analysis

CTBS. *See* Comprehensive Test of Basic Skills

CULTURE-FREE TESTS, 17–18

CURRICULUM: connectedness of, 34*t*, 38*t*. *See also* specific curricula

CURRICULUM EVALUATION: deliberative approach to, 131

D

DATA: collection and analysis, 162–163; collection methods, 39; contamination of evidence, 48–49; interpreting and using, 41; policy makers' requests for, 163; on Yopp-Singer Test of Phoneme Segmentation, 169–172

DECISION MAKING: classroom, 116–117; using portfolios for, 116–117

DELIBERATIVE APPROACH, 131

DEVELOPMENT: knowledge about, 4–5

DIAGNOSTIC TEACHING, 73–76; evaluating, 75–76; executing, 74–75; planning for, 73–74; procedures, 73–76; purposes for, 73

DICTATION, 70

DISCUSSION QUESTIONS: for Retrospective Miscue Analysis, 144

DISCUSSIONS: Collaborative Retrospective Miscue Analysis, 146; Retrospective Miscue Analysis, 144–145

DISTRICT MEETINGS, 119–120

DIVERSITY, 17–18

Dr. Seuss's ABC (SEUSS), 173

DRAWING, 104; students' drawings, 104, 105*f*

E

EDUCATIONAL DESIGN, 248

EFFECTIVE READERS, 3–4

ELEMENTARY READING ATTITUDE SURVEY (ERAS), 199–214, 204*f*–208*f*, 234; administering and scoring, 200; characteristics of, 199–200; classroom plan, 201; descriptive statistics and internal consistency measures, 213*t*; development, 199–200; Directions for Use, 210*f*; "Directions for Use," 200; midyear percentile ranks, 211*t*–212*t*; norms, 211, 211*t*–212*t*; reliability, 213, 213*t*; response profiles, 201–202; scoring sheet, 210*f*; strengths and limitations, 201; technical aspects, 211–214; using, 200–202; validity, 213–214

ELKONIN BOXES, 174

EMILIA, REGGIO, 25

EMPOWERMENT, 26–27

ENGAGEMENT WITH TEXT: through reading, 33*t*, 34, 35*t*; through writing, 33*t*, 35*t*

ENGLISH AS A SECOND LANGUAGE (ESL) students: running records for, 69

EQUITY, 109–112; components of, 110; integration into assessment, 112

ERAS. *See* Elementary Reading Attitude Survey

(Lobel), 155*f*, 155–156; reading of *The Three Little Pigs* (Madden), 156, 157*f*; reading of "Upstairs and Downstairs" (Lobel), 156–157, 157*f*; supporting through Retrospective Miscue Analysis and strategy lessons, 156–157

N

O

P

101; in reading and language arts, 100–108. *See also* Assessment

PERFORMANCE INDICATORS: for literacy dimensions and attributes, 34, 35t–38t

PERFORMANCE-BASED ASSESSMENT: advantages of, 110–111; disadvantages of, 111; equity and, 109–112; portfolio, 123–124

PHONEMIC AWARENESS, 173; test for assessing, 166–176; Yopp-Singer Test of Phoneme Segmentation, 167–169, 168f, 169–175

PLANNING: for diagnostic teaching, 73–74; instructional, 88–89, 92; for portfolios, 115; students' plans for writing and reading, 77–79

POLICY, 254

POLICY MAKERS: recommendations for, 257–258; requests for data, 163

PORTFOLIO ASSESSMENT, 99–138; additional readings, 99; for young readers, 131–134

PORTFOLIOS, 49, 53–54, 135–138; appearance of, 114–115; booklist, 120, 121f; for classroom decision making, 116–117; conferences, 123; contents, 115–116; entry forms, 136f–137f; filling, 115–116; grading and evaluation, 123; guiding principles for, 113–114; initiating, 121–123; initiating through shared learning, 118–130; managing contents of, 116; need for, 113–114; organization of, 115–117; performance-based assessment, 123–124; perspectives on, 124–127; planning for, 115; rationale for, 113–114; reflection prompts for, 129f, 129–130; reflections on, 127–130; requirements for, 53–54; rubrics, 123–124; seminar activities, 120, 122f; seminar texts, 121f, 121; show, 45; student-managed, 135–138; suggested readings for, 120, 122f; teacher-student, 138; working, 45; workshop session topics, 120, 122f; writing checklist for, 127, 128f

PREDICTIVE VALIDITY: reading and spelling tests to determine, 170, 170t

PRINT: concepts about, 68–69

PROBLEM SOLVING, 106–107; rubric for, 106–107

PROFESSIONAL KNOWLEDGE: about reading, 1–5. *See also* Knowledge

PROFESSIONALISM, 13–14

PROGRAMS, 52–53

PROGRESS: communicating to parents, 163

PUBLIC: as assessment audience, 46, 47f

Q

QUESTIONNAIRES: Elementary Reading Attitude Survey (ERAS), 199–214, 204f–210f, 211t–214t; to measure children's awareness of strategic reading process, 189–198; Metacomprehension Strategy Index (MSI), 189–198, 196f–198f. *See also* Tests

QUESTIONS: assessment, 89–90; discussion, 144; generating, 89–90

R

READ-ALOUD BOOKS, 173

READER SELF-PERCEPTION SCALE (RSPS), 216, 233–246, 242f–243f; administration of, 236–237, 244t; assessment and instructional uses, 237–239; description of, 236; descriptive statistics, 237, 238t; directions for, 244t; example use, 239–240; interpretation of, 244t; items and internal consistency reliabilities, 237t; rationale for, 235–236; scoring, 236–237, 244t; scoring sheet, 245f; validation of, 246t

READERS: idealized, 216; ineffective and effective, 3–4; Michael's beliefs about himself as, 154–156; revaluing, 140–151; young, 131–134, 166–176

READERS' WORKSHOP, 85

READING: attitudes toward, 36t, 199–214, 234; constructive, 35t; engagement with text through, 33t, 34, 35t; evaluative, 35t; language-based model of, 2, 3f; Michael's, 152, 153f, 155f, 155–157, 157f, 157–158, 158f; Michael's beliefs about, 154–156; motivation for, 36t, 133, 215–232; performance assessment in, 100–108; process of, 2–3; professional knowledge about, 1–5; record-

hension, 107–108; Reader Self-Perception Scale (RSPS), 236–237, 244*t*; Reading Survey (Motivation to Read Profile, MRP), 224–227, 226*f*; rubrics, 71; Stanford Achievement Test (SAT) declines, 45; student work samples, 39–41; subscores, 20

SCORING SHEETS: Elementary Reading Attitude Survey (ERAS), 210*f*; Reader Self-Perception Scale (RSPS), 245*f*; Reading Survey (Motivation to Read Profile, MRP), 227*f*

SCRAPBOOK COLLECTIONS, 123

SEARCH, 102

SEARCH LOGS, 102–103, 103*t*–104*t*

SELF-ASSESSMENT, 37*t*; interviews, 70–71

SELF-EFFICACY, 234; factors, 234

SELF-PERCEPTION, 234; Reader Self-Perception Scale (RSPS), 216, 233–246, 242*f*–243*f*

SELF-REFLECTION: in first-grade classroom, 135–138

SEMINARS: activities for, 121, 122*f*; texts for, 121*f*, 121

SETTINGS, 74

SEUSS, DR.: *Dr. Seuss's ABC*, 173; *There's a Wocket in My Pocket*, 173

SHARED LEARNING: follow-up sessions, 120; initiating portfolios through, 118–130; model for, 119–124

SHOW PORTFOLIOS, 45. *See also* Portfolios

SONGS, 174

SOUTHWEST REGIONAL EDUCATIONAL LABORATORY, 30–31

SPELLING TESTS: correlation with Yopp-Singer Test of Phoneme Segmentation, 171*t*, 171–172, 172*t*; to determine predictive validity, 170, 170*t*. *See also* Tests

STAIR (SYSTEM FOR TEACHING AND ASSESSING INTERACTIVELY AND REFLECTIVELY), 91–98; example, 92, 93*f*; planning instruction and checking hypothesis, 92, 94*f*; questions, 91; reflecting on instruction and updating hypothesis, 92–94, 95*f*, 96*f*

STANDARDIZED TESTS: criterion-referenced, 250; rationale for, 248–249; results, 249–250

STANDARDS, 24–25

STANFORD ACHIEVEMENT TEST (SAT), 31–32; score declines, 45

STATE BASIC SKILL ASSESSMENTS: high-stakes, 251. *See also* Assessment

STATEMENT OF PRIOR KNOWLEDGE, 101–102; rubric for, 101–102

STRAND FORMAT, 57

"STRANGE BUMPS" (LOBEL): Michael's reading of, 155*f*, 155–156

STRATEGIC READING, 132; Metacomprehension Strategy Index (MSI), 189–198, 196*f*–198*f*; questionnaire to measure awareness of, 189–198; strategies measured by MSI, 190, 191*t*

STRATEGY ASSESSMENTS, 132

STRATEGY LESSONS: supporting Michael through, 156–157

STRENGTHS AND WEAKNESSES, 87–88

STUDENT PERFORMANCE, 101–108; tasks, 101. *See also* Performance

STUDENT PORTFOLIOS. *See* Portfolios

STUDENT WORK SAMPLES: scoring, 39–41

STUDENT-MANAGED PORTFOLIOS, 135–138; entry forms, 136*f*–137*f*

STUDENTS: as assessment audience, 46–47, 47*f*; drawings, 104, 105*f*; evaluations, 77–82; plans for writing and reading, 77–79; promotion, 254; questions about literacy dimensions and attributes, 39; responsibilities related to report cards, 64; retention, 254; teachers as advocates for, 15–16; views of each other, 81–82; who don't pass, 254. *See also* English as a Second Language (ESL) students

SUBSCORES, 20

SURVEYS: Elementary Reading Attitude Survey (ERAS), 199–214, 204*f*–210*f*, 211*t*–213*t*, 234; Metacomprehension Strategy Index (MSI), 189–198; Reading Survey (Motivation to Read Profile, MRP), 216–217, 217*f*, 221, 224–228, 225*f*–227*f*, 229. *See also* Tests

SUSTAINED SILENT READING, 85

SYSTEM FOR TEACHING AND ASSESSING INTER-
ACTIVELY AND REFLECTIVELY. *See* STAIR

T

TEACHER-GENERATED OBSERVATION GUIDES, 85,
86*f*

TEACHERS: as advocates for students, 15–16; as
assessment audience, 46, 47*f*; as learners,
13–14;classroom assessment choices, 68–
72; miscues by, 147; professionalism of,
13–14; recommendations for, 257; responsibilities related to report cards, 63–64; selection of miscues, 143–146

TEACHER-STUDENT PORTFOLIOS, 138

TEACHING: critical moment, 146–150; diagnostic,
73–76; questions related to becoming experts in, 91; STAIR (System for Teaching
and Assessing Interactively and Reflectively), 91–98; to test, 48, 252. *See also*
Instruction

TESTS, 48–49; Comprehensive Test of Basic
Skills (CTBS), 170, 171*t*, 171–172, 172*t*;
culture-free, 17–18; Elementary Reading
Attitude Survey (ERAS), 199–214,
204*f*–210*f*, 211*t*–214*t*, 234; high-stakes,
250–251, 253–258; importance of, 248;
Iowa Test of Basic Skills, 180, 183*t*,
182–184; Metacomprehension Strategy
Index (MSI), 189–198, 196*f*–198*f*; Motivation to Read Profile (MRP), 215–232,
217*f*–220*f*; Names Test, 177–188, 183*t*;
National Assessment of Educational
Progress (NAEP), 255–256; norm-referenced, 52; norm-referenced global comprehension, 50, 51*f*; objectives, 49; of phonemic
awareness in young children, 166–176; potential problems, 48–49; of predictive validity, 170, 170*t*; Reader Self-Perception Scale
(RSPS), 216, 233–246, 237*t*–238*t*, 242*f*–
243*f*, 244*t*, 245*f*, 246*t*; requirements for,
13–14; standardized, 248–250; students who
don't pass, 254; teaching to, 48, 252; Yopp-
Singer Test of Phoneme Segmentation,
167–169, 168*f*, 169–175. *See also* Assessment

TEXT, ENGAGEMENT WITH: through reading, 33*t*,
34, 35*t*; through writing, 33*t*, 35*t*

TEXT COMPREHENSION: informational, 107; narrative, 107–108

THERE'S A WOCKET IN MY POCKET (SEUSS), 173

THE THREE LITTLE PIGS (MADDEN): Michael's
reading of, 156, 157*f*

*TINKER V. DES MOINES INDEPENDENT SCHOOL
DISTRICT*, 15–16

U

UNITED STATES: federal government, 255–256;
National Assessment of Educational
Progress (NAEP), 255–256; national report
cards, 256; Supreme Court, 15–16

"UPSTAIRS AND DOWNSTAIRS" (LOBEL): Michael's
reading of, 156–157, 157*f*

UTAH: performance assessments, 53

V

VALIDITY: consequential, 256; predictive, 170,
170*t*

VOCABULARY, 70

W

WEAKNESSES, 87–88

"WHAT AM I THINKING OF?" (GUESSING GAME),
173–174

WHOLE LITERACY, 32

WORD DICTATION, 70

WORK SAMPLES: scoring, 39–41

WORKING PORTFOLIOS, 45. *See also* Portfolios

WORKSHOPS: Readers' Workshop, 85; session
topics, 121, 122*f*

WRITERS' WORKSHOP, 85

WRITING, 106; attitudes about, 36*t*; constructive,
35*t*; engagement with text through, 33*t*, 35*t*;
motivation for, 36*t*; self-assessment of, 37*t*;
students' plans for, 77–79; technically appropriate, 35*t*

WRITING ANECDOTAL RECORDS: techniques for, 84–85

WRITING CHECKLISTS: for portfolio entries, 127, 128*f*

WRITING VOCABULARY, 70

Y

YOPP-SINGER TEST OF PHONEME SEGMENTATION, 167–169, 168*f*; correlation with reading and spelling subtests, 171*t*, 171–172, 172*t*; data on, 169–172; directions, 167; implications, 172–174; use of, 174–175

YOUNG READERS: portfolio assessment for, 131–134; test for assessing phonemic awareness in, 166–176. *See also* Readers